Education and the Many Faces of the Disadvantaged:

cultural and historical perspectives

Education and the Many Faces of the Disadvantaged:

cultural and historical perspectives

edited by

William W. Brickman

*Professor of Educational History
and Comparative Education,
Graduate School of Education,
University of Pennsylvania
Editor of* School & Society

Stanley Lehrer

*President, Society for the
Advancement of Education
Publisher of* School & Society *and* School & Society Books

John Wiley & Sons, Inc.
New York • London • Sydney • Toronto

Library of Congress Catalogue Card Number: 74-37166

ISBN 0-471-10350-0 (Cloth); ISBN 0-471-10355-1 (Paper)

Printed in the United States of America.

10 9 8 7 6 5 4 3 2 1

TO

Lawrence S. and **Huguette Braverman**
artistic contributors
to man and his culture

Harry and **Dorothy Kochman**
achievers of a heartfelt dream—
finding in America the freedom and happiness
unfulfilled in a dictatorial homeland

Abraham A. and **Adele Schnitzer**
parents-in-law
and community benefactors

Preface

Human beings in civilized society are capable of achieving success in almost every endeavor, such as landing on the moon, and yet are culpable for their failure to avoid inglorious waste in large numbers of human resources. Millions of people in the United States are unable to contribute very much to society or to their own support. They are labeled "disadvantaged" or "culturally deprived" because their racial or cultural backgrounds have left them inadequately prepared for the schools of a white-oriented nation. The education to which they are exposed is mostly irrelevant to their special needs as people in poverty and, therefore, cannot prepare them properly for a constructive life in American society. As human beings, we should listen to our conscience: we must develop the potentialities of the poor through qualitative education, consisting of excellent teachers and appropriate curricula. If the United States is to continue to thrive in the future, the abilities of all our people must be encouraged to blossom through equal educational opportunity.

The mass media have focused on the plight of the disadvantaged. Newspapers, magazines, radio, and television have noted the desperation of the poor black and Spanish-speaking Americans within their grimy ghettos and the Indians on their ruinous reservations as they aspire to improve their lot through the great American uplifter—education. Group W—Westinghouse Broadcasting Company and WNEW-TV in New York devoted three hours one evening in 1968 to a special documentary program, "One Nation, Indivisible," which probed the racial crisis in the United States. CBS-TV, concerned about the seriousness of another aspect of the dilemma of the disadvantaged—hunger—presented during the same year a shocking report on starvation in the wealthiest country in the world and the dire effect of malnutrition on the physical and mental health of children[1] of tenant farmers in Virginia, black Americans in Alabama, Mexican-Americans in Texas, and Navaho Indians in Arizona. A clinical study has proven that malnourished babies experience limited brain growth, leading to mental retardation.[2] In addition to being financially and educationally starved, the poor are unmistakably the dietary disadvantaged of America.

To neglect the needs of the disadvantaged is not only cruel and undemocratic; it debilitates the well-being of the entire nation. This book examines various types of the disadvantaged in the United States, uncovers reasons for the multifaceted problem of societal deprivation, and indicates constructive ways, through education, to help the disadvantaged. Attention also is focused on the poor and disadvantaged in foreign lands.

The uniqueness of the book is in its comprehensive treatment of the subject of the disadvantaged. There are ten parts to the volume: the disadvantaged in urban America; the black American; the Spanish-speaking American; the North American Indian; the immigrant and refugee in America; the rural poor and America's undereducated adult; the middle class as culturally deprived; the culturally disadvantaged reader; the teacher and Federal programs for the disadvantaged; and the disadvantaged in international perspective. Also included is an extensive bibliography on the school and the children of the poor.

This book will be useful as a text or general reference work in undergraduate and graduate courses in the foundations of education, social foundations of education, sociology of education, urban education, teacher education, and educational administration. Readers will find the book helpful in learning more about disadvantaged persons and how the right kinds of education should be able to infuse into them the knowledge and skills they need to rise above their despair.

Stanley Lehrer

[1] See Nevin S. Scrimshaw, "When Young Children Go Hungry: Effects on Learning and Behavior," in *1970 Britannica Yearbook of Science and the Future* (Chicago: Encyclopaedia Britannica, Inc., 1969), pp. 345–355.

[2] Jane E. Brody, "Study Finds Malnutrition Stunts Growth of Brain," *The New York Times*, July 12, 1968, p. 37.

Acknowledgments

During the creation of this book, it was an honor for the editors to be associated, via correspondence and telephone, with the many professional individuals who generously contributed the thousands of words that constitute the contents. No invitation to write for specific parts of the book was refused. Several authors willingly granted permission to reprint their essays on some aspect of the disadvantaged that originally had appeared in various issues of *School & Society*. Without the cooperation of these contributors, whom the editors proudly list below, the book could not have been produced.

MICHAEL ANELLO, *Director, Program in Higher Education, Boston College*

CLARA ANTHONY, *Instructor, Center for Inner City Studies, Northeastern Illinois State College*

NANCY L. ARNEZ, *Director, Center for Inner City Studies, Northeastern Illinois State College*

ROBERT L. BAILEY, *Administrative Assistant, University of Oklahoma*

RICHARD M. BOSSONE, *Professor of English, Bernard M. Baruch College of The City University of New York*

WILLIAM H. BOYER, *Associate Professor, Department of Educational Foundations, University of Hawaii*

THOMAS P. CARTER, *Professor of Sociology and Education, University of Texas at El Paso*

J. DAVID COLFAX, *Assistant Professor of Sociology, University of Connecticut*

FRANCESCO CORDASCO, *Professor of Education, Montclair State Col-*

lege, and Educational Consultant, Migration Division, Commonwealth of Puerto Rico

MARGARET L. CORMACK, *Professor of South Asian Studies, Callison College, University of the Pacific*

NICHOLAS P. CRISCUOLO, *Supervisor of Reading, New Haven (Conn.) Public Schools*

J. MICHAEL DAVIS, *Assistant Director, Cuban Teacher Program, School of Education, University of Miami*

RICHARD G. DURNIN, *Assistant Professor of Education, The City College of The City University of New York*

ROBERT FISHER, *Professor of Education, Eastern Michigan University*

ASHLEY FOSTER, *Behavioral Scientist, Indian Health Service, U.S. Public Health Service*

PHILIP I. FREEDMAN, *Associate Professor of Education, Herbert H. Lehman College of The City University of New York*

ROBERT FULTON, *Professor of Sociology, University of Minnesota*

A. BRUCE GAARDER, *Chief, Basic Studies Branch, U.S. Office of Education*

THOMAS E. HARRIS, *Program Analysis Officer, Division of Student Financial Aid, U.S. Office of Education*

KENNETH T. HENSON, *Assistant Professor of Education, Indiana State University*

MAURIE HILLSON, *Professor of Education, Rutgers, The State University*

SEYMOUR W. ITZKOFF, *Associate Professor of Education, Smith College, and Director, Smith College Day Schools*

NEAL JUSTIN, *Assistant Professor of Education, College of Education, Florida Atlantic University*

ROBERT B. KAPLAN, *Associate Professor of English and Linguistics and Director, English Communication Program for Foreign Students, University of Southern California*

NATHAN KRAVETZ, *Associate Professor of Education, Herbert H. Lehman College of The City University of New York*

EUGENE KRUSZYNSKI, *Supervisor of Student Teaching, University of San Francisco*

NORMAN D. KURLAND, *Director, Center for Planning and Innovation, New York State Education Department*

WILLIAM E. KUSCHMAN, *Professor of Education, Northern Illinois University*

ARTHUR LAING *was Minister of Indian Affairs and Northern Development, Canada, at the time his essay was written. He now is Minister of Public Works*

JOHN H. LANGER, *Educational Programs Specialist, Bureau of Narcotics and Dangerous Drugs, U.S. Department of Justice*

DANIEL U. LEVINE, *Director, Center for the Study of Metropolitan Problems in Education, University of Missouri—Kansas City*

HERSCHEL T. MANUEL, *Professor Emeritus of Educational Psychology, University of Texas*

LEONARD NADLER, *Associate Professor of Adult Education, George Washington University*

BARBARA W. NEWELL, *Acting Vice-President for Student Affairs and Associate Professor of Economics, University of Michigan*

EDWARD G. OLSEN, *Professor of Education, California State College at Hayward*

ALLAN C. ORNSTEIN, *Assistant Professor of Education, Chicago State College*

HOWARD OZMON, *Chairman, Department of Education, Chicago State College*

FRANKLIN PARKER, *Benedum Professor of Education, West Virginia University*

RICHARD R. RENNER, *Associate Professor of Comparative Education, College of Education, University of Florida*

BARBARA A. RHODES, *Assistant Professor of Afro-American Studies, San Fernando Valley State College*

RAMON SANCHEZ, *Assistant Professor of Education, Hunter College of The City University of New York*

MITCHELL SHARP *was Minister of Finance, Canada, at the time his essay was written. He now is Minister of External Affairs*

RUDIE TRETTEN, *Assistant Principal—Instruction, Jefferson High School, Daly City, Calif.*

PAUL WALSH, *Assistant Professor of Education, University of Hawaii*

LAMBERT N. WENNER, *Assistant Professor of Sociology and Anthropology, University of Idaho*

LAWRENCE A. WENZEL, *Associate Professor of Sociology, Chicago State College*

THOMAS P. WILBUR, *U.S. Office of Education Research Trainee, Institute of Administrative Research, Teachers College, Columbia University*

The editors are grateful, indeed, to these contributors for all their kindness and helpfulness.

Robert S. Rothenberg of the Society for the Advancement of Education deserves special acknowledgment for his accuracy in proofreading, skill in indexing, and efficiency in obtaining formal permission from authors to include their essays in the book.

My collaborator undertook the important tasks of requesting and editing manuscripts for the volume. During the editing process, he frequently outlined the revisions that were necessary, and the authors complied. In addition to selecting, recommending, and editing many essays, I had the responsibility of dividing the book into appropriate parts for study and organizing all the material within the framework of these parts.

Many helpful suggestions were made by my wife, Laurel, concerning the book's manuscript. Of inestimable value was her encouragement, which she offered readily when the goal of completing the book seemed unattainable.

Stanley Lehrer

June, 1971

Contents

PART 10
The Disadvantaged
in International Perspective

Education and the Many Faces of the Disadvantaged:

cultural and historical perspectives

Varieties of
the Educationally Disadvantaged:
An Introduction

The disadvantaged, the deprived, the despised, the downtrodden, and the discriminated against always have been with us. So has human concern and action for these unfortunates. Efforts to remedy social, economic, and other types of wrongs perpetuated by man upon man have been going on ever since the dawn of man's conscience. That these attempts did not bring about a permanent solution everywhere is beyond question. At most, they were able to bring relief to some, perhaps even to many, but the problem of human suffering remained a persistent one all through history.

A careful inquiry into the past of the human race will reveal, no doubt, that the economically poor have been the disadvantaged group common to all nations and all periods. In fact, the patient searcher also will learn that other types of people were subject to deprivation, among them persons of particular races and religions, for example. Nor can one overlook any more the fact that the female sex has been subject to various disabilities in various parts of the world.

During the past decade, when the plight of those who are culturally and educationally disadvantaged has impressed itself upon government, society, and the educational profession, the focus of discussions and action programs has been, by and large, on the children and the adolescents of the lower economic levels. In many, if not in most instances, the emphasis has been placed on aid to members of minority racial, ethnic, or linguistic groups, such as the Negroes, the Puerto Ricans, the Mexican-Americans of Southwestern United States, and, most recently, the American Indians and Eskimos. Few will insist that adequate justice has been shown to any one of these groups, let alone the minority population of the United States as a whole.

It is only right to applaud the labors of those who are concerned with rectifying the wrongs committed with respect to all kinds of disadvantaged youngsters. The work of removing artificial barriers to the development of human beings must go on at more accelerated and more efficient pace than ever before if mankind is to live in an environment of justice, fairness, and equality.

The preoccupation with the problems of the poor, however necessary and justified, has resulted in a situation whereby less attention has been paid to other types of disadvantaged individuals who have received less than their full and fair share of educational opportunities and benefits. In a study dedicated to the dire status of the disadvantaged, it is only right to take account of all persons who, for whatever reason, poverty or otherwise, fall within the category of the deprived with regard to matters of culture and education.

Before proceeding further, it would be appropriate to comment on the terms used in the course of the discussion. When the concept of deprivation is coupled with that of culture to produce the expression culturally disadvantaged, there is no intention to imply that there is a lack of culture. An immigrant who is an heir to an ancient culture will be at a disadvantage in his new community, the members of which do not share his heritage. However cultured or educated he may be, he lacks the knowledge or appreciation of the culture of the majority of his neighbors. The expression culturally or educationally disadvantaged, then, is by no means a value judgment, but rather a description of a relative state of affairs. It also must be recognized that there are situations where a disadvantage exists in an absolute sense. As others have done,[1] the writer will feel free to use interchangeably the adjectives *deprived, disadvantaged,* and *underprivileged* in connection with the lack of the knowledge, ideas, and materials which are characteristic of the culture of persons who have had more than a basic education and who have leisure time. But once again, this definition is too limited, even if it appears to correspond to the common conception of the culturally and educationally disadvantaged. What has to be done is to broaden the interpretation of disadvantaged to encompass a variety of persons who have not been able to enjoy culture and education to the fullest on account of various disabilities, whether social, ideological, religious, or of any other origin. This position of all-inclusive consideration of the disadvantaged is not to underestimate the importance of the poor, but rather to provide some sort of a balance.

To begin with, let us consider the dwellers in the rural areas as culturally disadvantaged. It may be true that the one-room school now belongs to history, that buses bring children to centrally located, well-equipped schools, and that

[1] See Frank Riessman, *The Culturally Deprived Child* (New York: Harper & Row, 1962), p. 1, note 1.

radio and television have brought drama, music, and other cultural features to remote farm regions. Nonetheless, there are vast areas in various parts of the world in which children still are taught under conditions far less favorable than in urban centers. One recalls the complaints of a Soviet educational leader not so long ago that it was very difficult to get good teachers to want to settle in the distant Siberian settlements. In the newer or developing countries, we have observed the gap between the school facilities of the cities and the country, as well as the difference between the teaching done in these areas. Clearly, children who get their initial education in a rural environment may not be as fortunate as their city cousins, even if they may enjoy pollution-free air and the opportunity coming directly from nature. In the modernized, technologized world, they are at a distinct disadvantage if they do not have access to the urban educational resources. Moreover, there is no substitute for the opportunity to visit art and science museums, work in well stocked libraries, attend musical and theatrical performances, and otherwise obtain tridimensional and multisensory cultural experiences. This situation, it is clear, requires remedies to permit children and young persons to overcome the disadvantages of living in an environment which does not provide for the full enjoyment of culture and education such as is the privilege of persons in the larger centers of population. Something concrete can be done by members of a society that professes the ideal of giving all of its members the maximum possible in education and culture. No doubt, there will be problems of various kinds, not the least of which is likely to be that of finance. However, the difficulties do not absolve the leadership in society and government from the task of giving the most and the best to the most.

The problem of the rural child and adolescent also suggests the disadvantage of geography with respect to the smaller settlements. Many localities in most countries are at some distance from the metropolitan centers. It is hard to visualize how the inhabitants of the Faeroe Islands or of Greenland can obtain the same type of education, or one remotely similar, as the young people of Denmark proper. The children whose parents migrate from one place to another in search of work also present a problem. In the Netherlands, the canal boat children seem to have a carefully organized program of study; yet, even they might be described as disadvantaged as compared to their peers whose mobility is limited to walking a few blocks or taking a bus to school. The problem of Bedouin children in the Middle Eastern countries represents an even greater source of deprivation. It is possible that ministries of education cannot do away with all the disadvantages of geography for all pupils. Nevertheless, it does seem incumbent, in every situation, for the leaders to reduce the difficulties by the greatest effort of which they are capable.

A historical disadvantage of very long standing is due to discrimination on the basis of sex. In past periods, there were many societies which did not provide any formal educational or cultural experiences for females. Despite the disability of sex, there always were women who managed to obtain some education, first by way of tutoring and then by autodidactic procedures. As can well be understood, such women belonged, as a rule, to the upper and middle levels of society. Most females, however, had to remain content, if they were permitted to have any ambitions at all, with the barest rudiments of formal learning. It has been something of an eighth wonder of the world that some women were able, throughout the various ages of history, to attain high educational and cultural status. At once there come to mind the medieval dramatist, Hroswitha of Gandersheim, doubly disadvantaged as a nun; St. Catherine of Siena, the mystical thinker and author of 11 published works; Queen Margaret of Navarre, renowned for the "Heptameron"; Anna Maria van Schuurman, polyglot, theologian, upholder of the right of women for a higher education; Madame de Staël, woman of letters and leader of thought; and others too numerous to list.[2] It may be argued that these outstanding women had opportunities denied to those of lower social and economic status. Even if this be conceded, there still remains the matter of the multitudes of the upper classes who did not have the benefits enjoyed by the learned ladies. Furthermore, we must recall that, until around the middle of the 19th century, it was a rare female who would be admitted to an institution of higher education. It is difficult not to admire the struggle of a Sofia Kovalevskaya to leave Russia and to acquire a Ph.D. in mathematics *summa cum laude* at the University of Göttingen, in spite of having been unable to gain admission to the University of Berlin. Even the high-born were subject to disadvantages, merely because of having been born female. There is no wonderment at a growing activism of women in the later decades of the 19th century and subsequently.

We now are approaching the last quarter of the 20th century, that era of enlightenment in which there still are to be found substantial pockets of resistance to the idea that girls and young women should be given little beyond a basic education. It is only rather recently that girls were permitted in some Middle Eastern countries to obtain an education on the secondary level. In time to come, there even may be more opportunities for girls, both in secondary and higher education.

Even where members of the female sex are not prevented or dissuaded from embarking upon educational careers, there still exist direct or subtle pressures and procedures that operate to maintain a gap in educational equality between the sexes. But those who delight in depriving females of their full rights in education, culture, and society may be facing hard times ahead. The new Women's Liberation Movement may bring to an end any practice which discriminates against girls and women. It is likely that, in some countries at least,

---

2 For a convenient compilation of women who were eminent in culture, see *Grosse Frauen der Weltgeschichte* (Murnau vor München: Verlag Sebastian Lux, n.d.).

being a woman would not involve being disadvantaged any more. Perhaps symptomatic of what is to come is the appointment, for the first time in the history of the institution, of a young woman as dean of a residential college at Yale University. The Master of this college, which consists of 340 male and 70 female students, was quoted in the press as follows: "We didn't choose her because she was a woman. She was a very strong candidate and she seemed to be the right person for the appointment."[3] Such a judgment is a model of objectivity, one which may well teach other appointing and selecting authorities to consider the person, rather than his race, religion, sex, or social and economic status.

From earliest times down to the present, when religious groups came into contact with each other, it was inevitable for members of the minority to be denied access to the educational institutions of the dominant society. There have been numerous instances when Catholics were disadvantaged in a Protestant environment, and vice versa. Discrimination also has been practiced against deviationist groups or individuals within the major sect.

Examples of interreligious or intrareligious discrimination are not hard to find in history. The persecution and the execution of heretics by the Catholic authorities are well known. The cultural and educational limitations upon Catholics and dissenters are equally familiar. Among the results of this policy was the migration of Calvinists to the Netherlands, where they were able to study at the University of Leiden, and the departure of Catholics to such hospitable locations as Louvain, Douai, Paris, and Valladolid, where they were able to study in the regular universities or to set up their own. The founding of the University College in London in 1826 ". . . initiated a revolution, for it was the first university institution in England to admit students without a religious 'test.' "[4] Not until the bill introduced by Prime Minister William E. Gladstone became law in 1871 were the religious tests abolished for all degrees except for divinity at the Universities of Cambridge, Oxford, and Durham.[5] The final disabilities of those who did not subscribe to the Thirty-Nine Articles of the Church of England were not removed until 1915 at Cambridge and 1920 at Oxford.

The Jewish religious group has experienced discrimination to an extent which apparently surpassed any other form in history. For centuries, it was virtually impossible for a believing and practicing Jew to gain admission to a university in Christian Europe, let alone to teach in an institution of higher learning. Even the Lutheran professors of Germany, who rejected the regime

---

[3] "First Woman Dean Is Named at Yale," *New York Times*, April 1, 1970.

[4] W. H. G. Armytage, *Four Hundred Years of English Education*, second edition (Cambridge: University Press, 1970), p. 103.

[5] S. J. Curtis, *History of Education in Great Britain*, seventh edition (London: University Tutorial Press, 1967), p. 457.

of Rome, accepted the ruling of the Catholic Council of Basel in 1434 that "no Jew may be given any honorable and learned degree."[6] The Italian universities, especially the University of Padua, although Catholic, did not heed the decision of the Council of Basel and permitted Jews to study and to gain their degrees. When, for whatever reason, it was not feasible for young European Jews to travel to Italy, they would have to obtain books, or the aid of an unbiased Christian scholar, or instruction from Jewish graduates of the University of Padua if they wanted to get any advanced learning. Not that all knowledge-avid Jews felt disadvantaged at the lack of university facilities. Most of them were satisfied with the parallel system of higher learning, that of the *Yeshivah*, or Talmudical College, in which the Holy Scriptures, the Talmud, and the respective commentaries were studied in depth. But this did not alter the fact of discrimination, which prevented those who desired a secular higher education from getting it. A small number of Russian Jews were able to win admission to the University of St. Petersburg and the University of Moscow during the Tsarist regime by submitting to conversion to the Russian Orthodox Church. It is not so long ago that, even when admitted to the universities of Central and Eastern Europe in the 20th century, Jewish students and applicants suffered from the policy of *numerus clausus*, ghetto benches, and other forms of bias. Nor was it rare, until rather recently, for American young people of the Jewish faith to go abroad in order to be admitted to a medical school. This form of religious prejudice, evidently, has been overcome in the United States, although probably not all over the world. There is hope that other forms of bias and discrimination also will vanish and each person would be judged as to his capabilities without reference to such factors as race, religion, ethnic background, and the like.

We need to heed the experience of the past, not only with respect to learning how improvements were brought about, but also because of the possibility that bias, once it has been removed, might return if vigilance is not exercised by those who are committed to the principle of the equal treatment of all members of the human race. One also learns from history that those who disagreed with the political policy of a closed, dictatorial society were subject to discrimination in various ways. The politically independent thinker, even in a democratic country, who lives in an area where another political viewpoint is dominant, may not be appointed to boards of education, committees, or other bodies which are concerned with the making of decisions affecting the community. Obviously, a totalitarian nation, by the very definition of the term, cannot tolerate any disagreement with the official doctrine, and any upholder of a dissenting opinion cannot expect to be granted full, or perhaps any,

6 Johann Jacob Schudt, *Jüdischer Merckwürdigkeiten* . . . *II. Theil* (Frankfurt, 1714), p. 403; David Kaufmann, *Dr. Israel Conegliano und seine Verdienste um die Republik Venedig bis nach dem Frieden von Carlowitz* (Vienna: Konegen, 1895), p. 8.

opportunity to study and to teach. History is full of examples in all parts of the globe. Let us recall some instances of the current century to illustrate the progress in man's inhumanity to man. The advent of Adolf Hitler and the National Socialist Party to power in Germany in 1933 led to the dismissal or, at best, the pensioning of university professors who were identified as active proponents of the viewpoints of other political parties. Even prior to this *Machtübernahme*, the Nazi students made matters uncomfortable for fellow students and for professors who were known to be in opposition to their ideology. The exodus from Germany, which resulted from the repressive Nazi decrees and practices, enriched the scholarship and education of England, Turkey, the United States, and other host countries. At the same time, the departure of the politically and religiously disadvantaged left Germany culturally and educationally in a state of deprivation, but this was its sovereign choice.

It also is pertinent to recall, in this connection, the exodus of non-Fascist and anti-Fascist scholars from Mussolini's Italy and Franco's Spain, as well as from other countries which turned into territories of totalitarianism. But what about those nations that did not permit easy egress to its no-saying intellectuals? The locality that comes quickest to mind is the Soviet Union, where the Communist Party succeeded, for over more than half a century, in imposing its ideology on the population by controlling the entire educational system, the nonscholastic agencies of education, and all the mass media of disseminating information. In addition, it has suppressed all organizations and institutions, such as the noncommunist youth groups and the religious schools for children—all in the name of the Constitution, Article 124, which guarantees "freedom of religious worship and freedom of antireligious [but not religious] propaganda" for all citizens; and Article 123, which declares that "equality of the rights of citizens of the U.S.S.R., irrespective of their nationality or race, in all spheres of economic, government, cultural, political and other social activity, is an indefeasible law."[7] These provisions are in the nature of exaggerated rhetoric, in view of the incarceration in mental hospitals, Siberian camps, or prisons of writers and thinkers who have questioned one or more of the Communist articles of faith which have been propagated in the Soviet Union. It does not take much to recall the mass murders under Stalin[8] and the lesser known or possibly unrecorded instances of execution and inner exile during the more than five decades of Soviet existence. Nor can we forget the crackdown on culture, scholarship, and education in the years immediately following the end of World War II—the era of *Zhdanovshchina*

[7] *Constitution: Fundamental Law of the Union of Soviet Socialist Republics* (Moscow: Foreign Languages Publishing House, 1962), p. 101.

[8] Robert Conquest, *The Great Purge: Stalin's Purge of the Thirties* (New York: Macmillan, 1968). For a brief record of the cultural, educational, and scholarly purge, see pp. 317–331.

and its aftermath—until the death of Stalin in 1953. But it would be misleading to think that those who were not punished were spared disadvantage. The very fact that the individual feared to give expression to his thoughts because of sure reprisals certainly deprived him of his fundamental rights as a man and as a citizen. Creative work which does not correlate with the current policy of the Communist Party must be unpublicized and unwritten; or, if written, cannot be published unless by way of the *Samizdat*, the privately duplicated and disseminated manuscript or typescript. Unlike the Nazi and Fascist dictatorships, the Soviet state does not permit the disadvantaged dissenters to embark upon a new life and career in another country. They are left under police watch and may be harassed in numerous ways. There have been cases of discrimination, moreover, in accessibility to higher and professional education against the children of political dissenters or of the clergy. In sum, the cultural and educational level of quite a few citizens of the Communist state would seem to be circumscribed if they betrayed by an act, or did anything to arouse suspicion, which could be interpreted as antagonistic to the ideological status quo.

Let no one imagine that this brief study of the politically disadvantaged is confined to, or is chiefly characteristic of, states with a totalitarian orientation, whether of the right or the left. There is considerable evidence of discrimination along political lines even in pluralistic, free, and democratic countries, with the result that some persons are relegated to the status of the disadvantaged. The scholarly study published in 1941 by Howard K. Beale, professor of history at the University of North Carolina, on more than three centuries of teacher freedom in the United States revealed that "political questions are still more restricted [than economic questions] unless one is on the orthodox side."[9] In an earlier and more detailed monograph, Professor Beale devoted about 800 pages to documenting his thesis that there have been numerous cases of restraints upon the freedom of teaching and expression, with reference to political, economic, social, and other issues and problems during the two decades since the beginning of World War I.[10] More recent evidence of this sort can be found in the abundant books, reports, and articles. Changes have taken place toward more freedom for teachers, both in instruction and in their lives as citizens in the community. However, as political and other types of crises take place in a democratic society, there are strains and stresses which might lead to a discouraging of teachers and students in the expression of certain viewpoints.

The problem of the Negro as disadvantaged in culture and education has been receiving a justifiably increasing emphasis during the past decade. Few

[9] Howard K. Beale, *A History of Freedom of Teaching in American Schools* (New York: Scribner, 1941), p. 240.
[10] Howard K. Beale, *Are American Teachers Free?* (New York: Scribner, 1936).

will contest the historical fact that slavery first and segregation afterward prevented the children, youth, and adults of the downtrodden race from receiving the benefits which were available to the whites. This conclusion is not challenged by the recollection of cultured and educated Negroes prior to the Civil War and by the subsequent emergence of a Booker T. Washington, George W. Carver, W. E. B. DuBois, Carter G. Woodson, E. Franklin Frazier, John Hope Franklin, or Ralph J. Bunche. The vast majority of the Negro children and adolescents in the South attended separate but unequal schools, a circumstance which hindered their future development. In the Northern states, they often were neglected by reason of their residential patterns and by the educators' acceptance of the alleged natural inferiority of Negro learning ability. In fact, the so-called scientific conclusions of the psychologists who administered tests to American soldiers during World War I served, despite competent refutations by such scholars as William C. Bagley, to convince teachers and administrators for some time that little could be done to raise the cultural and educational level of the Negro pupils beyond a basic level.

Science and the times have changed. The accent in the United States is now on compensatory education and other plans to help the black pupils to advance, as many of them indeed have been doing. In the meantime, the question whether *de facto* segregation, *per se*, constitutes a disadvantage has become a moot matter. At one time, it was quite easy for liberals to cite the testimony of Professor Kenneth B. Clark to the U.S. Supreme Court before the desegregation decision of 1954 that segregation is inherently unequal, hence putting Negroes at an educational disadvantage. More recently, however, with the growth of the Black Power and the Black Muslim groups, Negroes have begun to demand separate facilities in educational and other affairs, so that their children and young people might learn in accordance with their way of life and thought. Such a development places white and black liberals in a dilemma and in a position in which they might have to defend segregation of a voluntary kind. Be that as it may, the current mood is such that the government, society, and education are determined to try to give the black minority equal cultural and educational opportunities with the other elements of the population.

The subject of the racially disadvantaged is not at all exhausted with the consideration of the Negro in the United States. First, one must think of the Bantu or African Negroes in the Republic of South Africa, where the policy of apartheid has been successfully keeping them in a lower cultural and educational status. Notwithstanding such superior schools as the University College of the North, in the Transvaal, where blacks are taught by an integrated faculty, the average Bantu gets fewer opportunities than those of the white groups in terms of cultural and educational development.[11] Nor should one

[11] There is a considerable amount of literature on the race question in education in

forget the discrimination in education suffered by the Coloured and the Asian minorities in South Africa.[12] In brief, disadvantages abound in education and culture in the modern, industrial Republic of South Africa.

Examples of the inequality of peoples also can be found in other areas. The Indian of North and South America, the Eskimo in the Arctics, and the Eta in Japan are some of the racial groups that have received less than their due in education. To some extent, one might explain the disadvantages on the ground of difficult and inaccessible terrain. However, such excuses seem less and less convincing as time goes on and transportation and communication improve. There still remains a latent suspicion that some degree of prejudice lurks behind the inadequate cultural and educational opportunities granted to these racial minorities. Before leaving the subject of race, moreover, it is well to reflect on the situation of the products of mixed racial unions, some of whom have been victimized in certain parts of the world by various forms of prejudice and deprived of cultural and educational advantages.

Another class that deserves consideration is that which is disadvantaged by reason of ethnic origin or language, especially as the result of immigration into another country. The struggles of the immigrants who left South and East Europe around the turn of the century for the American shores have been documented fully in studies by sociologists, ethnologists, historians, and other specialists. The human element is especially evident in the many auto-biographical accounts by the more literate immigrants and in the letters to the editor in the foreign language press. When the children of the new arrivals came into the public schools, they often had traumatic experiences through ridicule or disrespect by teachers and fellow-pupils toward their ancestral language, dress, and customs. One result was the development of the generation gap. It is not an exaggeration to trace some of the juvenile delinquency and crime to this situation. The loss of linguistic resources of the immigrant peoples, and the consequent cultural impoverishment, also can be attributed to the shabby treatment accorded by public schools to the children of the newcomers. During the course of time, these disabilities tended to disappear

South Africa. Only a few can be listed here: F. E. Auerbach, *The Power of Prejudice in South African Education* (Cape Town: Balkema, 1965); N. J. Rhoodie and J. H. Venter, *Die Apartheidsgedagte* (Cape Town: Haum, [1960]); *Onderwys vir Suid-Afrika* (Johannesburg: Witwatersrand University Press, 1961). The last two works also have appeared in English. See also H. J. Van Zyl, "The Education of Racial Minorities in South Africa," pp. 104–111, and William W. Brickman, "Racial Segregation in Education in South Africa," pp. 112–144, in William W. Brickman and Stanley Lehrer, editors, *The Countdown on Segregated Education* (New York: Society for the Advancement of Education, 1960).

12 How the South African policy affects racial minorities is illustrated by a recent study by Unesco: *Apartheid: Its Effects on Education, Science, Culture, and Information* (Paris: Unesco, 1967).

and were overcome by the more energetic and ambitious of the immigrant children, but considerable damage seems to have been done to many others.

The problem of minority language seems to persist. The Puerto Ricans and the Mexican-Americans[13] have to be bilingual if they are to live a full, integrated life in American society. The learning of English as a second language appears to be an added strain, another source of disadvantage, unless the educational administrators and the teachers make a serious effort to help the Spanish-speaking pupils. To the extent that this is not done, there exists a situation whereby persons are prevented from the exercise of the educational and cultural freedom which is theirs as a natural human right. There does not seem to be any defensible reason why such students should suffer when it is within the province of professional educators to undertake measures to eliminate the disadvantages due to the learning of language.

A recent development with regard to the teaching of English to children living in ghetto areas, particularly Negroes, is the recognition of dialect as a legitimate linguistic form of expression. The aim, apparently, is to give the pupils more confidence as they undergo learning experiences in language. What was—and in most places still is—regarded as ungrammatical is considered by some teachers to be correct because it is the linguistic style of the people living in the underprivileged environments. That the intention and the logic are good seems beyond doubt. What seems questionable, however, is whether the recognition of the ghetto or street language is, in fact, an advantage to the black boys and girls who will have to learn English when they grow older and unlearn the linguistic patterns and habits which, they were taught, were correct in their childhood. The advisability of teaching what amounts to an alternative and generally unacceptable form of English does not appear to be clear. Possibly, the expenditure of extra energy on the part of both the teachers and the pupils will make the learning of English a permanent acquisition by all. It would be interesting to ascertain the attitudes of teachers in other countries—Great Britain, for instance—where alternate forms of the national language are spoken by children enrolled in the state schools. The British educational authorities constantly are faced with the problems of Scottish, Irish, and rural English children with different intonations and usages. To these, they have had to add, in recent years, the West Indian, Pakistani, Indian, and African children with their variations of English.

---

[13] Thomas P. Carter, *Mexican Americans in School: A History of Educational Neglect* (New York: College Entrance Examination Board, 1970). For earlier efforts to teach English to Hawaiian and Mexican-American minorities, see Willis B. Coale and Madorah E. Smith, *Successful Practices in the Teaching of English to Bilingual Children in Hawaii.* Bulletin 1937, No. 14, U.S. Office of Education (Washington: U.S. Government Printing Office, 1938); and J. L. Meriam, *Learning English Incidentally: A Study of Bilingual Children.* Bulletin 1937, No. 15, U.S. Office of Education (Washington: U.S. Government Printing Office, 1938).

There is no doubt that each of these pupils is disadvantaged by the deviation of his language pattern. The British teachers try to help all of them to the best of their abilities, but it is doubtful if many will recognize the variations as equivalent to standard English. But perhaps, on this question of teaching ghetto English, it might be best to withhold final opinion until firm facts can be cited on the basis of experience in school and life.

The numerous discussions on the platform and in print of the educationally deprived have tended, during the past decade or so, to overlook the large numbers of children and young people who are handicapped in their learning ability by reason of various physical or mental factors. It is true that every system of education in whatever part of the world makes special provisions for the education of the blind, deaf, dumb, the brain injured, those with retarded mental development, and others with handicaps. The reading of the literature on special education, as well as the observation of the schools for the handicapped in several countries, raises the question as to whether the handicapped children and youth are being given everywhere the fullest measure of educational service to enable them to function as adults within the limits of their capability. It is to be hoped that the movement in behalf of the disadvantaged also will include the consideration of the many children and adolescents who have been handicapped physically and mentally. If each individual cannot be brought up to a level which is equal to that of the non-handicapped, he should be developed, at the very least, to his full capacity.

It is very probable that the academically and intellectually talented are not looked upon, in general, as disadvantaged persons. And yet, such children have not always been receiving the type of education which would fit their abilities. In some countries, as in the Soviet Union, heterogeneous classes are the rule because of ideological reasons, while, in others, such as the United States, there exists the fear that special attention to the superior student is somehow inconsistent with the democratic principles of education and society. However, if the pupil with exceptional ability is not allowed full opportunity to develop in line with his capacities, then we are faced with another category of disadvantaged. In a fair and equitable society, this also calls for correction.

From the standpoint of some circles, the lack of spiritual content in the curricula of public schools is a form of deprivation which diminishes the ability of an individual to live his life in a balanced way. We are aware that, in certain societies, religious instruction is banned from public education on account of the conviction that church and state must be separated by an impregnable wall. Under these circumstances, children whose parents want them to have religious teaching along with the secular, and cannot afford to send them to a private school, may be regarded as belonging to the category of the disadvantaged. The assurance by the proponents of separationism that keeping church, state, and school apart is a guarantee of religious freedom does not convince those who are observant of the inculcation of secularist *Weltanschauung* in the public schools.

One also should include the young people who are disadvantaged because of addiction to various types of drugs. The vaunted independence of the contemporary adolescents is not always manifest in actual practice, especially when too many of them jump on the bandwagon and imitate their peers in experimenting with L.S.D. and other drugs. There seems to be abundant evidence of damage, some of it possibly permanent, to the ability of drug-taking youths to use their intellectual abilities to the utmost. In some cases, the young persons do not know that they are disadvantaged. It would take considerable skill to guide them so that they could benefit themselves and society.

A final addition to the list of the disadvantaged, in this essay at least, is the juvenile delinquent and young criminal. Whatever causes may have brought a deviant and destructive pattern of behavior, it is not possible to absolve the school in relation to society. The cooperation of the educational system with all the agencies of the community is a necessary step in reducing and hopefully eliminating the delinquent as an educationally and culturally deprived group.

The list of the culturally and educationally underprivileged is quite extensive, as the preceding pages have demonstrated, but one's imagination cannot envision all of the possible forms deprivation might take. Does one usually think of the teacher or school administrator who lacks proper preparation with reference to knowledge of subject matter and of professional content as deprived? The disadvantaged, in such cases, breed disadvantaged. Similarly, there must be more instances of discrimination than have been recounted in this essay. What is needed is an up-to-date version of the excellent study made by Charles D. Ammoun[14] in 1957 for the United Nations on the various facets of educational discrimination: race, color, sex, religion, social origin, property, political or other opinion, rural location, nomadic nature of life, indigenous population, underdeveloped economy,[15] and minority language status. Possibly, since the completion of this study, there has been an increase in the number of discriminatory criteria.

It is only proper to be aware of the actions, such as Head Start and Upward Bound, that have been undertaken to reduce or eliminate disadvantages in culture and education. The literature on education is full of plans, programs, and experiments to aid the disadvantaged.[16] The teachers, admin-

[14] Charles D. Ammoun, *Study of Discrimination in Education* (New York: United Nations, 1957).

[15] Guy Hunter, *Modernizing Peasant Societies: A Comparative Study in Asia and Africa* (New York: Oxford University Press, 1969).

[16] See for example, the special issue, "The Disadvantaged and Education," *School & Society*, Vol. 96, March 30, 1968; A. Harry Passow, editor, *Reaching the Disadvantaged*

istrators, social workers, and others involved in working with the under-privileged face many problems—differentiation of curricula, methodology, and materials, to mention one basic issue. There are conflicts of values—desegregation as against individualized improvement toward excellence, multiplication of curricula versus a national common curriculum of essentials, priorities in finance, and many others. The understandable desire to meet the felt, or what is considered to be the felt, needs of underprivileged youngsters runs up against the problem of encircling the individual's vision and ambition with what may prove to be an iron curtain of immediacy. Clearly, the process of aid to the deprived is a long-term, concentrated, continuous, and costly activity. The improvement of the education of those against whom discrimination has been dispensed is likely to be gradual rather than sudden. The great pedagogical push needs persistence and power, but also some measure of patience. It is well to remember that the Universal Declaration of Human Rights, which declares that "everyone has the right to education" and that "higher education shall be equally accessible to all on the basis of merit," was proclaimed by the United Nations on December 10, 1948, well over two decades ago.[17] Furthermore, Unesco and the United Nations found it necessary in 1960 to adopt a Convention and a Recommendation, respectively, against discrimination in education.[18] Since then, the United Nations and its affiliated agencies have had to reaffirm these principles several times. On an international scale, the disappearance of discrimination and disadvantage is still an achievement to be realized in the unknown future. The latest reports on the state of education all over the world are by no means reassuring: 75–80% of the children in Africa, 60–75% in many Latin American nations, and 55–60% in Asia do not complete the elementary school.[19] The struggle to keep children in school is exemplified by the plight of Pakistan, which reported in July 1970 to Unesco's International Bureau of Education in Geneva a 70% dropout rate for the child population aged five to ten.[20] The campaign in behalf of the disadvantaged does not seem to have started in many areas of the world.

Learner (New York: Teachers College Press, 1970); and Edward L. McDill, et al., *Strategies for Success in Compensatory Education: An Appraisal of Evaluation Research* (Baltimore, Md.: Johns Hopkins Press, 1969).

17 F. M. Van Asbeck, editor, *The Universal Declaration of Human Rights and Its Predecessors (1679–1948)*, (Leiden: Brill, 1949), p. 97. The quotations are from Article 26. See especially Articles 1, 2, and 27, and indeed all 30 articles, each of which expresses the equality of all human beings.

18 These documents are reproduced in Pierre Juvigny, *The Fight Against Discrimination: Towards Equality in Education* (Paris: Unesco, 1962), pp. 67–77.

19 F. M. Newell, "World Dropout Rate Is Appalling," *Times Educational Supplement* (London), June 26, 1970.

20 Peter Newell, "Unesco Delegates Debate Educational Wastage," *Times Educational Supplement* (London), July 10, 1970. For a comprehensive coverage of the international

But it is time to conclude this presentation. As educators, we naturally would have to close on a note of hope, but also one of caution about the magnitude of the task.

In our preoccupation with the theme of the decade—the education of the disadvantaged—it is essential that, in our zeal to rectify the wrongs of the past, we must not forget the many varieties of persons who have lacked the advantages of most of the population. It is the duty of education and society everywhere to provide each person with the best upbringing and training of greatest benefit to him. This may require changes of policy and practice.

All human beings, by the law of nature, are equal. In actual practice, some have been less equal than others. These have been the disadvantaged—by reason of race, religion, sex, and other factors. It is our duty as educators and members of society to try to remove the barriers which divide humanity into the advantaged and the disadvantaged. Let us try to make human beings as equal as humanly possible.

WILLIAM W. BRICKMAN

literature on educational wastage on all levels, see the excellent bibliography in the *Bulletin of the International Bureau of Education*, Vol. 43, Fourth Quarter, 1969, pp. 205–337.

Part 1

The Disadvantaged in Urban America

1

Stratification, Segregation, and Children in the Inner-City School

Daniel U. Levine

That the nation's cities are in a state of tragic crisis is recognized by almost every American. Were the crisis not focused on youth in the inner core sections of our big cities, we could view our situation with some optimism and perhaps even wait for urban problems to work themselves out as a new generation grows to maturity. Unfortunately, however, urban disorder is being fueled by discontent among young people who, rather than acquiring the attitudes and skills needed to succeed in our society, are demonstrating an increasing tendency to behave in a self-destructive and socially destructive manner. From this point of view, the problem is getting worse rather than better.

To understand why this is so, it is necessary to recognize that there are a variety of forces which determine how well and whether youngsters will succeed in our society. In the language of the social scientist, these are the "socializing" institutions which should operate to prepare young people for positive personal adjustment and for social mobility. The most important of these institutions are the church, the school, community agencies which serve families and children, the adults and peers who provide "models" of behavior for the child to emulate, and, above all, the family—particularly the nuclear family which consists of both parents and their children living separately from all or most of their relatives and other people.

Living in the modern world, it is hard for us to realize that through most of history the typical family arrangement has been one in which many individuals related by blood or by close social ties live together in extended units. Until only a few hundred years ago, as Philippe Ariès has shown in his *Cen-*

SOURCE. Reprinted from *School & Society*, February 1970, by permission of the author and publisher.

turies of Childhood: A Social History of Family Life, "Life . . . was lived in public . . . privacy scarcely ever existed . . . [and] people lived on top of one another, masters and servants, children and adults, in houses open at all hours to the indiscretion of callers." Without privacy, and with many adults perpetually present, it was difficult to prevent children from seeking adult satisfactions and from copying the behavior of the adults around them rather than postponing adult goals and pleasures in order to acquire the self-control and the special knowledge needed for success in the emerging post-feudal economy.

As Ariès shows, it was not until many youngsters were removed at least temporarily from the "public world" to be educated in a variety of special school settings that childhood in the western world began to be conceived as a special period of life during which a child slowly learned specialized roles he would be called on to perform as an adult. This process was circular, because it was particularly the youngsters who were socialized according to the new pattern who were encouraged to form nuclear family units in which they better could control the socialization of their own children in order to provide them with the habits and values needed for success in modern society.

Having recognized the crucial importance of the parents' ability to shield children from forces that make it difficult to socialize them for success in a modern society, it is instructive to take note of the changes that have occurred in the "socializing environment" which now exists in the heart of American cities. The inner core of the city served for at least a century-and-a-half as the "port of entry" for migrants from rural areas and for immigrants from other lands. What happened in America's cities between 1800 and 1940 must be counted among the most glorious achievements in all of human history, for surely there was a unique beauty to the process wherein millions of people sought to build a more prosperous way of life for themselves and their children by exchanging one set of traditional customs and behaviors for a new set more suited to a free people and to an industrial economy. The family, the school, the church, the community agencies, and other institutions as well were knit together in a way that helped individuals acquire the skills and attitudes which equipped them to move out of the inner core and to prosper in the wider society. Low-income youngsters growing to maturity in the inner city could see this happening all around them, making it relatively easy to persuade them to adopt behavioral patterns which obviously had led to success for other people much like themselves.

Millions of our fellow middle-class citizens either grew up in poverty or are but one generation removed from ancestors who started in poverty or semi-poverty, but worked successfully to attain an improved station in life. For these millions, the "American Dream" was not so much a dream as a reality. Today, however, youngsters growing up in the inner core areas of our big cities live in a much different world than did their counterparts as recently as 30 or 40 years ago. Where low-income parents once were aided in raising their children by a whole web of reinforcing social institutions, conditions in the inner city have changed in many important respects, so that the social forces in the low-income sections of the big city now conspire to mire many youngsters ever deeper in despair and poverty.

Most of these changes are related very closely to the fact that urban areas in the U.S. have become more socially stratified and segregated in the past 20 or 25 years. The term "socially stratified" is one which social scientists use to describe a pattern wherein middle- and low-income citizens live geographically apart from one another, while the term segregation is used most often in describing a residential pattern wherein whites and Negroes live in separate communities. Because many of the newcomers to the cities since World War II have been Negroes, the increasing tendency toward stratification and segregation so characteristic of our metropolitan areas typically has been manifested in residential patterns wherein low-income Negroes live in older parts of the city which are surrounded by middle-income, white neighborhoods in the outlying parts of the city and suburbs. Some of the resulting changes with respect to the socialization of youngsters in the low-income areas are as follows:

1. No longer is there the highly motivating example set by large numbers of friends, relatives, and acquaintances who give up the habits of low-income life, acquire the skills of middle-income life, and move out into the wider society to compete on an equal basis with other Americans. It is very much harder today for the low-income individual, no matter how hard he may work, to make a meaningful career for himself. Automation and mechanization have done away with most of the unskilled jobs which traditionally enabled the poor to get a good start in life. Even where still available, unskilled and semi-skilled work generally represents a dead-end in life, a fact which is recognized quickly by young people. To make matters even worse, fields of work which enable a person to rise on the social ladder almost universally have come to require a better educational background than is being provided in schools in the inner core parts of the big cities.

2. The school, the church, and other social institutions no longer are able to exert as positive an influence in the low-income neighborhood as they did 30 or 40 years ago. In the case of the school, stratification has meant that middle-income students who set an example of good school behavior no longer are available to provide this needed stimulus. In the case of the church and the family agencies, stratification has meant that the financial support for these institutions, and often even their professional personnel, have moved far out to the suburbs, thus leaving community institutions in the inner city to struggle weakly along as best they can.

3. The family unit in the inner core parts of our big cities is less frequently of the nuclear family type than was true years ago, primarily because the black family was broken up systematically during the time of slavery and because the efforts of Negro adults to establish a nuclear pattern since then have been thwarted tragically by discrimination in employment and by government policies which have discouraged attempts to build strong nuclear ties.[1] In some low-income sections of the big cities, as a result, as many as three-quarters of the young people are growing up without the full support of family resources which most sociologists believe could help protect them from the negative influences in a socially and economically depressed community.

4. Today, the population of the inner-city ghetto consists in large part of a discriminated-against black minority. One result of this discrimination is that even those low-income citizens who do acquire middle-class habits and skills have been prevented from moving out to live and work wherever they prefer and from enjoying all the fruits of their hard-won success. This effectively destroys the influence of parents attempting to socialize their youngsters by arguing that "You can succeed and move out in the world if only you work hard and follow the advice of adults who have your best interests at heart."

5. Even if they had been able to exercise the full range of choices open to the white middle class, middle-class Negroes would not have been able to provide a sufficiently effective model for the black child merely because they belong to a group which historically was kept quite small by limiting the opportunities available to Negroes and which, therefore, was recognized—and thereby discredited—as being dependent on the favors of more powerful white groups. Since even the presidents of Negro colleges had to bow and scrape and practice uttering a properly servile "Yassuh, Yassuh," middle-class blacks were and are viewed by many low-income youth not as models to imitate, but as individuals who have gained their success by "selling out" their own people.

6. Since urban areas contain more people and are more stratified than was true years ago, the slum itself is naturally both larger and denser than it used to be. The low-income child, therefore, no longer lives in a low-income tenement or block which occasionally brings him into personal contact with alternate social environments; instead, the only universe which he knows at first hand is the world of the defeated and alienated.

7. To make matters still worse, the modern slum now is used explicitly as the "dumping ground" for society's misfits. In earlier times, "skid row" was a separate area clearly set apart from other parts of the community, but today "nice people" no longer are willing to tolerate having attention fixed on the disgusting behavior of its hopeless inhabitants. The skid row areas, as

---

[1] Jessie Bernard, *Marriage and Family Life Among Negroes* (Englewood Cliffs, N.J.: Prentice-Hall, 1966).

a result, are being demolished to make room for urban renewal projects, and the derelicts, perverts, and addicts who once lived there in exile are shifted to the nearby ghetto. Parents in the ghetto, in this situation, rightly feel that they have become "everybody's doormat," and their children are exposed still more pervasively to the example of social failures in order that youngsters in middle-income areas may be shielded completely from this harmful influence.

8. Forty or 50 years ago, inner-city parents striving to persuade their children to work hard to attain long-range goals in school and society were aided by newspapers, magazines, books, and other mass media which told the child to save for the future, to renounce worldly pleasures in favor of spiritual ones, and to view the satisfaction of many of his impulses as sinful and paganistic. Does anyone believe that this is still the case? Today the messages communicated to children by the mass media tell them to "buy now, pay later" and to regard the satisfaction of worldly desires as the most glorious and personally fulfilling of all human pursuits. These messages are directed, of course, at middle-class as well as low-income children, but it is the lower-class child who is victimized most by them because the inner-city environment does not, and at the present time can not, provide him with the alternate social support available to the middle-income child.

Considering all these changes together, it seems almost as if our society is determined to establish and maintain two nations at once, one of them the genteel and child-nurturing world of the middle-income suburb, but the other the medieval child-destroying world of the big city core. Is it any wonder that parents in big city ghettos throughout the U.S. are complaining bitterly that "I can't control my children"? Or that thousands of parents literally try to lock their children in confined quarters in a last-ditch, but seldom-successful, effort to protect them from the unwholesome environments into which so large a proportion of the black population—whether low-income or not—has been squeezed systematically? Or that we have produced a generation of youngsters in our big cities inclined to strike back violently and indiscriminately against a society which has condemned them to stand forever at the bottom of the social ladder? The anguish typical of parents striving desperately, but unsuccessfully, to protect their children against the hostile environment in the heart of the big city ghetto has been expressed forcefully by one bitter mother who attempted to describe the insuperable odds she faces every day in trying to raise her children:

I live on the ninth floor of Wayne Miner [a large housing project in Kansas City] and I think it's a concentration camp. When you're up there you can look down and see children of all ages without room enough to play so they have to fight. . . . [My youngest son is 17 and] won't work and won't go to school. When I ask him what he wants to do he says, "I want to die. What else?" . . . It's too late for me but my grandchildren must have a chance. I don't want to sit back and take it any longer. I'd rather die standing up in the street fighting for a chance for my grand-children.[2]

One need not look beyond the inner core part of the nearest large city to see what happens when large numbers of low-income citizens are massed together involuntarily to bear the twin brunts of pervasive racial discrimination and poverty in the midst of a modern economy. Thus, special Federal censuses conducted in Cleveland and Los Angeles, for example, have shown that:

Outside of the poor neighborhoods in Cleveland, Negro families made major gains between 1960 and 1965. Average incomes rose, the incidence of poverty and the number of broken families were reduced.

But in the poorest neighborhoods, all of the social indicators showed decline. In Hough, which is one of the worst of the poor neighborhoods, the incidence of poverty increased, the proportion of broken homes increased, and the male unemployment rate was virtually unchanged. A similar study was made in various neighborhoods in South Los Angeles after the riot in Watts several years ago, and showed much the same pattern. Despite the general improvements in the conditions of life for Negroes nationally, conditions have grown worse in places like Hough and Watts. As Negro families succeed, they tend to move out of these economically and socially depressed areas to better neighborhoods where they and their children have the opportunity to lead a better life. They leave behind increasing problems of deprivation in the heart of our cities.[3]

Described neutrally, the crisis can be enumerated primarily in impersonal statistics which tell us, for example, that in September of 1967 there were 56,000 unemployed citizens seeking jobs in Detroit, and that 70,000 others had dropped out of the labor force entirely;[4] that employment among young adults in the Woodlawn section of Chicago has held steady at 30-35% throughout a period of enormous increase in the gross national product;[5] or that researchers making an intense study of the 640 households on a single block in Spanish Harlem found that half the residents heading households were unemployed and another third were working at jobs paying less than $60 a week.[6] Described more personally and meaningfully, what Lyford calls

[2] Patricia DeZutter, "Life in the K. C. Ghetto," *The New People*, April 26, 1968, p. 5A.

[3] *Social and Economic Conditions of Negroes in the United States*, Current Population Reports, Series P-23, No. 24, p. XI (Washington: U.S. Government Printing Office, October, 1967).

[4] Sar A. Levitan and Garth L. Mangum, "Programs and Priorities," *The Reporter*, Sept. 7, 1967, p. 21.

[5] Julian Levi, "The Greatest Domestic Challenge," *Chicago Today*, **5**: 3, Summer, 1968.

[6] David Burnham, "Heroin Traps 33 Percent on Harlem 'Addict Block,'" *The New York Times*, Oct. 13, 1968.

the "tidal fact" in the inner city is the "waste and loss of human life" and "the destruction of children" brought about among the unfortunate masses of people who have been condemned to live there.[7]

Most Americans are aware of the fact that poverty and social disorganization are widespread in the inner city. All too often, however, this awareness tends to be shallow and unidimensional. Have we really understood, one might ask, what it means to grow up or live in the inner city? Do we really understand how seriously stratification and segregation inhibit the operation of educational programs in settings where—to enumerate some particularly glaring examples—adult basic education classes are poorly attended because large numbers of clients who would like to take advantage of such opportunities may be afraid to leave their homes to go to evening classes?[8] Have we really recognized the plight of parents and children striving to improve their lot in life in environments in which one-third of the teenagers interviewed in a 1965 study had become heroin addicts by 1968, and in which these addicted youngsters tended to be drawn disproportionately from those families with *more* rather than *less* "economic and social stability . . . perhaps . . . because the kids from the stronger families are better able to see the world they will never succeed in."[9] Do we really appreciate the situation in elementary schools where serious troubles requiring almost daily police action have culminated in the type of "educational" environment to which one frightened principal has drawn attention in describing how:

Two boys opened an attache case, pulled out a sawed-off shotgun and began firing away on the playground. You should have seen that sight. You would have thought you were in Vietnam. . . . [as the bullets were flying] youngsters were diving for cover. . . . I have police in the building and they responded immediately. They came out firing, too. It is by the grace of God that nobody was hurt.[10]

At the present time, observers disagree on what must be done so that children who are the victims of poverty and discrimination can grow to maturity with mind and soul whole and undestroyed. Some believe that giving the poor the power to make decisions which determine their future will enable them to build a community favorable for socializing the young. Others believe that inhabitants of the ghetto can seize control of their community only if roused by emotional appeals to "Black Power" and only after taking "therapeutic" revenge against the wider society. Still others believe that the more constructive course of action—and possibly the only effective one—would be to elimi-

[7] Joseph Lyford, *The Airtight Cage* (New York: Harper & Row, 1966), p. 344.

[8] Peter Deuel, "Street Terror Blocks Training of Reliefers-County Aid Boss," *Chicago Daily News*, Sept. 19, 1966.

[9] Burnham, loc. cit.

[10] Basil Talbott, Jr., "Principal Describes His Playground: A Viet Battlefield," *Chicago Sun-Times*, Jan. 11, 1968.

nate the forces of stratification and segregation which result in the psychological murder of young people in the inner city.

No one can say for sure which of these alternatives, if any, can solve the crisis in our cities. One thing, however, is certain: those who would do nothing but conduct small anti-poverty programs in the inner city while righteously telling its inhabitants that they will have to "shape up" and redouble their already desperate efforts to educate their children are prescribing a remedy appropriate to a world which no longer exists, and to follow this course of action may result in disasters far greater than any we yet have imagined. Stratification, segregation, and other changes in our society have made the world of the inner city a qualitatively different place from what it was years ago. It is no more realistic to expect the child condemned to live in the new world of the inner city to "pull himself up by his bootstraps" than it would have been to expect most corner grocery stores to have competed successfully with the A&P or other giant food retailers. In this context, for a citizen to write off the problem of growing up in the inner city as it now exists by reiterating the statement that "My people did it and so can you" constitutes little more than blind rationalization for the pattern of stratification and segregation which has come to dominate our national existence.

Implications for the educator concerned with the inner-city school should be immediately obvious. The most important of these implications is that efforts to raise the achievement of disadvantaged students in the inner city must be far more wide-ranging and comprehensive than those we have tended to focus on in the past. On the one hand, educational programs designed to compensate for the inner-city child's particular problems in the school must be intensified to a level which will require the expenditure of many billions of dollars per year. Smaller classes, more suitable curricular materials and instructional methods, new school buildings, prekindergarten classes emphasizing the development of cognitive skills, tutoring, sophisticated new equipment and technology such as the Edison Response Environment or other multimedia educational systems, more and better-trained counselors, teacher training programs, pupil assignment policies which take account of the damage done to children growing up in the inner city,[11] and a variety of compensatory services and actions must be expanded greatly if they are to have much impact on the learning performance of students in the inner-city school.

[11] As Foster pointed out in a recent issue of the *Phi Delta Kappan*, unless we make teacher education more realistic and ". . . Until we admit to the incidents that do take place in our schools, perform action research, and devise methods of excluding but educating the disruptive disturbed pupil minority so that those who may want to learn may do so, we will compound our failures with the disadvantaged school population." Herbert L. Foster, "The Inner-City Teacher and Violence: Suggestions for Action Research," *Phi Delta Kappan*, November 1968, p. 175.

In a very real sense, however, compensatory education represents little more than the educator's equivalent of the "bootstraps" philosophy inasmuch as, taken by itself, it does nothing to attack or modify the root problems of stratification and segregation which have made the inner city a horribly damaging environment in which to raise or educate children. Unless we address our solutions more directly to these root causes, we may find that all our efforts and money will continue to produce little more than bitterness and frustration among every party—student, teacher, parent, etc.—concerned with improving educational performance in the inner city.

A comprehensive program which recognizes stratification and segregation as a primary source of the educational disadvantage of low-income children in the inner city should be visualized as centering on two conceptually distant dimensions. One of these dimensions is concerned with reducing the existence of segregation and stratification to whatever extent this can be achieved. Components under this dimension should include the following:

1. Vigorous efforts to place as many inner-city students as possible in classrooms which are neither socioeconomically stratified nor racially segregated.

2. Strong actions to reduce stratification and segregation in the residential and employment patterns of the metropolitan area. In some cases, these actions should include a refusal to build new schools for predominantly middle-income or white student bodies as well as new schools in the inner city. In general, educators should work closely with many other groups to enforce open housing and other anti-discrimination laws and to build cities in which neither housing nor schools would be stratified or segregated.

The second dimension in a comprehensive program to provide an effective education for disadvantaged students involves efforts to overcome the out-of-school effects of stratification and segregation in every way possible. Components under this dimension should comprise the following: support for community and group development movements variously referred to under such headings as "Black Power," "Chicano Power," "Power of the Poor," etc., which are aimed at achieving the political, social, and cultural unity needed to develop viable communities in the inner city; initiation of community school programs incorporating adult literacy, recreational, home-making, and other services in the inner-city school; decentralization plans which give parents in the inner city sufficient voice in educational decision-making to enable them to hold administrators and teachers accountable for any glaring failures in the implementation of instructional programs in the classroom; systematic programs to help parents in the inner city learn how to provide more effective educational environments in their own homes; active and vigorous support—including lobbying and other forms of political pressure—

for programs of the Office of Economic Opportunity or other anti-poverty organizations, particularly those which focus on the creation of well-paying jobs
or on other approaches to reduce the economic powerlessness of the inhabitants of the inner city.

The basic argument of this essay is that the low-income child in the inner
city—and particularly the low-income black child—is a victim of underlying
social processes which place him in an environment even less conducive to
academic achievement than was true in previous historical eras and that educators must take this very explicitly into account in framing programs to help
children residing and attending school in the poverty core of the big city
ghetto. It is difficult to make this argument without being misunderstood. For
one thing, the argument of this paper is not that all or even most youngsters in
the inner city have succumbed irretrievably to the negative forces set in motion
by stratification and segregation. In a way, the argument is just the opposite:
the number of clearly deviant youngsters and adults is sufficiently large so as
to constitute a "critical mass" which defeats the efforts of the objectively
larger numbers striving desperately to survive against the social forces and
traditions that have placed them in today's big city ghetto. Second, it also
must be noted that many teachers are only too ready to acknowledge how
difficult it is to educate a child whose family or neighborhood background
has not prepared him well for success in the school—but to acknowledge this
primarily in a superficial way, without taking steps to help change or improve
the child's environment while doing everything possible to improve instruction in the classroom. Starting from a shallow recognition of this sort, some
teachers who have experienced frustration in the difficult task of teaching the
inner-city child sit back and blame the child or his parents and conclude that
the inner-city child cannot be expected to learn very much in the school.
Understandable though this reaction may be, it is neither justified nor constructive. To say that most inner-city students are not learning in the big city
school districts as they presently are organized and operated is not to say
that they are incapable of performing at an adequate level in the school.
Indeed, educational researchers are providing data which suggest that inner-
city students who possess the particular kinds of abilities and behavioral
orientations which happen to be favored in the school do fairly well there,
but little has been done to tap the divergent abilities and build on high aspirations of low-income pupils;[12] that the way teachers respond to pupils can
help generate a process wherein students internalize the negative expectations
held for them by others; and that in some cases progress is being made in
counteracting the well-known pattern according to which low-income pupils

[12] Helen H. Davidson and Judith W. Greenberg, *School Achievers from a Deprived
Background* (New York: City College of the City University of New York, 1967),
processed.

fall progressively further behind national achievement norms with every year they remain in school.[13]

Certainly we must recognize how destructive the inner-city environment often is for children who grow up and go to school there, but a logical and professional response based on this understanding is not to conclude that inner-city students are unable to learn very much, but rather to bend every effort to help change the psychological, sociological, and physical environments in which inner-city students function both inside and outside the school. On the one hand, this means that the inner-city educator stands ready to give up any instructional or curricular approach which is not working in favor of approaches which possibly might be more effective. On the other hand, it means that he perceives all of a child's experiences as having an effect on mental and emotional development, and, therefore, that he does not withhold vigorous support for the anti-poverty program, the Black Power movement, school integration plans, or other possible attacks on segregation and stratification on the fallacious grounds that these activities have little or nothing to do with education in the classroom.

[13] *Title I/Year II: The Second Annual Report of Title I of the Elementary and Secondary Education Act of 1965. School Year 1966–67* (Washington: U.S. Government Printing Office, 1968).

2

Cultural Pluralism
in Urban Education

Seymour W. Itzkoff

The educational failure we are witnessing in our urban centers is not due alone to the raw prejudice encountered by the new minorities—Negro, Puerto Rican, and Mexican. Nor is it caused by a lack of economic and social opportunities for advancement. While these factors, certainly, are elements in dampening youth's sense of possibility, there is another and more important aspect of the cause for the lassitude, indifference, and degradation which symbolize the educational failure we are now confronting belatedly.

Recent educational solutions proposed for these minorities buttress and serve to institutionalize the subtle inferiorities these minority young feel. This is due to our interpretation of the concept of integration, which, as promulgated in recent school directives, tacitly supports a denigrating self-image, since equality can be achieved only through assimilation into the majority. To obtain their inherent rights as human beings, the minorities must surrender their cultural integrity and identity, and pass into that which they now are not. Is it any wonder that public education has not been accepted with the same enthusiasm with which it has been offered?

There is an alternative position in the philosophy of pluralism. However, in the context of the current hysteria, the values inherent in this position virtually have been ignored. In a symposium devoted to the issue of subsidized pluralism in education, Fishman traced this value to its European roots, noting the strong tradition of acknowledgment by various nations of the cultural rights of minorities.[1] Americans have discussed cultural pluralism in the past, but

SOURCE. Reprinted from *School & Society*, November 12, 1966, by permission of the author and publisher.

[1] Joshua A. Fishman, "Publicly Subsidized Pluralism: The European and the American Context," *School and Society*, **87**: 246–248, May 23, 1959.

rarely have put it into practice.[2,3] As Fishman correctly noted, once our earlier minorities—Irish, Italians, Jews, etc.—became assimilated into the larger stream of American social, political, and economic life, their concern for their own cultural integrity waned.

Today, discussions of pluralism tend to center around issues that derive from religious, social, and political concerns.[4] Yet, cultural pluralism is a value that transcends the parochial demands of sectarian groups. Potentially, pluralism is an answer to the question of how a vast and variegated mass society can succor diversity and avoid drifting into a miasma of anonymity, conformity, and totalitarianism. However, diversity and pluralism are anathema in the liberal liturgy. True equality, we are told, must result in a fully integrated society. The schools have become the focus of this endeavor and their reconstruction according to the models proposed by integrationist spokesmen has become the first order of social business.

It is reasonable to expect that, given those high-minded ideals of freedom and equality now being promulgated, the youngsters of minority origins would be mobilized into positive action to take ideological advantage of the situation. The schools would be centers of a vigorous endeavor to enable them to move into active participation in our society. Obviously, the urban schools are not achieving these purported goals.

There have been some gains, of course, stimulated by open enrollment policies, school pairing, and new school construction in slum areas. And yet, as some brutally frank observers have noted, the Puerto Ricans, the Negroes, and the Mexicans are not grateful for our efforts. The juvenile delinquency, the academic apathy (when it is not interrupted by violence against the teachers), the racial and ethnic hatred have not been ameliorated. The reasons for this lack of gratitude are twofold. First, in our contemporary social existence where it really counts, the American people are unwilling to accept these minorities into those contextual interminglings and interactions through which real integration and assimilation can take place. At the heart of the problem is a deadly fear of miscegenation. This stigma corrupts the entire range of social relations between majority white and minority "colored" today.

Secondly, the inequality of the integrationists' program is apparent to the most naive member of the minorities. It does not take much sophistication to understand that planned integration, whether in housing or schooling, implies an existing inequality that goes much deeper than just being poor. These

---

[2] Isaac B. Berkson, *Theories of Americanization* (New York: Bureau of Publications, Teachers College, Columbia University, 1920).

[3] Horace M. Kallen, *Cultural Pluralism and the American Idea* (Philadelphia: University of Pennsylvania Press, 1956).

[4] Nathan Glazer and Daniel Moynihan, *Beyond the Melting Pot* (Cambridge: MIT Press, 1963).

minorities are being asked to divest themselves of their identity and to accept in the intermingling process the "civilized," bourgeois values of the white majority.

We must face the democratic issue. People may be poor, ignorant, and despised, but they are people nonetheless. They have an inherent respect for themselves, for their individuality. No matter how this is rationalized away, they *do* fight for their cultural integrity. We recognize economic and racial facts, but seem to be blind to the fact of culture, and, as a result, a stigma has attached to the values of these groups. This stigma has persisted because of the generalization that equates, quite erroneously, the minority culture with the material and educational degradation of its people.[5] And yet, all fine cultures have risen out of similar deprivation. The raw material is there, untilled, but still rich. It needs cultivation, not elimination.[6]

A sensitive understanding of this fact, unfortunately not implemented in the schools, is shown in this excerpt from the Puerto Rican Study of the New York City Board of Education:

"Education of the non-English-speaking child involves more than giving him a seat with the chance to work out his own salvation, more than teaching him English as it is taught to mainland children, more than providing him a bilingual teacher, more than helping him to become adept in practice of the custom and mores of the teacher. Does his education involve helping him to forget the language of his fathers? Does it involve creation of barriers between him and his parents? Does it subconsciously leave him to discover a 'color-line'? Does it quietly demonstrate that integration of ethnic groups is a two-way process? These questions purposely cut two ways. They are intended to challenge the remnants of a philosophy long since outmoded. They lie at the roots of the integration of ethnic groups in the school."[7]

All of these groups—the Negroes, the Puerto Ricans, and the Mexicans—have a history, art forms, and language and vernacular modes that can be built into expressive literary forms.[8] That these groups first need enormous material help is obvious. They also need aid in identifying and cultivating those latent community values out of which a richer cultural tradition could be built. We could help to make them conscious of their history, the raw material of self-consciousness, without which no people can raise itself as a creative or truly equal component of the democratic society.

The first order of educational business should be the development of a curriculum which would reach into and illuminate the lives of these minority

---

[5] New York City Board of Education, *The Puerto Rican Study, 1953–1957* (New York, 1958), p. 108.

[6] Ruth Landes, *Culture in American Education* (New York: Wiley, 1965).

[7] New York City Board of Education, op. cit., pp. 237–238.

[8] Margaret Butcher, *The Negro in American Culture* (New York: Mentor, 1956).

children. The curriculum should concentrate on building up their powers of self-discipline, their sense of structure and meaning to the world. In short, it should give them a sense of futurity through knowledge. In our present educational system, we foist upon these children curricula not only irrelevant to their needs, but representative of a vision of life that they see as hostile to their own sense of identity. These supposedly objective curricula become just one more affront by the majority culture.

We have a difficult educational problem: to build a set of subject matters which, while it is contributive to the larger ends of our society, still has intrinsic cultural validity to these students. Perhaps it can be solved by recognizing that all successful curricular systems have had both their universal categories as well as their particular symbolic flavors. Today we recognize the existence of mathematics, the physical and biological sciences, political, social, and economic theory as forms of knowledge that are common to all civilized nations. Yet, in each nation or cultural community there are forms of thought which are nondiscursive and specific in their cultural orientation.[9] These latter subjects—language, history, music, drama, fine and applied arts, literature, social and personal relations—can be taught in a meaningful way only by taking into account the particular experiences and traditions of the community. We do not demand that members of the United Nations surrender their cultural identity in order to live in peace and equality with other nations. And we ought not demand the extirpation of the cultural identity of these minorities as the price of U.S. citizenship.

There is an ingrained hostility to pluralism that has been buttressed continuously by various appeals to the conception of national unity. And it has been fed by the valid recognition of the hatreds and fears which have infected the Western world throughout its long history of cultural togetherness. Chworowsky has expressed the concern that subsidized pluralism could lead to a kind of apartheid or cultural parallelism.[10] He implied that, were we to gear our educational system to the creation and sustenance of difference, we would divide ourselves into a hundred encapsulated splinter groups and cliques producing a society riven by suspicion, conflict, and the enervating contentions of these groups for national dominance. In fact, were the government to support affirmatively a philosophy of pluralism, it not only would enlarge the welfare state, so he claims, but it would lead to a type of totalitarianism that eliminates those voluntary associations that always have buttressed individualism.

[9] Ernst Cassirer, *An Essay on Man* (New Haven: Yale University Press, 1944) ; also, Susanne Langer, *Philosophy in a New Key* (Cambridge: Harvard University Press, 1957).

[10] Martin Chworowsky, "Subsidized Pluralism: Its Implications for Intergroup Relations," *School and Society*, **87**: 247–260, May 23, 1959.

His is an important contention, one with deep roots in the legitimate concerns of all men for the preservation of the stability and peace of their society. However, it does presuppose that differences necessarily breed conflict and that, therefore, the role of government being to establish peace and security, necessitates the latter's role in the support of homogeneity. Ethel Albert has noted that this has been the dominant implicit belief in the West.[11] Unlike the East, the Western tradition has not found a method of coexistence between cultures living under one political order. The West always has equated harmony with similarity. Even across borders, the absence of tolerance and respect for differences has caused many unnecessary wars.

Another difficulty of the position that peace must be equated with homogeneity (integration) is that it necessitates that government take an active stand for one set of values over another, an action which is prohibited for religion by the First Amendment. It means that, inevitably, the cultural freedoms of certain groups will be abandoned in favor of a majority cultural system.[12]

This attitude has been part of the American social system since its inception under the Puritans of New England. Benjamin Franklin himself was suspicious of any other tongue but English and wanted the schools to wean the Pennsylvania Dutch from their foreign accents. In the 1840's and 1850's, we used the then youthful common school to assimilate the new immigrant groups which were adding linguistic and religious dimensions to our national fabric.[13] In fact, the usefulness of the public schools for this task enabled the common school movement to take hold and spread rapidly beyond its Massachusetts origins. It was important that these newcomers be Americanized, as, supposedly, they constituted a threat to our democratic ideals. Towards this end, they would be forced to adopt the English tongue and, possibly, the Protestant religion. This assimilationist endeavor became the principal activity of the public schools throughout the last century and well into our own.[14]

Perhaps the use of the schools for this purpose was valid in the context of the times. After all, the U.S. was still a new experiment, and, perhaps, a fragile one at that, considering that most nations of the world still lived under autocracies of various forms. Our ideals of social and political democracy certainly were new to these immigrant peoples, yet, unfortunately, but understandably, we confused their ethnic and cultural identities with their political and social

11 Ethel M. Albert, "Conflict and Change in American Values: A Cultural Historical Approach," *Ethics*, **74**: 19–33, October 1963.

12 Ibid., p. 30.

13 Lawrence A. Cremin, *The Transformation of the School* (New York: Knopf, 1961), pp. 66ff.

14 Mary Antin, *The Promised Land* (Boston: Houghton Mifflin, 1912).

experiences. Presumably, members of immigrant cultural communities were undemocratic, politically and socially:

"These Southern and Eastern Europeans were of a very different type from the North and West Europeans who preceded them. Largely illiterate, docile, often lacking in initiative, and almost wholly without the Anglo-Saxon conceptions of righteousness, liberty, law, order, public decency, and government, their coming has served to dilute tremendously our national stock and to weaken and corrupt our political life."[15] Theoretically, to Americanize them would rid them of their political, as well as their cultural allegiances. But certainly, in the 20th century, in the context of the United Nations, we are aware that economic and sociopolitical forms of democracy can thrive under a variety of cultural orders.

We live in a new era. Our world is heading towards larger political and economic associations (the European Common Market, NATO, etc.). The entire issue of what constitutes national unity in an age of mass democracy needs to be redefined.[16] We must ask ourselves to what extent do we demand similarity of values within a nation such as ours, which by the year 2000 will have close to 300,000,000 people. Our consciousness has been so preoccupied by those social, economic, and political antagonisms of history that we find it difficult to contemplate that, in a world tending increasingly towards the settlement of those discrepancies of power which have bred the above antagonisms, we may have to redirect our attention to those important aspects of experience in which diversity (as in language) is the natural mode of human perception and expression.[17]

Our principles of nationhood were formulated in the 1790's, when we had a scant 4,000,000 people scattered along a 1,000-mile seacoast. Thus, the political and cultural unity that seemed to need careful nourishing in our first century might need reconsideration today. A clarification of the principle of unity in diversity is essential, and it very well might take place first in our schools. Above all, we must secure for ourselves some assurances that a national school system might not produce a national orthodoxy of either intellectual or social dimensions.

The forces of centralization and homogenization never have been stronger. We are passing out of an age of individualism and into an era of mass society. All of our institutions are beset by this social phenomenon as the bureaucratic machinery of society seeks to manage the rapidly proliferating and uncon-

[15] Ellwood P. Cubberley, *Public Education in the United States*, revised edition (Boston: Houghton Mifflin, 1934), pp. 485–486.

[16] Edward H. Carr, *The New Society* (Boston: Beacon, 1957).

[17] Benjamin L. Whorf, *Language, Thought, and Reality: Selected Writings* (Cambridge: MIT Press, 1956).

trollable numbers of people and things in our world. In education, this phenomenon manifests itself through proposals for, among other things, nationally uniform curricula, standards, and tests. The arguments for local control of education, and for community and neighborhood schools, seem to be enveloped and obliterated in a host of social and political pressures having little to do with intrinsic educational issues.

In our urban centers, we have the most substantial concentrations of minority cultural opinion in the nation. In the rotting slums of these cities, we are confronted also with the greatest educational failure we have experienced as yet. The only solution thus far presented has been couched in administrative terms—to mix our schools racially and thus, *de facto*, eliminate the minority problem. It is doubtful that the problem will be so resolved. The self-hate that has been conjured up in the minds of these children will not be removed. Their intellectual capacities are not likely to be mobilized in this atmosphere of inferiority in both the racial and cultural areas. Can we honestly say we find nothing in the lives, personalities, and histories of these people worth noting, and therefore worth teaching to them about themselves?

This seems to be the central issue: can human beings who have been destroyed psychically be expected to grasp artificial and imposed educational experiences to lift themselves up? Can an essentially foreign educational program be used to help these children attain a fuller awareness of themselves? The schools are not mere agents in this social process of psychical destruction; they have been a central causative force.

To most of us, our urban slum dwellers are the contemporary dregs of society, crying out for rescue from their fate. Perhaps, if we considered a moment, we might realize that, instead, they represent an important opportunity to build into our social system democratic values which are reflective of a new era of history.

3

The Nature
of Urban Education

Eugene Kruszynski

Urban education, a recent entry in the educational glossary, already has outlived its usefulness. This is not to deny its legitimate value as a descriptive concept serving to focus attention on the contemporary problems of big-city schooling, but to caution against its possible development into a definition as a kind of education, which it is not.

In this connection, I am reminded of the statement once made to me by the late Prof. Harvey Eby of UCLA, who had taught courses in rural education for two decades at the University of California: "Gene," he stated earnestly, "there is no such thing as Rural Education." Was I to understand from this apparent contradiction that professional maturity disturbingly had revealed an academic lifetime misspent in teaching a hoax? Certainly not. He simply was indicating that the problems which faced his future teachers of farm youth in the 1920's and 1930's were, in the final analysis, educational (teaching) problems; their context was rural. These courses merely prepared the teacher to understand the cultural and social setting as a sort of language in which his students could be expected to express their problems, problems which the teacher then had to translate into educational terms. For these teachers, the educational task was not the training of successful husbandmen in some special content, but the teaching of standard school subjects to future citizens of a complex society, some of whom, to be sure, might choose agricultural pursuits. In other words, rural education differed from education anywhere only in its setting—rural America.

A people's most sophisticated formal education takes place in its population centers as a result of cultural determinants and demands. There, the temple,

SOURCE. Reprinted from *School & Society*, March 1970, by permission of the author and publisher.

marketplace, school, and university initiate future participants into the life of the tribe and nation. So long as these rudimentary educational institutions were primarily urban and drew their students from the immediate area, few unusual problems were encountered. In the United States, the rapid growth of industrialization, technology, and urbanization, coupled with the extension of political and social democracy, soon forced expansion of educational opportunities into the countryside. Primitive rural schools, traditionally staffed with their own graduates, proved unequal to the new legislative, curricular, and societal demands, and professional reform accelerated. However, the rather rapid qualitative improvement sought via increased appropriations and an upgraded teacher corps fell short of expectations, so attention was directed to the relation of the classroom problems of this "new" teacher and his professional preparation.

In brief, there emerged strong indications that teacher training was geared largely to the production of teachers who were "effective" in teaching that proportion of the urban population which remained in school—students who resembled their teachers in many crucial attitudes and habits, all based upon urban drives and expectations. Teachers trained to adjust to the problems inherent in taking the typical city dweller through the standard curriculum could not cope easily with the "backwardness" of farm youth seeking the same diploma. It was the recognition that rural youth differed from their city cousins in educationally significant factors related to environment that prompted the development of rural education courses for teachers entering that field of endeavor.

The differences between teaching urban and rural youth, which previously had focussed professional concern on rural education, have their parallel in our time, except that the disparate groups now exist side-by-side. Both groups today are urban, seeking an education within a single school district, and not infrequently attending the same school. Who are these groups of neighbors, only one of which is apparently in need of urban education?

The positively defined city-dwelling group, and the one which establishes the norm, needs but brief elaboration: teachers not only identify it readily, most identify with it as successful alumni. Its latest arrivals to academia are representatives of the group for whom schools always have existed. Western history marks the steady extension of educational opportunities to groups which see themselves as hard-working, responsible, conforming, ambitious, and virtuous bearers of what has become known as "the contemporary wisdom"—the middle class. Its youth adjust readily to schooling, since it is but an extension of home and all its values; they understand it, and it understands them. Their variations in behavior are familiar, seldom exceed well-established limits, and are within the teachers' expectations. It is for them that the curriculum was selected and for the learning of which their teachers have developed traditional methodologies. The situation is stable, predictable, and, on the whole, satisfying. What they experience is called education—not urban education—as they move confidently toward graduation.

Accompanying these pupils in the urban school setting is another group, composed of those originally thought to be culturally deprived, but now more accurately described as being culturally different, or educationally disadvantaged. They are the late arrivals: Negroes, poor whites, Mexican-Americans, and other minority groups seeking membership in the defining group—the middle class. They arrived late not only to the city and to participation in its life and culture, but, more significantly, they are the latest group to seek education beyond the rudiments. Near-universal compulsory education, among other factors, has determined their continuing presence through secondary education, where their differences increasingly become magnified. They are identified quickly by teachers as being "difficult to teach," and from then on find themselves defined negatively.

It was the evident inability of the disadvantaged to amalgamate easily with their middle-class schoolmates without necessitating significant instructional modifications that led to the apparent need for urban education. Their unfamiliar attitudes, values, habits, and responses were upsetting to established teaching methods, though not enough to encourage much variation. Evidence that teaching still was taking place was available in that those who always had learned still were learning; only the late arrivals were not—they merely failed. But, as the teachers took credit for the one, they did not take the blame for the latter, citing superficial sociological analysis as indicating that the fault lay with the pupils. The situation intensified as various minority groups supplanted the suburb-bound middle class in its old city neighborhoods, and the proportion of ill-prepared youth increased alarmingly. The very magnitude of the problem now supported the rationale which discouraged instructional innovation, as the pedagogical consensus seemed to indicate a different kind of education for the disadvantaged—Urban Education.

Urban education is based on the theory that the teacher must be familiar with the culture of the taught, especially to the degree it differs significantly from his own. Armed with this knowledge—family background and traditions, self-concept, value system, and expectations—he better is able to make the vital psychological contact required to lead the pupil intellectually through the subject matter. The function of the teacher everywhere is that of intermediary between the pupil's experience and course objectives, as he alone commands a view of both. For middle-class pupils, the task is familiar, since course objectives, textbooks, and appropriate activities are based on long-established assumptions about their experiences, both in and out of school. Now this is what effective teachers always have done, except that inertia and institutional practices in middle-class education have transferred much of this burden to the members of the relatively homogeneous student body. The successful pupil soon learns to learn the teacher, since there is less teaching of individuals than there is of classes. Teachers, therefore, have reasons for developing rigidity in their procedures, since comparatively few pupils fail to measure up and give cause for any serious professional self-evaluation. Such security, however, does not exist in teaching the disadvantaged, where the standard assumptions are distinctly less valid for pupils whose scholastic disabilities are the result of an environment which cannot find expression in the curriculum easily. Unfortunately, hurriedly mobilized teachers of the disadvantaged perform as though their sole purpose in learning the pupils' culture is to be able to recognize it when it rears its ugly head and then teach "around it."

The true urban educator must be willing not only to learn this other culture, but to relearn his specialty in its terms in order to design classroom activities which will result in understanding, i.e., learning. After all, it is the quality of what pupils do that results in learning. The teacher either will seek to teach his subject matter in terms of the pupil's culture—a difficult task for the teacher; or he may require that the pupil deny his own past and accept the teacher's along with the content—a difficult task for the pupil. The former alone constitutes teaching and is in keeping with the ideals of urban education, while the latter becomes a pseudo-remedial process which negates both as it deteriorates to busy-work and the keeping of order. Such teaching will produce memorization at best and, at worst, confusion, hostility, and failure. Superficial success here would be an indication of mechanical rather than thoughtful learning, equivalent to the remedial work considered valid for middle-class pupils. With the truly disadvantaged, such memoriter-based progress will be devoid of the experiential involvement so necessary to understanding, and of no value as a basis for further intellectual growth. Pupils so taught never will "catch up," though they may lead that class; their very accomplishments would tend to mask the deeper problem as they continue to require remedial instruction year-after-year. Effective teaching of the disadvantaged can be measured best by a decreasing demand or need for its services.

Now, has anything been stated here which applies to teaching disadvantaged youth, but not to teaching the advantaged middle class? Is it not true that every principle of education found to be effective in the instruction of the former is as valid for the latter? If so, then urban education as a kind of education indeed does not exist; it is merely a matter of the application of that degree of pedagogical expertise necessary to produce desired changes in disadvantaged, i.e., non-middle-class youth. Furthermore, it is a matter of instructional involvement and intensity equally applicable in classrooms on both sides of the tracks.

In other words, urban education is but education conducted under certain conditions—in the slum, the ghetto, the inner city—much as rural education was education for farm folk. And, as such, it operates under the same principles, seeks solutions to the same kinds of problems, and pursues the same goal: the reduction of ignorance.

4

Educational Alternatives
for the Disadvantaged Child

Daniel U. Levine

During the next few years, the American people will be making some crucial decisions about education in the big cities. These decisions will have an important bearing on what happens in our economy, our politics, our social relationships, and in the public treasury. Very few people, however, understand exactly what is involved in these decisions, or what the implications are for the future.

The most basic of these decisions involves the very poor level of academic achievement among the students from low-income families who attend schools in the central core or "inner city" sections of every large city. Because few middle-income families live in these areas, the schools there are correctly referred to as socially and economically "stratified." In many cases, of course, such schools also are racially segregated, consisting almost entirely of either white or Negro students.

With only rare exceptions, achievement levels in these schools are abysmally low. In some inner city schools in Chicago and New York, for example, over 75% of the pupils are at least two years below the national average in reading by the time they reach the seventh or eighth grade. In one high school which we studied in Chicago, more than half the entering ninth-graders were reading at the fifth-grade level or below. Similarly, there are schools in Kansas City in which only one of every 20 children has scored above average in reading at a particular grade level, and there are other schools in which probably less than half the student body will graduate from high school. Over a ten-year period, moreover, reading scores in the inner city have tended to fall a little more with each passing year.

Unless they begin to perform better in reading and other basic skills, few children in these schools ever will be qualified for anything but the most menial work. The large majority, instead, will sink into the apathy or oblivion of the welfare list, or will become bitter participants in the violent life of the streets in the inner city, or both.

It is not hard to understand why the level of achievement in these schools is so low. Most competent observers who have studied the problem believe that youngsters in the inner city possess as much native intellectual ability as do youngsters in schools elsewhere in the metropolitan area. Pupils in the inner city, however, are educationally disadvantaged in the sense that they have not been prepared to succeed in traditional school programs. For the most part, their parents try hard to encourage them to do well in school, but a majority enter first grade without having learned words and concepts which they need to know to understand instruction in the classroom. In many cases they have not learned to follow verbal directions individually or in groups, and the hardships they experience throughout their childhood have prevented them from acquiring the habit of working persistently to achieve abstract, long-range goals. Merely attending a predominantly low-income school—particularly if it is a segregated nonwhite school—suggests to a child that he has a definite "place" in life, that the place reserved for him is a very low one, and, therefore, that he has little to gain by working hard to be a good student. As a result, most inner city classes do not function well, and research has shown that teachers and administrators in the inner city spend twice as much time keeping order and half as much time actually teaching as do their colleagues in more privileged communities.

Unless great changes are made to modify the school program in the inner city and to prepare disadvantaged children to succeed there by overcoming—or compensating—for their educational handicaps, achievement in the inner city cannot be expected to improve. For this reason, local districts have begun to spend extra money in inner city schools, and the federal government recently has provided more than $2,000,000,000 to support compensatory education in schools with large concentrations of disadvantaged students.

The simple fact, however, is that, so far, compensatory education has not resulted generally in significant and consistent achievement gains in the inner city. In part, this may be because these programs have not had time to be effective, but even their firmest supporters (of which I am one) admit that the inner city presents very difficult educational problems for which we do not as yet possess final answers and which will require enormous sums of money to solve. Based on conversations with officials in a number of cities and reports from schools in many parts of the country, I guess that it will cost at least twice as much to make compensatory education effective as is currently being spent. In a city like Detroit, this would amount to perhaps $100,000,000 more per year; in Kansas City, it might run on the order of $15–$20,000,000 per year.

At the same time that research has failed to show disadvantaged pupils making dramatic improvement as a result of compensatory programs in inner city schools, other studies have shown that disadvantaged students who have been enrolled for a number of years in predominantly middle-income schools often achieve at a higher level than do similar students in schools attended predominantly by other low-income students. Again, it is not hard to understand why this should be so. In a class in which middle-income pupils are in the majority, for example, a disadvantaged child has many models of how to behave in the classroom—and it is well known that pupils can learn as much from their classmates as from their teachers. Still more important, the teacher who has only a minority of disadvantaged students is less likely to be overwhelmed by learning and behavior problems among her pupils than is her harassed colleague in the inner city. Placing a disadvantaged child in a predominantly middle-income classroom, therefore, tends to improve his achievement, and many studies in all parts of the United States have shown that this happens without harming in any way the performance of students already in the class.

Considering the practical implications of these findings, it is clear that only a limited number of general responses can be made in connection with the educational problems of the inner city:

1. The problem can be largely ignored and disadvantaged students can continue to receive a grossly inadequate education. This does not seem a very rational response, however, because, in the long run, a population of poorly educated citizens in the big cities will constitute a malignant cancer at the heart of our society, and it is possible that the peace in such a society can be kept only by turning it into a gigantic concentration camp.

2. Far greater sums of money can be spent for compensatory education programs. These sums, almost certainly, would involve substantial increases in the local property tax, the state sales tax, and the federal income tax. This alternative assumes, of course, that it is possible for educators to find more effective ways of teaching disadvantaged youth.

3. A systematic effort can be made to place disadvantaged students in predominantly middle-income schools. This is a relatively inexpensive way to improve the academic achievement of disadvantaged youth, though it will not eliminate completely the need to provide a number of expensive compensatory services for them irrespective of what school they attend. Whereas the cost of compensatory education services (*e.g.*, reducing class sizes, adding guidance counselors) needed to raise achievement to acceptable levels probably will prove to be in the neighborhood of $1,000 per year per student, the cost of bringing about a comparable improvement in the academic performance of low-income youth by placing them in predominantly middle-class schools might amount to about $700 or $750 per year (including expenditures on

transportation or other administrative arrangements for destratifying the schools).

4. By appealing directly and emotionally to the "power of the poor" and to Black Power, educators possibly might succeed in convincing low-income pupils that they do have opportunities to succeed in school and society, thereby reducing the all-embracing feeling of defeat and hopelessness which is partly responsible for the scholastic problems in the inner city school. But, aside from the fact that this alternative does not get at some of the basic underlying handicaps of the disadvantaged child, occurrences in several big cities have shown that this kind of effort easily can get "out of hand" and even can result in building up hostilities which make the educator's job still more difficult.

Several points not specifically commented on above deserve special emphasis. First, the issues raised in this essay have been concerned primarily with academic achievement and have ignored very important considerations which deal with the impact of the school on students' attitudes toward one another. Second, my estimates of the amount of money needed to improve the achievement level of disadvantaged youth under various conditions are very rough guesses based on the best evidence now available. Many more studies are needed before it will be possible to cite precise and definitive figures. Nevertheless, the alternative to using estimates based on existing research is to continue the present practice of determining school policies almost entirely by "flying blind." (This practice is unlikely to change, however, until more citizens realize that school officials are prying many billions of dollars from the public treasury for the annual operation of the schools while generally blocking serious proposals to determine exactly how well students are achieving; from this point of view, today's school administrators certainly must be considered among the most talented salesmen of all time.)

Third, and perhaps most important, the problem of educating disadvantaged youth and eliminating the heavy concentrations of poorly educated, low-income groups in the big cities are nearly as important to citizens who live in the suburbs as to those who live in the cities. If these problems are not solved in a very short time, suburban as well as city residents soon will be paying "through the nose," so to speak, either to finance federal activities, greatly expanding the scope of compensatory education in the big cities, or to assume such costs as will arise from the need to double or triple the number of law enforcement personnel in the cities and to erect Berlin-type walls to protect the suburbs from violent explosions ignited by hostile and embittered subgroups in the central city.

As a taxpayer, as an educator who believes that children do not have equal educational opportunities when the disadvantages of their background condemn them to fail from the first day they enter school, and as a citizen who believes that we cannot afford to have our children grow up hating and fearing each other, I believe that the first alternative is unacceptable and that the second is preferable to the other two. The choice, however, is one which eventually must be made by every adult American, and the future of our nation certainly will ride on its outcome.

5

The Disadvantaged, the Three R's, and Individual Differences

John H. Langer

Are the schools in urban areas attempting the hopeless task of teaching disadvantaged children to become semiliterate and socially adjusted? Has the curriculum of urban schools changed enough to accommodate the individual differences of the disadvantaged? And are the schools unwilling or unable to meet the needs of these "different" children because society and local communities will not pay the cost?

These questions arise with increasing frequency in discussions of what is to be done for the disadvantaged. The schools have been criticized in recent years for not providing adequately for the education of the gifted. These critics, in their "pursuit of excellence," attacked the "social adjustment" aspects of the typical school curriculum. However, their quest for additional training was for pupils at the opposite end of the normal curve. It is ironic that their rationale was based on "national survival." Today, the cancer of urban decay has become a problem of social survival in the most real sense, for millions of Americans. And the cry is for additional training for the disadvantaged.

There always has been some truth in the accusation that, when the schools make social adjustment a co-equal objective with the three R's, neither objective can be as effectively met. In ghetto schools especially, the standard curriculum does not fit pupil needs. Providing for individual differences is a major article of the teachers' credo. It is strange indeed that the schools should be reluctant to provide for the individual differences of large numbers of pupils.

Arguments over what the schools should teach have generated much heat and a great deal of smoke which obscures most of what little light there is. However, attempts to establish some basis for evaluation have been made.

The Conant study has had some effect on secondary schools,[1] but the Tyler study for national assessment of our total population is being resisted by educators on many grounds.[2] This reluctance to face facts (assuming that the Tyler study will provide them) is a symptom of the basic problem, resistance to change.

Whatever the arguments over excellence and social education, there are none over whether the schools should teach the three R's. Yet, in many areas, both urban and rural, it is not being done very well. The issue which politicians and educators are reluctant to face is that different segments of our population have very different needs. Especially, they have not faced the needs nor the costs of basic education for disadvantaged children.

The major stated objection to direct confrontation of this problem is cost. Whenever funds become available, they have been allocated in such a way as to dilute their effectiveness. A recent example is the distribution by the states of hundreds of thousands of dollars to suburban districts under the Elementary and Secondary Education Act of 1965. Many of these districts, allocated amounts based on welfare lists of 1960, had such difficulty in finding sufficient numbers of economically disadvantaged that the qualification was in effect raised or ignored. It is difficult to equate the "poverty" in cities like Grosse Pointe and Birmingham, Mich., with that in the 12th Street area of Detroit. "Pork-barrel" rules which provide "something for everyone" result in big city ghettos getting much less than they need, while affluent communities write fiction to qualify their pupils for aid.

Riessman feels the basic need for disadvantaged children is the "know-how" to function in society. He argues that basic learning skills are essential for them to compete on an equal basis. Attempts to change values, to insist on social adjustment, meet with hostility and negate efforts to teach skills. Riessman concludes, "I have indicated the basic weaknesses of the disadvantaged children which the school must work to overcome: lack of school know-how, anti-intellectualism, the limited experience with formal language. There are others which should be noted: poor auditory attention, poor time perspective, inefficient test-taking skills, limited reading ability. The school must recognize these deficiencies and work assiduously to combat them."[3]

There is ample evidence of the need to emphasize basic learning skills. Hentoff found that, "this year, nearly 85% of all sixth-grade children in

[1] James B. Conant, *The American High School Today* (New York: McGraw-Hill, 1959).

[2] *AASA Convention Reporter* (Washington: National School Public Relations Association, 1966), p. 6.

[3] Frank Riessman, "The Culturally Deprived Child: A New View," in U.S. Office of Education, *Programs for the Educationally Disadvantaged, OE 35044* (Washington: U.S. Government Printing Office, 1963), p. 9.

Harlem are two years or more below the city-wide average in reading achieve-ment. Two-thirds of the Harlem children who will go on to high school this year will drop out."[4]

Studies of Detroit schools show that pupils in predominantly Negro areas averaged two grades below their grade placement on reading tests. Studies in other large cities revealed similar deficiencies in basic language skills. The disadvantaged child, deprived of good instruction in reading, and presumably in the other two R's, is thus doomed to exclusion from higher education, some-times even high school, and most likely from legitimate opportunities to earn a higher income.

Joseph Alsop examined the problems of ghetto schools. He pointed out the inadequacy of busing, school pairing, and other makeshift methods to force desegregation of city schools, and noted that the District of Columbia schools, with a student population 93% Negro, has been ordered to desegregate. The superghetto, as Alsop terms Washington, is to be the fate of cities like Detroit, Baltimore, Cleveland, and others, where Negroes are already a major-ity of the school population. The flight of the middle class whites to the suburbs, the apparently stiffening resistance to open housing legislation, and the reluctance of many liberals to allow much to be done for ghetto schools unless some plan for total desegregation is included—all these are indications that Alsop's predictions may come to pass.[5] The evidence points to the need for direct, compensatory efforts. Delay is costly to society and to the thousands of children left without adequate educational opportunities.

Another part of Alsop's data is highly significant. The More Effective Schools Program has been, he says, the most effective approach to the educa-tional problems of disadvantaged children in New York City. Pupils in the 21 schools in the program averaged at or above grade level in basic skills. However, the cost was $430 per pupil *above* the regular per-pupil expenditure. Unfortunately, there was a cut back in this program in September, 1967.

Alsop's recommendations for immediate assistance to children in the ghetto, like Reissman's, are simple, realistic, and clear: "First, face the facts as they are, and deal with them as they are. Second, spend no more than is needed for [ghetto] children to perform, on the average, at grade level. . . . But, third, invest until it hurts cruelly, if need be, . . . for there is no other cure for the cancer that threatens American urban life."[6] Although More Effective Schools, Higher Horizons, Great Cities, and other projects are helpful, they are not panaceas. A massive, total effort is needed, with the major burden borne by

[4] Nat Hentoff, "Making Schools Accountable," *Phi Delta Kappan*, **48**: 332, March, 1967.

[5] Joseph Alsop, "No More Nonsense About Ghetto Education," *New Republic*, **157**: 18–23, July 22, 1967.

[6] Ibid., p. 22.

local and state agencies. The slow progress and limited success of many experimental projects should serve as warnings and guides for future efforts. Spectacular short-range results are not to be expected, but there must be steady progress and continued experimentation.

Educators of disadvantaged children face several problems. First, these children come to school with limited experiences and concept developments. Second, their verbal ability is low. Third, the teachers of these children do not usually have the same backgrounds of experience, nor the same labels for the concepts they do share. Fourth, some teachers are fearful of or anxious about these children, give the impression that they dislike them, and may reject them. Fifth, the facilities, equipment, and materials provided for teaching disadvantaged children are often neither appropriate nor available. Sixth, class size and the organization of pupil and teacher time are unreasonable for success. Many teachers in ghetto schools, frustrated at every turn, quickly leave. The result is that large numbers of inner-city teachers are inexperienced and stay only until they can manage to get transferred.

If teachers are to help disadvantaged children to learn, they need the tools and a reasonable task. Reduction in class size, one of the major issues in big-city contract negotiations in Detroit, New York, and elsewhere, has become a political issue. But, with the present use of buildings and materials, this is an immediate solution to many of the learning problems of the disadvantaged. These children cannot wait for improved technology and facilities. They need help now, and the source of that help is the teacher and her skill. What disadvantaged children need are more and better teachers, and more and better materials—now.

Special help to children does give better results. Short-term evaluations of Head Start pupils have shown that there are significant gains on IQ and readiness tests. The Head Start Program is based on the premise that a child will do better in kindergarten if he has the experience necessary for success in kindergarten activities. It has been found, however, that the advantage of such compensatory education does not persist, and follow-up programs have been initiated to provide experiences needed for success in first grade. However, funds for these programs have been pitifully inadequate. Sargent Shriver has urged school districts to follow up on the advantage provided by the Head Start Program.[7]

Disadvantaged children lack sufficient concept development to perform well at ordinary school tasks which develop reading and other learning skills. The essential difference is lack of experience and the vocabulary to describe experience. Both experience and the symbols that represent it must be provided and related. To compound the difficulty, the vocabulary of the typical

[7] William F. Brazziel, "Two Years of Head Start," *Phi Delta Kappan,* **48**: 347, March 1967.

college-trained teacher differs markedly from the vocabulary of the typical disadvantaged child in meaning, and often in pronunciation. Mutual learning must occur or there can be little communication.

Many barriers to learning are placed in the way of disadvantaged children, and difficult tasks are set for their teachers. In our concern for the needs of the articulate majority, very like ourselves, we ignore the needs of those who cannot express them clearly, and who have not until recently found ways even to demand attention. The disadvantaged have individual needs. Essentially, these needs are the basic skills with which to continue their own learning, to permit them to participate in the dialogue of society.

Perhaps this solution will appear to be simplistic and not immediately effective. It is certain to appear so to those who will be charged with providing funds for it and for making policy decisions regarding it. It will appear to be too slow to the militants who want results today. But the problems of disadvantaged children and their teachers must be separated from the complexities of making the solutions socially acceptable and feasible. Getting the money and reorganizing the schools will be complex indeed; however, alternatives to compensatory education are even more difficult to face. The millions of dollars in riot destruction in Detroit and other cities in the summer of 1967 is only the monetary toll. The human cost in dislocation, misery, and the development of antagonisms and hatred has yet to be fully assessed.

Let us admit that we can change the life opportunities of disadvantaged children, if we will. The experiences of More Effective Schools, the Great Cities projects, Head Start, and of thousands of individual teachers have provided promising alternatives to inaction. The Federal government has attempted to prime the pump, as have many private foundations. Now it is time for local and state governments to meet their responsibilities in the long process of educating a new generation.

Lack of funds may be in many cases a valid objection. Yet, when the need is faced for other problems such as roads, sewers, and other local emergencies, the funds are found. Perhaps if the threat to our society that ignorance has raised was faced by all our people, not just those near the ghettos, society and its leaders would be more willing to sacrifice to defeat it. A massive, local effort here may clear the way for work in other problem areas such as the rural slum, where voices have yet to be raised. The means are available, the problem is clear; only the will to accept the challenge is lacking. But, for our cities at least, time is short.

6

Financing Urban Schools:
A Continuing Crisis

Thomas P. Wilbur

The most important demographic fact of 20th-century America has been the population explosion in her metropolitan areas. Automation and technology have combined with healthy birth and longevity rates to transform our rural, small-town society into an increasingly urban one. What Jean Gottman called "megalopolis" is clearly with us and spreading rapidly. It has been estimated that by 1970 two-thirds of our people will be living in metropolitan areas,[1] and the Regional Plan Association predicts that the New York City area alone will contain 11,000,000 additional people by 2000.[2]

The big cities are the centers of our populous metropolitan areas. They provide home for a large number of Americans and work, recreation, and cultural space for a great many more. Because quality education is a presumed necessity for entrance into contemporary American society and because of the vast number of people involved, it is important that large cities offer excellent public educational opportunities. Our central cities have more educational problems to solve than affluent districts and less money to solve them with. Therefore, they are not meeting this challenge.[3]

Large cities, with their concentrations of wealth and talent, were once the educational leaders of the nation, but no longer. Their educational decline has resulted partially from increasing demands and problems: large numbers of "educationally disadvantaged" children and those with special problems; teacher shortages and militancy; and rising school site and construction costs.

[1] Catherine Baer Wurster, "Framework for an Urban Society," in *Goals for Americans* (Englewood Cliffs, N.J.: Prentice-Hall, 1960), p. 255.

[2] According to William B. Shore, Information Director, Regional Plan Association, at the December, 1966, Arden House Conference, Metropolitan School Study Council.

[3] The arguments presented in this chapter are generalizations drawn from several studies using different data and they do not necessarily hold true in all cases.

As the demographic revolution in America sends large numbers of rural poor to the cities and large numbers of the rising middle classes to the suburbs, city schools are being given a greater number of problem children to work with than more socioeconomically favored school districts. A related factor in this population shift is that city schools are increasingly dominated by nonwhite youngsters, which might not be bad except that, as Miller has pointed out, "All figures collected in the census . . . on housing, education, occupation, income . . . show that the Negro still ranks among the poorest of the poor."[4]

A typical study of achievement related to social status conducted in Pennsylvania showed that "A significantly larger proportion of urban school children achieve one half grade level or more below the 1963 standard achievement test scores examined. . . ."[5] We see, thus, the effects on an increasing racial and socioeconomic imbalance on city schools. To counter these disadvantages, urban districts will have to provide more educational help and excellent teachers. This obviously will require immense expenditures.

Other expenditure-raising children who are treated in urban schools more often than elsewhere are those who require trade, vocational, and technical schooling or other special services. The Research Council of the Great Cities has shown that ". . . the higher cost of special and vocational educational programs are largely concentrated in major cities."[6] The financial implications of these statements should be clear. If urban children need, on the average, more and better educational services than children in other areas, we either are going to have to raise expenditure levels or fail to provide them with what they need.

Because of the difficult classroom problems faced by teachers in many urban schools and the attractiveness of teaching in suburban systems, central city personnel administrators face a more serious teacher shortage than their fellows in more favored circumstances. In addition, central city teachers have been generally more militant and demanding than their suburban and rural brethren. Teacher shortages and militancy have combined to drive teacher salaries in the cities to high levels. Usually 55–70% of a district's budget is spent on professional salaries, and these factors, therefore, have compounded the urban financial dilemma.

Another factor in the cost of education in cities has been the skyrocketing cost of some nonpersonnel budget items. City boards of education have been

[4] Herman P. Miller, *Rich Man Poor Man* (New York: Signet Books, 1965), p. 97.

[5] *Special Education and Requirements of Urban School Districts in Pennsylvania* (Philadelphia: Fels Institute of Local and State Government, 1964), p. 6.

[6] The Research Council of the Great Cities, *The Challenge of Financing Public Schools in Great Cities* (Chicago: Research Council of the Great Cities Program for School Impovement, 1964), p. 6.

especially hard hit in the area of school site and building construction costs. The Research Council of the Great Cities notes that ". . . substantial differences in school site costs between the large cities and other districts constitute a handicap in providing adequate facilities in the districts with higher costs. Construction costs and restrictive building codes are additional factors which contribute to the high cost of school plants in large cities."[7]

One side of the financial crisis in large cities, then, is that they are facing more costly problems than most districts. As needs and prices have risen in the cities, unfortunately, available resources have not kept pace. Three major factors contribute to the comparative reduction of available resources: the available tax base in the cities has not kept up with educational demand; "municipal overburden" robs schools of money in large cities; and state aid formulas do not effectively consider urban educational problems.

While the past few years have witnessed a tremendous growth in metropolitan regions, all parts of these areas have not been affected in the same way. The middle classes, with their affluent tax base, are concentrating largely in the burgeoning metropolitan suburbs as the poor inherit the central city. This unequal diffusion of people not only has made city problems more acute, but is ". . . removing to inaccessible suburbs the very resource base which is necessary to solve city problems."[8]

Two other factors cripple the tax base in large cities. First, many valuable city properties belong to church and educational institutions and are, therefore, tax exempt. Secondly, cities, in general, have been lowering their rates of tax assessment. James, Garms, and Kelly have shown that average property assessment in cities has dropped from 72% of market value in 1930 to 51% in 1960. Expansion of property values is, thus, ". . . undercut by limiting the exposure of property to taxation."[9]

Big cities have tremendous financial problems in areas other than education. They often feature air and water pollution, poor transportation facilities, and substandard and overcrowded housing. In addition, they must supply costly amounts of police, fire, health, and welfare services. These difficult problems and necessary extra services cost a great deal of money. The Fels Institute has described the result of this municipal overburden on city education: "The high cost of municipal services which produce much higher total tax burdens in the urban districts significantly reduces the ability of

[7] Ibid., p. 9.

[8] Alan K. Campbell, "Financing Education: Matching Resources to Needs," in *Leadership for Education* (Washington: National Committee for Support of the Public Schools, 1967), pp. 29–30.

[9] H. Thomas James, James A. Kelly, and Walter L. Garms, *Why City Schools Need More Money* (Chicago: Research Council of the Great Cities Program for School Improvement, 1967), p. 5.

urban districts to provide comparable fiscal support for educational services."[10]

State government provides a large amount of the financial base to local school districts in many states, and the urban school difficulties mentioned above would lead us to expect that city districts would receive proportionately more of this money than their wealthier neighbors. Because state legislatures usually are dominated by rural and suburban interests, however, the distribution is not what we logically would expect. "As recently as 1957," wrote Campbell, "annual expenditures in 35 of the largest metropolitan areas were roughly equal in the cities and their suburbs. By 1963, the suburbs were spending, on the average, $145 more per pupil than the central cities. This differential is primarily a reflection of the fact that during those years the disparity in wealth between suburbs and cities was growing. The shocker, however, is that state aid to the schools, which one might think would be designed to redress this imbalance, somewhat discriminates *against* the cities. On the average, the suburbs receive $40 more in state aid than the cities."[11]

The studies presented in this brief chapter are typical of those that have been made on the financing of urban public school systems. They indicate beyond a doubt that these districts have proportionately more demanded of them and fewer available resources to meet these demands than most other districts. The urban districts' financial position appears to be especially poor in comparison with its suburban neighbors, and this obvious educational differential, along with the knowledge that great numbers of children are involved and that the central city has revealed its capability for socially disruptive violence, have led to much discussion on the part of educators and other professional commentators as to what courses of action will best "solve" or at least "alleviate" the urban educational crisis. Not all of these plans involve more money. Socioeconomic and racial integration, big city school decentralization, the employment of computers and systems analysis techniques, and so on would cost nothing and might even save money in the large district. Assuming a significant relationship between educational quality and school system expenditure level, however, it is doubtful that we can improve the quality of city schools without more money. Most educators argue, therefore, for more state and federal aid to the cities along with an expansion of the urban tax base.

While the proposal for more money is, thus, a rational one and theoretically could create an equitable American school system, past experience forces us to be doubtful that the actual flow of new money can keep pace with the social decay of our inner cities, let alone conquer it. Given the competitive nature of our culture and its formal system for socializing young people, we would

---

[10] Fels Institute, op. cit., pp. 6–7.

[11] "The Rich Get Richer and the Poor Get Poorer . . . Schools," *Carnegie Quarterly*, **XIV**, Fall, 1966, p. 1.

have to spend substantially more money on the disadvantaged city child than on his suburban peers if we were to offer him anything approaching an "equal" education. As long as we persist in extending the ideal of free enterprise into our public school system, however, there is little hope of dramatically narrowing the gap between what we spend on city and suburban children.

Our society and its leadership does not appear eager to radically redistribute educational and other public dollars or, equally necessary, to mount a concerted drive for socioeconomically and racially integrated schools. This reticence on the part of the majority does not offer much comfort to the parents of disadvantaged children. Nor does it comfort those concerned Americans of every class who would have their children educated into a multiracial, egalitarian society.

7

Open Versus Closed Schools

Rudie Tretten

Success or failure of a school is a hard thing to define. However, we seem to agree that academic achievement is success. On this basis, urban schools are increasingly failing and suburban schools are succeeding.

Since we have a model of success—the suburban school—the city simply could adopt and adapt the successful model for use within the city. But the suburbs took their model from the successful city school of the past. While there have been innovations in both school design and the curriculum, the changes are not so startling as are the current school's similarities to the schools of the 1940s, the 1930s, or the 1920s. It is this model which is failing in the central city today.[1]

If this model is failing, we can proceed on one of two assumptions: the essential model is an accurate picture of good schooling and will bring success if it is reformed a bit and recast to take account of any new difficulties the schools may be having, or the model is faulty and needs to be eliminated entirely.

Current practice in the large city systems seems to indicate that it is the first line of thought which is being followed. Programs are being grafted onto programs, and millions of dollars are being spent to upgrade the educational practices of the city schools. Compensatory education designed to serve the poor has created new bureaucracies almost overnight to deal with the problem. Some improvements are seen; some scores do rise, but the general impression obtained from reading the Civil Rights Commission Report, *Racial Isolation in the Public Schools*, is that, while there is a lot of activity, there is not very much happening.[2]

[1] This essay was done while the author was a consultant on urban education with Stanford Research Institute, Stanford, Calif., in the summer of 1967. It is printed with the institute's approval.

[2] U.S. Commission on Civil Rights, *Racial Isolation in the Public Schools* (Washington: U.S. Government Printing Office, 1967), pp. 115–140.

In the meantime, self-styled spokesmen for the Negro students and families trapped in the core city ghetto appeal to the various boards of education for integrated schools, better schools, a chance for their young to enjoy the affluence they see around them. The schools listen, study, take under advisement, refuse to be dictated to, and then go on about their business feeling that, since the people have had their say, the democratic process has been served. Now, most frightening of all, Black Power has become a watchword for militant young Negroes, and the schools, like the rest of white society, gird themselves for the onslaught of demands, riots, and outright rebellions.

There is, then, a conflict situation: on the one hand, the establishment (the school board, school bureaucracy, taxpayer groups, and their sundry allies), and on the other, the poor (large organizations like the National Association for the Advancement of Colored People or Mexican American Political Association, ad hoc committees, concerned members of the middle class, and Black Power advocates). The goal of both sides is the same thing—good education. They both would define the goal in roughly the same terms: an equal opportunity to succeed and live a "good" productive life. The desire for academic excellence is as much a part of the upward aspiring ghetto mother's hopes for her children as it is among suburban mothers. The problem is that something happens in the translation of aspiration into reality. ("Between the idea/And the reality/Between the motion/And the act/Falls the shadow.")

The aspirations of the suburbs are realized; the aspirations of the ghetto are unfulfilled; and the pleas and imprecations about the necessity of staying in school and of going on to college sound increasingly hollow. Perhaps the model of the school which we have been using is, in some way, to blame, for surely we are confronted with a failure of the imagination and of our vision as much as by our inability to do.

In pursuit of another model, we must look first at urban life as it is today. The slum conditions, the lack of hope, the general contrast to the way of life of the majority of American society have been chronicled almost ad nauseum. But they are the problems of urban education. We might say that the problem of urban schools is urban life. The lessons taught within the confines of any slum are greater and more powerful by far than the feeble preachments of the school marms and masters. It is to the very nature of life in the city that we must look if we wish to have any appreciable impact on the schools of the city.

Robert Havighurst has said that the schools have a choice to make between what he called the "four walls school" and the "urban community" school.[3] His essential distinction between the "four walls" school and the "urban community" school is the degree of relationship that each bears to the imme-

[3] Quoted in Peter Schrag, *Voices in the Classroom* (Boston: Beacon, 1965), pp. 58–59.

diate community it serves. The "four walls" concept demands that the boundary between school and community be clear and respected by all. The "urban community" school concept sets out to break down the barriers between the school and those it serves. It demands great participation on the part of school people in working on a give-and-take basis with individual citizens and organizations on a whole range of problems affecting city life.

The "four walls" notion is roughly analogous to the suburban school model. Certainly the suburban schools are not simply cut off from the communities which they serve. There are the PTAs, the father-and-son banquets, the football teams, the dependence by parents on the school to see that the youngsters make it into college, and the general interest of concerned parents over what their children are doing. But this does not correspond with the "urban community" school idea.

What Havighurst envisions is a dynamic interaction between the school and the people it serves. It requires the recognition by both school authorities and local political officials that the quality of education available is one of the determiners of the quality of life in the city and that the people to be served must have a responsible say in what goes on in the educational program. This is not to say that all school decisions should be made by the poor or that school people are incompetent. Rather, the schools must open themselves to the community and that together they should attempt to deal with the problems that beset them both.

In a fashion similar to Havighurst's, Richard Derr has proposed two models for consideration by school policy-makers. Derr refers to his policy alternatives as the "strategy of integration" and the "strategy of functional autonomy." Like the "urban community school," the "strategy of integration" implies "the belief that the most effective solution to the problem which the urban school has in securing community reinforcement is to aid the other public and private agencies in the reconstruction of the community so that such reconstruction will be forthcoming."[4]

Derr feels that his "strategy of integration" will bring about closer relationships between the formal and informal socializing influences forming the lives of urban youngsters. Greater cooperation with parents, changes in parental attitudes, and a general restructuring of the home-school relationship all would aid the school.

The alternative policy formulation, the "strategy of functional autonomy," is analogous to Havighurst's "four walls school." "The strategy of functional autonomy suggests . . . that the school can be aided better by changing its status as a dependent institution in the community . . . the basic premise is

[4] Richard Derr, "Urban Educational Problems: Models and Strategies," in Marilyn Gittell, ed., *Educating an Urban Population* (Beverly Hills, Calif.: Sage Publications, 1967), p. 278.

that the means are at hand for transforming the school into a dominant source of socializing influence."[5]

It should be noted that the idea of using the schools as a means of remaking the society is not a new idea, nor is it one without a philosophic base. George S. Counts in 1932 wrote *Dare the Schools Build a New Social Order?* in which he postulated, somewhat utopianly, a new collectivist society created in large part through the educational system. Theodore Brameld is currently the leader of the philosophical school called "reconstructionism," which proposes that the schools actively seek out a role in bringing about social change.

Carried out, Havighurst's or Derr's notion would greatly expand the current provisions in the Elementary and Secondary Education Act for consultation with the parents of children to be served and with the local Community Action Councils. The school would move deliberately toward a position of partnership as opposed to its present role as an implacable and unassailable dictator to the community.

Development of the "urban community" school would mean changes in the daily pedagogical routine. School might remain open from eight in the morning to midnight, with course offerings covering the spectrum from advanced composition to janitorial service. The present distinctions between high school and junior college would end, since people would be enrolled in both institutions simultaneously. There would be a real stress on community self-help, and attempts would be made to study the dynamics of city life and to seek out positive means of alleviating distress. Teachers would come to see one of their roles as cooperative workers with the poor, and teacher organizations would become deeply involved in the life of the community. Ideas for curricular change would come from the people served and would be worked out jointly with teachers and administrators. The school would serve as a center for cultural and social life so that art, theater, and music become readily available to all.

Additionally, there would be significant changes in school buildings. Most central city schools are old and have been in operation for many years. With the school and the community working together, there would be sufficient political heat generated so that old schools would be torn down and in their place would rise new and architecturally exciting buildings reflecting the general concern for environmental values which would be a part of the community. Because the excuse for maintaining the "fortress school" no longer would be available, the new schools would reflect an openness and freedom now lacking. It will become appropriate to speak of the school campus, for campus it will be, combining educational and community facilities in such a way as to create and nourish a spirit of intellectual and artistic endeavor.

But before this becomes a reality in the mid-1970s, there will have to occur

[5] Ibid., p. 279.

three extremely significant developments: school districts will have to be re-organized within the urban complex, the politics of education will have to become more clearly defined, and the federal commitment to education and its commitment to restoring the quality of life in our cities will have to become fused and seen as part and parcel of the same thing.

Part 2

The Black American

8

Historical Perspective
on Negro Deprivation, Protest,
and Segregated Education

Franklin Parker

During the summer race riots in 1967 in dozens of American cities with many deaths and some $1,000,000,000 damages, I was challenged by 30 European students and teachers attending a folk high school seminar in Lower Saxony, West Germany. These thoughtful Europeans, ostensibly friendly to America, pointed to *Life* photographs of burned and gutted sections of American cities and wanted to know *why* such destruction had happened and *how* such a thing could have happened in affluent and democratic America. With the comparison in mind of bombed German cities at the end of World War II, the Europeans had reason to be stunned by apparent revolution in the United States. It was then that the following chronology of dates and events was recorded to explain Negro deprivation, protest, and segregated education.

The year was 1619; the place, Jamestown, Va. A Dutch ship dropped anchor and the captain sold ashore nine African slaves. Why had this happened? The Dutch, French, and English, competing with Spain and Portugal for land and trade in the New World, had introduced new money-making crops into the Caribbean, crops which required hard field work. Slavery did not at first catch hold in British North America; white bond servants were sufficient for growing tobacco. The introduction of rice, indigo, and cotton changed this picture and sowed the seed of the present racial problem. Slavery then and racial discrimination since arose and persisted for economic reasons.

The year was 1792; the place, Georgia. A young Connecticut Yankee who had taught school and graduated from Yale College had heard of a tutoring position in Georgia and had gone there only to find the job filled. Invited to visit a plantation, he saw the great difficulty being experienced in separating cotton lint from its seed. Within a few days, Eli Whitney, who had tinkered with tools as a boy in his father's workshop, made a simple and cheap cotton gin. In 1811, the South raised 80,000,000 pounds of cotton, mainly in the Carolinas and Georgia. In 1861, the South grew 2,300,000,000 pounds of cotton in a great cotton belt stretching from the Carolinas to Texas, and cotton accounted for two-thirds of the total United States exports. King Cotton fastened slavery on the South, and this economic fact of life was to help precipitate civil war. This war, essentially fought to deny the South's separation from the Union, led to the adoption of important amendments to the Constitution: the 13th Amendment, abolishing slavery; the 14th Amendment, granting citizenship to Negroes; and the 15th Amendment, giving Negroes the right to vote. In southern communities, where Negroes sometimes outnumbered whites, Jim Crow segregation laws were instituted to perpetuate the southern way of life. The question awaiting an answer was whether or not the federal courts, and particularly the U.S. Supreme Court, would uphold southern segregation laws.

The year was 1896; the place, the U.S. Supreme Court Building, Washington, D.C. At issue was a court case known as *Plessy v. Ferguson.* The Louisiana legislature had passed a law in 1890 providing separate railway cars for whites and Negroes. When Homer Adolph Plessy, a light-skinned Negro, entered a railway car reserved for whites, he was arrested and decided to challenge the law through the courts. The U.S. Supreme Court upheld Louisiana's separate railway facilities, and, by implication, approved separate facilities in restaurants, hotels, schools, and other public places, on the theory that separate-but-equal facilities did not violate the Negro's constitutional rights. Undoubtedly, all, including the Supreme Court justices, knew that segregated facilities were in fact not equal. Why, then, did the court uphold Louisiana's discrimination law? The answer lies partially in the fact that Northern sentiment wanted reconciliation with the South 30 years after the divisive Civil War. To keep the peace, to promote national unity, and perhaps to accommodate the enlarged country's industrial growth, the Court went along with discriminatory legislation, preferring not to disturb the South's traditional structure. However, one Supreme Court justice, Kentucky-born John Marshall Harlan, dissented, and in his brave minority stand he anticipated reversal of the *Plessy v. Ferguson* decision 58 years later.

The year was 1905; the place, the Canadian side of Niagara Falls. The occasion was a meeting of young Negro leaders who had decided to protest legally for Negro rights. The leader of this movement was Massachusetts-born W. E. B. DuBois, then age 37, who had attended Fisk University and Harvard University and the University of Berlin. His doctoral dissertation was and remains the acknowledged definitive history of the slave trade. Militant in his views, DuBois came into direct confrontation with the older Negro leader, Booker T. Washington, who had followed the agricultural-vocational bias in

Negro education favored by southern whites. In a major address a year before the *Plessy v. Ferguson* decision, Washington called on Negroes to develop work habits and noncompetitive skills that would win the respect and friendship of southern whites. DuBois' opposing and militant call was for academic education and equal rights. His all-Negro Niagara Movement paved the way for the establishment of the National Association for the Advancement of Colored People (NAACP) in 1909, formed mainly by white liberals with DuBois as the organization's only Negro officer. The next year, 1910, the National Urban League was formed to help rural Negroes find jobs and adjust to city life. Up to World War II, these two organizations, the NAACP and the National Urban League, dominated the civil rights movement. Both were interracial and middle class in membership and outlook. Both were northern-based and urged education to advance Negroes economically and relied on the courts to redress wrongs.

The year was 1916; the place, New York. The occasion was the establishment by Marcus Garvey, a Jamaican, of a chapter of the Universal Negro Improvement Association. Asserting that Africans had a noble past, Garvey appealed to Negroes' racial pride and urged their return to Africa. But American Negroes, by and large, rejected Garvey's back-to-Africa movement, and his swift rise was matched by his quick fall. He was jailed for fraud and deported to Jamaica. His death in 1940 was little noticed.

The year was 1930; the place, Detroit, Mich. The occasion was the first year of the Great Depression. Hardest hit were Negroes who had migrated to northern cities. Between 1900 and 1930, 2,400,000 Negroes left the South for northern cities. Detroit's Negro population increased 400% during those 30 years. Having fled the paternal and poverty-stricken rural South in hope, these Negroes found themselves jobless and in despair in the cold and indifferent slums of the North. In the black ghetto of Detroit, Wallace Fard, a Negro, appeared and spoke a new message to small groups of Negroes. Calling himself W. D. Farad Muhammad and claiming to be from Mecca, he spun an elaborate myth, the gist of which was that black men were good and white men were devils. The Prophet, as he was also called, dropped out of sight four years after he appeared, leaving behind some 8,000 converts led by a hand-picked successor and disciple, Elijah Muhammad, originally Elijah Poole, son of a Georgia Baptist minister who had come to Detroit in the early 1920s.

The Black Muslims rejected white Christianity and the American creed, and had as their goal physical and political separation as a black nation. There has been much self help and a moral tone in this movement: no liquor drinking or eating of unclean food; cleanliness of body; honest work; the establishment of schools teaching homemaking, Negro history, Arabic, and other subjects; the publication of newspapers and magazines; and the establishment of temples. C. Eric Lincoln, Professor of Social Relations, Clark College, Atlanta,

Ga., historian of the movement, described it as composed of neurotics who, frustrated by the white society, have created for themselves new names, new lives, new self help agencies, and a new myth about being a superior black nation. The martyred Malcolm X and prize fighter Mohammed Ali (Cassius Clay) are recent leaders of this movement, which continues to operate within the context of the American society.

The year was 1954; the place, again the Supreme Court Building, Washington, D.C. The occasion was a decision involving five cases on school segregation brought before the court by the NAACP's Legal Defense Fund. What made the decision historic was the fact that it unanimously and unequivocally reversed the 1896 *Plessy v. Ferguson* separate-but-equal doctrine. The court had attacked this doctrine piecemeal in the cases of Gaines seeking entry into the University of Missouri Law School in 1938 and McLaurin and Sweatt, respectively seeking entry into the law schools of the University of Oklahoma and the University of Texas in 1950. Though the court ruled favorably in these cases, it never had attacked boldly and frontally the separate-but-equal doctrine. Why was the 1954 decision different? After Chief Justice Fred M. Vinson died in the summer of 1953, President Eisenhower replaced him with California's Governor Earl Warren. Some believe that this single reconstitution of the court largely led to the unanimous decision. "We conclude," Chief Justice Warren said, "that in the field of public education the doctrine of 'separate-but-equal' has no place. Separate educational facilities are inherently unequal." The decision was bold, but the order to integrate with all deliberate speed was resisted, as seen in the violence which erupted at Central High School in Little Rock, Ark., in 1957. Desegregation in the South is still only token, while in the North *de facto* segregation actually has increased.

The year was 1955; the place, Greensboro, North Carolina. The occasion concerned Joseph McNeill, a Negro college freshman, who tried to eat at a downtown bus terminal and was refused service. Hurt and humiliated, he went with three classmates the next day and sat at the lunch counter in Woolworth's department store. They were not served, but did stay several hours while a crowd gathered. This was the beginning of the sit-in movement which spread from lunch counters to hotels, movie theaters, and amusement parks. The sit-ins gave rise to the freedom riders in the spring of 1961, led by the Congress of Racial Equality (CORE), which filled buses in trips through the South to challenge segregation at bus terminals. Many participants were beaten and arrested. A young college student who entered the civil rights movement in 1961 was Stokely Carmichael who, five years later, was to emerge as the champion of Black Power.

The year was 1963; the place, Washington, D.C. The occasion was "The March on Washington for Jobs and Freedom," the largest public demonstration ever held in the nation's capital. Over 200,000 persons marched from the Washington Monument to the Lincoln Memorial. About 15% of the marchers were whites. Ten organizations sponsored the march: six Negro civil rights groups—the National Association for the Advancement of Colored People (NAACP), the Congress of Racial Equality (CORE), the National Urban League, the Student Nonviolent Coordinating Committee (SNCC), the Southern Christian Leadership Conference, and the Negro American Labor Council; three groups representing the Jewish, Catholic, and Protestant faiths; and the AFL-CIO Industrial Union Department. This march marked a high point of hope in the Negro protest movement, a hope turned by unfulfilled events to frustration and disturbances.

The year was 1965; the place, again, Washington, D.C. The occasion was the publication of a government report, *The Negro Family: The Case for National Action,* familiarly called the Moynihan Report. Its author, Daniel P. Moynihan, was then Assistant Secretary of Labor. Using data from the U.S. Census of Population, 1960, Moynihan put forward with striking clarity some facts about the basic weakness of the Negro family. It was a story sociologists had long recorded, but which Americans seldom had read or heard. Few knew of the many ways Negro family life had been broken up when slaves were brought to the New World: at the time of capture in some interior African village, during the long forced march to some coastal port, in the crowded, dark hold of a filthy slave ship, during the terror-filled month-long voyage, on landing, at slave auctions, and on plantations. Husbands, wives, and children were separated and sold.

Not only the tradition of family life, but the American patriarchal family pattern was kept from the Negro. Negro males seldom have received a fair and steady wage. Negro women have been more regularly paid to cook, clean, and care for white families and their children. By forcing the role of main breadwinner on the wife, American society also forced a matriarchal pattern on the Negro family. She who earned the living was the head of the house, while he who could not earn a living and was the first to be fired and the last hired frequently drank, was belligerent, deserted the family, lived with other women, and fathered illegitimate children. One-fourth of Negro families are headed by a woman. Of all married Negro women, 20.4% have absent husbands, as against 4.4% of all white married women. Over one-third of all Negro children live in broken homes or with a relative.

The effect on school work and on life expectancy is shocking. In central Harlem, by the eighth grade, Negro pupils' I.Q. averages 87.7 as against the national norm of 100. Four times as many Negroes fail the army entrance mental tests as do whites who take the same tests. Life expectancy of white males was 48 years in 1900; that of Negro males, 32 years. Whites lived an average of 67 years in 1960; Negroes averaged 61 years, a six-year difference.

Six lost years multiplied by 20,000,000 Negroes equals 120,000,000 years of life lost.

In short, the Moynihan Report was a strong indictment of American society's rooting out almost every stable element in the Negro family. It pointed out that the situation was getting worse, not better, and indicated that equal treatment would not change the picture fast enough, but rather that preferential treatment alone could speed up the recovery of wholesome Negro family life. This suggested preferential treatment in jobs, salaries, and benefits was criticized, of course, by many whites. Negro leaders, too, out of new-born Negro pride, disdained the sordid picture painted by the report, which never reached the audience it deserved.

The year was 1966; the place, again Washington, D.C. The occasion was the publication of a report sponsored by the U.S. Office of Education, *Equality of Educational Opportunity*, commonly called the Coleman Report after its principal author, James Coleman, sociologist at Johns Hopkins University. The report was commissioned by Congress under the 1964 Civil Rights Act to uncover the degree of segregation in public schools and any connected educational shortcomings. This lengthy, statistics-laden, controversial document deserves full study. Many reviews of it have appeared. In essence, the report shows that American schools are still overwhelmingly segregated, that both Negro and white students do better academically in integrated schools, that pupil attitude and self-concept are more important to achievement than are all other school factors taken together, and that this attitude of control over one's own destiny comes more from the family and neighborhood outside the school than from all factors inside the school. Even good schools cannot compensate for the loss of self-esteem that inhibits Negro children's achievement. The Moynihan and Coleman reports, taken together, indicate the cumulative needs of Negroes for integrated schools, quality education, and for a strengthened family and environment.

The year was again 1966; the place, northern Mississippi. The occasion was not so much a civil rights march led by James Meredith, first Negro to enter and graduate from the University of Mississippi, as it was the chant of Black Power voiced by Stokely Carmichael, then SNCC chairman. He used the Black Power slogan again at a University of California, Berkeley, speech in October, 1966, and the phrase has since been popularized. A position paper by SNCC on the philosophy behind Black Power indicated that the term originally was used to explain why white liberal policy-makers and financial supporters no longer were wanted in SNCC, the feeling having grown among Negro members that whites, no matter how sincere, naturally act superior and take over direction of Negro rights organizations. Moderate Negro leaders have used Black Power to mean Negro self-respect and political influence. Carmichael, an emotional speaker and effective demagogue, has increasingly used Black Power as a revolutionary slogan to promote rebellion and sedition. In a Cleveland speech he said, "When you talk of Black Power, you talk of bringing this country to its knees. When you talk of Black Power, you talk of building a movement that will smash everything Western civilization has created." Carmichael's militancy, and that of H. Rap Brown, his successor as SNCC's chairman, had lost for SNCC many of its liberal white financial backers as well as moderate Negro followers, even before Carmichael's late 1967 overseas tour, which included Cuba and North Vietnam.

Born in Port of Spain, Trinidad, Carmichael was 11 when his family moved to Harlem in 1952. He became a citizen by derivation when his parents were naturalized. His father, a carpenter and taxi driver, moved the family from Harlem to the East Bronx, where young Carmichael was bright enough to be admitted to the Bronx High School of Science. There he read Marx, associated with young Socialists, and first came in contact with liberal whites. After some sit-in experiences in 1961, he was solidly in the civil rights movement, taking time to earn an A.B. degree in philosophy from Howard University in 1964. After Howard, he plunged into direct action and rose rapidly, aided perhaps by Negro disappointment over the slowdown of Great Society funds.

Many middle-class Negroes still favor the NAACP, which has the largest Negro and liberal white membership, is financially solvent, and is dedicated to working nonviolently for legal redress. The late Martin Luther King, Jr., was a magnetic leader, though he had alienated some followers by merging his anti-Vietnam war stand with the civil rights movement. Roy Wilkins of NAACP has pointed out that the civil rights movement has moved from protest to politics, a view reinforced by the unprecedented November, 1967, election of Negro mayors in Cleveland, Ohio, and Gary, Indiana. Whitney Young of the National Urban League has said that civil rights issues today are rent supplements, demonstration cities, antipoverty programs, and educational aid to deprived areas. Both leaders see the mainstream Negro protest as a supporting part of the Great Society effort, temporarily stalled because funds are being diverted to the Vietnam effort.

The year was 1967; the place, the United States Congress. The occasion was a coalition of southern Democrats and Republicans who, in May, forced public school desegregation guidelines from the administration of the U.S. Commissioner of Education, where it had been placed by Title VI of the 1964 Civil Rights Act, to the broader responsibility of the Secretary of Health, Education, and Welfare. This transfer of responsibility from Commissioner Howe, accused of pushing integration too hard and too fast, slowed the tempo of school integration. In 1968, 14 years since the 1954 decision, only 15.9% of Negro students attended integrated schools in 11 southern states. Texas led with 44.9% integration; Tennessee had 28.6%; Virginia, 25.3%; Florida, 22.3%; North Carolina, 15.4%; Arkansas, 15.1%; Georgia, 8.8%;

South Carolina, 5.6%; Alabama, 4.4%; Louisiana, 3.4%; and Mississippi, 2.5%. Negro voter registrants in these 11 southern states, averaging 52.8%, represented a much better record than had been attained in school integration.

While the South slowly desegregates its schools, the North in its residential patterns actually has increased its segregated schools. Reinforcing this none-too-bright desegregation rate is the growing urban Negro concentration: Washington, D.C., 63% Negro; Newark, N.J., 55%; Baltimore, Md., 41%; St. Louis, Mo., 37% and Philadelphia, Pa., and Chicago, Ill., both 30%. Poor Negroes, lacking taxable incomes, move into the cities; affluent whites take their taxable wealth with them to suburbia. How to halt and reverse this opposing flow is one of America's unresolved problems.

The year is 1968—and beyond; the place, 100,000 American homes. The question is the future of the country. How fares the Union? America's message to the world has been one of hope, refuge, and a new start. That was the real gold that glittered in the streets for millions of immigrants who in time enriched the American dream. Some 20,000,000 Negro Americans want to get in, not out, of the American stream. They want to come into the house, not bomb it; to join the white man's system, not upset it. They are the inheritors of the American gospel of work at a time when our society is shifting from an industrial to an automated economy. The fear that haunts the Negro is less discrimination, with which he has lived for 350 years, than it is in not being needed, of becoming irrelevant, of being, in Ralph Ellison's phrase, a permanent "Invisible Man." In the urban ghetto, the Negro is America's orphan—forgotten, ignored, denied. He revolts to establish his identity and worth, and all he can find to revolt against is in the city. To deny him further is to shorten the sizzling fuse of mammoth revolution, to fan the flames of the fire next time. To absorb him is to enrich America, to add 20,000,000 pairs of hands to the building of a better tomorrow. As the American Negro prospers, so do we all.

Bibliographical Note

The two major reports mentioned are Daniel P. Moynihan (now director, Joint Center of Urban Affairs of Harvard University and Massachusetts Institute of Technology), *The Negro Family: The Case for National Action*, March, 1965; and James Coleman, *Equality of Educational Opportunity*, 1966, both available from the U.S. Government Printing Office, Washington, D.C. A 33-page abstract of the Coleman Report is also available from the same source. Good analyses of recent race riots are Robert Conot, *Rivers of Blood, Years of Darkness* (New York: Bantam Books, 1967), probing the 1965 Los Angeles riots; and Fred Powledge, *Black Power—White Resistance:*

Notes on the New Civil War (Cleveland: World Publishing Co., 1967), dealing with more recent disturbances in other cities. A useful account of the Negro movement before the summer, 1967, riots, is "Which Way for the Negro Now?," *Newsweek*, **69**:27–34, March 15, 1967. One of the best recent in-depth reports on the Negro movement is "The Negro in America: What Must Be Done," *Newsweek*, **70**:32–65, November 20, 1967. Useful background information is contained in Leon H. Keyserling, *Progress or Poverty* (Washington, D.C.: Conference on Economic Progress, 1964). An invaluable comprehensive study, done at the request of President Johnson, is *Racial Isolation in the Public Schools,* two volumes, both published in 1967 by the U.S. Commission on Civil Rights and available from the U.S. Government Printing Office, Washington, D.C. Sidney M. Willhelm and Edwin H. Powell, in "Who Needs the Negro?" *Trans-action*, I:3–6, September/October, 1964, present the interesting thesis that automation will make common labor superfluous and that the present Negro revolt presages later poor white revolt against being unwanted.

9

On the Significance
of *Hobson v. Hansen*

Ramon Sanchez

If one event could be singled out as the main cause of the most dramatic and important social change in postwar America, it probably would be the *Brown* decision by the Supreme Court in 1954. The Negro revolution dates from that decision which cut away the legal basis for segregation in public schools. The civil rights organizations followed through by attacking discrimination in public accommodations, interstate transportation, and voting. Their legal suits, sit-ins, pray-ins, marches, and bus rides culminated in the Civil Rights Acts of 1957, 1960, 1964, and 1965. But, by 1966 and 1967, the civil rights people realized that they had not won the Negroes' battle for the right to be treated as human beings; they had won only a few skirmishes. They hardly had touched the economic, political, social, and professional structure of racial separation which is still the practice in this society.

On June 19, 1967, in the case now known as *Hobson v. Hansen*, Judge J. Skelly Wright of the U.S. District Court for the District of Columbia handed down a decision which seems destined to figure prominently in all future histories of American education. He permanently enjoined the District of Columbia school system from discrimination on the basis of race or economic status and ordered that the track system be abolished. In short, he outlawed *de facto* segregation. This decision, so far applicable only to Washington, D.C., could affect all of American society even more profoundly than did *Brown v. Board of Education of Topeka,* for *de facto* segregation exists in almost every city in America. It is increasing in large cities and small ones, and includes the suburbs, too. Challenges to this "norm" will be made in other courts, and so, whatever their outcome, the seeds of a new era in education and politics have been planted.

Judge Wright found that the Washington school system, which apparently had complied with the desegregation ruling of 1954, was actually denying the great majority of its students, mostly Negro and mostly poor, an education as good as that given to the white, middle-class students. It was doing this by following such professional educational practices as the neighborhood school, ability groupings, and optional school zones for white students. The result was to keep the mostly depressed group on the bottom by stacking the educational cards against them. Judge Wright enjoined Washington from further discrimination on the basis of racial or economic status. Specifically, he ordered that the track system be abolished, an open enrollment system be instituted, certain racially homogeneous school zones be abolished, and the teachers of the District of Columbia school system be integrated.

Anyone who reads *Hobson v. Hansen*[1] will find that it documents beyond any further doubt, quibbling, or excuses that public school desegregation has been evaded in Washington and that the school system has been distributing its educational favors on the basis of racial and economic status, with the poor and the nonwhite getting the least. The high points of this unequal education include the following: Negro-poor schools receive approximately $100 less per pupil than white schools; Negro schools are filled to 115% of capacity while the predominantly white middle-class schools are at 70% of capacity; Negro schools have lower paid, less experienced, and fewer certified teachers than do white schools; Negro schools have fewer kindergarten facilities than do white schools, and usually they are too crowded to spare the space for kindergarten; and Negro students are trapped, for the most part, into what Superintendent Hansen called "blue collar" tracks, to which they are assigned after scoring low on aptitude tests standardized primarily on white middle-class children ("They are denied equal opportunity to obtain the white-collar education available to the white and more affluent children").

The fact that a school system could treat its less advantaged majority in such a consistently unjust manner led Judge Wright to exclaim: "The school system is a monument to the cynicism of the power structure which governs the voteless capital of the greatest country on earth!" Despite the fact that 90% of the school children in Washington are Negroes, there had been an unwritten rule (until the recent changes) that the school board would not and could not have a Negro majority.

This decision reveals about education what the *Miranda* and *Gideon* cases revealed about the legal rights of accused persons: all the poor face discrimination—poor whites, Negroes, Puerto Ricans, Mexicans, Indians. The traditional belief in America as the land of opportunity for all keeps us from recognizing that our society always has had a definite hierarchy of wealth and power and each ethnic group has had its more or less permanent place within it. The crucial elements in the perpetuation of the American dream are

[1] The decision can be found in its entirety in the *Congressional Record*, Vol. 113, No. 98, June 21, 1967, H 7655–7700.

our dynamic, growing economy and our free educational system. But, to a cynical observer or a devil's advocate, the schools might seem to have been a relatively cheap investment which has paid off well until now. The lower classes have been nonrevolutionary, peaceful, and hopeful. In place of such expensive amenities as good wages, unemployment insurance, health insurance, family allowances, and low-cost housing, the poor and the immigrants have received free schools. Not necessarily good schools, but free ones.

We often forget that the promises of the American dream—justice and opportunity—were not intended for Negroes. They were not lured to this country by hope; they came in chains as a cheap labor force. When slavery was abolished, they became a surplus labor force and so they have remained. To climb out of their oppressed condition, Negroes since Emancipation, like most other Americans, have placed their hopes on education, but even there they have found themselves not really equal—not in the education received nor in the opportunities available after its completion. In the 1940s the leaders of the N.A.A.C.P. began their long legal struggle against the whole edifice of segregated education which had been standing without challenge since the *Plessy v. Ferguson* decision of 1896 (separate but equal).[2] Their basic assumption, that the end of legal segregation automatically would improve public education and open up innumerable new opportunities for Negroes, now seems incredibly naive. In this second decade after the *Brown* decision, such a dream has been exploded effectively by no less an authority than Dr. Kenneth Clark, one of the main formulators of the legal and psychological thinking which resulted in the 1954 decision: "One cannot now escape the conclusion that the early hope for an effective and orderly transition from a system of segregated public schools to a more humane, efficient, and economical system of nonsegregated schools was wishful thinking; and particularly wishful in believing that litigation or legislation would be effective instruments in bringing about desegregation. . . . The facts are that public school desegregation has been aborted, evaded, subjected to the mockery of tokenism, equivocation, and seemingly endless litigation, while generations of Negro children in these segregated schools continue to be damaged irrevocably by a society which now knows clearly that it is damaging and destroying them solely on the basis of their color."[3]

The overwhelming evidence of the discriminatory education received by the Negro students in the Washington school system led Judge Wright to "act in

[2] A 1938 case, *Missouri ex rel. Gaines v. Canada*, concerned a Negro's complaint that his state had provided a law school for whites but none for Negroes. This case did not challenge the idea of separate but equal education.

[3] Kenneth B. Clark, "An Address to the Conference on The City College School of Education and the Urban Community," Tarrytown, N.Y., December 3–4, 1966. *Conference Journal* (New York: City College, 1967), pp. 17–18.

an area so alien to its [the court's] expertise. In such situations, under our system, the judiciary must bear a hand and accept its responsibility to assist in the solution where constitutional rights hang in the balance." The constitutional rights referred to are those of the Fourteenth Amendment: "No state shall make or enforce any law which shall abridge the privileges or immunities of citizens of the United States; nor shall any state deny any person of life, liberty or property without due process of law; nor deny to any person within its jurisdiction the equal protection of the law." This amendment was applied in the *Brown* case to establish the doctrine of equal educational opportunities for all persons. "Therefore, we hold that the plaintiffs and others similarly situated for whom the actions have been brought are, by reason of the segregation complained of, deprived of the equal protection of the laws guaranteed by the Fourteenth Amendment." But the *Brown* case applied only to segregation imposed by law. Judge Wright has applied the doctrine of equal educational opportunities to *de facto* segregation. He has asserted that the courts have the right and duty to probe the inner machinery of the schools (*e.g.*, the track system, teacher assignments, school district lines, per pupil expenditures) to make sure that they are providing equal protection of the laws and equal opportunities for all children.

This new and expanded role for the courts could open up endless possibilities for challenging and changing the present system. Perhaps any parent with a child in an overcrowded slum school could sue the board of education for subjecting his child to double sessions, lack of textbooks, laboratories, kindergartens, and experienced teachers when these things are available to children of more affluent parents in other districts within the same school system. Perhaps, too, parents or a board of education of a poor rural area or a crowded city could sue the state for not providing an equalization formula that truly equalizes the financial resources of towns, cities, and suburbs in different parts of the same state. The results could be chaos—recriminations, boycotts, strikes, mass resignations of school boards and teachers—or could be the beginning of a new era in American education, volatile to be sure, but one in which the schools would be accountable to the parents of *all* the children.

Optimism, however, is not in order. The school system is only one institution in American life; it cannot create profound social changes. The migrations from the South (10,000,000 persons have left that region in the past decade) and from Puerto Rico will continue to bring unskilled, poor persons to the cities where the market for untrained muscle power is drying up. Our great cities are more and more becoming the centers of the culture of poverty. The Washington public schools soon will be 100% black and mostly poor, and the New York City, Cleveland, and Chicago school populations will be increasingly poor and black, too. The past failures of education compounded by radical changes in work patterns in the North and South are the sources of the most serious domestic problem our nation ever has faced. It is unknown as yet whether wé will face the problem or contrive to ignore it. Black cities surrounded by white belts; white residents fleeing the cities and taking with them the factories, the warehouses, and the jobs; technological revolution on the farms and factories making even a high school diploma a passport to nothing in particular. With it all there are rising expectations and rising dissatisfactions. The Wright decision, *Hobson v. Hansen,* stands as a voice of reason and hopefulness. It says that the poor have, at least, a friend in court.

10

The Negro Child
and Public Education

Robert Fulton

We are witness to a revolution in America, a revolution in which the educator, if he is willing, can play a significant part. This revolution is the struggle for unfettered citizenship and dignity of self now being waged by the Negro and other disadvantaged members of our society. It is a revolution that is being fought on many different fronts and in many different arenas. For the educator, however, the task is not that of Medgar Evers, Martin Luther King, or James Reeb. Rather, his task is the more prosaic, but nevertheless important, one of making secure the rights won at such a cost by men such as these.

It is for us, as educators and teachers, to challenge not the barricades to the body, but rather the barricades to the mind. For only when man learns to respect his fellow man are the public rights and private lives of all secure.

As members of the educational profession, we are—or should be—clear about the ideological or value premises that serve as foundations for our efforts and the objectives or goals that we seek to achieve. It is fair and correct to summarize our ideological position with Myrdal's now famous phrase, "The American Creed"; that is, underlying what we seek to do is the belief in the rights and privileges regarded as ethically, morally, and socially legitimate for all Americans.[1]

Our objectives are derived directly from this "Creed." Through the instrumentality of the educative process we seek to lower or to remove the social

SOURCE. Reprinted from *School & Society*, February 18, 1967, by permission of the author and publisher. This essay is a revised version of the first of five lectures presented originally at the NDEA Institute held at California State College at Los Angeles during the summer of 1965. The author is grateful to the director, Elsa May Smith, and the staff members of the School of Education for their cooperation and support.

[1] Gunnar Myrdal, et al., *An American Dilemma* (New York: Harper, 1944), pp. xlv–xlvii.

and emotional barriers to full realization of these rights and privileges by all disadvantaged groups.

Such objectives, however, are expressed much more readily than achieved. The painfully slow admission of the Negro to full participation in the public life of America gives stark testimony to this fact. The shrill voice of hatred is still heard in America. Men, women, and children are being assaulted and killed for striving to achieve equal rights for Negroes. As teachers, it is not for us to turn away from such ugly facts, but rather to confront them directly and, in doing so, to recognize the depth and tenacity of feelings hostile to minority group members in many sectors of this country.

However, it is necessary for us to bear in mind that, although the dynamics of prejudice are complex and the roots of hostility deep and often beyond our power to control, there is a part we can play in mitigating and lessening the effects of prejudice and hostility upon the minority-group student. Our success in this venture will depend not only upon our awareness of the many problems that confront these students, but also upon our courage and our creativity in making the appropriate efforts to overcome them.

To look directly and specifically at the dimensions and dynamics of public education for the Negro child in America compels us to recognize the part played by the containing culture and, more specifically, those social institutions which contribute a vital part to our national milieu. For instance, the struggle for equal-status participation by the Negro in American life is thwarted and frustrated in part by the identity sometimes given him by interpretations of Christian doctrine. As the putative descendant of Ham, the Negro is believed by some churches to be accursed and to derive his inferior position in society by Divine ordinance. Yet, at the same time, it also must be said that Christianity has been the fount of much of the emotional fervor and rationale for the long civil rights movement. The striking divergence within the Judaeo-Christian ethic, on the one hand recognizing the worth and dignity of every man and, on the other, giving rise to self-righteous certitude and intolerance, cannot be ignored by the educator.

The emergence of the Black Muslim movement is an example of the way many Negroes have reacted to the dual image of "inferior but equal" imposed upon them by the dominant white majority. The Muslim's repudiation of the white-Christian civilization as incurably corrupt is, in part, a reaction to this ambivalence. Moreover, the glorification of the black man and the rejection of all things white is the reverse image of a bias deeply ingrained in our culture—namely, the pre-eminence of white over black. In our culture, God, truth, beauty, virtue, chastity, and honesty are associated with whiteness, while the Devil, falsehood, ugliness, evil, promiscuity, and dishonesty are expressed by various shades of black. Examples are familiar to us all. Polite people tell "white" lies, hold "white-collar" jobs, visit the "White House" in Washington, and proudly announce on occasion that they are "free, white, and 21." On the other hand, disliked individuals are "black-listed" or "black-balled" from clubs and associations. Every family has its "black sheep" who may, on occasion, be hauled off in a "Black Maria" to the accompaniment of "black looks" from relatives and friends.

These examples of color bias serve to remind us of the force of language in our lives and of the very significant part it plays in structuring our relations with others. In the case of Negro-white relations in this country, it need not be pointed out that language often has served to keep the races apart as effectively as any physical barricade.

However, language also has a potentiality for growth and change. The examples offered above are "live" words that evoke an emotion or stimulate an attitude. But there are in our language words and phrases now "dead," which lack the power to evoke a feeling or an attitude where they once had the force to do so. Who among us today has been to a "Dutch auction"? We are unfamiliar with that expression; it has no emotional significance for us. How many of us, however, have ever been "Jewed-down"? Here the meaning is known and the phrase is "alive" with emotion. And yet, both expressions mean the same thing—to be taken advantage of unfairly. The difference is, of course, that the Dutch-English wars are over, while Jewish-Gentile feelings still simmer.

When we appreciate that a Dutch treat is not a treat at all, a Dutch door is only half a door, a Dutch oven is a pot, and a Dutch widow is not an attractive, warm individual, but rather a bamboo and cotton contraption to keep one cool while sleeping, we become aware of words as weapons which sometimes can be beaten into useful and colorful tools of the language. Inasmuch as teachers are keepers of the language, we can make a significant contribution to greatly improving relationships between people by remaining alert to the power and force of language and resisting its influence when it is used to the detriment of our fellow citizens. In this regard, we can point with some satisfaction and optimism to the disappearance of the "Uncle Tom" shows, to the waning of derogatory cartoons and prints, such as those by Currier and Ives, to the virtual end of the minstrel show, and to the end of the "Amos and Andy" image of the Negro which, until quite recently, was standard fare in all communications media.

At a more immediate and personal level, there are aspects of a child's experience with language that also deserve mention. In discussing the socialization of the lower-class Negro child, Basil Bernstein of the University of London identifies two forms of communication or styles of verbal behavior— one of which may encourage and the other of which may thwart a child's capacity and desire to learn.[2] He identifies these as "restrictive" and "elaborate" styles of communication. The "restrictive" style is stereotyped, limited, and condensed—a language of implicit meanings and of non-specific cliches. "Elaborate" styles of speech, on the other hand, are those in which communication is individualized and specific, allowing for a wider and more complex range of thought and discrimination among cognitive and affective content. In Bernstein's opinion, the "restrictive" style of communication is outstandingly characteristic of lower-class Negro family life. The result is that the imagination, curiosity, and intellectual assertiveness of the Negro child is blunted and discouraged. The lower-class Negro child, therefore, is doubly "trapped" by language—that of other people as well as by his own.

What may be said of the language barriers facing the lower-class Negro child and their subsequent effect upon his motivation and capacity to learn can be extended to the other dimensions of Negro life. The caste line in America has denied the Negro access to the mainstream of the economy. While this situation has improved recently, it is, nevertheless, true that the average Negro child has little contact with people who have meaningful, satisfying, or secure employment. His family life does not include the typical work pattern of the white, middle-class family. Instead, his parents and other adult models are restricted to the periphery of the occupational structure and have little share in the tenets and rationalizations of the work ethos. The relationship between effort and advancement goes unexperienced by the Negro child. In addition, there are few rungs on the Negroes' occupational ladder. Though one works hard and makes an extra effort to keep a job, neither hard work nor extra effort necessarily promise promotion or advancement. The middle-class white child, on the other hand, has had demonstrated to him, both in his home and in his school environment, the direct relationship between effort and achievement. The work reserved for the Negro child, however, often is without value or importance and, more often than not, is uninspiring, fatiguing, and poorly rewarded. The Negro child soon learns that effort or aspiration or deferred gratification need be neither good nor rewarding.[3]

Further, the number of Negro families without fathers also is of great importance. The Negro child often comes from a mother- or female-dominated household. As a result, many Negro children have few, if any, close male models of behavior. Negro children may suffer further handicaps inhibiting learning and satisfactory living because of anxieties over broken homes and poverty, superimposed upon the twin burdens of racial prejudice and discrimination. That Negro children are often low achievers and early school

[2] Basil Bernstein, "A Public Language: Some Sociological Implications of a Linguistic Form," *British Journal of Sociology*, **10**: 311–327, January 1965.

[3] Allison Davis, *Social Class Influence on Learning* (Cambridge: Harvard University Press, 1962), passim.

dropouts should come as no surprise. What should surprise us is that their learning efficiency, aspiration levels, and attainment levels are as high as they are.

As Paul Lazarsfeld has written, "The underprivileged youth has seen less, read less, heard about less, his or her whole environment experiences fewer changes than the socially privileged and he simply knows of fewer possibilities."[4] But, as Adams and Friedrich caution about Negro children, "Unless the gap between the culture level of the white middle-class and these children lessens, they will continue to be cheated out of the full richness of whatever educational opportunities are presented them. They will bring to their learning less motivation, less background to give it meaning, and far less expectation of success than does the average school pupil—with the result that they will learn far less as they go along and will 'drop out' of school *mentally* years before they, as teenagers, drop out *physically*."[5]

We cannot leave this discussion without reference to the larger social context within which the private struggle of the disadvantaged student goes on. This struggle does not occur *in vacuo*, but, rather, it is part of a social network which ultimately both enfolds and affects us all.

Americans are becoming an urban people; 61% of the population lived in metropolitan areas in 1960. By 1980, it is estimated that 70–75% of our total population will be living in cities of 50,000 or more or in areas which feed into these cities.[6] Many observers have noted that this metropolitan growth has served to give rise to, as well as to intensify, many social problems in education. The schools presently must cope with growing socio-economic and social segregation of the urban communities. Such segregation, if allowed to go unchecked, constitutes not only a threat to our ideal of an equal educational opportunity for all, but also, conceivably, to the basic democratic structure of our society.

The process whereby this social segregation of our urban communities occurs may be described as follows: the growth of a city sees an increased concentration of lower-class people in areas of poorest housing—typically in the central or oldest part of the city. Persons whose income permits it move out of these slum neighborhoods and locate farther from the city's center. In the same fashion, people in middle-class neighborhoods of the central city

---

[4] Quoted in Genevieve Knupfer, "Portrait of the Underdog," in *Class, Status and Power*, ed. by Reinhard Bendix and Seymour M. Lipset (Glencoe, Ill.: Free Press, 1963), p. 263.

[5] Fern Adams and Jeanette Friedrich. "Summary of Literature and Development of Guidelines for Diagnosis of Culturally Disadvantaged Pupils," Office of the Los Angeles County Superintendent of Schools, Division of Research and Guidance, Summer, 1963, p. 1.

[6] Robert Havighurst, "Metropolitan Development and the Educational System," *School Review*, **60**: 251, March 1961.

move to the suburbs and to what they believe to be a more congenial environment. Thus, the city's growing population proceeds to divide itself along social class lines, with the lower classes at the center of the city and successively higher socio-economic groups at greater distances around the suburban periphery. Discrimination, restrictive housing practices, private covenants, and designated ghettos merely add to and complicate this process—the end result of which is even greater stratification of residential areas along ethnic, racial, and class lines. The schools tend to become homogeneous enclaves assuming the quality and character of the areas in which they are located. Some schools become entirely middle-class in character, while others become lower-class. It is the urban, lower-class school, a product of the growth of low economic areas in the great urban centers, that confronts us with our greatest problems.

Conant reports that half of the children from deprived neighborhoods drop out of school in grades nine, 10, and 11. Moreover, he points out that the per-pupil expenditure in deprived schools is less than half the per-pupil expenditure in privileged schools, and that there are 70 professionals per 1,000 pupils in privileged schools, while there are only 40 or fewer professionals per 1,000 pupils in deprived schools.[7]

Such economic segregation in American public schools has been growing since 1940, and is reflected particularly in the increasing percentage of middle- and lower-class schools and a decreasing percentage of mixed-class schools.[8] The question arises whether equality of opportunity can exist in economically and racially segregated schools. Opportunity for upward social mobility, a characteristic which we regard as essential for a democracy, is undermined by lower-class schools. Mingling youth of different backgrounds in the same school is an experience, recent findings indicate, which contributes to a sense of democracy.

Wilson reports on research, conducted in eight high schools of the San Francisco-Oakland area, which supports the proposition that pupils of a lower-class school have lower educational aspirations than they would have if they were in a mixed- or middle-class school. He found that a boy with a given I.Q. is more likely to go to college if he is in a mixed-class school or a middle-class school than if he is in a lower-class school.[9]

Complementing Wilson's findings are Sexton's data which demonstrate that curricula, educational standards, equality of teaching, educational facilities and materials, and academic achievement of the children are directly related

[7] James B. Conant, *Slums and Suburbs* (New York: McGraw-Hill, 1961), p. 3.

[8] Robert Havighurst and Bernice Neugarten, eds., *Society and Education*, second edition (Boston: Allyn and Bacon, 1962), ch. 13.

[9] Alan B. Wilson, "Class Segregation and Aspirations of Youth," *American Sociological Review*, **24**: 835–840, September, 1959.

to the socio-economic status of the majority of children attending a particular school. Sexton's findings support the proposition that academic achievement varies directly with socio-economic status.[10]

Goodwin Watson has said somewhere that the American public school is a curious hybrid. "It is managed by a school board drawn largely from upper-class circles; it is taught by teachers who come largely from middle-class backgrounds; and it is attended mainly by children from working-class homes. These three groups do not talk the same language. They differ in their manners, power and values."

These studies suggest the extent and complexity of the problems presently confronting our society in its search for equal education for all. The solutions to these multi-dimensional problems, however, will not come to hand readily. While recent events in the fields of civil rights, employment, law, and legislation invite optimism toward the future, the task of assuring equality of opportunity in education, as elsewhere, is far from completed.

As teachers, we see the school as the crucible in which the citizens and workers of tomorrow are prepared. It is, therefore, incumbent upon us to understand and to view realistically the life opportunities, or their absence, available to our different citizens. If we are to use the school successfully as a mortar in which new formulas for citizenship and participation in American life are developed, we must be prepared to work to bring about a closer union between what is practiced in the closed society and what is espoused in the open classroom.

[10] Patricia C. Sexton, *Education and Income: Inequalities of Opportunity in Our Public Schools* (New York: Viking Press, 1961), passim.

11

Working with
Disadvantaged Negro Youth
in Urban Schools

Nancy L. Arnez and Clara Anthony

The unique identity of every person negates the collective term "disadvantaged youth." Therefore, each characteristic described has some relation to various disadvantaged youth to a certain degree, but in relationship to their own specific personalities. It is impossible to make a total group of youngsters fit into the same mold. Educators, especially, should be cognizant of this fact. Since there is no such human as the typical, then it is reasonable to assume that disadvantaged children come in various sizes and shapes and can be found in various places. They have varying moods, attitudes, aspirations, frustrations, and desires, as do all children.

The term disadvantaged youth, however, is not useless entirely. It can help us to describe some of the behavior that results from the cultural conditioning that often is an inherent part of slum dwelling. When we speak of the culturally disadvantaged child then, we are abstracting a set of statistical possibilities that may be found in many children who are slum dwellers. We are not describing, however, what necessarily is true of any particular child.

As we view the youth of our disadvantaged communities, we often wonder about their purposes in life. Why do they form gangs? Why do they maim and kill one another? Why do they look glum and mean? Why are their nerves always at a trigger pitch? What are they seeking? Why can they not mold themselves into our image, and thus fade into the background in anonymity? Why must they make us so aware of them through their misdeeds? The complexity, the ambivalence, and the perplexity underlying these ques-

SOURCE. Reprinted from *School & Society*, March 30, 1968, by permission of the authors and publisher.

tions result, it seems, from their efforts toward identification of self. These youth are beginning a quest, perhaps a lifelong one, that is man's inescapable heritage. The inevitable trauma associated with the conflict between adolescent expectations and adult realities is increased for these youth because, too often, reality for them is a grim spectre foreboding continued poverty, frustration, and despair. They are seeking an identity with life, as are other adolescents, but the life with which they usually must identify is unpleasant at best, defeating at worst. Yet, in spite of their awareness of these grim realities, many disadvantaged youth feel unable to profit from their perceptions. They often are powerless to redirect or abort what seems to lie ahead. Often they have no hand in decisions made concerning them.

The job of the teacher, then, is to help these youth who—seeing the reality of their present positions—need to understand the causes and formulate plans to change positively the course of their lives. We must be as realistic as they are about the alternatives which are open to them, and we must help them see that present reality not necessarily is future reality. Therefore, the obstacles preventing them from becoming a contributing part of the larger society must be confronted realistically by both groups.

In addition to seeking their identity, these youth are seeking a meaningful place in society. They are tired of the education game. Education often particularly is meaningless to lower-class Negro youth. And perhaps it is just plain meaningless; for, if the education of the *haves* in our society can permit them to make the kinds of decisions they make about the *have-nots*, then there certainly is something wrong with education in our country. Furthermore, what realistic concerns does the curriculum focus on? Does it deal with what to do about being hungry all of the time? No! It simply admonishes against stealing. It advocates getting a job when there are not any jobs to be had for most of our youth and even fewer for minority youth. Does it explain how to handle a drunken father and keep him from viciously beating his child each night? No! It answers back, "Honor thy father." Does it tell what to do about a mother who is a prostitute? Again we must answer, "No!" It preaches, "Honor thy mother, too." How does one heat a house without coal or oil? The curriculum teaches children to rub two sticks together in early American Indian fashion. It simply does not focus on the real concerns of students. It conscientiously avoids such provocative concerns as: How can we eat without stealing? How can we control our sexual urges? How can we equip ourselves for a good job without having to involve ourselves in the mumbo-jumbo taught in most classrooms? How can I arrive at self-fulfillment? Who am I? Where am I going? How do I get there? These are our concerns, our youth shout. What does the school propose to do about helping us with these problems? The point is that today's youngsters, disadvantaged or not, are a questioning brood—a probing group.

This generation of young people, whether advantaged or disadvantaged, being more pressured by time and opportunity than were past generations, can not afford to waste time shifting through layers of unreality and phoniness. They want to come to immediate grips with reality. Living in an age which has seen the creation of fantastic frontiers in space, technology, communications, and in man's ability to control the physical environment, they seem to demand the same progress in man's understanding of himself. They seek to hasten the breaching of the psychological frontier, and to ensure society's wiser use of each individual's human potential and right to self-realization, in spite of accidents of birth.

The irrelevant middle-class values and middle-class-oriented school system are academically, socially, economically, and psychologically irrelevant for lower-class children. Relevancy has become a new philosophy for today's rebels and social critics in the civil rights movement. View our youth's participation in sit-ins, freedom rides, passive resistance movements, and mass protests. They are fed up with dilly-dallying, pussyfooting, compromising approaches. They are impatient with all equivocation, evasion, hypocrisy, and subterfuge. They no longer can be satisfied with mere empty survival. Their reaction is a drive to make a worthwhile contribution to the larger society.

Our disadvantaged Negro young people are more realistic than we are. They are aware of the structure of our society and their place in it, or perhaps non-place in it.

They know that they are not respected in our middle-class schools with white middle-class standards. We must be realistic, too. We must find a way to let our Negro disadvantaged youth know that we, too, are aware of the economic and social pressures that govern their lives. The masque must be ended, because our youth and we are caught fast in the bitterness of hard reality. They think we are crazy. They think we do not know what is happening. They say, "Tell it like it is." And we keep on avoiding doing so. We keep our heads buried in the sand. An example of this is the following case. In one of the typical Negro ghetto schools, there was a seventh grader who had a most original ending for the Pledge of Allegiance. Each morning this lad stood with the other students, faced the flag, put his hand over his heart, and recited the pledge in the traditional sing-song fashion; but he added daily to the ending the words "white people"—that is, ". . . with liberty and justice for all *white people*." He said it loud and clear. Each and every morning he did this. No amount of admonishing, explaining, or threatening—as we teachers are prone to do—deterred him from his stance. It was as if his mission in life was to make his teacher and his classmates see the hypocrisy involved in black people pledging allegiance to prejudice, discrimination, and segregation.

Who were the misguided in this case, this disadvantaged Negro youth or his

middle-class teacher and middle-class-oriented classmates? His constant aston-
ishment at our failure to understand that liberty and justice in America were
not meant for black people truly was unsettling.

And the fact remained that there was little that he would accept in the way
of book-learning from this teacher or the rest of his hypocritical elders. There
was complete closure of the mind operating in his case, and perhaps in the
case of many others. And it probably was then that the teacher began to
question what she was teaching—the relevancy of it for these Negro children.

Surely, if we are going to work effectively with disadvantaged Negro youth,
we must face life squarely and admit to its many hypocrisies, for they truly see
them and lose faith before our refusal to acknowledge their existence. Being
constantly faced with uncaring, often unscrupulous, white-oriented, middle-
class society, whether in social, political, or educational institutions; confronted by necessary, but irrelevant choices and alternatives; wishing to
achieve, to succeed, to consume, to be accepted, to be relevant, and to destroy
the irrelevant, lower-class children devise ways to cope with the paradoxes and
frustrations. They learn to tune out middle-class teachers and middle-class
schools.

The problem of lower-class Negro children in middle-class, white value-
oriented schools must be solved. And middle-class teachers need to reappraise
and to reexamine their own cultural backgrounds if they are to help children
solve the problems realistically. Realism consists of understanding the child's
awareness of reality and in helping him achieve as much as his potential and
life expectancies will allow. When necessary, teachers must modify and extend
the horizons of these children. They must not indoctrinate, though. They
should not use the child's lower-class culture to motivate him to achieve the
teacher's own preconceived middle-class standards. Teaching of lower-class
children should not be an attempt dictatorially to change the life style of these
children. The function of schools should be to focus on reality and to make
the child aware of the nature of reality. If a child chooses not to learn to read,
for example, he should not be threatened or punished, but he should be told
of the alternatives which realistically are open to him. He should be told, for
example, that, without verbal skills, he may limit his chances or reduce statistically the chances of his owning that Mercedes Benz or buying that Brooks
Brothers suit. We should not tell him that he can not buy these commodities
without an education, because he knows better. He knows of those slightly
outside the law, for example, or jazz artists or popular singers who have
achieved material success without an education. But these are the exceptions.
Statistically, people with only a high school education can expect to earn less
than those with a college education. And, of course, those without a high
school education earn substantially less than both groups.

We do not mean to suggest that only those with a college education are the ones who can achieve material success. There are, of course, the talented few who, without a college education or even a high school education, achieve success in business. Why should a child so trust to luck or divine providence to believe that he, too, will not be a poverty statistic. Therefore, teachers must focus on realism, by explaining the alternatives and the roads which most likely can lead to accomplishment of desired objectives. Only when we remove the phony and irrelevant from the curriculum of the lower-class child, can we hope to "move" him to make a difference in his scheme of things.

Here we only are touching upon the most obvious and tangible goals of most people, no matter what their socioeconomic class. We believe that economic needs motivate human beings to such an extent that they interfere with their higher and more noble aspirations. Each child deserves the right to self-fulfillment; perhaps to love, to play, to hope, to laugh, to find, and to respond to beauty. No teacher, however, has the right to tell her pupils what to love, to play with, to hope for, to laugh at, to find beauty in. Can we be so sure that our tastes represent the ultimate? Cultural differences and environmental backgrounds shape our tastes. Each teacher, though, can help the child refine his personal values so that he is not ashamed to love what he loves, to hope what he hopes, to laugh when he laughs; that is, teachers must teach the child not to be ashamed of whatever is uniquely him, but, if necessary, to modify and change himself for greater self-fulfillment. Thus, if teachers expose the child to enough alternatives, he will desire and respond to noble and high aspirations. If they teach him to think, to discriminate, they will have helped him to recognize present realities, and to recognize and cope with future realities as well.

12

Special College Entry Programs for Afro-Americans

Barbara A. Rhodes

"Who is this creature we would educate so joyfully? What are his ca-pacities? Can he really be changed? Will great efforts yield us great gains? History tells us more than we want to know about what is wrong with man, and we can hardly turn a page in the daily press without learning the specific time, place and name of evil. But perhaps the most pervasive evil of all rarely appears in the news. This evil, the waste of human potential, is particularly painful to recognize, for it strikes our parents and children, our friends and brothers, ourselves."[1]

The problem of the waste of human potential among Afro-Americans in the U.S. has been a problem since slavery. The struggle for human and civil rights has been an effort that perpetuates this waste. Afro-Americans are demanding the opportunity to develop and utilize their potential. Much of the push has been in the area of education. In a speech at Washington, D.C., in 1965, the late Dr. Martin Luther King, Jr., said: "The Negro today is not struggling for some abstract, vague rights but for concrete and prompt improvement in his way of life. . . . Education and learning have become tools for shaping the future and not devices of privilege for an exclusive few."

How can the slum child be helped to join the mainstream of meaningful life in America? Civil rights rallied around the theme that integration would provide quality education for all pupils. Civil rights forces reasoned that integration was the only way to grasp equal opportunity. Corollary to this thinking was that commitment to educating Afro-Americans was so low that the Afro-American school as a separate entity had to be eliminated.

Although some efforts, such as busing of students and gerrymandering of

SOURCE. Reprinted from *School & Society*, October 1970, by permission of the author and publisher.

[1] George B. Leonard, *Education and Ecstasy* (New York: Delacorte Press, 1968), p. 24.

92   The Black American

school boundary lines, were made to integrate schools, a large-scale integration effort was not made. For example, in Detroit in 1961, 46% of the public school pupils were Afro-American; in 1967, the figure had grown to more than 60%.[2] Other large cities reflected similar statistics. White parents were putting their children in private schools or transporting them to schools where there were few or no Afro-Americans. Integration was not being achieved.

In 1965, the theory of compensatory education was introduced as a means to make up for the past neglect and to assist the student while the slow process of integration was taking place. A report by Harlem Youth Opportunities Unlimited, Inc., financed by the President's Committee on Juvenile Delinquency and Youth Crime, supports this view. According to this report, general integration is necessary in the long run, but, in the short run, compensatory education is needed for all Harlem children. The Elementary and Secondary Education Act of 1965 designated $1,250,000,000 a year[3] to aid education, with money for more supplies, special teachers, and new remedial clinics. With the money, compensatory programs were initiated in many schools at the primary and secondary levels.

Compensatory education has continued to be directed to the elementary and secondary levels as prescribed by the 1965 act. However, few educational programs have been developed for the child who has completed 12 years of an inferior education and is ill-prepared for the fullest possible participation in American life, or for the young person who has dropped out of school before completion of the 12th grade. Programs that address themselves to this part of the population are generally vocational or job-training programs. (In 1962, the Manpower Development and Training Act was passed. Its purpose was to identify current and future manpower shortages and to help in recruiting and training people to fill the jobs. In 1963, Congress passed the Morse-Perkins Vocational Education Act, thereby increasing the subsidy to, and broadening the scope of, vocational programs.)

Several important factors must be considered that reflect the need for another type of educational program for the ill-prepared part of the population. First, many of these young have a high native intelligence and have the potential to contribute to society in more effective functions than in those of semi-skilled, skilled, or other vocational capacities. Many are actively involved in the community and possibly will emerge as leaders. It is the responsibility of society to prepare those young people for leadership, or the society will reap the seed sown by uneducated, miseducated, bitter, and frustrated leaders. American society cannot waste the untapped resource represented by many youngsters in this segment of the population, and must accept large responsibility for the cultivation of their potential ability. This segment of the popula-

[2] Irwin Eisenberg, *The City in Crisis* (New York: Wilson, 1968), p. 110.
[3] David Cushman Coyle, *Breakthrough to the Great Society* (San Francisco: Oceana, 1965), p. 76.

tion cannot benefit from the early childhood programs or the improvements and special programs being implemented in primary and secondary schools. Many of the unstimulated students have passed through, or dropped out of, the educational system. A program is needed to give these young people the opportunity to realize their potential intelligence and, with special assistance, upgrade themselves educationally so that they can enter higher education, be successful in higher educational pursuits, and then function in society at a level compatible with their realized potential. Such a program should be a special entry program at the college or university level with the objective of making up educational deficiencies and in other ways preparing the student for successful matriculation in higher education.

On July 28, 1967, Pres. Lyndon B. Johnson, in the aftermath of major racial disorders that summer in Newark, Detroit, and neighboring communities, established the National Advisory Commission on Civil Disorders to investigate three basic questions: What happened? Why did it happen? What can be done to prevent it from happening again? The commission reached the basic conclusion that "Our nation is moving toward two societies, one black, one white, separate and unequal." Their recommendation was to mount programs on a scale equal to the dimension of the problem, to aim these programs for high impact in the immediate future in order to close the gap between promise and performance, and to undertake new initiatives and experiments that can change the system of failure and frustration that now dominates the ghetto and weakens our society.

The commission reported: "Education in a democratic society must equip children to develop their potential and to participate fully in American life." It presented recommendations in this area. One of these was, "Expand opportunities for higher education through increased federal assistance to disadvantaged students."[4] This also included the conclusion that new experiments should be initiated to change the system of failure and frustration that now dominates the black community and weakens the American society.

A seminar reported that, "Despite rising standards of American education, the problem of national education failure—whether measured through dropouts, grade retardation, evaluations of levels of literacy, unemployment of youth, or any other indice, is becoming increasingly apparent. . . . The problem is widespread, but it is also concentrated in certain groups and locations. Education failure is interlaced with social problems, such as poverty, racial discrimination, and political inequality. It is most dramatically apparent in the ghettoes of large cities."[5]

The Association of Urban Universities stated in 1965: "It is the problem of

---

[4] National Advisory Commission on Civil Disorders, *Report of the Commission* (Washington: U.S. Government Printing Office, 1968), p. 25.

[5] Report of a seminar by Bank Street College, *Education of the Deprived and Segregated* (Boston: Northeastern University Press, 1963), p. 28.

providing post-high school educational opportunities for thousands of young-sters from underprivileged groups and ethnic minorities who can be expected to graduate from big city schools over the next few years but whose educa-tional attainments are likely to be equivalent to only the tenth or eleventh grade accomplishments—or even lower. . . . This is an educational problem true, but it is more than that; it has political, social, economic, civil rights and psychological overtones as well."[6]

The above three statements reflect the need for academic programs at the level of higher education. Failure in education does not occur in a vacuum, but is related to other problems. Educational programs are needed that can relate to these other problems and achieve their educational goals. Educational programs are needed that can upgrade students from a tenth grade or lower level to a level necessary for college or university success.

The need for this type of program is reflected further by the high dropout rate of Afro-Americans at the secondary level. "The high school dropout prob-lem is not basically a question of the high school. It has become abundantly clear throughout studies that the damage has already been done to the child even before he has entered first grade. The typical dropout's problems are those of weak self-image, weak communications skills, and inability to get along pleasurably with others."[7] Educational programs are needed that can relate to the needs of these youngsters.

According to Broom and Glenn,

An improvement in education, occupation, and economic condition has occurred in the past half century and in these respects, the gap between Negroes and Whites has been considerably reduced. The most pronounced and striking change in the Negro, however, has been a sharp rise in Negro aspirations, a shift from accommo-dation and quiet resignation to an urgent demand and struggle for equality. There is increased discontent and restiveness which is more and more being expressed outwardly rather than inwardly. The well educated and well qualified Negro can look to the future with optimism. The uneducated and unskilled (and this group represents the majority of Negroes) look to a dismal future. The latter group of Negroes have caught the spirit of the protest movement, but their discontent is not tempered by optimism. Their aspirations have been raised by mass media and by observing the advancement of better educated Negroes. However, they have attained no appreciable fulfillment of their ambitions. These Negroes remain ob-servers of an affluent society. The civil rights movement has given them a tem-porary psychological lift, but they have gained few tangible benefits. The tendency for the underprivileged Negro is an inclination toward violence, a susceptibility to the appeals of demagogues, and a rejection of moderate Negro leaders.[8]

[6] National Advisory Commission on Civil Disorders, op. cit., p. 26.

[7] Lucius Cervantes, The Dropout: Causes and Cures (Ann Arbor: University of Mich-igan Press, 1966), p. 92.

[8] Leonard Broom and Norval Glenn, Transformation of the Negro American (New York: Harper & Row, 1967), p. 185.

This is another dimension of the problem. Programs are needed that will attempt to engage the underprivileged Afro-American in higher education, and to have him return to the community and participate meaningfully and effectively in its uplift.

The success of any educational program designed to meet the needs of the Afro-American is dependent, in the final analysis, on its bringing to maturity the potential of the black youngsters who have not had previous success in academic life and preparing them for success in higher education. The need for such programs is an immediate problem confronting the institutions of education in America. On some campuses, an effort is being made to implement programs that will serve the Afro-American student in terms of the needs presented in this essay. However, to date, programs have not been mounted on a scale equal to the dimension of the problem. Until creativity, experimentation, and innovation are permitted in the institutions of higher education in this country, the problems of the educational needs of a large segment of Afro-Americans will not be met.

13

More Negroes in College:
A Program for Action Now

Norman D. Kurland

Every discussion today of the Negro in higher education begins with the fact that there are very few Negro students in the supposedly integrated colleges and universities of this land. When the small numbers of Negroes among their students were brought to the attention of colleges, the first response was usually to point with pride to the nondiscriminatory policy of the institution, its liberal faculty, and the star Negro athlete who was president of his class. When pressed on numbers, some institutions could even come up with a small number of Negro students who, on investigation, turned out to have found it easier to get admitted via the U.S. embassy in Ghana or Nigeria than via the high school across town.

When further pressed on the evident failure of a nondiscriminatory policy to produce more Negroes on campus, colleges blamed poor preparation in the high schools, lack of job opportunities for Negro college graduates, the low income level of Negroes, low Negro aspirations—everything but themselves. When asked if they might make some special efforts to get more Negro students, many reacted in horror to the implied suggestion that they should take race into account in the decisions. Even to the suggestion that a statistical study be made of the situation, the response was an offended, "We do not keep records by race!"

Given the tenacity with which nondiscrimination has been used as a defense for inaction, a biased observer might conclude that its use was a deliberate device for the exclusion of Negroes from higher education. How better explain the success with which higher institutions have preserved their reputations

SOURCE. Reprinted from *School & Society*, January 22, 1966, by permission of the author and publisher. Remarks at a conference of liberal arts colleges, Albion (Mich.) College, February 24, 1965.

for liberalism, yet effectively avoided disturbing the caste system of American society?

Let us admit, however, the good intentions of the colleges. What we are forced to conclude is that on so fundamental a matter as racial understanding, our colleges and universities proved to be no better than other institutions in our society. Fortunately, this sad truth is now widely recognized and a will to do something about it is certainly manifesting itself.

To date, however, the program has been slow and the way to go is far. Announced programs number their beneficiaries by tens and fifties when the needs are in the hundreds and thousands. A dozen distinguished institutions announce proudly that they each have 10 Negroes this year when they had only one apiece last year. A less selective institution, however, keeps quiet about the fact that its 100 Negro freshmen of past years are down to 10 this year.

What might higher education do to make its record better? As a starting point, something could be done about admissions where actions can make an immediate and decisive difference. What would be a reasonable admissions figure to aim for if higher education really wanted to make a significant break with the past now?

We can start with the requirement that the applicants for admission at least should have graduated from high school. Although Negro performance in this regard is below whites (median years of school completed: White 10.9, non-white 8.2 according to 1960 census), because Negro high school graduates do not go to college in nearly the same proportions as white high school graduates, the potential "pool" of Negro applicants is proportionally larger than for white. An immediate and realizable goal would be, therefore, to bring the proportion of Negroes in each college freshman class to the same proportion that Negroes were in the preceding year's high school graduating class. This is a slightly more modest goal than would be one based on equalization with the percentage of white in the age group attending college or the percentage of white high school graduates attending college. Yet, even this modest goal will require effort in face of the fact, for example, that in New York State it would require raising the percentage of Negro students from the less than 2% total student bodies that it is now to about 8%.

If this goal were realized in New York in the fall of 1965, instead of the estimated 1,200 Negroes in a total freshman class of some 77,000, there would be 6,000 (based on an estimated 17,800 Negroes in the 1965 high school graduating class of 227,500).

Can the colleges handle an increase of this dimension? If so, how would they get Negro candidates and overcome the obstacles that previously had kept them out?

To the first question, the answer is certainly an unqualified *yes, provided* that the colleges really wanted to achieve this goal.

As to the second question, the answer in one way is simple—by admitting as many Negro students as necessary to achieve intended proportions. But then come the thundering cries of "lowered standards," "reverse discrimination," and "special privilege." In answer, it first must be recognized that some significant proportion of the "new" Negro students will be capable of achieving success in college as regularly admitted freshmen. Their only problem is that standard I.Q. tests, admissions tests, and other "predictors" are not accurate measures of their capabilities.

Some sizable proportion of the new Negro students will, however, be below the standards of performance normally required for success. For these students, compensatory action will be required either in the form of a precollege program or of a program carried on concurrent with regular college attendance. In either case, the lowering of admissions standards does not require lowering of graduation standards. The first groups admitted may require help during much of their college career and may take more time to complete a degree program. The provision of such help is not beyond the capacity and should not be beyond the will of most colleges.

It can be predicted with confidence that the extent of compensatory action required in the future will rapidly decline under the combined impact of the increased college opportunity itself, the improvement of elementary and secondary education for Negroes, and the generally improved social climate. In fact, where a climate for achievement is generated on a campus the extent of formal compensatory action required will be much less than expected.

New selection procedures for Negro students will not by themselves bring Negroes to the colleges. There also will have to be changes in the climate of acceptance both on and off campus. Colleges will need to review all social arrangements to insure full participation for Negro students in the life of the college and community. Negro applicants will have to be sought out and the determination of the college to make success possible will have to be made clear. For a college ready to take the first step of altering its selection policies, there need be little concern about its ability to handle this second step.

This still leaves the problem of economics. Most of the new Negro students will need substantial financial help, particularly to attend private colleges. Effective use of loan programs, work-study and special scholarship funds will close the gap for some, but many students still will be short and most colleges will be unable to help, particularly if they also try to carry the burden of the extra expense of compensatory programs. The scholarship provisions of the Higher Education Act of 1965, coupled with the Work-Study Program of the Economic Opportunity Act, should go a long way to solve this problem.

Finally, there is the matter of space and faculty. The press for increased Negro enrollments comes just at the time when pressure on college facilities is increasing. Will not more Negroes mean the denial of opportunity to better qualified whites? It may in some instances, but considering the number of better qualified Negroes who in the past have had to make way for less qualified whites, not only in college but in employment and everything else, this might be viewed as only just compensation.

But even this sacrifice may not be necessary. Shortage of facilities and faculty is a function of our readiness to use both as effectively as possible. More efficient use of facilities would create spaces for more students; the teaching needs can be met by imaginative deployment of faculty, willingness to seek out untapped sources of faculty talent (women, retired professors, industrial people with advanced degrees), and greater emphasis on independent study, self-instructional materials, and new teaching media.

Nothing has been said to this point about the advantages to the colleges that participate in the proposed effort. The entire history of race relations in America has demonstrated a flaw in higher education that involves more than a lack of social consciousness. In matters of knowledge, which many would say is higher education's only legitimate concern, there has been a nearly total failure to seek, see, or teach the truth about the Negro in America. When one area of truth is so systematically ignored, questions cannot help but be raised about the integrity of the entire enterprise. Inclusion of the excluded offers higher education a chance for a wholeness that many recent critics have found it lacking. It offers to each student, faculty and community member a chance to prepare for the multiracial international society in which he will live. Such a prize is a thing of great worth. Are we ready to seize it?

In summary, higher education in the U.S. has shared with the rest of our society a blindness to the rights and needs of colored citizens. A readiness to change is widely in evidence and small steps have already been taken by many institutions. A major effort is still needed, however, if the numbers of Negroes in college is to be increased significantly soon. Such an effort would be the determination by all colleges to admit enough Negroes to bring their proportion in freshman classes up to their proportion in high school graduating classes. For individual institutions, depending on present Negro enrollment, this would mean a four-fold or more increase of Negroes in freshman classes. This increase is easily possible if the colleges wish to do it. Do they?

14

Parallels of
Negro and Women's Education

Barbara W. Newell

In the current unprecedented thrust to give recognition to black scholarship, white institutions are raiding Negro colleges for staff. The fervor of this quest has given rise to the query: Will this raiding merely lower the already undistinguished academic standards of those schools which today educate the majority of black students?

Student power movements are notably strongest in predominantly Negro colleges. Why is this? What should be the role of these schools in the 1970's?

These are some of the questions the blacks are forcing the community at large to consider. The purpose of this essay is to explore one parallel which may help in the search for answers. The often unnoticed parallel the writer chooses to examine is that between Negro education and women's education.

The comparison between the assimilation of Negroes and past immigrant groups into the American educational process is most common. Some, for example, facetiously affirm that it was football that effectively democratized the Ivy League. First the Irish, then the Poles, and the South Europeans gained entry to the hallowed halls because of their gridiron prowess. Over time, each ethnic group has become accepted in its own right, and now forms a functioning part of the Establishment. As immigrant groups in the past have earned entry, so may the Negro.

Yet, with each such analogy there is one basic difficulty—the Negro is black. The aim of past groups has been to "pass," to be assimilated. For the black man, this is impossible. To draw a more valid comparison, one only needs to choose another minority group which could not "pass." Let us face it: in the field of education, the problems of women are, historically, closest to those

SOURCE. Reprinted from *School & Society*, October 1970, by permission of the author and publisher.

of the American Negro and are, therefore, of great value in exploring some of the pertinent questions of our day.

Educational opportunities for women began in the first half of the 19th century. Opportunity emerged both as a coeducational experience (Oberlin, 1837) and as a segregated school at the collegiate level (Mt. Holyoke, 1836). With the expansion of state institutions after the Civil War, coeducation spread. The long-run impact of this expansion into coeducation was without question crucial to the eventual quantity and quality of women's education. The political battles to open the doors of the University of Wisconsin or the University of Michigan to coeducation assured the education of more women in a year in a wider variety of fields and levels than Mt. Holyoke could enroll in a decade.

Yet, the staging ground for the feminist revolution was primarily the women's colleges of the 19th and early 20th centuries. Indeed, the re-examination of human values which accompanied the abolitionist movement brought about an awakening of women, out of which emerged a concern for women's education and for the development of women's colleges. More students than the new institutions could readily accommodate were attracted to higher education. As the activists helped to found and to populate these new institutions, so they also gained substance from these colleges. Graduates of Vassar, Mt. Holyoke, and their sister schools provided both leaders and followers for the feminist crusade.

Why have the segregated institutions been the militant communities of scholars? Let us hypothesize that the most critical question appears to be: Did the institution directly challenge the existing system or did it attempt rather to bring change without direct confrontation with deeply held values? Those institutions which educated women to play more adequately the role of "perpetuator of culture" greatly enriched our country, but they did not spearhead social change. The argument to open state university doors to women was made initially on the group of educating "the hand that rocks the cradle." The expanding schools of home economics and nursing which arose in the coeducational institutions drastically altered and improved their respective disciplines and, in the process, challenged tradition, but their approach was through accepted avenues of feminine endeavor. These approaches did not challenge the existing status or the current employment patterns of women. They expressed little of the dream of education as the essential preparation for a new society with which "to open opportunities to women as human beings on an equal basis with men."[1] Commitment to the then radical dream of eliminating all academic, social, and employment barriers appears to have

[1] Mary Woolley's statement on the reasons given by Mary Lyon for establishing Mt. Holyoke, in Jeannette Marks, *Life and Letters of Mary Emma Woolley* (Washington, D.C.: Public Affairs Press, 1955), p. 161.

been essential for the creation of a sufficiently charged environment to produce militant feminist agitators. Here emerged the unique role of the women's college.

The maintenance of feminist extremists was assured by the employment of activists on segregated women's campuses. Such employment served two roles. First, it provided professional status to able women who did receive competent training, but who were not welcome in the coeducational world. Secondly, it provided an asylum for dissenters. There dissenters could retreat, find refreshment and re-enforcement for their minority stance.

Activists established the educational milieu of women's colleges, but of most lasting importance was the unique training which they provided. Only within the protected environment of an all-female college could women gain the experience of self-government and complete self-direction. Leadership was, traditionally, an exclusively male role. One could not learn the "how" of leadership without practice. To this day, coeducational settings have not offered women adequate practice. Tradition has changed sufficiently to include women secretaries and a scattering of vice-presidents and sometimes editors, but the experiences utilized by women students normally are limited in the coeducational setting. Typical was the recent University of Michigan Regents' hearing on women's hours, at which some 20 students spoke, only one of whom was a woman. Not even the women's sororities were represented, although the Interfraternity Council had much to say.

Social conduct, of necessity, is markedly different in a women's college. Isolation accords four years in which to speak up without being considered pushy, to choose careers without the question of appropriateness for women being raised. In a society which often questioned the ability of women to perform, such isolation provided the time and the place for feminists to gain the tools of full participation and, perhaps, more importantly, to prove to each student her own capability to perform—her own dignity.

Integration of students and staff in coeducational institutions has, as well, some interesting parallels with present Negro demands. The position of Dean of Women was established originally as an aid in governing a separate, but unequal, clientele. As students have been treated increasingly alike, the need for such a separate administration has diminished. Instead of crying utopia, a substantial fraction of the earlier militants now maintain that the last bastion for protecting minority rights is disappearing from the scene. Women are being dropped from academic administration.

Academic arguments for restructuring traditional schools of home economics are now so strong that, like the office of Dean of Women, this second outpost of female power is losing to the male majority. Today, the assumption is that women have been accepted sufficiently in academia to constitute an articulate minority which no longer needs institutional protection. This degree of staff integration emerged only after teaching demands brought the recruitment by coeducational campuses of many potential members of women's college faculties. In recent years, although women by no means have maintained their earlier portion of the total professional market, they have increased their academic rank, and are making their voice more distinctly heard in academic halls today. Newcomers feel less need for feminist protections, thus leaving the militants more isolated on the coeducational campus.

Parallels such as this always have their difficulties—Negro education and white female education span much the same period, but the balance sheets are different. One cannot say whether for better or worse. For how does one weigh a Supreme Court Justice against a Senator or a UN delegate? How does one measure acceptability in our medical schools? The feminists had the great advantage of emerging from a middle-class environment. Negro schools and scholars began with a far more educationally deprived population.

Howard, Tuskegee, and other Negro institutions across the country are experiencing turmoil today. Black students may not know it, but they are asking that Negro colleges do for the black community what Mt. Holyoke, Vassar, Smith, Bryn Mawr, *et al.* did for the feminists—define the cause and train the leaders for their minority protest. True, Fisk, Tuskegee, and Howard have played this role in the past. Yet, as civil rights increasingly are attained, the new generation wishes a rededication to the cause of Negro rights, an identification with black values and self-interest, and, very specifically, a recognition of the importance of student training in the processes of democracy. Such leadership training, such a sense of control of one's life, is critical if these schools are to give students the tools and direction they need for militant leadership upon graduation. The argument often is not stated so frankly, but is this not a valid interpretation?

On integrated campuses, in churches, and in politics, the blacks are affirming that, as a permanent minority, they never can hope to gain leadership. "Let us restructure institutions so we can control our own destiny and learn from our own mistakes," they assert.

Negro institutions which receive their basic support from government may be able to increase the training of their students in democratic procedures, but they will be less able to become sanctuaries for black militants. Only the privately endowed schools may have the essential freedom to become black activist centers for the development of a black intelligentsia which, in turn, spawns and directs a significant social movement.

Many of the problems faced by women and Negroes are the same, even though the fields in which they are encountered may vary. In the area of student training, for example, long-run job expectations and models for entrants to a field are needed to encourage both Negroes and women to the sciences. The Negro who wishes to upgrade himself faces many of the same hurdles as the woman wishing to enter the employment market after the establishment of her family. Both groups wish the system to make exceptions. Concessions for part-time students and remedial work are common demands.

In the field of the integration of academic staffs, the parallel also may be useful. Female recruitment has augmented coeducational faculties across the country. If integration is the long-run goal, why, then, should this not be the employment pattern for Negro academic recruitment? It is the dead-end job with few alternate employers that repels a potential entrant. If we want Negroes to enter education, give those in the field adequate mobility and opportunities. Let us employ high market wages and expanded competition to encourage new entrants to the academic profession. Only through a total increase in the number of Negroes choosing academia can we integrate in the long run. In the meantime, the predominantly Negro schools need not be stripped of the staffs they need in the task of formulating Negro community objectives and training black leaders. The militants would not be so prone to transfer from Negro institutions if these Negro institutions were to spearhead the civil rights movement.

In the long run, the integration of both students and staff in all institutions of higher learning is crucial in the creation of that freedom of choice necessary for an open society. Effective integration of the large state institutions which grant the majority of degrees can enhance Negro educational opportunities substantially. Within these institutions, Negroes always will be a minority. Negro interests frequently will be modified to meet majority needs. If black militants are to have their own academic base, Negro institutions are best adapted for their role.

In conclusion, an irony of this parallel is that, in the long run, although the black power movement of today is in part an assertion of masculinity, the two minority groups who cannot "pass" may have more to gain in common than either presently recognizes.

15

The Cognitive Self-Concept
and School Segregation:
Some Preliminary Findings

J. David Colfax

This essay reports some preliminary results of an inquiry into the "cognitive self-concept" of more than 2,500 white and Negro sixth-graders in the five largest cities in Connecticut. Our purpose is to identify Negro and white differences in the content, direction, and elaboration of the pre-adolescent self-concept, and to examine these patterns within the context of contemporary Northern, urban, *de facto* school segregation.

Given the generally acknowledged limitations of the data which served as the basis for the United States Supreme Court decision (1954) regarding *de jure* school segregation, it is remarkable that greater research efforts have not been devoted to a systematic assessment of the effects of school segregation—*de facto* or *de jure*—on the self-concept of the child. Although the deleterious effects of segregated school experience on the child's sense of self have been taken as given in educational and public policy planning, there is surprisingly little hard data on Negro-white differences in self-concept, and even less on the topic of the tripartite relationships among school segregation, the self-concept and race. Much of what is available consists primarily of comparisons within a few schools, or secondary analyses of data that permit inferences about, rather than direct examination of, various facets of the self-concept. Theories about the social psychological consequences of segregation remain relatively underdeveloped. This is related, to some extent, to the fact that the study of Negro and white ego development has remained narrowly practical, methodologically unsophisticated, and theoretically vague.[1]

SOURCE. Revised version of a paper presented at annual meeting, American Association for the Advancement of Science, New York City, December 29, 1967.

[1] See, e.g., Thomas F. Pettigrew, "Negro American Personality: Why Isn't More Known?" *Journal of Social Issues*, **20**: 4–23, April 1964.

In late 1965, we undertook a broad-gauged study of the sources and effects of *de facto* school segregation in Bridgeport, Hartford, New Haven, Stamford, and Waterbury.[2] Each of these cities experienced substantial nonwhite in-migration over the last decade and a half. Ranging from seven to 16% of the total population in 1960, the nonwhite population of these cities appeared to have been increasing at approximately the same rate in the 1960's as it did during the 1950–1960 decade. *De facto* school segregation at the elementary level was extensive; in 1965, two-thirds of Negro elementary school children attended schools that were more than 50% Negro; 42% attended schools that were more than 75% Negro.

One of our objectives was to identify the effects of various levels of school imbalance on the self-concept. A battery of tests and questionnaires was administered to a stratified sample of 2,554—1,458 whites and 1,096 Negroes—sixth-graders. Included among the items intended to tap various dimensions of the self-concept was the "Who-Am-I" (WAI) or "Twenty-Sentence-Test" (TST) developed by the late Manford H. Kuhn and his associates.[3] This consists simply of a page on which the respondent is asked to complete, as many times as possible, a sentence beginning with the words, "I am." We provided 25 lines, which gave the respondent an opportunity to provide up to 25 spontaneous self-definitions in their order of salience. The open-ended nature of the test permits the respondent to order his self-definitions, with as much elaboration and emotion as he cares to provide. No time limit was set for the completion of the task.

Self-references were coded in three ways. First, responses were classified into one of 28 content categories, 17 of which were social roles, and 11 psychological states.[4] The latter group was regarded as a set of residual categories, with an effort being made to code self-conception in terms of social roles as often as possible. "I am a boy," for example, was classified as a sex role reference, and "I am angry" was coded as a psychological state. Psychological states comprised only six percent of all responses.

Second, the "valence," or positive-neutral-negative dimension of each self-reference was coded. For example, "I am a good student," "I am a student,"

[2] The research was supported in part by the U.S. Office of Education, Basic Research Branch, and the University of Connecticut Research Foundation, under the joint direction of Professors Irving L. Allen, Henry G. Stetler, and the author.

[3] The test was first described in Manford H. Kuhn and T. S. McPartland, "An Investigation of Self-Attitudes," *American Sociological Review*, **19**: 68–76, February, 1954. See also, *Sociological Quarterly*, **5**, Winter, 1964, whole issue.

[4] The social roles coded were: Sex, intellectual, physical, literal self, peer group, racial, age, family, recreational, athletic, occupational fantasy, other fantasy, religious, occupational, nationality, occupational aspirations, economic, and political. Psychological stages included anger, fear, distress, etc. For a discussion of some of the considerations involved, see Philip J. Stone, et al., *The General Inquirer* (Cambridge: MIT Press, 1966), pp. 170–186.

and "I am a poor student" were coded positive, neutral, and negative, respectively. No attempt was made to record the intensity of positive or negative self-references; thus "I am a good student," and "I am the best student in my class" were similarly coded as positive. Third, the salience of each response was established by coding the order in which each self-reference occurred.

In order to eliminate intercoder variability, each self-reference was listed in a "dictionary" to which coders referred in classifying responses. Unlisted terms were referred to the coding supervisor, who gave them content and valence codes and entered them in the operational dictionary.

Content: Negro and White Differences

Nearly 28,000 self-references were made by the 2,500 children. White children gave an average of 11.5, compared with 9.2 for Negroes.

The most frequently occurring self-reference among both white and Negro students involved some aspect of the student's intellectual or classroom role. Twelve percent of all white responses, and nine percent of Negro responses, involved this dimension. References to the physical self were next in order: 10% of white responses, and eight percent of Negro responses referred to self-perceptions of size or appearance.

When we examine responses in terms of individuals, rather than in terms of the total number of responses, we find that more than half of both Negro and white students made reference to their sex roles—"I am a boy" or "I am a girl." The intellectual or classroom role was mentioned one or more times by 59% of white students, compared with only 39% of Negro students. Negro students mentioned nonracial physical characteristics (48%) more often than whites (36%).

The fourth ranking role among Negro students was the literal self—*i.e.*, "I am me," "I am John Smith"—which was mentioned by nearly 36%, followed by peer group mentions (27%), race (23%), age (23%), family roles (21%), and athletic roles (16%). White students provided a somewhat different ordering of roles: 38% mentioned peer group relations, 35% recreational interests, 34% literal-self references, 32% age, 30% athletic skills, and 27% mentioned family roles. Interestingly, Negro students were nearly twice as likely as whites to provide fantasy-references. Thirteen percent of Negroes mentioned occupational fantasies—e.g., "I am a famous scientist"—compared with seven percent of whites; and 10% mentioned other fantasies—"I am dead"—compared with only six percent of whites. Most other roles were infrequently mentioned. Religious identities were expressed by 11% of the students, followed by occupational roles (7%), occupational role aspirations (7%), nationality (6%), economic (4%), and political roles (1%). With the exception of religious identity, which was mentioned by 15% of whites and only seven percent of Negroes, these roles were approximately equally salient among both groups.

Sheldon Stryker has suggested that the self, as an object to itself, can be regarded as existing "in a hierarchy of salience, such that other things equal we can expect behavioral products to the degree that a given identity ranks high in this hierarchy."[5] The fact that the Negro preadolescent self includes fewer reflexively applied positional designations in general, and fewer classroom and peer group roles in particular, implies that these roles occupy a less central place in the repertoire of the self and has certain obvious implications for role performance.

The Evaluative Self

Most of the self-identities expressed by Negroes and whites embodied no evaluation dimension. The major difference between the two groups was that Negroes referred to themselves neither in positive nor negative terms as frequently as did whites. Of Negro responses, 61% were neutral, compared with 54% of the white responses. Of both white and Negro responses, 8% were negative. However, Negroes expressed fewer positive self-references: 38% of white responses, and 31% of Negro responses were positive.

The mean number of positive expressions among whites was 4.4, compared with only 2.9 among Negroes. The tendency of Negro children to refer to themselves in affectively neutral terms becomes even clearer when we look at the response patterns of individuals. Of the white students, 76% referred to themselves in positive terms one or more times, compared with only 59% of Negro children.

We suspected that the lower proportion of positive self-references among Negroes might be related to the fact that their overall response rate was approximately 25% lower than that of white students. However, when we controlled for the number of self-references and compared whites and Negroes, no significant differences emerged: Negro children made fewer positive self-references at every level than did whites.

The Self-Concept and School Segregation

The often-vague and frequently controversial terms "segregation" and "racial imbalance" were employed in this analysis in an operational sense.

---

[5] Sheldon Stryker, "Identity Salience and Role Performance: The Relevance of Symbolic Interactionist Theory for Family Research," paper presented at the American Sociological Association meetings, Chicago, 1965, p. 4.

We divided schools into three groups after empirically establishing that in this instance, at least, finer distinctions did not provide additional clarification of relationships between school segregation and the self-concept. The option of dividing schools into two groups seemed to obscure more differences than it clarified, since schools in the intermediate range typically possess some of the best and some of the worst features of schools at either end of the continuum. Therefore, we divided schools into those in which fewer than one-third of the students were Negro, those in which from one- to two-thirds were Negro, and those in which more than two-thirds of the students were Negro. Our middle group thus refers to what is likely to become the typical inner-city elementary school of the future—that in which between a third and two-thirds of the students are Negroes.

Contrary to what some of the more speculative literature might have led us to expect, we found no relationships between *negative* self-identities and the racial composition of the school attended. One-third of Negro children in predominantly white schools expressed one or more negative self-reference, compared to 30% of Negro children in schools in which more than two-thirds of the pupils were Negro.

However, Negro students who attended predominately Negro schools expressed positive self-identities less often than did those in racially heterogeneous or predominantly white schools. Of the Negroes in the white schools, 80% referred to themselves in positive terms one or more times, compared with only 57% of those attending predominately Negro schools. Thus negative self-references constituted a larger proportion of all *valenced* responses.

When role content and valence are jointly considered, it becomes clear that the ratio of negative-to-positive self-references varies with school segregation in some role designations, but not in others. For example, the ratio of Negro negative-to-positive school or intellectual role responses increases with school segregation from .36 to .41. Similarly, the level of racial imbalance is associated with the ratio of negative-to-positive responses in relation to the literal self (2.80 to 14.00), physical attributes (.31 to .42) and fantasies (.23 to 1.25). Other aspects of the self which are perhaps less directly related to school experiences, such as family, race, and sex roles, were unrelated to levels of racial imbalance. Thus, it is precisely in the areas in which school experiences presumably exert the greatest influence that the negative-positive ratios are the most closely related to levels of school segregation.

Some Implications

Differences in the Negro and white preadolescent self-concept as reviewed here take on a somewhat different aspect insofar as the Negro sense of self appears to be less elaborate and less evaluative than that of whites. The more constrained, affectively neutral self-concept of the Negro might usefully be interpreted as a result of the psychological costs of relating the self to a wide variety of social roles and contexts, and is to this extent consistent with some more impressionistic interpretations. Here, however, relatively little support is provided for the idea that the Negro sense-of-self is one that is self-stigmatizing and self-derogating. In our sample, the self-derogating preadolescent Negro was, in fact, rarer than the self-derogating white. However, we should not lose sight of the fact that self-derogation requires an evaluation of self relative to various external criteria. We therefore might speculate that at the age of 11 or 12, when the sense of self is determined by family and formal school roles to a greater extent than by peers or by participation in the larger society, the preadolescent's cognition of self is expressed in narrower and more neutral terms. Perhaps only later, partially as a result of wider experience, does self-derogation find greater articulation. We would suggest that the Negro preadolescent sense of self, under conditions of segregation, is not so much negativistic as neutralized and constrained, an interpretation which has a number of implications for the design and implementation of remedial programs. This notion can be tested further by comparing the responses of an older group of Negro and white adolescents.

16

Black Power and Education

Rudie Tretten

"Only a new self-image which reveals to the child that black can also be beautiful, only this can create in him a feeling that he too can make it. Black men must free themselves from the cultural imperialism of white power. To do this they can best make a beginning by taking over schools in their own ghettoes."

This expression of Black Power is by one white man, a recently retired principal of a New York City school. His remarks echo or are echoed by those of the foremost advocate of Black Power, Stokely Carmichael. "Black people do not want to 'take over' this country. They don't want to get 'whitey'; they just want to get him off their backs, as the saying goes. The white man is irrelevant to blacks, except as an oppressive force. Blacks want to be in his place, yes, but not in order to terrorize and lynch and starve him. They want to be in his place because that is where a decent life can be had." Similarly, Bayard Rustin, in speaking to a group of school people, noted the ambivalence among Negroes who want "in" to the dominant society, but who also are afraid of being hurt again in the attempt.

Black Power, then, has something to do with the ability to live the good life and gain the rewards that this society has to offer. And inevitably, because of the way the society distributes its rewards, Black Power has to do with education. Because of deficiencies long assumed to be theirs and only recently assigned to the schools, Negro students do less well in school than do white students. They go on to higher education in smaller numbers, and thus are limited in their ability to compete in the certification-oriented society in which they live.

Haunted by a history that has told them repeatedly that black is bad, faced with a racist society preaching equality and practicing inequality, surrounded by the evidence that a white skin is equivalent to power, the Negro now seeks

SOURCE. Reprinted from *School & Society*, November 23, 1968, by permission of the author and publisher.

power through the very thing which has made him powerless—his color. Color is not the only one of the white man's categories and judgments the Negro has adopted. Evidence abounds that many Negroes have gone so far as to internalize the white stereotype of Negro inferiority.

Sociologists have done numerous studies indicating the existence of some kind of interaction disability on the part of Negroes in their contacts with whites. Such disability leads to a feeling of weakness or powerlessness in a world perceived as unfriendly. The Coleman report revealed that ". . . responses of pupils to questions in the survey show that minority pupils, except for orientals, have far less conviction than whites that they can affect their own environments and futures. When they do, however, their achievement is higher than that of whites who lack that conviction."[1]

Coleman's findings are borne out in other studies, which indicate that Negroes as a group are more likely to feel that what they do in a situation has little impact on any outcome forthcoming: "Success in externally controlled situations (luck or fate determined) seems more controllable for the Negro who believes that goals derived through achievement will be denied him regardless of his effort, while externally controlled goals are, at least, obtained fairly."[2]

Unfortunately, there has not been a great deal of social psychological study done on power, so that search for a theoretical framework for dealing with power, or, more exactly, a perceived powerlessness, is not very rewarding. It is likely that the work being done on alienation will reveal some useful descriptions of the phenomena without pointing the way to specific solutions to the problem. Suffice it to say that it is not specifically a Negro phenomenon, and is apparently more associated with poverty, or relative poverty, than with race. Dahl showed the way in which the poor see themselves as unable to influence their environment and thus fail to take advantage of those opportunities which are available.[3] All around them the poor, and perhaps particularly the Negro poor, see that they lack both affluence and influence, and so why bother?

The impact on young people when they see themselves as unworthy has been reported by Rosenberg. Quoting a study by Andras Angyal, he observes, "In the neurotic development there are always a number of unfortunate circumstances which instill in the child a self-derogatory feeling. This involves on the one hand a feeling of weakness which discourages him from the free expres-

1 James S. Coleman, *Equality of Educational Opportunity* (Washington: U.S. Government Printing Office, 1966), p. 23.

2 Herbert M. Lefcourt, "Internal Versus External Control of Reinforcement: A Review," *Psychological Bulletin,* **65**: 215, April 1966.

3 Robert Dahl, *Who Governs?* (New Haven: Yale University Press, 1961), p. 292.

sion of his wish for mastery, and on the other the feeling there is something fundamentally wrong with him and that, therefore, he cannot be loved. The whole complicated structure of neurosis appears to be founded on this secret feeling of worthlessness, that is, on the belief that one is inadequate to master the situations that confront him and that he is undeserving of love. . . ."[4]

Black Power, then, is a corrective on two levels. It is designed to provide the Negro with an image of himself consonant with that of a participating decision-making adult, and, at the same time, to serve as a rallying cry for the kind of power which will result in social and economic elevation. The schools must respond on both of these levels.

Negro history, literature, art, music, and success stories have been made a part of the curriculum in many large cities. Negro teachers and administrators have been sought out to "up-grade the self-image of Negro students." In-service courses have proliferated, with the aim of informing white teachers about the culture of the ghetto and the values which ghetto youngsters have internalized. These devices are all necessary and all inadequate.

"The Negro's experiences in America have produced in him a mass social neurosis that can only become more morbid as the frustrations of trying to cope with the problem of color and identity are intensified by education and increased marginality at the top of the social pyramid, and by increasing poverty and the concomitant loss of personhood at the bottom."[5]

For C. Eric Lincoln, the task at hand is, literally, the building of persons. The question which must be answered is whether or not the schools are willing and able to participate in the undertaking. The willingness part of the question has been answered almost by default; the able part will be answered over time in the classrooms of the nation.

While schools may prove effective in the building of effective persons, their present capacity for aiding in the quest for black political, social, and economic power is laden with doubt. But, whether the schools will it or not, they will find themselves increasingly the center of both hope and controversy.

In their pursuit of power, Negro leaders have adopted and adapted various techniques based upon different sources of their perceived strength. There are at least five sources of power which have been tapped. One, which apparently has passed its peak of effectiveness, is the moral power symbolized by the non-violent protest tactics of the late Rev. Martin Luther King, Jr. Another, closely allied to the first since the time of the Montgomery bus boycott of the mid-1950's, is the power of the Negro pocketbook.

[4] Morris Rosenberg, *Society and the Adolescent Self Image* (Princeton, N.J.: Princeton University Press, 1965), p. 22.

[5] C. Eric Lincoln, "Color and Group Identity in the United States," *Daedalus*, **96**: 539, Spring, 1967.

A third kind of power is that to be found in the streets. The "long hot summer" seems to have become an American urban institution only very loosely tied to the Fourth of July.

The fourth source of power for the Negro is politics. Here the housing patterns imposed by white America aid in the pursuit of power. With vast numbers of black voters concentrated in the various city ghettoes, there is an opportunity for election of Negro Congressmen, state legislators, and city officials. But, here, too, the Negro sees himself as still at the whim of the majority. Adam Clayton Powell was the most powerful Negro in the American Congress and, in Negro eyes, it did him little good in the face of a racist legislature. He may have been abusing his power, he may have been a very poor Congressman, but he was more than a symbol of power—he was power.

The fifth source of power which is available is that supplied by education. In an economy which demands trained personnel and which cannot afford to wantonly waste whatever talent exists, education is seemingly a permanent detour from the road to serfdom. It is, however, the failure of education to provide the hoped-for power which has occasioned the recent soul-searching at all levels of the big-city educational establishment.

However, since the educational system is part of the political system, the way to power through education well may be via the political path. About 73% of American Negroes now live in urban areas, and 80% of urban Negroes live in the core city. Over 11,250,000 Negroes live in the city ghettoes of the nation. The political activation of this mass is the prerequisite without which Black Power will remain only a rallying cry, and a decreasingly effective one at that.

Properly mobilized, the Negro vote can swing electoral votes in Presidential elections; it can elect governors; it can, and it has, elected Negroes to Congress and to state houses around the nation. It can provide the bargaining power for Negro leaders through which they can obtain for the Negro community those things which it needs and wants. However, the above formulation postulates the continuation of white-imposed ghetto life for the majority of Negroes. The integration rhetoric, if adopted as policy, would spell the end of effective elective Black Power. Seen in this light, the Negro politician owes his very existence to the housing and social discrimination which create the ghettoes of the nation. It is within the ghetto itself that Black Power can approximate most closely the ability to control the environment. And, if the proper institutional arrangements are made, it is in control of education that this power can be most effective—effective in terms of providing a tangible asset to the ghetto community and effective in providing training for wider political leadership.

Nathan Wright, Jr., Plans Committee Chairman of the National Conference on Black Power, held at Newark, N.J., in July 1967, holds out hope that the white culture ultimately will accept black power. "Thoughtful white people thus will readily be open to accept black-engineered organization for black influence and for the creation of new power relationships which will reflect to the benefit of all. . . ."[6]

Recent disputes in New York City, Chicago, and other large cities over control of educational policy, and even over the appointment of personnel, have brought attention to the over-centralization of most school systems. To counter this tendency, New York City is sub-dividing itself into many smaller districts, each with its own board of education and superintendent. Whether or not this tactic eventuates in meaningful power dispersal will depend upon the kinds of decisions that the local boards will be allowed to make. It is precisely this matter which may cause the entire movement to decentralization to founder before it even hits the water.

It is not likely that local district boards will have a great deal of fiscal power. They will be allowed, in all probability, to allocate funds within districts to meet needs perceived by the inhabitants. They also can serve as a vehicle for exerting pressure upward within the over-all system. If decentralization of schools is to be meaningful at all, either to the school system involved or to the Black Power movement and the ghetto populace, the local boards must be more than just a means for sounding off. They must represent an honest effort to provide a power base for improving educational services and a legitimate out-growth of the black American's desire to control his destiny. Wright says, "Black Power means black development into self-sufficiency for the good of Negroes and for the good of the whole nation. We want —as others must want—to replace the helping hand which now aids us with our own hand—to sustain ourselves and not be burdens to others."

In terms of curriculum, the decentralized school system might evolve what current curriculum makers would consider to be aberrant versions of the present offerings. Ghetto schools probably would specialize in dealing with the practical politics of Black Power. It is of little value to talk about the virtues of American democracy with youngsters who see only the worst that the system has spawned. The Negro of the ghetto needs to know the ways in which he can use his numbers to get what he wants. To this end, all of the various Negro movements, from the most extremely nationalist to the most ardently integrationist, must present their case through spokesmen with whom the youngsters can identify. The entire social studies curriculum could be devoted to creating not just the stereotype good citizen, but the effective, involved participant, aware that what he does politically will have a substantive effect on his life.

If decentralization does not work, and if changes in structure and offerings

[6] Nathan Wright, Jr., *Black Power and Urban Unrest* (New York: Hawthorne Books, 1967), p. 44.

are not made, serious thought will be given by Negro leaders to setting up rival school systems which will meet their demands. Kenneth Clark has argued that there is a real need for competitive systems and that unions, business, foundations—even the army—might set up their own schools.

In a somewhat similar vein, Edgar Friedenberg has put forth a tripartite approach. He would continue to improve the present system, provide tuition grants for attendance at private and parochial schools, and create Federally funded boarding schools which would take youngsters from the ghetto environment and attempt to free them from its debilitating effects.

Still another approach might involve the creation of experimental schools in the ghetto by foundations interested in education. Such schools, in cooperation with local academic institutions, would have direct ties with the people in the area to be served. California is contemplating such a program.

Perhaps Wright overstates the imperative for revitalized ghetto education, but he is not alone in the alternatives he perceives. "Liberate us or exterminate us," says Whitney Young.

Finally, in the words of Wright, "A reasonable ultimate alternative to provision of full training and full opportunity is genocide. Some feel that—as genocide was possible with white Christian Germany when extremist feelings held the day—it will be possible in America when white myopia and white lethargy and unwillingness to make the most of American potential meet the deadly monster of a mass of millions of resentful, angry, and untutored Negro poor caught in a vicious cycle of illegitimacy and vice causing almost total demoralization and outrage."[7]

[7] Ibid., p. 55.

Part 3

The Spanish-Speaking American

17

The Challenge of
the Non-English-Speaking Child
in American Schools

Francesco Cordasco

In an open-ended American society, education has afforded the essential entry point into the mainstream of American identity. Education has provided social mobility, and it has extended opportunity. In the peopling of the American continent and the creation of a democratic society, the schools have served as a basic vehicle of cohesion; in the transmission of a society's values, the American schools have ministered to children who brought with them myriad cultures and a multiplicity of tongues. More often than not (almost always in the urban immigrant citadels), the American school found its children in poverty and neglect; increasingly, the schools recognized that their success in the absorption of the child lay not only in meeting his cognitive needs, but equally in confronting the reality of the social context in which the child was found. A definite correlation existed between the cognitive achievement of the child *vis-à-vis* the socio-economic disadvantagement which he suffered.

The cornucopia of Federal legislation of the last few years did not discover poverty as a new or rare phenomenon in American society. What the Congress perceptively recognized was that many of our social institutions (particularly, our schools) only partially were successful, and that many of our democratic ideals were mauled severely in the grim pathology of social disaffection, cultural assault, and enforced assimilation. It was not that our schools failed, but rather that their recorded failures were to be measured in the inadequacy

SOURCE. Reprinted from *School & Society*, March 30, 1968, by permission of the author and publisher. Based on testimony before the Committee on Education and Labor, U.S. House of Representatives, Washington, D.C., June 29, 1967.

of their response to the child who came to them formed in the context of another heritage, or in the articulation of a strange tongue. If there is a common denominator which must be sought in the millions of American children who presented themselves to a society's schools, it is poverty. And its ingredients (within the parameters of this poverty) were cultural differences, language handicaps, social alienation, and disaffection. In this sense, the Negro in-migrant rural poor huddled in the urban ghettoes of the 1960's, the Puerto Rican migrant poor who seek economic opportunity on the mainland, and the Mexican-American poor, largely an urban minority, are not newcomers to the American schools, nor do they present American educators with new problems. The American poor, traditionally, are the ingredients out of which our social institutions have fashioned the sinews of greatness.

A vast literature on the schools and poor children is being assembled.[1] The children of poverty have been described euphemistically as "culturally deprived," "disadvantaged," "disaffected," "alienated," "socially unready"; yet, what most educational historians have not seen and have not recorded is the continuing historical confrontation of American social institutions and the poor. The American "common" school evolved in a free society to train citizens "to live adequately in a republican society and to exercise effectively the prerogatives of citizenship . . . ,"[2] and in the process it encountered many difficulties. The greatest of these difficulties lay in its treatment of the "minority child" whose minority status was affirmed by his cultural, ethnic, religious, and linguistic differences, and all related to his presence in a social sector of severe socio-economic disadvantagement.

In its efforts to assimilate all of its charges, the American school assaulted (and, in consequence, very often destroyed) the cultural identity of the child; it forced him to leave his ancestral language at the schoolhouse door; it developed in the child a haunting ambivalence of language, of culture, of ethnicity, and of personal self-affirmation. It held up to its children mirrors in which they saw not themselves, but the stereotype middle-class, white, English-speaking child, who embodied the essences of what the American child was (or ought) to be. For the minority child, the images which the school fash-

---

[1] See Yeshiva University, Informational Retrieval Center on the Disadvantaged, *Bulletins*; also, *The Education of Disadvantaged Children: A Bibliography* . . . (Washington: Office of Education, U.S. Dept. of Health, Education, and Welfare, Aug. 15, 1966) ; and Helen Randolph, *Urban Education Bibliography* (New York: Center For Urban Education, 1967). We are witnessing a proliferation of books (mostly collections of articles) on the schools and the children of the poor, the best of which is the review of current issues and research edited by Harry L. Miller, *Education for the Disadvantaged* (New York: Free Press, 1967).

[2] Lawrence A. Cremin, *The American Common School: An Historic Conception* (New York: Bureau of Publications, Teachers College, Columbia University, 1951), pp. 213–214.

ioned were cruel deceptions. In the enforced acculturation, there was bitterness and confusion, but tragically, too, there was the rejection of the wellsprings of identity and, more often than not, the failure of achievement. The ghettoization of the European immigrant, in substance, is exactly analogous to the ghettoization of the Negro, Puerto Rican, and Mexican-American poor. A long time ago, Louis Wirth called attention to the vitality of the ghetto in its maintenance of the life-styles, languages, and cultures of a minority people assaulted by the main institutions of a dominant society.

The schools, if only because of the sensitivity of their role, measured their successes sparingly; for it increasingly became apparent that, if the schools truly were to be successful, they would have to build on the strengths which the children brought with them—on ancestral pride, on native language, and on the multiplicity of needs and identities which the community of the children afforded.[3]

The imposition of immigration quotas during 1920–24 largely ended the confrontation of the American school and the European immigrant bilingual child. In the course of the past quarter-century, the bilingual child in America, in the main, has been Spanish-speaking, encountered in growing numbers in the classrooms of American schools. In the major cities of the U.S. at the present time, it is the Spanish-speaking child (Mexican-American or Puerto Rican) who is the bilingual child, almost inevitably found in a context of poverty and reflecting a constellation of unmet myriad needs.

Faye L. Bumpass, Texas Technological University, recently testified before a Senate subcommittee on bilingual education. She observed: "In the five state area [Texas, New Mexico, Colorado, Arizona, and California], there exist today at least 1.75 million school children with Spanish surnames, whose linguistic, cultural and psychological handicaps cause them to experience, in general, academic failure in our schools or at best limit them to only mediocre success."[4] The average number of school years completed by the Anglo child in the Southwest is 12.1 years, for the Negro it is nine years, and for the

---

[3] It is instructive to note that the immigrant Catholic minority of the 19th century created its own schools as a direct response to the social disenfranchisement of its children by the dominant society. See J. A. Burns and Bernard Kohlbrenner, *A History of Catholic Education in the United States* (New York: Benziger, 1937). For an in-depth study of the acculturation of a minority's children, ethnicity and the American school, and the context of poverty and its challenge to the schools, see Leonard Covello, *The Social Background of the Italo-American School Child: A Study of the Southern Italian Mores and Their Effect on the School Situation in Italy and America*, edited and with an introduction by F. Cordasco (Leiden [The Netherlands]: E. J. Brill, 1967). A graphic picture of the failings of the school in meeting the needs of children of the immigrant poor is in the address of Jane Addams before the National Education Association in 1897 (*Proceedings*, 1897, pp. 104–112).

[4] *The New York Times*, June 18, 1967.

Mexican-American it is 7.1 years. "The problems of the group [Mexican-Americans] include all of the inter-related complexities of low income, unemployment, migration, school retardation, low occupational aspirations, delinquency, discrimination and all of the problems that attend the intrusion of one culture upon another."[5] The Mexican-American child classically demonstrates that an almost inevitable concomitant of poverty is low educational achievement.[6]

The Commonwealth of Puerto Rico neither encourages nor discourages migration. As an American citizen, the Puerto Rican moves between the island and the mainland with complete freedom. If his movement is vulnerable to anything, it fluctuates only with reference to the economy on the mainland. Any economic recession or contraction graphically shows in the migration statistics.[7] How the Puerto Rican child has fared in the mainland schools is best illustrated in the experience in New York City, where Puerto Ricans have the lowest level of formal education of any identifiable ethnic or color group. Only 13% of Puerto Rican men and women 25 years of age and older in 1960 had completed either high school or more advanced study. Among New York's nonwhite (predominantly Negro) population, 31.2% had completed high school; and the other white population (excluding Puerto Ricans) did even better. Over 40% at least had completed high school.[8] In 1960, more than half (52.9%) of Puerto Ricans in New York City 25 years of age and older had less than an eighth-grade education. In contrast, 29.5% of the

[5] From a development proposal submitted to the U.S. Commissioner of Education by the Department of Rural Education, National Education Association. Reported in *Congressional Record*, Jan. 17, 1967, p. S 357. See generally, Sen. Ralph Yarborough, "Two Proposals for a Better Way of Life for Mexican-Americans of the Southwest," *Congressional Record*, Jan. 17, 1967, pp. S 352–S 361.

[6] The best source on the educational problems of Mexican-American children is Herschel T. Manuel, *Spanish Speaking Children of the Southwest: Their Education and the Public Welfare* (Austin: University of Texas Press, 1958).

[7] The best source on Puerto Rican migration is the Migration Division of the Department of Labor, Commonwealth of Puerto Rico, which maintains a central mainland office in New York City and offices in other U.S. cities. It also maintains an office in Puerto Rico to carry out a program of orientation for persons who intend to migrate to the mainland. See Joseph Monserrat, *Puerto Ricans in New York City* (New York: Department of Labor, Migration Division, Commonwealth of Puerto Rico, 1967). See also *Bibliography on Puerto Ricans in the United States* (New York: Department of Labor, Migration Division, Commonwealth of Puerto Rico, April, 1959). In 1964, the New York City Department of Health placed the Puerto Rican population in New York City at 701,500, representing 9.3% of the city's population. A projection of this study by the Migration Division of the Puerto Rico Department of Labor estimated the 1966 Puerto Rican population at 762,000.

[8] The statistical indices of Puerto Rican poverty (and the related needs) are assembled best in *The Puerto Rican Community Development Project* (New York: Puerto Rican Forum, 1964), pp. 26–75. See also Monserrat, op. cit.

nonwhite population had not finished the eighth grade, and only 19.3% of the other whites had so little academic preparation.[9] Clearly, the critical issue for the Puerto Rican community is the education of its children, for the experience in New York City is a macrocosm which illustrates all the facets of the mainland experience.

In the confrontation of the problems faced by Mexican-American and by Puerto Rican children, educators have not been without specific proposals. If one allows for these essential differences which relate to the history of both groups and their relationships *vis-à-vis* the dominant American society, the major problem presented to the American schools has been the legacy of poverty and the context of debilitating deprivation in which the children are found. In this sense, it cannot be reiterated too strongly that the Spanish-speaking child is not unlike the child of poverty who presented himself to the American school in other eras. It is not that the school is inadequate to the needs of these children; the tragedy lies in the failure to use the experience gained by the schools, and the lessons learned, in the many decades past.

A persistent theme in all of the literature which deals with the minority child is the *absolute necessity* for the school to build on the cultural strengths which the child brings to the classroom: to cultivate in him ancestral pride; to reinforce (not destroy) the language he natively speaks; to capitalize on the bicultural situation; to plan bilingual instruction in Spanish and English for the Spanish-speaking child in the cultivation of his inherent strengths; to make use of a curriculum to reflect Spanish (and Puerto Rican) as well as American traditions; and to retain as teachers those trained and identified with both cultures. Only through such education can the Spanish-speaking child be given the sense of personal identification so essential to his educational maturation.[10] We only can lament the lost opportunities of other eras;[11] there

[9] *The Puerto Rican Community Development Project*, pp. 34–35, 39–41, and tables, pp. 43–44; see also F. Cordasco, "Puerto Rican Pupils and American Education," *School & Society*, Feb. 18, 1967, pp. 116–119; and F. Cordasco, "The Puerto Rican Child in the American School," *Journal of Negro Education*, **36**: 181–186, Spring, 1967.

[10] See Herschel T. Manuel, op. cit.; also, "Bilingualism and the Bilingual Child: A Symposium," *Modern Language Journal*, **49**: 143-239, March–April, 1965; Yarborough, op. cit., particularly, pp. S 358–S 361. Eight colleges and universities in Texas are co-operating to develop a model for teaching Mexican-American children. Teachers from selected Texas public school systems attended a 1967 summer institute (NDEA, Title XI) at St. Mary's University, San Antonio, followed by inservice training during the school year, in the use of Spanish and English in first-grade teaching of children of Mexican ancestry. The institute is the first step toward the establishment of a number of demonstration centers featuring bilingual schooling. A New York City-sponsored Puerto Rican conference (April 15–16, 1967) called for bilingual education programs for Puerto Rican children, and the inclusion of Puerto Rican history and culture in the curriculum of the schools (*The New York Times*, April 17, 1967).

[11] See Covello, *The Social Background of the Italo-American School Child*. Looking

is no excuse for failure at this historical and critical juncture in our society.

Congress has put forward a number of proposed bills to deal with the critical problem of the non-English-speaking child. In addition to H.R. 9840, introduced by Rep. James H. Scheuer (D.-N.Y.), bills have been introduced by Rep. Edward R. Roybal (D.-Calif.), Rep. Henry B. Gonzalez (D.-Tex.), and by others in the House, and by Sen. Ralph Yarborough (D.-Tex.). These bills seek to amend the Elementary and Secondary Education Act of 1965 to provide assistance to local educational agencies in establishing bilingual education programs.

In essence, the bills confront the basic problems of the non-English-speaking child in our schools. The bills seem to agree in the critical needs, not only in the categoric allocation of funds, but in the provision of programs which would promote closer home-school cooperation and provide high quality educational opportunities for children from non-English-speaking homes. If any basic difference exists in the bills, it remains primarily in the proposed Yarborough bill's limitation of its provisions to Spanish-speaking students, and its recommendation that Spanish be taught as the native language and English as a second language.

Neither of these differences is irresolvable. The limitation of the Yarborough bill to Spanish-speaking children quite obviously is a recognition that it is the Spanish-speaking child in our schools who, in the main, is non-English-speaking; and this is true not only in the Southwest, but in the major cities and many of the rural areas of America. However, nothing is lost by extending our definition to ". . . children from non-English-speaking, low income families" (H.R. 9840). On the matter of which primacy of language for instruction (Spanish or English?), attention must be paid to the needs of the children involved. It really is not a problem of which language is to be used, but rather of which language is most effective use to be made. It long has been an "ethnocentric illusion" in the U.S. that for a child born in this country English is not a foreign language, and virtually all instruction in schools must be through the medium of English.[12] All of the bills provide for planning and development of programs, including pilot projects to test the

back over a near half-century of service in the New York City public schools, Dr. Covello recently observed: "The Italian Department at the DeWitt Clinton High School began with one class in 1920 and by 1928 had a register of 1,000 students with a full four year course, and two 4th year classes. Cooperating with the Italian Teachers Association, parity for the Italian language was established in 1922 after a ten year campaign. *For during that period school authorities felt that having Italian students study the Italian language would segregate them from other students and retard their 'Americanization'—an old and often repeated story—an idea with which we very definitely took issue.*" (*Congressional Record*, May 16, 1967 [italics added]).

[12] See A. Bruce Gaarder, "Teaching the Bilingual Child: Research, Development, and Policy," in "Bilingualism and the Bilingual Child: A Symposium," loc. cit., pp. 165–175.

effectiveness of plans. Against this provision, the provisions of a final bill should allow for that flexibility out of which sound and effective programs will evolve. It really is not the primacy of language in the instructional process, but rather how a child is to be moved into an area of effective educational growth which will dictate practice.

The Scheuer Bill (H.R. 9840) provides a practicable vehicle to confront the critical needs of the non-English-speaking child. It provides for planning and development of programs, including pilot projects to test the effectiveness of plans, and the development and dissemination of special instructional materials; pre-service and in-service training programs for teachers and teacher aides involved in bilingual education programs; programs to upgrade the quality of the entire program of schools where large proportions of the children come from non-English-speaking, low-income families, including construction, remodelling, or renovation of facilities; intensive early childhood programs; and bilingual and bicultural education programs for elementary and secondary school children to acquaint students from both English-speaking and non-English-speaking homes with the history and culture associated with each language. It also provides a whole range of supportive service for students, with participation by full-time nonpublic school students assured.

For millions of disadvantaged children, a Bilingual Educational Act promises fuller participation in a free society.

18

Puerto Rican Pupils
and American Education

Francesco Cordasco

In 1960, some 900,000 Puerto Ricans lived in the U.S., including not only those born on the island, but also those born to Puerto Rican parents in the states. Until 1940, the Puerto Rican community numbered only 70,000, but, by 1950, this had risen to 226,000, and over the decade to 1960, the net gain due to migration from the island amounted to nearly 390,000. The census of 1950 began the recording of second-generation Puerto Ricans (those born on the continent to island-born parents) and counted 75,000; in 1960, the figure stood at 272,000, so that, by 1960, three out of every 10 Puerto Rican residents in the U.S. were born in the states.

Although there has been a dispersal of the migration outside greater New York City, the overwhelming number of Puerto Ricans are New Yorkers; the 1960 census showed 612,574 living in New York City (68.6% of the U.S. total). New York City's proportion had dropped from 88% in 1940, to 83% in 1950, and to 69% in 1960. If there is no serious setback in the American economy, the dispersion undoubtedly will continue.[1]

The Commonwealth of Puerto Rico neither encourages nor discourages migration. As an American citizen, the Puerto Rican moves between the island and the mainland with complete freedom. If his movement is vulnerable to anything, it fluctuates only with reference to the economy on the mainland.

SOURCE. Reprinted from *School & Society*, February 18, 1967, by permission of the author and publisher. Based on a paper presented at 61st annual convention, American Sociological Association, Miami, Fla., August 30, 1966.

[1] U.S. Bureau of the Census, *U.S. Census of Population: 1960 Subject Reports. Puerto Ricans in the United States*. Final Report, PC (2)-1 D. (Washington, D.C.: U.S. Government Printing Office, 1963). The 1960 census reported Puerto Rican born persons living in all but one (Duluth-Superior) of the 101 Standard Metropolitan Statistical Areas of over 250,000 population.

Any economic recession or contraction graphically shows in the migration statistics.[2] It is invidious at best to suggest that "The Puerto Rican migration to *Nueva York*, unchecked by immigrant quotas, is a major source of the island's prosperity," but there is truth in the appended observation that the migration ". . . upgraded the migrants, converted them from rural to urban people, relieved the island of some of its labor surplus, and sent lots of cash back home."[3]

For the mainland schools, the Puerto Rican migration presented a distinct and yet, in many ways, a recurrent phenomenon. With the imposition of immigration quotas in the early 1920's, the non-English speaking student gradually had disappeared. The great European migration and the manifold educational problems to which the American schools had addressed themselves had been resolved in a manner; with the increasing Puerto Rican migration and the recurrent pattern of the ghettoization of the new arrivals, the migrant child, non-English speaking and nurtured by a different culture, presented the schools with a new, yet very old, challenge.[4]

The Puerto Rican "journey" to the mainland has been (and continues to be) the subject of vast literature.[5] For the most part, the Puerto Rican child reflects a context of bitter deprivation, poor housing, high unemployment, and a record of disappointing educational achievement. It is the poverty context, to which the Puerto Rican community has been relegated, that explains its problems and graphically underscores its poor achievement in the schools. Not only is the Puerto Rican child asked to adapt to a "cultural

[2] See, in this connection, migration figures for 1953–54. The best source on Puerto Rican migration is the Migration Division of the Department of Labor, Commonwealth of Puerto Rico, which maintains a central mainland office in New York City and offices in other U.S. cities. It also maintains an office in Puerto Rico to carry out a program of orientation for persons who intend to migrate to the states.

[3] Patricia Sexton, *Spanish Harlem: Anatomy of Poverty* (New York: Harper & Row, 1965), p. 15.

[4] Although one of the greatest achievements of the American common school has been the acculturation and assimilation of the children of non-English speaking immigrants (largely European), it has received little study. See F. Cordasco and L. Covello, *Educational Sociology: A Subject Index of Doctoral Dissertations Completed at American Universities, 1941–1963* (New York: Scarecrow Press, 1965). Of over 2,000 dissertations listed, only a few clearly concern themselves with the non-English immigrant child, or generally with the educational problems of the children of immigrants.

[5] One of the best accounts is Clarence Senior, *The Puerto Ricans* (Chicago: Quadrangle Books, 1965), which includes an extensive bibliography. See also Christopher Rand, *The Puerto Ricans* (New York: Oxford, 1958); Don Wakefield, *Island In The City* (Boston: Houghton Mifflin, 1959); Elena Padilla, *Up From Puerto Rico* (New York: Columbia University Press, 1958); Jesus Colon, *A Puerto Rican In New York and Other Sketches* (New York: Mainstream Publications, 1964); an older, but invaluable, documented study of Puerto Ricans in New York City is that of C. Wright Mills, Clarence Senior, and Rose Kohn Goldsen, *The Puerto Rican Journey* (New York: Harper, 1950).

ambience" which is strange and new, but he remains further burdened by all the negative pressures of a ghetto milieu which educators have discerned as inimical to even the most rudimentary educational accomplishment.[6]

How the Puerto Rican child has fared in the mainland schools is illustrated best in the experience in New York City, where Puerto Ricans have the lowest level of formal education of any identifiable ethnic or color group. Only 13% of Puerto Rican men and women 25 years of age and older in 1960 had completed either high school or more advanced education. Among New York's non-white (predominantly Negro) population, 31.2% had completed high school; and the other white population (excluding Puerto Ricans) did even better. Over 40% at least had completed high school.[7]

In 1960 more than half—52.9%—of Puerto Ricans in New York City 25 years of age and older had less than an eighth-grade education. In contrast, 29.5% of the non-white population had not finished the eighth grade, and only 19.3% of the other whites had so low an academic preparation.

If the schools in New York City were to correct all of this (the numbers in the second generation who have reached adult years is still small, only 6.4% of persons 20 years of age and older in 1960), there is still evidence that Puerto Rican youth, more than any other group, is handicapped severely in achieving an education in the New York City public schools. A 1961 study of a Manhattan neighborhood showed that fewer than 10% of Puerto Ricans in the third grade were reading at their grade level or above. The degree of retardation was extreme. Three in 10 were retarded one and one-half years or more and were, in the middle of their third school year, therefore, reading at a level only appropriate for entry into the second grade. By the eighth grade the degree of retardation was even more severe, with almost two-thirds of the Puerto Rican youngsters retarded more than three years.

Of the nearly 21,000 academic diplomas granted in 1963, only 331 went to Puerto Ricans and 762 to Negroes, representing only 1.6% and 3.7% respectively, of the total academic diplomas. In contrast, Puerto Ricans received 7.4% of the vocational school diplomas, and Negroes, 15.2%. For the Puerto Rican community, these figures have critical significance, since Puerto Rican children constituted, in 1963, about 20% of the public elementary school register; 18% of the junior high school register; and, in keeping with long-discerned trends, Puerto Rican youngsters made up 23% of the student body in vocational schools and 29% of that in special (difficult) schools.

[6] For a graphic commentary on the debilitating environmental pressures and the "ghetto milieu" see David Barry, *Our Christian Mission Among Spanish Americans*, mimeo., Princeton University Consultation, Feb. 21–23, 1965. The statistical indices of Puerto Rican poverty (and the related needs) are assembled best in *The Puerto Rican Community Development Project* (New York: Puerto Rican Forum, 1964), pp. 26–75.

[7] *The Puerto Rican Community Development Project*, op. cit., p. 34.

Clearly, the critical issue for the Puerto Rican community is the education of its children, for the experience in New York City is a macrocosm which illustrates all the facets of the mainland experience.

In the last decade, a wide range of articles have reported special educational programs to meet the needs of Puerto Rican children. Although many of these have been of value, the more ambitious theoretic constructs have come largely from the school boards and staffs which have had to deal with the basic problem of communication in classes where a growing (and at times preponderant) number of Spanish-speaking children were found. As early as 1951 in New York City, a "Mayor's Advisory Committee on Puerto Rican Affairs" turned its attention to this major problem of communication; and this problem was periodically re-examined during the years which followed.

In New York City, as in other cities, the Board of Education turned its attention to the Puerto Rican child because communications *had* to be established, and, in this context, the most ambitious study of the educational problems presented by the Puerto Rican migration became (for New York City) ". . . a four-year inquiry into the education and adjustment of Puerto Rican pupils in the public schools of New York City . . . a major effort . . . to establish on a sound basis a city-wide program for the continuing improvement of the educational opportunities of all non-English speaking pupils in the public schools."[8]

If the major emphasis of *The Puerto Rican Study* was to have been the basic problem of language (English), its objectives soon were extended to include the equally important areas of community orientation and acculturation. The *Study's* objectives were summed up in three main problems: What are the more effective ways (methods) and materials for teaching English as a second language to newly arrived Puerto Rican pupils? What are the most effective techniques with which the schools can promote a more rapid and more effective adjustment of Puerto Rican parents and children to the community and the community to them? Who are the Puerto Rican pupils in the New York City public schools? For each of these problems, *The Puerto Rican Study* made detailed recommendations. The third problem, above, largely an ethnic survey, resulted in a profile of characteristics of pupils of Puerto Rican background and fused into Problems I and II.

Problem I: How Effectively to Teach English as a Second Language? The Puerto Rican Study concluded that an integrated method (vocabulary method; structured or language patterns method; and the functional situations or experiential method) was to be employed, and it developed two series of related curriculum bulletins, keyed to the prescribed New York City course

[8] J. Cayce Morrison, director, *The Puerto Rican Study (1953–1957): A Report on the Education and Adjustment of Puerto Rican Pupils in the Public Schools of the City of New York* (New York: Board of Education, 1958), p. 1.

of study. But, in the course of its considerations, it dealt with the ancillary and vital need ". . . to formulate a uniform policy for the reception, screening, placement and periodic assessment of non-English speaking pupils." It recommended, until such time as the Bureau of Educational Research may find or develop better tests or tests of equal value, the use of the USE Test —Ability to Understand Spoken English; the Gates Reading Test—Primary and Advanced; and the Lorge-Thorndike Non-Verbal Test. It proposed, also, three broad categories of class organization; considered the need of adequate staffing (Substitute Auxiliary Teachers [SAT]; Puerto Rican Coordinators; School-Community Coordinators and Other Teaching Positions [OTP]; and guidance counselors, particularly in the senior high schools), and found essential the ". . . coordinating [of] efforts of colleges and universities . . . to achieve greater unity of purpose and effort in developing both undergraduate and graduate programs for teachers who will work with non-English speaking pupils. . . ."

Problem II: How to Promote a More Rapid and More Effective Adjustment of Puerto Rican Parents and Children to the Community and the Community to Them? In its recognition of this problem, *The Puerto Rican Study* struggled with providing answers to the basic anxieties and preoccupations of a group of people beset with problems of housing, adequate employment, health, and "assimilation." That the study found difficulty in providing answers is perhaps explained in its inability to relate the answers it found most effective to the mandate of the school. If it were possible to revise curricula and discern the problems implicit in the learning experience of the Puerto Rican child, it remained an altogether different matter to attempt the solution of broad socio-economic problems, or to attempt the amelioration of community ills. In essence, the following statement suggests how far the schools have retreated from the community: "On the relation of Puerto Rican parents to schools, *The Puerto Rican Study* holds that because Puerto Rican parents are preoccupied with problems of learning English, finding apartments, finding employment, and with problems of providing their families with food, clothing, and proper health protection, they are not ready to set a high priority on their children's school problems. The schools can't wait until they are ready."

If *The Puerto Rican Study* is not thought of as a finished guide to the solution of the problems it investigates, but rather as a beginning, it must be characterized as the best assessment of the educational challenges which the Spanish-speaking child poses to the mainland school. In this sense, it is both a guide and a blueprint for effective reform.

Basically, the Puerto Rican child is not a newcomer to the continental school. In many ways, he presents himself to a school and a society whose very nature is heterogeneous and variegated, and to which the non-English speaking child is no stranger. In this sense, the acquisition of English for the Puerto Rican child (if necessary and inevitable) is not a great problem; certainly, it is a soluble problem to which the American school brings a rich and successful experience, and *The Puerto Rican Study* affirms how successful and resourceful American schools can and have been. What is more important to the Puerto Rican child and to American society is the process of acculturation. How does the Puerto Rican child retain his identity, his language, and his culture? In substance, this remains the *crucial* problem, and, in this crucial context, the role of the school in American society needs to be assessed carefully. If the Puerto Rican child is sinned against today, the tragedy lies in the continued assault against his identity, his language, and his cultural wellsprings. In this sense, his experience is not different fundamentally from that of millions of other children to whom the American school was a mixed blessing. This is in no way a deprecation of the egalitarianism of the American common school, but, rather, a reaffirmation of the loss of the great opportunity that a free society afforded its schools to nurture and treasure the rich and varied traditions of its charges. The melting pot theory is, at best, an illusion measured against the realities of American society and a true discernment of its strengths.

In another light, the Puerto Rican child is the creature of his social context —its opportunities or lack of opportunities. If his needs are to be met, they only can be met effectively insofar as the needs of this context are met. A school which is not community-oriented is a poor school. If this is so for the middle-class suburban school, it is even more so for the urban school, which is the heir of the myriad complexities of a rapidly deteriorating central city. More important than the Puerto Rican child's lack of English is the lack of that economic security and well-being that relates him to a viable family structure. If the Puerto Rican child's major disenchantment does not result from segregated schools into which his poverty has placed him, still one would have to deplore the school's inability to cope with the alienation that segregation spawns and the bitter destitution that poverty brings to its children. Perhaps, the "great society" really emerges from a strengthening of the school by its joining hands with all the creative agencies of the community.

19

Culture Conflict
and Mexican-American Achievement

Neal Justin

It appears that the least-educated citizens in the U.S. are the Mexican-Americans. Nearly 1,000,000 Spanish-speaking children in the Southwest never will go beyond the eighth grade.[1] In some areas, up to 90% of the Mexican-Americans fail to complete high school.[2]

What are some of the causes of deprivation and failure among the Mexican-Americans? Four closely related areas are of concern: language, discrimination, lower socioeconomic status, and culture.

The most obvious identifying characteristic of the Mexican-Americans is their language. The Tucson Survey of the Teaching of Spanish to the Spanish-Speaking by the National Education Association placed great emphasis on the influence of the Spanish language and its use as related to academic achievement.[3] In fact, the language barrier currently is given more attention than any other factor affecting Mexican-American achievement.

The use of the Spanish language by the Mexican-Americans has played a definite role in the isolation and discrimination of these people by the Anglos. The preservation of the Spanish language has been interpreted by

---

SOURCE. Reprinted from *School & Society*, January 1970, by permission of the author and publisher.

[1] Department of Rural Education, National Education Association, *The Invisible Minority*, Report of the National Education Association-Tucson Survey on the Teaching of Spanish to the Spanish-Speaking (Washington: National Education Association, 1966), p. 6.

[2] John H. Chilcott, "Some Perspectives for Teaching First Generation Mexican-Americans," in John H. Chilcott, et al., eds., *Readings in the Socio-Cultural Foundations of Education* (Belmont, Calif.: Wadsworth, 1968) p. 359.

[3] *The Invisible Minority*, ibid.

the dominant group as "a persistent symbol and instrument of isolation."[4] While the Anglo tends to consider the use of Spanish as an indication of foreignness, the Mexican-Americans consider it a symbol of their unity and loyalty to *La Raza*.[5]

In his discussion on barriers to Mexican integration, Officer stated that "the greatest hindrance to complete cultural assimilation of Tucson's Mexicans is the language problem."[6] Apparently, this opinion has been shared widely by educators, if we can judge from the adjustments made for Mexican-Americans in curricula.

There is evidence that the language barrier, although important, may be overrated. Available research shows that language need not be an insurmountable barrier to the academic and intellectual achievement of youngsters who come from foreign language-speaking homes.[7] Henderson points out that "the current mania for structural linguistics as a panacea for educational problems of Mexican-American children is another example of a language centered curriculum emphasis."[8] Moreover, he shows that the Mexican-American pupils who spoke the most Spanish also could speak the most English.[9] Nevertheless, most educators consider the language barrier as the major obstacle to the Mexican-American's success and achievement in school.

There is substantial evidence, however, that the greater emphasis should be placed on the socio-cultural problems of the Mexican-American. The ugly factors of discrimination and prejudice have played and continue to play an important role in keeping the Mexican-Americans in a subservient position. The Mexican coming to the U.S. is confronted with a double problem of prejudice. In Mexico, class discrimination is commonplace, but discrimination against color is unusual. Here, unfortunately, discrimination and prejudice commonly are based on both class and color.

Prejudice against the Mexicans and Mexican-Americans in the Southwest generally follows this pattern: lack of job opportunities, lack of educational opportunities, segregation in housing, lack of equality before the law, and

[4] Leonard Broom and Eshref Shevsky, "Mexicans in the United States . . . A Problem in Social Differentiation," *Sociology and Social Research*, **36**: 153, January-February, 1952.

[5] William Madsen, *The Mexicans of South Texas* (New York: Holt, Rinehart, and Winston, 1965), p. 106.

[6] James Officer, "Barriers to Mexican Integration in Tucson," *The Kiva*, **17**: 7, May, 1951.

[7] Leona Elizabeth Tyler, *The Psychology of Human Differences* (New York: Appleton-Century-Crofts, 1956), p. 305.

[8] Ronald W. Henderson, *Environmental Stimulation and Intellectual Development of Mexican-American Children: An Exploratory Study* (Unpublished Ph.D. dissertation, University of Arizona, 1966), p. 142.

[9] Ibid., p. 144.

various kinds of social discrimination.[10] Among the major reasons for this situation are a strong history of lower socioeconomic status, darker skin color, language, conflicting cultural traits and customs, and religion.

For the most part, discrimination against the Mexican-Americans is subtle in nature. While the Mexican-American enjoys all the legal rights of citizenship, he is the victim of extralegal discrimination. It is this special type of discrimination which led Tuck to call her book *Not with the Fist*. In it, she comments: "Rather than having the job of battering down a wall, the Mexican-American finds himself entangled in a spider web, whose outlines are difficult to see but whose clean, silken strands hold tight."[11]

The inferior socioeconomic status of the Mexican-Americans may be greater than most Americans would like to admit. Although Mexican-Americans are found in all walks of life, an examination of the 1960 U.S. Census data shows that they occupy an overwhelmingly large position in the lower-ranking occupations. Almost 75% of the Mexican-Americans are employed as manual workers. This concentration in the unskilled occupations has had a severe effect upon their incomes. The 1960 Census data indicate that the Mexican-Americans in the Southwest earned between $1,000 and $2,000 less per year than did the Anglo unskilled workers. In all of the five Southwestern states, the average incomes of Mexican-Americans are far below that of the population in general.

The greatest barrier to the acculturation, assimilation, and achievement of the Mexican-Americans probably is culture conflict. Other immigrant groups to the U.S. have felt the blow of discrimination.[12] The Chinese, Jews, Italians, Irish, Polish, etc., are common examples. However, the faster the immigrant group moves toward adopting the customs and language of the dominant culture, the less discrimination they seem to experience.[13] Madsen believes that any ethnic group that fails to show a maximum faith in America, science, and progress will be subject to discrimination. It would be additionally difficult for the members of this group to assimilate if they are physically distinguishable, if they use a foreign language, and if they hold to cultural ways that are not compatible with the dominant culture.[14]

Unlike other immigrant groups, the Mexican-Americans have preferred to hold to their Mexican cultural ways and Spanish language. This may be attributed to their close proximity to Mexico.

[10] John H. Burma, *Spanish-Speaking Groups in the United States* (Durham, N.C.: Duke University Press, 1954), p. 107.

[11] Ruth Tuck, *Not with the Fist* (New York: Harcourt, Brace, 1946), p. 198.

[12] Raymond W. Mack, *Race, Class and Power* (New York: American Book Co., 1963), p. 118.

[13] Ibid., p. 118.

[14] Madsen, op. cit., p. 1.

The question then arises: Which of the Mexican-American cultural ways is in greatest conflict with the dominant Anglo culture? Extensive and careful review of numerous studies by Angell, Chilcott, Kluckhohn, Madsen, Simmons, Strodtbeck, Zintz, and others indicates that there are two Mexican cultural characteristics that are the mirror image of the Anglo culture. These are concerned with feelings of personal control (fatalism) and delay of gratification (future orientation). Could it be that even third- or fourth-generation Mexican-American students are actually more fatalistic and present-time oriented than their Anglo peers? What might this mean in terms of curriculums and cultural conflict?

To answer these questions, the writer set up an exploratory study at the College of Education, University of Arizona.[15] A total of 168 male, Mexican-American seniors and 209 male, Anglo seniors were selected randomly for testing at four urban Tucson high schools. A special questionnaire, adapted from a similar instrument developed by the Institute of Behavioral Science, University of Colorado, was revised, judged for content validity, tested for reliability, and then administered to the sample population.

The statistical analysis of the data pertaining to the two cultural characteristics of delayed gratification (future orientation) and feelings of personal control (fatalism) provided a number of significant differences when the means of the two sample populations were subjected to independent tests.

The Mexican-Americans showed a mean of 6.90 on the measurement of their feelings of personal control, while their Anglo peers had a mean of 8.51. Measurement of the tendency to delay gratification provided a mean of 3.99 for the Mexican-Americans and 4.63 for the Anglos. In each case, the differences between these means were significant at the .05 level.

Marked contrast, therefore, is seen between the Mexican-Americans and the Anglos. The Mexican-Americans are significantly lacking in feelings of personal control and concern with delayed gratification when compared to their Anglo peers. These finding indicate that, whatever culture change has taken place among the second-, third-, and fourth-generation Mexican-Americans, it has not been great with reference to these two characteristics. It also should be considered that the students selected for this study were second-semester seniors and were, therefore, a select group of achievers in relation to their many peers who already have dropped out of school. One may have good cause to wonder how great these differences would have been if the study had been done with junior high students. Even with these very conservative results, the Mexican-Americans are seen to be significantly different from their Anglo peers.

[15] Neal Justin, *The Relationships of Certain Socio-Cultural Factors to the Academic Achievement of Male, Mexican-American, High School Seniors* (unpublished Ed.D. dissertation, University of Arizona, 1969).

Assuming that most of our school curricula are constructed by Anglos who apparently have significantly different orientations to life, then what over-all effect does this have upon the Mexican-American youngsters? What conflicts may be built into the curriculum that could permeate the whole subculture of education. Kneller provides a word to the wise when he asserts that, before we can attain our educational goals, we must be aware of the internalized antagonisms of the culture that may thwart the efforts of teachers.[16] Could it be that our Anglo-dominated curricula inadvertently thwart the efforts of both the Mexican-American students and their teachers? There may be a good reason to consider the findings of this study. Perhaps, we should examine the appropriateness of our curricula as they apply to the Mexican-American student in particular.

[16] George F. Kneller, *Educational Anthropology: An Introduction* (New York: Wiley, 1965), p. 14.

20

The Negative Self-Concept
of Mexican-American Students

Thomas P. Carter

Most educators who deal with Mexican-American children are convinced that the group contains a larger than normal percentage of individuals who view themselves negatively. This negative self-image is seen as being a principal reason for the group's lack of school success. Contacts with Mexican-American youth in one area of California, however, do not support the notion that they perceive themselves more negatively than do their "Anglo" peers.

What causes the individual Mexican-American's self-image to be negative? The usual answer stresses that such a child is marginal, caught between two ways of life—the Mexican and the American. This marginality presents the individual with more than normal difficulty in establishing his self-identity, leading the child to assume he is inferior. Often not accepted by the "Anglo" group, he concludes that he is as that group views him—lazy, unambitious, not very intelligent, etc. It is assumed that the child internalizes the "Anglo" stereotype of the "Mexican." Other causes are seen as contributing. Constant frustration and disappointment in school are regarded by Prof. Manuel as promoting feelings of inferiority. He contends that the child caught in such a syndrome of failure withdraws from the battle and assumes the inferior feelings ascribed to him by the school.[1] The child is perceived as judging himself against the "Anglo" school's norms of success.

The search for identity is real and traumatic for most youth in our kinetic world. The search for self for the marginal youth is, without doubt, more real and more traumatic. The Mexican-American suffers many frustrations and problems. Yet, experience indicates that such youth are quite resilient as

SOURCE. Reprinted from *School & Society*, March 30, 1968, by permission of the author and publisher.

[1] Herschel T. Manuel, *Spanish Speaking Children of the Southwest* (Austin: University of Texas Press, 1965), p. 189.

a group, and seem fairly successful in withstanding the temptation to think of themselves negatively. Rather than judge themselves solely by "Anglo" standards, they appear to judge by norms established by their own peer society or by the Mexican-American society of which they are part. They seem to reject "Anglo" society's and the school's opinion of them, and maintain individual integrity at least as well as their "Anglo" peers. A strong suggestion must be made that the supposed negative self-image of the Mexican-American is, in reality, our own stereotype projected onto him. "Anglos" tend to think of Mexican-Americans in negative ways, and conclude they see themselves in the same light.

From September, 1964, to June, 1966, the author conducted research in the secondary schools of one of California's rich agricultural valleys. The study involved the feeder seventh- and eighth-grade schools and the one union high school. School population in the area is approximately 65% Mexican-American, the vast majority are children of low-paid agricultural workers. The "Anglo" school population's parents follow a much more normal distribution of occupations and income. During the study, parents, students, teachers, and administrators were interviewed, some a number of times. Classes were observed repeatedly. Three sets of socio-psychological instruments were administered. Nothing supported the belief that the Mexican-American students saw themselves more negatively than "Anglo" students. However, it was very obvious that teachers and administrators believed them to be inferior and to conclude they saw themselves that way.

A demonstration of self-concept parity between the two ethnic groups was the analysis of data collected from a questionnaire administered to 190 Mexican-American and 98 "Anglo" high school ninth graders. It was hypothesized that important components of self-image involved the elements of personal intelligence, goodness, happiness, and power. The individual student rated himself on a five-point semantic differential. The adjectives used were: good-bad, wise-foolish, happy-sad, and strong-weak. Students told how they felt about themselves by indicating where they fell on the five-point continuum between the two adjectives. Little or no difference, in self-view as assumed to be measured by the instrument, was found to exist between the two groups.

Percentages of the two groups rating themselves on each of the five points between the four sets of differentials were calculated. In some cases, the Mexican-Americans had a slightly larger percentage rating themselves on the positive extreme. For example, 21% of the Mexican-Americans, contrasted to 13% of the "Anglos," rated themselves on the extreme good side of the good-bad differential. Even on the wise-foolish continuum, a slightly larger percentage of the Mexican-Americans than of "Anglos" saw themselves as extremely wise. On the other dimensions, both groups had similar percentages. Median scores for the two groups were very close. On the good-bad scale, both groups had a median score of 3.1. On the wise-foolish and strong-weak scales, the differences were practically nil. Mexican-American median on the intelligence item was 2.9, as contrasted to 2.8. The power item reflected the same magnitude of difference—the Mexican-American median being 2.2, the "Anglo" 2.1. Only on the happy-sad scale did a larger difference exist, the Mexican-American median being 3.6, a little less happy than the "Anglo" 3.3.

The students interviewed supported the notion that as a group they did not suffer from a negative view of themselves. Admittedly, individuals did. Yet, the Mexican-American students were well aware of the way teachers and others viewed their group. They knew the stereotype. Numerous students reported examples of derogatory statements about "Mexicans" made by teachers and fellow students. Many were school failures—having long histories of low achievement, poor grades, and repeated years. Yet, the majority of these children appeared to be doing a magnificent job of maintaining a positive view of themselves against the onslaught of the beliefs of the "Anglo" and the judgments of the school.

Two societies, the Mexican-American and the "Anglo," exist in the area served by the schools studied. The school, its teachers, content, and methods, represent the middle-class "Anglo" culture. The Mexican-American child often sees much of what is taught as irrelevant or in conflict with what he learns at home. The child caught between the home and school culture readily learns his reference group's methods of coping with the conflict situation. The reference group of most Mexican-Americans is their own sub-society. Such actions as a boy hanging his head and playing dumb often are interpreted by teachers as manifesting a negative self-view, yet well may be "tricks" developed by the subordinate group in order to coexist with the "Anglo." From the boy's point of view, the action may insulate and protect the boy's feelings. The apparent submissiveness of some Mexican-American girls often is judged as reflecting the girl's negative view of herself. However, this behavior may be well established in the girl's home culture as normal and desirable. Educators tend to interpret a minority's behavior from the "Anglo" frame of reference. Actions which may manifest negative self-view in one society are interpreted equally in children from another ethnic group.

The Mexican-American child may remove himself subjectively from the environment that depreciates him, and place himself in the valid community that supports and maintains the individual. What becomes relevant to him is either his ethnic peer group, the adult Mexican-American community, or both. This point was well taken by José Villarreal when he stated, ". . . discrimination, prejudice and poverty have not made him [Mexican-American youth] feel inferior. He can be traumatized by these things, but he is not broken by them. The Anglo may lull himself into believing the opposite, but the boy who is forced to drop out of the eighth grade because he was ignored, discouraged, or misdirected does not feel inferior."[2] Such a youth is lucky, as he has a sanctuary in a society existing adjacent to the "Anglo" world. The child's home and peer society teaches him who he is and what is expected of him. The Mexican-Americans studied seem to follow a rather normal distribution in regards to how well they perceive of themselves as meeting these standards.

The limitations of this research must be recognized. The area studied is rural and agricultural, with a numerical majority of Mexican-Americans. Other situations, where percentages are different, where there is a less close-knit Mexican-American community, or where the setting is urban and industrial, may present other findings as to how the Mexican-Americans view themselves. While no definite conclusions can be reached, a few assumptions are suggested. Every school and community is distinct; each must be examined carefully. Generalizations concerning Mexican-American students are misleading at their best. Mexican-Americans are a very heterogeneous group of people. Mexican-American youth does not necessarily internalize the "Anglo's" image of him, nor does he necessarily judge himself against school norms of success and failure. Educators must re-examine the school and the students they serve to test such currently held beliefs as the group negative self-image concept. Too ready acceptance of such notions serves to protect educators from the in-depth examination of other problems relative to the success and failure of Mexican-American students in the "Anglo" school.

[2] José Villarreal, "Mexican-Americans and the Leadership Crisis," *Los Angeles Times West magazine*, Sept. 25, 1966, p. 45.

Part 4

The North American Indian

21

The American Indian
and Formal Education

Lambert N. Wenner

Several generations of poverty-stricken, demoralized, and dependent people attest to the deficiencies of a national policy of segregating Indians on resources-poor reservations. It now seems clear that ultimate assimilation of the American Indians to the main stream of national culture is unavoidable and in some ways desirable. With the expansion of Euro-American civilization to the more remote regions of the West, it is becoming increasingly imperative for the Indian to become operational within the broader context of national life.

For several decades, concerned government officials have regarded education as a possible solution to the Indian's dilemma, but only during the past generation has there been much serious effort to extend and improve the facilities and the quality of instruction available to reservation youth and adults. At the present time, there is mounting concern that the conventional curricular content and methods of teaching may be inappropriate to the Indian student's personality, present cultural milieu, or future needs.

This essay surveys contemporary Indian education, both in its local and national contexts. It assesses the degree and quality of Indian participation in American life, some of his future alternatives, and the possible role of education in shaping his future. Some attention is devoted to specific educational situations, since American Indians vary in their tribal autonomy, economic self-sufficiency, and degree of present assimilation.

The necessity to adapt to a radically changing environment is hardly a challenge unique to the Indians of the 20th century. Both archaeology and history reveal that many Indian groups of earlier periods were forced to choose between innovation and extinction. Climatic changes, hostile neighbors, or the encroachments of the Euro-American pioneers forced migration, dietary adjustments, and even technological revolutions. In more recent times, the introduction of the horse and the rifle caused a major socioeconomic revolution among many of the Great Plains Indians within the space of a generation or two. Alternatively, one may cite the valiant efforts of the "Five Civilized Tribes," the Cherokee, Choctaw, and others, who selectively "Europeanized" while attempting to retain tribal identity and integrity.

This essay will not attempt to establish why many contemporary Indian groups have failed to make equally impressive adaptations to their changing physical and social environments. Such an explanation would doubtless deal with such factors as the compulsory assignment of Indians to inhospitable regions, the gradual depletion of traditional economic resources, the onslaught of alien diseases, resulting social disorganization, the complexity of Euro-American culture, discriminatory barriers, and the like. What is significant here is that the kind of maladaptation suggested by widespread poverty, alcoholism, and suppressed pride has important implications for Indian education.

Unlike the European immigrant, who was roughly acculturated to Anglo-American civilization before leaving his homeland, the New World Indian perceived the ways of the white American as strange, unpredictable, and sometimes threatening. Often, when the expansionist tendencies and private property orientation of the alien invader became apparent, the Indians resisted with all of the resources at their disposal. Small wonder that, when ultimately defeated and "exiled" to remote areas, they have been reluctant to adopt the ways of their former adversary.

If one examines Indian life today, at least four modes of adjustment to the Anglo-American culture are discernible. As a first step in assessing the educational needs of Indian-Americans, we describe the ideal types—namely, acculturated, marginal, traditional, and bicultural man.[1]

Roughly 200,000 Americans may be classified as acculturated Indians.[2] Relatively well-educated and gainfully employed in numerous occupations, they are self-sufficient, without close tribal affiliations, and in most ways indistinguishable from other community residents of similar socioeconomic status. While some, often subtle, discrimination may be experienced, acculturated Indians generally fare much better than more visible minority group members, e.g., Negroes or Mexican-Americans. Moreover, social and economic opportunities seem to be increasing for those at the upper educational or skill levels.

---

[1] Although it is recognized that these categories are simplifications or polarizations of social reality, it is believed they are suggestive of the range of American Indian adaptations to Euro-American culture.

[2] A more precise figure would require a definition of an Indian. Federal statutes specify $\frac{1}{2}$, $\frac{1}{4}$, $\frac{1}{8}$, or $\frac{1}{16}$ Indian ancestry and some states employ such terms as "a trace" or "colored" in their definitions.

An unfortunate feature of this life style, in the view of advocates of cultural pluralism, is that frequently such Indians almost completely abandon their ancestral heritage. Isolation from Indian traditions and perhaps a desire to "fit in" elsewhere eventually produce a generation of children who know only the Western patterns of social life. It is a tragedy that such pressures for conformity exist (or are thought to exist), it is argued, in a society which promises some real opportunities for individual and group expression and self-realization.

This type of adaptation is most evident among Indians whose reservations are adjacent to Euro-American communities of fairly recent origin, as in Northern Minnesota, South Dakota, parts of Montana and California, and elsewhere. Marginal man is partially shaped by a badly eroded traditional culture and is not yet assimilated adequately into the national or regional culture. He has had very little formal education, is frequently unemployed, lives in a log house or shack, and occupies a fringe status in the local community. Commonly, marginal man regards striving as tedious and futile, or quite uncritically follows a life style pioneered by his defeated parents.

There is no retreat, for the traditional life is no longer viable; neither are there fertile prospects for fulfillment in the larger society. The result is a hopeless cycle of frustration or self-doubt for the man-between-cultures, continued dependence, increased alienation, and renewed self-doubt.

A number of Indian societies have reacted to the problems and threats encountered as a cultural minority by withdrawing as much as possible from Euro-American society and attempting to be self-sufficient. This tradition-maintenance pattern has been most evident among sizable, stable societies such as the Hopi, extremely isolated groups like the Polar Eskimos, and certain stubborn tribes with a tradition of fierce independence, e.g., the Navaho. Though most of these groups have selectively borrowed ideas, equipment, and techniques from their alien neighbors, they have still managed to retain their integrity as a social unit, their language, some traditional institutions, and their arts.

During and since World War II, however, the traditionalists have experienced a dramatic increase in external influences, both in number and degree of pervasiveness. Returning servicemen, the mass media, public education, and expanded tourism are all affecting their life style. Present agricultural, mineral, and hydroelectric power developments and improved roads in these once remote areas result in a continued infusion of Anglo-American traits.

Some Indians have acquired the facility of participating equally well in their native and adopted cultures. These are often people with extensive formal education but with pride in their aboriginal heritage. In addition, certain wilderness guides, local museum curators, and artisans have appeared to be almost equally at home in two very different cultural contexts.

A second and perhaps more common version of biculturalism is enthusiastic identification with one's original or parent culture, even to cultivating its traditions, while simultaneously participating in quite another social milieu. But in the absence of social mechanisms to reinforce the original life style, it is likely to decline in its relative importance.

Education, including formal education, is not alien to Indian culture, but the Western institutional form with its career teachers, distinct facilities, and separation from family life is not fully consistent with the Indian way, even today. In some instances, traditional Indian education was an involved process with an extensive body of knowledge organized for a specific maturity level. Sometimes the child would be turned over to relatives or acknowledged experts for particular types of training. But more often, education consisted largely of repeated exhortations and demonstration as various family members, at opportune moments, emphasized the role of the good wife or explained how "humans" behave in contrast to other beings. Even at age five or six, the child had learned something of most adult roles[3] and could be expected to assume adult responsibilities much earlier than his Western counterparts.

Spindler, Mead, and others have reported several widely practiced patterns of primitive education which may have implications for modern elementary education. Small children are allowed extensive freedom and are fed on demand and sleep when tired. While they may receive considerable attention and affection, there seems to be no urgency in socializing them. But when the child has matured sufficiently to accept some responsibilities, usually about six or seven, the educational process dramatically intensifies. Soon the child learns to make real contributions to his household by gathering foods, tending animals, caring for small children, and other simple but necessary tasks. Apparently, the child seldom resents these assignments and may regard them as a form of play.[4] At the other extreme, the premanhood education of boys in their early teens may be a grueling experience, as among some of the Plains and Pueblo Indians, and serves to make the transition from youth to adulthood both clearcut and profound.

A most significant aspect of primitive education—in contrast to much Western schooling—is the ever-present meaningful context for learning. Almost everything learned has immediate, useful applications with little necessity to "store" presently meaningless content for future use. Moreover,

[3] George D. Spindler, ed., *Education and Culture* (New York: Holt, Rinehart and Winston, 1963), p. 381.

[4] Robert J. Havighurst, "Education Among American Indians: Individual and Cultural Aspects," in George E. Simpson and J. Milton Yinger, eds., "American Indians and American Life," *Annals of the American Academy of Political and Social Science*, **311**: 105, May, 1957.

the child is subject to far less contradictions than in Western pluralistic society, *e.g.*, the "Hopi way" is rather clearly and consistently defined.

The acculturated and bicultural Indians of contemporary Anglo-America usually send their children to the local public schools where they encounter few special problems relating to their racial difference. Cultural differences of the sort that nourish prejudice and discrimination have all but vanished and physical appearance alone is a much less formidable barrier. Even so, one might expect occasional obstacles in the informal social life of the school and community, *e.g.*, dating or friendship choice.

Children of marginal Indian parentage most often attend public schools but also enroll in Bureau of Indian Affairs, private, or parochial schools, depending upon the child's special needs and the availability of public facilities. Since 1950, Congress has provided financial incentives to encourage states to assume responsibility for the education and assistance of Indian youth and, when judged adequate, state programs replace earlier federal ventures.[5] While the initial cultural barriers these children face in the integrated public school may be considerable, there is a growing consensus that this is the most feasible solution to the problem of marginality.

Whatever talents and skills the marginal child may have, his public school experience is likely to be frustrating. His crude command of English, lesser competitive spirit, and limited experience in the Anglo-American milieu may result in student or teacher judgments of backwardness or inferiority. Thus, despite increasing recognition among educators that Indian children do have academic potential, special programs may be necessary if such children are to be brought up to appropriate grade levels.[6] The alternative may be an unruly, sullen, or passive lot of children whose "confinement" in the school presents numerous problems but little future promise. The Bureau of Indian Affairs, aware of this situation for over three decades, has made some progress in adapting its schools to the special requirements of Indian students.[7] The public schools have just recently begun to respond to this challenge.

Bringing modern education to the more traditional reservation Indians necessitates making certain assumptions about the future life of the students, some of whom speak only the native Indian language and are but vaguely acquainted with the "outside" world through missionaries, tradesmen, health officials, or other occasional visitors. For such a child, the federal or mission school is at once a wonderous, mysterious, and often frightening adventure.

[5] Miles V. Zintz, *The Indian Research Study*, Vols. I and II (Albuquerque: University of New Mexico, College of Education, 1960), pp. 2–3. Mimeographed.

[6] Recent availability of federal funds for education has stimulated increased interest in special programs for equalizing Indian education outside of the federal sector.

[7] M. L. Wax, R. H. Wax, and R. V. Dumont, Jr., "Formal Education in an Indian Community," *Social Problems*, 1964, pp. 53–54, 71–101.

Polingaysi Qoyawayma White vividly has described her personal school experiences in a moving account which traces her life from the village of Old Oraibi to a successful professional career in Anglo-American society.[8] Few people have bridged the vast gap between Hopi and Anglo cultures as effectively, a fact which leads one to conclude that Mrs. White may have managed the transition in spite of—rather than because of—her formal school experience.

Thus, for most traditional Indians, formal education seems to have been an either-or confrontation. Either one accepts the white man's school program, rejecting his own, or he avoids attending school by "hiding out" with a remotely situated relative, if necessary. This seems to have been most true in the case of certain mission schools, those in which zealous, doctrinaire personnel attempted to separate the "heathen" from their savage ways. Mrs. White's experience was less traumatic than some because her educators were at least as human and understanding as they were conversion-minded. Even so, the ordeal—shared by many youth of her generation—of being uprooted and transported to another state for a boarding school education was extremely upsetting and adjustment took months or even years.

Such factors as compulsory education, advances in scientific knowledge, and improved transportation and communications facilities combine to break down the traditional barriers that have existed between Indian and white Americans. Very likely great strides toward mutual understanding and assimilation will occur during the next generation or two. Considerable attention should be given to the needs and shortcomings of present programs for Indian education, if we wish to minimize the stresses and hardships that are likely to be generated in the interim.

A persistent problem throughout Indian educational history has been their limited, often nonexistent control of the educative process. Schools have been established, administered, and staffed by Anglo-Americans with only minimal attention to realities of Indian culture and social life. Exceptions to this generalization sometimes occur, as when a husband and wife team was assigned to a one-room reservation school to teach agriculture, homemaking, and the three R's. Cut off from other social opportunities, the teachers turned to their Indian neighbors and soon knew them well, even becoming fluent in their language.[9]

In most instances, educational programs have been similar to those in schools of comparable size elsewhere and children have tended to drop out as soon as possible. Often their services were needed at home. Thus, in 1950, the median years of education for Indians over 26 was under six years. But the

[8] Polingaysi Qoyawayma (Mrs. Elizabeth White), *No Turning Back* (Albuquerque: University of New Mexico Press, 1964).

[9] Wax, Wax, and Dumont, op. cit., pp. 58–59.

Bureau of Indian Affairs deserves some credit for trying. Following the 1928 Meriam Survey of Indian schools, the Bureau concluded that an Indian's education should be consistent with his life situation. It was decided that family units should remain intact whenever possible, the native language might be used in the schools, and Indians should be encouraged to take pride in their heritage.

Even though some of the more objectionable features of Indian education were thus mitigated, the present-day reservation schools are still the object of considerable criticism. At issue are the quality of teaching, the often low standards of student achievement, and the teacher's limited appreciation of student potential. The Bureau appears to be interested in these problems and has cooperated in some of the studies of Indian education in order to learn of deficiencies. But with the modern trend toward bigger schools with more offerings and equipment—and the practice of long-distance busing—one wonders what adaptations to Indian needs will be made. Beyond the availability of more courses of interest to Indians, e.g., English as a foreign language or Indian history or culture, will any advantages result?

Facilities for Indian education should continue to expand, for Indian populations have been growing rapidly for over a generation. The Navaho, a large tribe, are especially prolific. There are now 150,000 to 200,000 school-age children and federal facilities are already taxed even though about two-thirds of these young people attend the state, private, or parochial schools.[10] There is a growing conviction among concerned individuals that Indian children profit from their association with a cross-section of American youth and that they achieve better in the integrated school setting. Thus many states have responded to Great Society legislative inducements to improve facilities and offerings for Indian youth.[11] Of New Mexico's 90 eligible districts, 89 have had one or more Title I (of the 1965 Elementary and Secondary Education Act) supported projects, including special language programs, bus service, and liaison officials to keep parents informed of educational developments.

Education is easily the largest item of the budget of the Bureau of Indian Affairs, more than one-third of the total. Since 1961, there has been a "crash program" to improve reservation school facilities which now include 258 boarding and day schools, including high schools and 4,200 dormitory spaces for children from remote areas. Three post-secondary technical schools in Kansas, Oklahoma, and New Mexico feature vocational training and the Santa Fe school is also gaining a reputation as an Indian handicrafts and fine

[10] John Crow, "Schools for the First Americans," *American Education*, **1**: 15–22, October, 1965.

[11] Byron Fielding, "Federal Funds to Meet Local Needs," *NEA Journal*, **55**: 23–26, September, 1966.

arts center.[12] Bureau facilities are steadily improving in quality and some imaginative solutions to vexing problems are now in evidence, *e.g.*, house trailer schools in remote areas which hitherto have lacked schools due to the high initial costs and maintenance expense.[13]

There is considerable variety among the federal Indian schools, ranging from impressive modern complexes to one-room schools. Some are surrounded by rows of modern homes for teachers and resemble segments of suburbia except that many stand in stark contrast to the hogans, huts, or adobe houses of the nearby Indian population. Perhaps this contrast symbolizes, even solidifies, the gap between the worlds of the teacher and the students.

Beyond its efforts in conventional education, the Bureau provided, in 1965, summer enrichment programs for 20,000 children and adult education for 32,800 men and women in 115 job categories.[14] The educational program was coordinated with plans for industrial development, promotion of tourism, development of arts and crafts, reclamation and conservation programs, and real estate leasing projects. Finally, other federal agencies have become active on the reservation, including Neighborhood Youth Corps units, Job Corps centers, Operation Head Start classes, VISTA volunteers, and Community Action Programs to combat poverty.

For a really graphic view of the impact of Anglo-American educational content and methods upon Indian students, especially in reservation schools, it is necessary to visit the schools or to survey the reports of other observers. Indian schools, like schools everywhere, face the problems of raising public and professional expectations and lack funds for the special programs and "fringe" activities which round out a school. However, as Coleman has recently emphasized, following a study of Negro schools, it is not so much the quality of the physical facilities or the cultural origins of the students that makes for effective education; it is the quality of the teacher and the student-teacher relationship.[15] Roughly stated, the teacher must successfully relate to the student and to his class, discern the level of present achievement, and assist the students in raising it.

On the surface, this sounds like a simple, perhaps obvious formula and may actually be rather easy for a competent, experienced teacher who is himself emotionally secure. But the Bureau schools, even more than other rural

---

12 *Indian Affairs, 1965*, Commissioner of Indian Affairs (Washington: U.S. Government Printing Office, 1966), pp. 3–4.

13 For descriptions of Indian schools, see Mamie L. Mizen, *Federal Facilities for Indians* (Washington: U.S. Government Printing Office, 1962).

14 *Indian Affairs, 1965*, op. cit., pp. 5–6.

15 James S. Coleman, *Equality of Educational Opportunity* (Washington: U.S. Government Printing Office, 1966).

schools, have difficulty attracting and retaining such teachers. Moreover, in the reservation schools a new dimension has been added to the normal school situation—the formidable cultural barrier between the teacher and student. Most of the teachers are Anglo-American, some of them from other parts of the country. Even when Indian teachers are available, they are often of a different heritage. An accumulative result is that the students in the lower grades tend to be noisy and confused, then gradually withdraw as they recognize their inadequacies in the upper elementary grades. This has been the Sioux experience and similar or at least functionally equivalent reactions take place elsewhere as the youth experience difficulties in school and the teachers are not fully able (or willing) to meet the situation.

Over time, the more successful teachers and educational researchers have identified a number of the special handicaps which retard Indian students. English is ordinarily the language of instruction and, of course, reservation students are almost always deficient in this area. Most of them have not used English prior to elementary school. Much of what the student reads or hears is not fully comprehended. By now, most schools have remedial English programs and a few pioneering systems are experimenting with English taught as a foreign language.

A second major problem is the student's quite naturally uncritical acceptance of traditional lore, customs, and values. The nature and seriousness of this problem varies with the tribe involved. For example, the Hopi Indian child tries to do minimally satisfactory work but shuns outstanding achievement which will reflect unfavorably upon less gifted classmates. Another student may be convinced that witches, rather than bacteria, cause certain diseases. A third thinks ceremonials held at spaced intervals cause the seasons and rain dances bring rain. In short, potential value conflicts are found in many school situations due to differing conceptions of family structure, ideal behavior, religion, the good life, and adequate dress and personal habits. An interesting illustration of differing world views has been provided by Kluckhohn, who explained that in the Southwest, Spanish-Americans have a "subjugation-to-nature" orientation, the Navaho a "harmony-with-nature" outlook, and the Anglos think in terms of "mastery-over-nature."[16]

A third hardship is the Indian child's often total unfamiliarity with the "outside" world. Rural Navaho children sometimes have not seen a white person, except from a distance, and have no visual experience of towns, cities, modern transportation, and the like. Yet, many of the typical textual materials make this assumption.

There is also an Indian conception of morality—as Navaho permissiveness toward adolescent sexual relations and unmarried motherhood—which Anglo-

---

[16] Quoted by Zintz, op. cit., p. 42.

American teachers and students find difficult to accept, even though many have themselves had such liaisons in secret. Then there are communal notions about property that is not at the moment being used which may lead to forbidden behavior in the formal school.

Thus, the teacher in the Indian school faces a difficult challenge. He must make great efforts to understand his charges if he hopes to succeed moderately well. Even in the area of student discipline, the use of distinctly Western methods is likely to be ineffective for conceptions of shame and punishment vary. But continued research and the lessons of past experience make the task somewhat easier and suggest that the difficulties are not insurmountable.

A number of the findings of anthropological and educational research presented in this essay are supported by the present writer. It seems inescapable that all American Indians, eventually even the Polar Eskimo, must work out a rapprochement with the mainstream of Western culture, though the degree of urgency is not everywhere the same. But it should be a problem of mutual adjustment of both parties and employ no more compromise than is really necessary.

The mode of adjustment which shows most promise is the bicultural pattern described earlier. It combines active and responsible participation as an equal in the national culture with the opportunity to retain a familiar, often treasured heritage. This would seem to be a suitable goal for education in an Indian school. The writer finds it desirable to increase the Indian heritage content in the public schools and to use the Indian language for instruction, when appropriate, introducing English as a foreign language. In time, a transition to English as the language of instruction would be necessary, but only after considerable facility has been attained.[17]

Further research on the feasibility of such a proposal would seem desirable, however. It would be well to know if bicultural people are indeed accepted readily in their respective communities and if people of average intelligence and education can become bicultural. We also should know the time and expense involved in a transition to teaching in the native language in those areas where English is not understood.

[17] Incidentally, this is hardly a revolutionary idea. Many nations with several domestic languages follow this pattern.

22

The Present Failure
to Educate the American Indian

Robert B. Kaplan

The anomie exemplified in the following poem, which was written by
Daveen Graybeal, a 12th-grade Indian boy from Rapid City, S. Dak., is
typical of the central psychological problem of the American Indian today,
caught as he is between two worlds.

LISTEN TO THE DRUMS

i sit here all alone trying to
find myself.
from the distant hills i hear the
drums of my people.
they are calling out to me, i hear
them but i can't answer.
i am a half-breed, part of me belongs to my tribe but . . .
the other part does not. do i have
the right to answer,
to claim the heritage i have in my
blood?
do i have the right to answer the
call of the drums?
i have been raised away from the
drums.
by color, i am white, in my heart
i am both.
can i expect my people to honor my
blood when i have never honored it.
only now has it become real . . . and
a part of me.

i only know how to be white, never
before have i been red.
i hear the drums, they're louder.
i want to answer them,
to go to the holy men of the tribe,
they are wise.
i know they can help me, if they only
would . . .
i want to learn the old ways and
teach my people the new
but i am not sure they can be patient
with me till the knowledge comes.
the drums are dying now.
they have set me wondering of new
problems,
and knowing the goal i must fight
to obtain,
the answer to the call of the
drums, the drums of my people.
i sit here all alone trying to
find myself.
it is silent.
i no longer hear the drums.

The situation, the state of mind, of this young boy may be demonstrated in its implications by a look at some cold, hard facts. Bruce Gaarder, chief, Modern Foreign Language Section, U.S. Office of Education, speaking before the Senate Special Subcommittee on Indian Education in the 90th Congress, December, 1967, cited the following "Salient Facts": Total population of all ages (Bureau of Indian Affairs, 1960), 553,000; total age 6–18 (Bureau of Indian Affairs, 1966), 152,114; enrolled in public schools, 86,827; enrolled in federal schools, 46,154; enrolled in Mission and other schools, 8,713; not in school, 7,757; not located, 2,663.[1] Senator Paul J. Fannin, testifying before the same Senate subcommittee, stated that, ". . . of the 142,000 Indian children in school, 50% drop out before the 12th grade. In 1966 it was determined that at least 16,000 school age Indian children did not attend school at all. . . . Among the Navaho, our largest tribe, it is estimated that 40,000 are illiterate and cannot speak English. . . . 50% [of all Indians] are unemployed, housing is 90% substandard, average life span is 42 years (compared to national average of 62.3 years), infant mortality is five times the national average, one in five deaths result from infectious diseases, incidence of tuberculosis is

[1] *Indian Education:* Hearings before the Special Subcommittee on Indian Education of the Committee on Labor and Public Welfare (Washington: U.S. Government Printing Office, 1969), Vol. I, p. 67.

seven times the national average, the birthrate . . . is more than double the national average. . . ."[2]

Estelle Fuchs reports: "In 1900 when most children in this country had at least an elementary education, only one out of every ten Navaho children was in school and then for only a year or two. In 1949, one out of every four Navahos was attending school. By 1950, there were schools available for only half of the eligible Navaho children. . . . By 1964 there were 38,117 Navaho children in school, an increase of 23,000 [since] 1953. Symptomatic of the deficiency is the fact that among Navahos twenty-five years or older, the average length of schooling has been two years. . . ."[3]

Senator Fannin testifies that "the median number of school years completed by the adult Cherokee population as a whole is only 5.5."[4] He points out that 40% of all adult Cherokee are functionally illiterate in English and that only 39% have had an eighth grade education. In 1963, the median annual income per person among the Cherokee people was less than $550.

Ronnie Lupe, chairman, White Mountain Apache Tribe, testifies that the unemployment rate among the 5,300 White Mountain Apaches is 50%, that the infant mortality rate is 99.2 per 1,000, and that the average life expectancy is between 40 and 46.[5] According to Henry Montague, president, Quechon Tribal Council, the Pima Community ". . . more and more has a need for college trained individuals but has not had a college graduate in over 30 years."[6]

These facts are, indeed, almost incredible. That one of the most technically developed nations in the world, a nation capable of sending men to the moon, of helping to feed the hungry all over the world, of maintaining an enormous military establishment, could ignore so completely more than half a million of its own citizens seems somehow unreal. Quite aside from any collective guilt feelings relating to the dispossession of the Indian from his ancestral lands, simple humanity cries out against an "oversight" of such magnitude.

Yet, the situation has improved. The schools at Rough Rock and at Many Farms, Arizona, are doing some remarkable things. Many of the agencies

---

[2] *Indian Education:* Hearings before the Special Subcommittee on Indian Education of the Committee on Labor and Public Welfare (Washington: U.S. Government Printing Office, 1969), Vol. I, p. 9.

[3] Estelle Fuchs, "Innovation at Rough Rock: Learning to Be Navaho-Americans," *Saturday Review,* 82–84, September 16, 1967.

[4] *Indian Education:* Hearings before the Special Subcommittee on Indian Education of the Committee on Labor and Public Welfare (Washington: U.S. Government Printing Office, 1969), Vol. II, p. 540.

[5] *Indian Education:* Hearings before the Special Subcommittee on Indian Education of the Committee on Labor and Public Welfare (Washington: U.S. Government Printing Office, 1969), Vol. III, p. 1007.

[6] Ibid., p. 1013.

involved in Indian education have developed more realistic attitudes toward the Indians in general. There are hardly any instances of strict prohibition of the use of the tribal language; there are only isolated instances of corporal punishment of Indian children for minor infractions, and there is a growing tendency to recognize the validity of the Indian cultures and languages.

These forward steps have been many years in coming. Like the young militants among the black communities and among the Mexican-American communities, the younger Indians are rapidly growing impatient. The pressures they have exerted and will continue to exert will, as they have in other minority communities, tend to produce hasty and half-baked efforts to expedite the process. Panaceas are being proposed which have the expected efficacy—nothing.

We need massive, but carefully planned activities that will attack the root of the problem instead of leveling out a few surface blemishes. Language is a basic problem and, since language and culture are inseparable, culture is a problem.

In 1962, Wallace Chafe said that nearly 300 different recognizable American Indian languages were in use in the United States and Alaska. (That means that there were also nearly 300 different tribal groups.) However, only about 40% of these are spoken by more than 100 persons.[7] In about half of these language-tribal groups, the only remaining speakers are of advanced age. Thus, within a generation, some 160 of these languages may perish, may become extinct, may never again be heard by men. Chafe also found that about 45 of the languages are presently spoken by more than 1,000 people.[8] An estimate made in 1964 indicates that some 60% of school age (6–18) children in states with special Indian schools and 20% in states which put Indian children in public schools retain some use of their native languages.[9] These estimates may be low since individual tribal groups may have retained the language in as much as 91% of the population. Hard data are almost impossible to get because individuals may, for a variety of reasons, conceal information.

Of the 45 languages spoken by more than 1,000 persons, only seven have adequate reading and considerable literacy among the speakers; two do not even have written forms, 29 have no reading materials and no literacy among native speakers. The remainder have some materials and some literacy. Thus, some 85,000 Indian people, speaking 29 separate major languages, have nothing to read in their native languages and would be unable to read it if

[7] "Estimates Regarding the Present Speakers of North American Indian Languages," *International Journal of American Linguistics*, **27**: 3, January, 1962.

[8] "Estimates Regarding the Present Speakers of North American Indian Languages," *International Journal of American Linguistics*, **31**: 4, January, 1965.

[9] Cited by Bruce Gaarder in *Indian Education*, 1969, loc. cit.

they had it.[10] And there are some 250 languages for which information is not available.

Tests administered to Indian children show that, in both verbal and non-verbal skills, they, like average pupils from other minority groups, score significantly lower than average Caucasian pupils at every grade level and that the gap is significantly greater in the twelfth grade than it is in the first. Thus, Indian children fall farther behind their Caucasian peers each year they remain in school. It is not surprising that the Navaho have produced only one professional with advanced academic degrees. It is not surprising that only one percent of Indian children in elementary school have Indian teachers and only one percent have Indian principals (in secondary school two percent have Indian teachers and none have Indian principals).

Indian children consistently characterize themselves as "below average" and "poorly prepared." Their self-image has consistently been beaten down by repeated failure and by the attitudes of Caucasian teachers and administrators. Some 25% of all teachers dealing with Indian children report that they would prefer not to teach them (they would prefer to teach Caucasian children). As a result, the Cherokee, for example, show a level of educational achievement two full school years lower than the black population. They are, in the words of Senator Fannin, ". . . the least educated group of people in the State [Oklahoma]. . . . Others of the Five Civilized Tribes—Creek, Choctaw, Chickasaw, Seminole—have roughly the same educational levels as do Cherokees."[11]

As noted above, massive efforts are needed in the area of language and culture. Some efforts are now being made. A number of schools offer courses in English as a second language (ESL), but that alone, on the basis on which it frequently is offered, is not nearly enough. Most commonly, English as a second language is offered as a remedial course, meeting three to five hours per week for as many terms as appear necessary to provide the student with enough English ability so that he can move into the main stream of the curriculum. Most commonly the approach employed is the oral/aural approach. This concept appears inadequate on three counts.

English as a second language is not in any sense remedial. It is often assumed that any student who is not prepared to read at grade level needs seem sort of remediation. That assumption is commonly in error, but it is especially so in the second-language situation. French or Spanish language instruction is not considered remedial for native English-speaking students. English is, on the same basis, not remedial for native speakers of Spanish, or Navaho, or

---

[10] "Extent of Literacy Materials for 45 Indian Languages Spoken by 1,000 or More Persons of All Ages in the United States," in *Indian Education* (Hearings of February 9, 1968), Vol. II, p. 541.

[11] Ibid.

Swahili. The attachment of the stigma of remediation to ESL courses tends to dispel the motivation of the student, to degrade the content of the course, and to malign the teacher.

A course which provides 48 hours of instruction over a period of four months (16 weeks, three hours per week) hardly can be considered successful. John Carroll has pointed out that somewhere between 400 and 800 continuous contact-hours of instruction are necessary to implement any significant change in language behavior. Furthermore, it has been shown that, if the 400–800 hours is administered too slowly, the rate of learning drops below the rate of forgetting; and that, if the instruction is administered too quickly, the psychological pressure may become so great as to produce anomie, identity crisis, or other serious problems. Depending on the age and motivation of the learner, somewhere between 20 and 30 hours per week appears optimal if the instructional period can be extended to 20 or 30 continuous weeks. Obviously, during this period of intensive instruction in language, the student will be unable to study other subjects and may drop behind his peer group. But, although the danger is admitted, it would appear to be far less a danger than allowing a student to fall behind in smaller increments over a period of twelve years so that by grade 12 or earlier he is literally forced to become a dropout.

The oral/aural approach, at least as it is currently practiced by most teachers, contains one or more factors which assure failure. The technique, as practiced, calls for the instructor to drill the student in oral structures of the language until the student internalizes the patterns. Properly used in just proportion with other approaches, this technique will produce adequate results. But used as it presently is, the approach succeeds only in making the learner into a parrot capable only of repeating the patterns generated by the instructor or by the textbook. Thus, the technique can produce relatively good performance but it is unlikely to produce competence in the language. Competence may be defined as the ability to use all aspects of the language with near-native skill to produce and to receive completely original and unique utterances expressive of the intellect and personality of the speaker.

It is exactly in relation to this third problem that the massive effort is necessary. The oral/aural approach contains the implicit assumption that language consists only of a phonology, a morphology, and a set of grammatical rules, of finite number, capable of being reduced to formuli and learned as formuli in a short time. That assumption, while it is in part valid, ignores vast areas in the communication process. It ignores all the concepts of nonverbal communication which act in any given situation to furnish the communicants with clues as to the relationship between them, the level of formality, the reaction of one to the other, and so on. In short, the oral/aural technique, as it is practiced, seems to ignore the fact that communication occurs between real people in real situations.

In real situations, among real people, the following areas (and many other) become real concerns. First, the physical distance between speakers. In each culture there exists, for the bulk of the individuals within that culture, a sense of the appropriate distances for specified kinds of communication. Thus, in the Anglo-culture, businessmen separate themselves by the physical barrier of the desk or the conference table; casual conversations occur at handshaking distance, and intimate conversations at hand-holding distance. But in other cultures other rules apply. Unacculturated Indians are made uncomfortable, for example, by the desk barrier.

Second, touch taboos. Anglo teachers who wish to express their affection for a child do so by patting the child or by an affectionate hug. Indian children do not expect such signs and may be embarrassed by them. People from the Middle East accept public hand-holding as a sign of affection among men; Anglos do not. It is perfectly acceptable for one football player to pat another on the posterior as a gesture of congratulation for a good play, but U.S. Senators do not use such contact on the floor of the Senate to congratulate each other for good speeches.

Third, eye contact. Anglo teachers expect to maintain eye contact with students. But students from other cultures, including some Indian cultures, have been taught to look down as a sign of respect for adults.

Fourth, linguistic matters. Often, a message is conveyed not so much by lexical content, by the words in the message, as by the suprasegmental characteristics of the message—the tone of voice, the inflection, the pitch. When English speakers greet each other in passing with some phrase as "Hi, How are you?" they characteristically raise pitch, increase rate, and slur. The vocal features carry the message, and other words can easily be substituted—even vulgar ones—so long as the vocal characteristics are maintained. But this same set of vocal characteristics may carry other messages in other languages. In some linguistic systems the same set of vocal features may indicate anger or irritation. The English speaker may thus appear to be hypocritical since his physical manner is not in accord with his vocal signals.

Indian children may lack the linguistic frames for certain types of polite utterances. The frame "Would you please . . ." does not exist in Navaho, for example. A Navaho child may say "Give me water," instead of "Would you please give me a drink of water." He is not trying to be rude; rather he is using English words in a frame familiar to him in his own language.

Fifth, control of units beyond the sentence. Once the student has learned to control individual syntactic units—that is, to write individual sentences containing proper word order, agreement, and modification—he still must learn to control larger structures. He must relate material in terms of subordination and coordination—in terms of logical relationship—in such a way that the logical expectations of native readers are not violated. Speakers of certain languages, for example, rely much more heavily on structures of coordination while native English speakers rely more heavily on structures of subordination. In part, this is a manifestation of grammar, since English contains many more syntactic devices for subordination than it does for coordination while other languages may have different distributions of the syntactic capabilities.[12]

Sixth, world view. Each language permits its speakers to view the phenomenological world in certain ways and only in those ways. Speakers of Eskimo have a far larger inventory of lexical items for the phenomenon English speakers designate with the one word "snow." That does not imply that Eskimo eyes are physiologically different from Caucasian eyes; rather it means that speakers of Eskimo are conditioned by the interaction of language and environment to view this "real" phenomenon in the phenomenological world quite differently than speakers of other languages. Speakers of English employ active voice statements to indicate that they view themselves as active operant entities in a universe in which they can initiate actions in terms of their own wills and in which the actions which they initiate can affect other beings, both animate and inanimate. But many speakers of Indian languages live in a world in which they function as passive recipients of action, in which their individual wills play no role (perhaps do not even exist), and in which they have no direct power to influence other beings. Thus, speakers of English can posit the meaningful utterance "I see you." But speakers of some Indian languages can neither generate the utterance in terms of the linguistic capabilities of their language nor understand it as meaningful when it is generated by another speaker. They can approximate the idea only by some such statement as "you appear to me."[13]

Seventh, conflicting views of the role of education. The way in which students and teacher view each other linguistically determines to a large extent the potential success of the educational process. Students (and parents) often view the teacher as an antagonistic force. This view may be related to economic or social origins in cultures of poverty in which labor provided by the child is an important factor in survival and in which the economic level of the teacher may be viewed as unattainable and therefore alien. But the problem is also likely to have a linguistic base. The Navaho, for example, have a world view which divides all human beings into two polarized sets—Navaho and others. The Navaho word which designates all non-Navahos, while it often is

[12] Robert B. Kaplan, "Cultural Thought Patterns in Inter-Cultural Education," *Language Learning*, **16**: 1–20, 1966.

[13] Leo Spitzer, "Language—The Basis of Science, Philosophy, and Poetry," in George Boas, et al., eds., *Studies in Intellectual History* (Baltimore: Johns Hopkins Press, 1953), pp. 83–84.

interpreted to mean "others," really means "enemies." It is easy for an Anglo teacher to regard any cultural group that has no written language, that lives at the level of subsistence economy, and that prefers to live in virtual isolation in an inhospitable climate and terrain, as primitive and, hence, childlike. The teacher is likely to view the learning of English as a maturation process leading to adulthood. Thus, the Eskimo or Indian who speaks English inadequately may be viewed as an adult by his own people but as a child by the Anglo teacher. The Eskimo child is treated in a more adult fashion at an earlier age in his own culture than Anglo children are. Indeed, the Eskimo family has far more real regard for individual differences than has the Anglo family. The child's thoughts and opinions are sacred. When the Eskimo child is placed in the situation of learning English from a teacher who regards him as a child, indeed who regards his parents as children, he associates the role of child with language. The Eskimo learns and uses English in a condition of dependency; it is a code used with authority figures—teachers, government figures, missionaries, job foremen. These authority figures frequently adopt parental roles. Thus, the teacher forces the child to regard language as role criteria.[14]

Many Indian cultural groups have no written language. Anglo children, of course, tend to come out of basically literate environments. Anglo children tend to respect literacy as a value in itself. Indeed, some of the more militant leaders in Indian communities are pressing for strong cultural identity among their people. Cultural identity is often related to values transmitted in the literary tradition. Even among those Indian languages which have been reduced to written form, no real written literary tradition exists; the tradition is oral. Thus, there is no special respect for or motivation toward learning a written form. An Indian child is educated, outside the school, by example. He receives a cooperative orientation toward life in his society. He learns from watching adults, from listening to stories in the oral tradition (stories which are often allegorical), from observation of members of his society in interaction with each other and with the environment. He is never consciously taught. His learning style is completely alien to the formal school situation.

Quite aside from learning style, these same factors militate against competition in the sense in which it is often fostered in the Anglo classroom. In a tribal society operating on the tightly knit group at the subsistence level of existence, communal activity is essential. The worst punishment possible is ostracism, ritual murder by the group when it ceases to recognize the existence of one of its members. A child so oriented cannot compete by being

---

[14] Lee H. Salisbury, "Role Conflict in Native Communication," *Teachers of English to Speakers of Other Languages Quarterly,* **2**: 187–192, April, 1969.

"better" or "cleverer" than the other members of his social group because he cannot risk the price.[15]

Eighth, problems in cognition. Both the nature of particular languages and the nature of poverty tend to affect cognitive processes. The Indian cuts up the spectrum in quite a different way than the native English speaker does. It is therefore not enough to tell a young Indian child that the apple in his picture book is "red." Anglo children are taught color and space concepts in kindergarten. The Indian child must be taught two sets of such concepts— his own and those appropriate to English. In cultures of poverty, individuals are likely to own only one of any particular kind of item. Under these circumstances the child may lack entirely, or be severely limited, in the conceptual ability to compare and contrast. He may even lack the lexical items "bigger" and "smaller."[16] On the same basis, the child from a culture of poverty may be unfamiliar with the concept "set" since his family probably does not possess a "set of dishes," or a "set of silver," or a "set of books." Modern mathematics is based on the concept of "set." If the child lacks the concept, he may be inhibited in learning in other areas which seem only vaguely related to language.

These are a few of the problems directly related to language learning which are presently ignored in language teaching.[17] But these problems are the

[15] Anita Pfeiffer, in a personal conversation, Rough Rock Demonstration School, Arizona, May 28, 1969.

[16] Newton Metfessel, in an unpublished report presented at the Second Annual Conference on Language Testing, Idyllwild, Calif., November, 1968.

[17] Pertinent additional reading: Jerome Bruner, "On Going Beyond the Information Given," in Robert J. C. Harper, et al., eds., Cognitive Processes: Readings (Englewood Cliffs, N.J.: Prentice-Hall, 1964); Francis Christensen, Notes Toward a New Rhetoric: Six Essays for Teachers (New York: Harper & Row, 1967); Mikel Dufrenne, Language and Philosophy, Henry B. Veatch, trans. (Bloomington: Indiana University Press, 1963); Alfred S. Hayes, "New Directions in Foreign Language Teaching," Modern Language Journal 49: 281–293, May 1965; Robert B. Kaplan, "Contrastive Grammar: Teaching Composition to the Chinese Student," Journal of English as a Second Language, 3: 1–14, 1968; "49139162516254125366l," Journal of English as a Second Language, 4: 7–18, Spring, 1969; "Contrastive Rhetoric and the Teaching of Composition," Teachers of English to Speakers of Other Languages Quarterly, 1: 10–16, December 1967; "On a Note of Protest . . . ," College English, 30: 386–389, February 1969; Paul Lorenzen, Logik und Grammatik (Mannheim: Bibliographisches Institut, 1965); William Ritchie, "Implications of Generative Grammar," Language Learning, 17: 45–69, July 1967, and 17: 111–131, December 1967; Edward Sapir, Culture, Language, and Personality (Los Angeles: University of California Press, 1964); Valter Tauli, ed., Proceedings of the Ninth International Congress of Linguistics (The Hague: Mouton, 1964); U.S. Department of the Interior, Bureau of Indian Affairs, Division of Education, Fiscal Year 1968 Statistics Concerning Indian Education (1968); Albert Valdman, Trends in Language Teaching (New York: McGraw-Hill, 1966); Benjamin Lee Whorf, Language, Thought, and Reality (Cambridge: MIT Press, 1956).

proper and immediate concern of language teachers. It should be obvious that no single methodology can possibly cope with such a broad spectrum of problems. As has been pointed out several times, what is urgently needed is a massive approach. Single methodologies, even intelligently applied, can only eliminate single aspects of the broad problem; in a way, partial solutions may be more dangerous than no solutions because they hold out to the deprived the promise of a relief which is illusory. A nation capable of sending men to the moon should be capable of learning to teach little children who only wish to aspire to what their Anglo peers have had long enough to take for granted. The cost of one average week's material losses in Vietnam would provide the teacher training and research necessary to implement the kind of massive approach required. This essay[18] is neither a pacifist plea nor a militant response. The references to political and military events in the real world outside of education are only points of reference from which to consider the value of 600,000 people in urgent need as opposed to developments in other sectors of society. The massive effort necessary to meet the problem is well within the capability of the government and the academic community.

The following steps could be undertaken in the immediate future: Research designed to preserve those languages which are on the verge of extinction; research in the linguistico-cultural structure of those larger language groups whose languages have not been adequately studied; development of pedagogical materials in both language and culture designed to meet the specific needs of particular language communities; training of teachers to use the new materials; training of teachers to understand the problems of the communities in which they are going to teach; training of Indian specialists to staff all of the preceding categories; training of Indian specialists to supervise all of the preceding activities; and training of Indian specialists to develop whatever steps are necessary beyond this point.

While there is a building pressure to institute immediate action programs, the panic for action must not be allowed to supercede the need for intelligent and organized action. Massive effort is necessary, but massive effort is time-consuming. Perhaps what is most necessary now is the courage to abjure seeming panaceas and to start toward ultimate solutions. The problem concerns all of us and demands the best efforts and talents our society can muster.

[18] The author would like to acknowledge the assistance of Mrs. Mary K. Ludwig in the preparation of the manuscript and some of the initial research.

23

Dick and Jane
on the Navaho Reservation

Paul Walsh

American Indians, having lost the war, continue to lose the system of honor, truth, and justice that was overwhelmed by the white man's economic superiority. Modern-day generals in the campaigns against the Indian world are the Bureau of Indian Affairs administrators of Navaho reservation schools. A principal battle force deployed is Scott, Foresman's Dick and Jane, symbols of the Great Society.

Dick and Jane are the idealized textbook characters in beginning readers who have long provided middle-class symbols for the elementary school children in America. In a period of national criticism over the state of reading failure in this country, critics felt that Dick and Jane reinforced the inferiority of the many students unlike the people of storyland.

Dick and Jane survived the attacks relatively unscathed to continue earning corporate dividends. Admittedly, their tenacity was partly ruled by the huge financial investment supporting them. But even enlightened school administrators often use Dick and Jane because they see no viable alternative. The possible substitute readers show remarkable resemblance to the Scott, Foresman books. To be sure, some multiethnic educations exist, but few seem to recognize the gross inadequacies that exist.

Identification with subject matter of reading is necessary. A child is at a disadvantage if he is expected to identify with imagery drawn from a different environment.

Navaho differences need to be respected in planning a reader. The running, jumping, playing, and the general togetherness of Dick and Jane is, perhaps, the height of ethnocentrism in dealing with the Navaho, for it violates the most severe taboo in Navaho culture, that of incest. Any type of contact— dancing or even walking with members of your father's clan—is prohibited and can be expected to bring about severe consequences such as insanity and, possibly, even death.

There seems to be an assumption that textbook depictions should represent the experiences common to most children. This methodology is increasingly out of place in larger society as well as on the reservation, for technological development makes for specialized behavior patterns. There is insufficient concern for the diversity of prior experience. What may be considered as "common" experience for the majority of children may be applicable, in fact, only to a few.

Although the Dick and Jane text often is assumed to have limited applicability for minority groups, it usually is believed to be adequate for the majority of so-called middle-class children. Actually, with a nationally standardized reader, the degree of identification made possible is very low. If identification is fundamental to learning, it would appear that any text, to be an aid in learning, should include experiences drawn from the cultural background of the student it intends to serve. If the Scott, Foresman book is unsuitable for Negroes living in a ghetto, the attempt to use it in beginning reading on a Navaho reservation involves pedagogical myopia. Though there is cultural variation between groups of Navahos, there are socially accepted values which will be found, in varying degrees, in virtually all Navaho groups.

Dick and Jane are mythical members of a family structure in which one set of parents and their children reside physically separate from other relatives. Navaho culture, however, is dominated by extended families, including a clanship arrangement in which family heads trace their lineage to a common source. In Navaho society, the emotional energies of the members of a group are concentrated on one another to the exclusion of other people. A member of the group is accepted totally. An outsider is viewed with suspicion and distrust. So strong is this feeling that adult Navahos who live apart from the group still return periodically to the clan for the "Great Sings," like "Blessing Way," and the emotional security it gives them.

In the absence of a codified legal system, the Navahos maintain a very complex system of myths and ceremonial ritual necessary of psychological stability if their social structure is to survive. Perhaps most prominent in the system is a belief in witchcraft. The Navaho attempts to live in harmony with the supernatural world. If an undesirable result occurs, the Navaho attributes this to a taboo violation or a ritual he omitted or performed incorrectly.

Material prosperity as revealed by Scott, Foresman readers is highly frowned upon by the Navaho because it suggests a failure in the individual's responsibility to his relatives. One of the key ethics of Navaho interpersonal relations is the need for reciprocal behavior, almost in direct contrast to the competitive ethic emphasized by Western culture. In contrast to the Christian view, life to the Navahos is in no way a preparation for further existence; in fact, there is an almost psychotic fear of death because it is the end of all good things.

Mental disorders are felt to be the results of taboo violation. In addition, the strong belief in supernatural beings affects the way in which individuals solve problems. They do not classify diseases according to symptoms as in Western culture, but more in terms of presumed causes.

The teacher's guide in use in the Navaho schools states, "The Scott, Foresman basic readers are as suitable as any." After some comments about not reading any book from cover to cover, the guide goes on: "In many cases chapters of books can be omitted if the subject matter is too foreign to them, even if the rest of the book is usable." A few pages later the guide continues: "The vocabulary development in the basic text is planned so that the books should be read in order."

Throughout the guide the central concern appears to be standardization and administrative efficiency. Only one statement refers to the fact that these children are different and that some attention should be paid to the specific differences.

The use of the Scott, Foresman book on the reservation is even more of a pedagogical blunder than using it in a city ghetto, for the scenes presented are distant from the city ghetto child but not necessarily alien to him. With the Navaho, the depicted values and models threaten the values by which he lives. It should not be assumed that Navaho culture no longer has value, yet that is what the school assumes when it ignores Navaho heritage and presents the child with materials radically opposed to his past culture.

Another factor ignored is that the Navaho language is exceptionally specific, making it impossible for the user to be abstract. In fact, there are no abstract words. The Scott, Foresman readers now in use in Indian schools present a system of vocabulary development which excludes consideration of the Navaho child's interpretation of symbols. Is it not to be expected that ambiguity created by such a method of instruction manifests itself in low levels of academic achievement?

All Navaho schools are boarding schools, and the overwhelming majority of the children arrive at school speaking only Navaho. English is a secondary language. The teachers, by and large, speak no Navaho, and the children are made to cope with this barrier as well. They are placed in the position of being forced to adapt to the white man's culture—of which they are naturally suspect—and their success is judged by the white man's, not Navaho, standards.

To function in 20th-century society, we must possess the ability to relate with some success to people of diverse social backgrounds. If we expect to foster such ability in students, we first must develop methods and materials which will have a meaningful interpretation and acceptance by children of diverse school situations.

This does not deny that there is some value in the use of commercial text-books. Indeed, from an economic standpoint, large publishing houses are in the best position to develop materials with differentiated applicability. If textbook irrelevance continues, the market for commercial texts may disappear as schools take over the responsibility for development of their own teaching materials.

Though it is a widespread American practice to impose middle-class materials on non-middle-class students, the Navahos especially must wonder what peculiar kind of civilization the white man offers. Historians have well documented our shoddy treatment of the Indian. In some ways we apparently have not progressed much past Lord Jeffrey Amherst's moderate suggestion for the solution to the problem of "savages." Amherst felt genocide was the answer and suggested the federal government should send blankets infected with smallpox to the Indians.[1] The present-day Amhersts may think they have more socially acceptable agents of genocide in Dick and Jane.

[1] Henry Steele Commager, "A Historian Looks at Our Political Morality," *Saturday Review,* July 10, 1965.

24

Changing Predispositions to Academic Success by Alaska Native People

Ashley Foster

Until very recently, in terms of United States history, the Alaska native[1] has lived in comparative isolation and, to a very large degree, he still does. Although the Russian colonization of present-day Alaska began early in the 18th century, large and sparsely populated areas of the state remained relatively isolated from the West and, even today, are very much in a transitional state. Newer customs have been superimposed upon the traditional ways, but, for example, in much of the Eskimo-inhabited lands, English is still a second language. Nevertheless, the most significant aspect of native life in Alaska is the fact that it is undergoing vast and far-reaching change. This essay is a description of one aspect of that change—the change in some of the unique predispositions which affect the success of the Alaska native at the university.

In most of the significant areas of the American way of life, living standards, health standards, or academic achievement, for example, the Alaska native is far below the mean of the United States population. The "worst slums in the United States" are in western Alaska.[2] The native population survives on a mixture of use-subsistence economy supplemented by a few jobs but principally by relief checks.[3] Although much positive progress has been made since the Parran Report in 1955 revolutionized the approach to

AUTHOR'S NOTE: This essay was supported in part by Vocational Rehabilitation Administration Research and Demonstration grant SAV No. 1054-68.

[1] Alaska natives who number about 55,000 and make up one-fifth of the state are Eskimos, Athabascan Indians, Aleuts, and the Thlingit and Haida Indians of the Southeast.

[2] Homer Bigart, *New York Times*, July 31, 1966.

[3] Douglas N. Jones, "Alaska's Economy," in *Alaska Review*, Fall/Winter, 1966–67, p. 6.

the health problems of the Alaska native,[4] his health standards are still among the worst in the country; the infant mortality rates among the highest.[5] As Margaret Lantis once pointed out, the native Alaskan culture no longer exists; what we see is primarily a poverty culture in the Alaskan environment.

Formal education is also a relatively new experience for the native Alaskan. The completion of the eighth grade is only a very recent event.[6] A little more than half the population who entered the first grade in 1954 completed elementary school at the end of eight years.[7] By 1950, 30% of the nonwhite population 25 years or older—93% of whom are Alaska native people—had received no schooling.[8] By 1960, the median education for the nonwhite population was 6.6 years and for the white population, 12.4 years. If we exclude the urban nonwhite population, the median figure drops to 5.6 years, and for at least one area of western Alaska, the figure drops to a median of 1.6 years of education.[9] Only 163 Alaska natives could be identified as college graduates in the 72–year period, from 1895 to 1967.[10] Only about 5.5% of the eligible Alaska native population now is enrolled at a college or university.[11]

---

[4] Thomas Parran, et al., *Alaska's Health, A Survey Report.* Graduate School of Public Health, University of Pittsburgh, 1954.

[5] James E. Maynard and Laurel M. Hammes, *Infant Morbidity and Mortality Study,* Arctic Health Research Center, Anchorage, Alaska, May 1964. There are areas of western Alaska where the infant mortality rate reached a staggering 121/1,000, which is in excess of most countries that publish statistics.

[6] Nulato, a fairly large village on the Yukon River with over 300 persons, for example, had its first person complete the eighth grade in 1951. Vide William J. Loyens, *The Changing Culture of the Koyukon Indians,* Ph.D. dissertation, University of Wisconsin, 1966, p. 154.

[7] William D. Overstreet, *A Study of Elementary School Dropouts Among the Native Population of Alaska for the Period 1955–1962,* unpublished manuscript, Bureau of Indian Affairs, Juneau, Alaska, 1962, 71 pp.

[8] Charles K. Ray, *A Program of Education for Alaskan Natives* (University of Alaska, 1959), p. 11.

[9] U.S. Bureau of the Census, *U.S. Census of Population 1960,* Vol. 1, Characteristics of the Population, Part 3, Alaska. U.S. Government Printing Office, Washington, D.C., 1963, p. 3–54.

[10] John I. Eichman, *Who's Who in Alaska 1895–1967,* mimeographed report, Bureau of Indian Affairs, November, 1967.

[11] These figures and the following are derived, it is hoped, with a minimum of statistical violence. In fiscal year 1966, 3,140 Alaska natives were between 20–24 and 4,780 between 15–19 years of age. Using the breakdown figures of the 1960 census when 19–year–olds made up 21.3% of the 15–19 year group, 21.3% of 4,780 (1,018) was assumed to be the 19–year–old population in 1966. *The Survey of Students Attending Schools of Higher Learning 1965–66,* compiled by John I. Eichman, Bureau of Indian Affairs, Juneau, Alaska, March, 1967, lists 229 Alaska native students enrolled in universities and colleges—many who are nonmatriculated students—hence the 5.5% figure. For the U.S. the data were handled similarly. Over 5,500,000 persons were enrolled in higher education and 17,400,000 was the total population 19–24 years of age. U.S. Bureau of

In the U.S., about 32% of this age group are enrolled in institutions of higher learning. Less than five percent of the Alaska native people who entered the University of Alaska in 1962, however, received a bachelor's degree in 1966, and only 4% of those who entered in 1964 received their degree in 1968.[12] A college education has not yet become a part of the Alaska native way of life.

In earlier studies made in 1967 and 1968, when some 68 students at the University of Alaska were interviewed, the Alaska native student at the university could be considered successful because he had progressed in school beyond 95% of his fellows. This assumption was untenable. There were too many individuals who merely remained longer in school. They had been able to drift on to the university as an alternative to entry into the mainstream of Alaskan economic life. The first study in 1967, however, did suggest that factors such as the home background, the student's ideas on the purpose of a university education, and what he hoped this education would do for him were significant in relation to success at the university.[13]

The second study which sought to follow up the earlier findings concluded that there were unique background factors which the Alaska native brought to the university which put him at greater risk of failure than the university population in general. These factors included his family's educational background, his own inferior scholastic background, his inability to see his future with clarity, and in the case of the women, an apparent contentment with the subordinate status of women in the Alaska native culture.[14]

There was a significant relationship between the educational background of the parents of these students and the degree of success at the university. Of the 68 persons interviewed only three persons averaged a "C" or better as freshmen when both parents together had less than 12 years of education.

The students who had come from rural Alaska had, for the most part, been educated in village schools in which the achievement level was generally well behind grade level.[15] Even the grades attained in the academic curriculum of the Bureau of Indian Affairs (BIA) high school at Mt. Edgecumbe—the major high school for Alaska native students—were less effective than any other high school grades in the prediction of university success.

the Census, *Statistical Abstract of the United States, 1967*, 88th edition. U.S. Government Printing Office, Washington, D.C., p. 133.

[12] Report: Study of Alaska native degree candidates, 1966–68, University of Alaska, May 29, 1968.

[13] Ashley Foster, "An Inquiry Into Predispositional Factors Incidental to Achievement Success by Alaska Native People," *Alaska Medicine*, **10**: 3, 121–127, September 1968.

[14] Ashley Foster, "Predispositions to Success by Alaska Native Students," *Alaska Medicine*, **10**: 4, 160–166, December 1968.

[15] Charles K. Ray, op. cit., pp. 79–83.

Differences in life-goals after university education also seemed to separate the successful from the unsuccessful student. The student who sought to pursue the same goal throughout his life seemed to fare better and be more persistent. The student who established a consciously transient goal and merely planned to make money to be able to do something else, fared worse. Although this may not be unique to the Alaska native it was, in 1967 and 1968, significantly related to academic persistence in a culture without an academic tradition.

Finally there were very significant differences both in the persistence and the grades achieved between men and women students. The women students left school in greater numbers and they did significantly poorer academic work. Their life goals seemed exclusively to be marriage and a family.

With these factors in mind, therefore, the writer undertook a prospective investigation. Alaska native freshmen entering the University of Alaska were to be interviewed as previously and a prediction of academic risk was to be made. Risk status was to be established by the following: the years of education of the parents, gender, school attended, near and distant future plans, and reason for attending school, *i.e.*, a job versus a "knowledge" orientation. These factors had proven significant in distinguishing students who succeeded at college from those who did not. For this purpose, 32 freshmen students were interviewed in September 1968. Success was defined as the ability to survive in an academic environment.

In the time between the first and last series of interviews, there were many changes in the areas originally thought to provide an index of risk—namely, family educational background, gender, location, high school graduated, vocational commitment, and ideas on purpose of education. Of these indices, the only area which changed little was the family educational background and, inferentially, the educational value system in which the Alaska native student grew up. A low level of educational achievement by parents is still a most significant risk in any aspiration to achieve academic parity. Consistently, it seems most unlikely that any student would achieve a college average better than "C" when neither parent had gone as far as the eighth grade in school.

If we combine the years of education for both parents, the parents of the "D" students averaged almost five years less education than those with a "C" or more (10.44 vs. 15.22 combined years of education). Although one can predict a poor academic showing when the parents have had little or no education, the reverse does not hold true; parents who have many years of schooling do not necessarily have children who do well in school.

Originally, the women were significantly poorer students. Although there were still some differences in favor of the men by spring of 1968, this difference was much less significant. This situation now, however, seems no longer true; the women conform to the more general academic picture and as entering freshmen they now do better academic work than the men. This is consistent with the subjective impression of many instructors that the incoming classes are better prepared for college life.

In earlier years, the students from the urban high schools, particularly Anchorage, Fairbanks, and Juneau, fared best at the university. There was relatively little difference between the high school grades and the college grades of the urban high school students. In the case of the rural high school students and those from the Bureau of Indian Affairs (BIA) high school, the high school grade point average bore only little relationship to achievement at the university. This led to an assumption that the urban high school students were best prepared and the BIA high school graduates most poorly prepared for university life. The most recent study strengthens the impression that the BIA high school graduates seem most poorly prepared for university life. The urban high school graduates, however, no longer rise to the top of the class. In the years since this study was first undertaken, the proliferation of the small rural high schools has had its effect and their graduates are now arriving at the university. These students are now doing the best academic work. These rural high schools hardly have a variety of course offerings and rarely have a total student body of 100 persons. Since it is hardly a tremendous academic richness, on the whole, which contributes to this comparatively good showing, it seems probable that there is an esprit at the small local high school. Its graduates have a better sense of academic purpose than those of either the urban or the BIA boarding high school. It is possible that this small regional high school attracts a type of student who, ordinarily, would not have attended secondary school.

Earlier there seemed to be a significant and positive relationship between the intensity of vocational commitment and academic success. Thus, the student who, while still a freshman, felt committed to a lifetime career in his already established university major, tended to do better academic work than the person who thought in terms of career change over a lifetime. This is related also, to the poorer performance of women since for them marriage was the ultimate career regardless of declared university major. Increasingly, for the Alaska native women attending the university, however, marriage seems less of an end and more as one aspect of living. In any case, the students who plan while undergraduates to change careers or are uncommitted as freshmen no longer do significantly poorer academic work than their fellows who feel committed to a single career when they enter the university.

Those who were interviewed in 1967 and 1968 and went to school to get a job did more poorly than those who sought an education for understanding. The frankly vocational aim to education then seemed to predict a poorer student. This distinction between those who succeeded and those who did not which was so significantly clear early in 1967 has become somewhat blurred over the years. At present, it seems to have become useless as a prognostic device.

Alaska natives have not been immune to the impact of national movements for racial identification. Upon the local scene, however, they have taken a turn more meaningful to Alaskans. If we consider the various shapes and forms of ethnic movements as attempts to attain cultural equality and a prestigious racial image based, if not on respect, then on strength, such a movement has not been without its Alaskan counterpart. Although Alaska native people make up about one-fifth the population of the State, they have not participated proportionately in the social, political, or economic life of this State. Only recently have they become aware of the need for political power. In Alaska, the direction of this search has been somewhat different from those of racial minority groups in other states. Alaska native people have not developed power movements to redress grievances by action in the streets or on the campus. Perhaps, as one dean remarked, it is difficult to carry on a demonstration in —50° F. weather. Whatever the reason, however, the Alaska native is increasingly aware of the significance of education in his life in relation to any attempt to achieve economic and social parity. He seems to seek this parity through an improvement of his educational status. His strong concern with the inadequacy of his present education was best expressed at a recent (1969) Senate Subcommittee hearing in Fairbanks when requests for ". . . more local control over our affairs, a greater voice in the operation of our school, respect [for] our judgment and honor [for] our request and suggestions" were presented. The Alaska native people wanted, they said, "Teachers who will accept the Alaska native as a human being and respect him as such" and not, ". . . the misfits, the untrained, the failures from other professions, the extremists, the draft evaders, and those who seek to demoralize our country and our children, the youth of our nation. Give us the best teachers that are obtainable and we will give you a people the world can be proud of." They pointed out too, that, "At present, we have no full time Guidance Counselor in our school system."[16]

The inadequacies of the curriculum are most apparent when we realize that there is not only a very poor survival rate by Alaska native students in the elementary and secondary school but even those few who finish high school and enter the university seem, by more conventional standards, to be grossly underprepared. Of the 100 students who were interviewed, only one had a "B" average in the freshman year.

A long pending claim for lands owned by various native groups seems to be approaching a settlement hastened, no doubt, by the discovery of oil-rich lands in the north. Potentially, this could make many native groups affluent.

[16] Report by Alaska Native Brotherhood Camp No. 68 to Special Senate Subcommittee on Indian Education, 1969.

The crisis of identity, however, does not seem to have had the same impact in Alaska as elsewhere. The entrance by the Alaska native into the political arena has been characterized chiefly by efforts to convert aboriginal title to legal title to the land and to effect reforms in the educational environment in which he had been raised. The Alaska native is in the process of social and economic change in which he sees himself acquiring a political voice increasingly through involvement with and improvement of his educational status. The prediction of academic success by Alaska native students at the university is increasingly fraught with hazard should one seek characteristics exclusive to that particular group. It is apparent that, in 1969, research studies two, three, and more years old on Alaska native attitudes toward education are obsolete since these attitudes are very much in a state of change. The freshman students who were interviewed in September 1968 were not the same as those who were interviewed in February of 1967 or February 1968. Because they are so much in the process of change, descriptions and predictions have little permanent value. In the ten years since Ray's classic book[17] on Alaskan education was written, the school-age population has doubled and the traditional economy cannot support this growth. It does not require perspicacity for the elders to encourage the learning of other nontraditional occupations. These, largely, must be learned in institutions away from the village.

For the students who have arrived at the university, a retreat to the village from the discouragements faced in the academic life is becoming less and less an option they can elect. Success is more imperative. The traditional means for gauging predispositions does not hold as true today as it did several years ago. The motivation to succeed has become more intense over the past few years and, because of this, negative predispositions have become poor negative prognosticators of success. In so far as any predictions can be made, it may well be that Alaska native students at the university will become in time like the other social, cultural, and/or ethnic groups of this country who have experienced deprivation. For the present, however, the experience of adaptation to university life is new. Alaska native students still hope to achieve success, however, and to participate actively in the burgeoning prosperity of their land as vital participants and not as an identifiable social, cultural, or ethnic group.

[17] Charles K. Ray, op. cit.

Educating Young Canadian Indians

Arthur Laing

It is in the schooling of the Indian children that the future of Canada's Indian people will be moulded. The teachers are the front-line soldiers in our efforts. In the words of Sir William Osler, "It is well for the young man to remember that no bubble is so iridescent or floats longer than that blown by the successful teacher." The conception of implanted knowledge as an iridescent bubble hovering above the tribulations of the world is a vivid image, one that bears much truth.

The teacher creates images in the minds of the pupils—images which float and soar, catching the inner eye and holding these minds fast to the ultimate truth that it is knowledge which sets man free. It is the magic of literacy that brings man directly into the world of thought, gives him power over his life pattern, and enables him to understand what has gone before and what is yet to come. It is a challenging and awful responsibility and it is more so when the youngsters come from a culture which is so different from that toward which they grope.

Our school system today has the responsibility for 64,000 Indian children, of whom 33,000 attend provincial schools. Here in British Columbia, 60% of the 12,500 school-age Indian children and young people are enrolled in provincial schools; the remaining 5,000 are in our own federal school system.

It is our policy to enroll as many children as possible in the provincial system. We are committed to the belief that it is better for the children if they gain as much of their schooling as possible in the classrooms with their fellow British Columbians. We believe they need the same learning experiences as other Canadian boys and girls. We believe this is part of equal opportunity.

In adopting this policy, we are aware that these children need something more than their non-Indian counterparts. We hope that our kindergarten system will fulfill a large part of this requirement. Part of this need will be

EDITORS' NOTE: This essay is based on an address to the Northern British Columbia Federal Teachers' Association, Terrace, B.C., Canada, October 6, 1967.

met through specialist counselling for young Indians who attend high school and post-high school educational institutions, whether these be university, technical, or other institutions.

We hope that the kindergarten experience will to a large degree overcome the cultural deprivation of those children who come from homes where both parents have limited education and we hope that they will offset the handicap of children who come from homes where English is seldom spoken. We will have to continue to operate our own schools for a number of Indian children for some years to come. We anticipate that enrollment in the federal schools will remain at 5,000 for some time, while enrollment in provincial schools will continue to rise, taking a larger and larger percentage of the children.

This will mean the closing of some schools and the enlargement of some. There will be some shifting around in our physical plant and some movement of teachers. However, we will have requirements for teachers in the federal school system for many years to come. No teacher who is experienced in the specialist task of teaching young Indians need worry about working. Quite apart from the needs of our own Indian Affairs Branch schools, the provinces which are more and more involved in the teaching of young Indians are going to be looking for the very kind of specialized experience you have gained.

More and more of the universities are looking at this specialized area of teaching and there are challenging opportunities to further advance your skills under the educational leave program. I advise any teacher who wishes to make a meaningful career in the field to investigate the possibilities of undertaking more training, to inquire of the universities of the special courses which are available, and to improve his capabilities.

While in our system we will require fewer and fewer high school teachers, for it is our policy to enroll the young Indian student in provincial high schools to as great an extent as possible, the opening of kindergartens, which apparently will be a federal responsibility for some years to come, provides opportunities for specialists at that level. The future of teachers in our federal schools depends to a large extent upon personal mobility. For a lifetime career in our system, one must be prepared to move to where we have requirements. Our needs across the country will not diminish so much as to mean there is no place for experienced teachers. They will change locale as the provincial systems develop. They will change, as I have said, to the extent that one expertise will replace another. However, teaching has always been a learning process; teachers have always been prepared to learn new things and to move ahead.

There is another field where special skills are needed. The emerging nations have need of teaching skills where cross-cultural problems exist. In the Commonwealth countries where English is the language of education, there is a great and growing need for teachers who are skilled, as many of you are, in teaching children of a different culture, of different language and who come from unlettered households. I have a selfish hope that not too many of our teachers will accept this challenge, for we need them, too. I hope that we can keep the best for our own urgent Canadian problem; but, as a country, we have an obligation to the less developed countries and this, too, must be honored.

We have pinned our faith in the educational process as being the key which will allow the Indian men and women of the future to take their place in the mainstream of Canadian life. It has become a commonplace that all workers in the future are going to have to be better educated. There is a lot of truth in this. The simplest task now may very well involve the operation of a piece of machinery. It is necessary that workers be able to read instructions, fill out maintenance reports and understand the machine they operate.

Education plays a growing role in every trade, in every walk of life. The educated worker produces more goods and earns more money. There are better reasons for supporting education, but I recognize that the economic reason will weigh heavily with any people who have for long lived on a substandard level. We must use such arguments to overcome the resistance to schooling which is still found in many homes where the parents have not had the advantage of education.

The barrier of the children growing up in a home where the language of instruction is a second language adds to and compounds the problem. Our kindergarten program must be a combined extension forward of home and play into a learning situation, and an extension to a younger group of the school. It must act as the bridge between these two experiences. This, in itself, will not overcome all the difficulties; it will alleviate some of them. It will help surmount the language barrier, but in the later grades it will not overcome the child's need for assistance with homework nor will it provide the support that children need to enable them to get the most out of school.

In the high school grades, our boarding home program is a considerable improvement on the old residential school which had many limitations, especially in the more advanced grades. Some of our residential schools are being given a new place in the educational system by conversion to hostels with the children attending at nearby provincial high schools. With a large number of students gathered under one roof, we are able to provide the supplemental assistance with homework and the necessary support often required if the pupils are to keep going in the more difficult work they face at the advanced levels.

Beyond high school, we are paying the cost for many young Indian people to get technical, vocational, and university education. Some of those who go into advanced education will return to the Indian community and make their leadership available to the Indian people. Some will want to make a life in the world at large and will apply their special knowledge and talents in fields outside the world of the reservation communities. All will be contributing to the well-being of the Indian people. We hope, naturally, that they all will find time to lend a helping hand to other young Indian boys and girls as they, too, go forward into the educational mainstream. It is the policy that all young Indian boys and girls shall be able to proceed as far with their schooling as their talents justify and that they shall be free to choose from all the alternatives which are open to any other Canadian.

The teachers have a vital role in making this policy work. It is the task of lighting the beacon of educational interest, in nursing the flame into the brilliance which illuminates the infinite capabilities of man. In doing so, the teachers are performing a task of enormous importance.

I want to thank those teachers who have served the Indian people so well. In doing so, they have also served the Indian Affairs Branch well, for our primary interest must always be the best interests of the Indian people. The Indian people are making great progress. They are working hard to achieve their aims. They are worthy of the support of all of us.

Part 5

The Immigrant and Refugee in America

26

The Education of Immigrants in the United States: Historical Background

Richard G. Durnin

Since America is a nation of immigrants, it would seem that a good portion of its history of education would concern the schooling offered to these new-comers and their children. The process of becoming an American, one that has persisted since the 17th century, is indeed a major theme in American social history. The historiography of education, dealing rather exclusively with schooling in this country, begins essentially with the early 20th century. The topic of the education of the immigrant seldom was treated as a discrete one.

The fact that America was, for the most part, an English-speaking land, with most people coming from a similar social-economic class in the British Isles in the 17th, 18th, and early 19th centuries, tended to erase the concept of these peoples as immigrants, in the latter 19th-century sense of the term. Presumably, these settlers were more or less quickly assimilated into the life of their towns and cities.

In whatever way the immigrants thought of themselves or were thought of by their contemporaries, the history of American education has not dealt with them and their schooling to any great degree. That Dutch settlements were extensive in New York and New Jersey, that German-speaking people made up a considerable portion of the population of the Province of Pennsylvania, that French Huguenots were present in several of the colonies, and that New York City always had a sizeable number of inhabitants of non-English language and culture have hardly concerned the educational historian seriously until recent years. It was, of course, the incursions of non-English speaking peoples during the second half of the 19th century that have affected American education the most.

Cubberley, in referring to the early immigrants—those who came during the 1840s—wrote glowingly: "All were from race stock not very different from our own, and all possessed courage, initiative, intelligence, adaptability, and self-reliance to a great degree. The willingness, good nature, and executive qualities of the Irish; the intellectual thoroughness of the German; the respect for law and order of the English; and the thrift, sobriety, and industry of the Scandinavians have been good additions to our national life."[1]

But, in the late 19th century, after 1882, there was a change in the nature of immigration. Cubberley wrote of these new people in strong and unfavorable terms. His observations and feelings, and no doubt those of many of his fellow Americans, were that these newcomers were "largely illiterate, docile, often lacking in initiative, and almost wholly without the Anglo-Saxon conceptions of righteousness, liberty, law, order, public decency, and government. . . ." He believed that their coming "served to dilute tremendously our national stock and to weaken and corrupt our political life . . ." and observed, as a result, that "foreign manners, customs, observances, and language have tended to supplant native ways and the English speech. . . ."[2] Apparently holding the "melting pot" theory, he felt that the nation had suffered from "racial indigestion," and that the mission of public education had indeed been made more difficult from the last two decades of the 19th century on.

The public schools, especially in the cities, were faced with problems of crowding, non-English speaking children (many illiterate in their own language), parents whose working conditions would not allow much concern with school progress, and alienation between parents and the educational establishment. But Cubberley's rather conclusive remarks about the immigrants themselves were written before much evidence became manifest and accepted regarding the enrichment of the American way: its cuisine, economy, language, literature, art, music, and life style in general. He lived through those years when the thrust of immigration was greatest, when its impact seemed almost overwhelming, and when restrictions on the movement of foreigners to America were being enacted into law.

It is interesting and pertinent to note that most of the disparaging characterizations directed at the late 19th-century immigrant have been said in recent decades (but perhaps not as often written) about the Negro, Puerto Rican, and Mexican-American in-migrant to our cities. The children and grandchildren of those European arrivals of the 1880s and 1890s are prospering in suburbia and usually form a bulwark of American "patriotism."

The early story of the education of immigrants in America is interwoven with the annals of the conventional pattern of American schooling. These

[1] Ellwood P. Cubberley, *Public Education in the United States* (Boston: Houghton Mifflin, 1919), p. 337.
[2] Ibid., p. 338.

immigrants were, for the most part, English-speaking, and so the transition was nominal. Much of the educational account of English-speaking immigrants, as well as for those from other cultures, in earlier periods has been blended into the chronicle of schooling in the city. Here the newcomers landed and many of them remained. Noninstitutional aspects of education (apprenticeships, ethnic mutual aid societies, the family, and self-study) were responsible for much of the adjustment to the new way of life. The history of immigrant education in America is often the history of schooling in the American city. Aside from being the place where they landed and where many remained, more provisions seem to have been made for them in the city and their educational experiences there are better documented.

The concept of the immigrant as "disadvantaged" or "deprived" is one that is closely associated with the study of specific immigrant groups in American history. A generalization can be made that all immigrants were disadvantaged to some degree, but not all were economically impoverished. The Huguenots who came to New York, Pennsylvania, and the Carolinas after the revocation of the Edict of Nantes in 1685 were skilled, industrious, and prosperous. The Immigration Act of 1965, abolishing the national quota system, admits new people who have the skills needed according to Department of Labor schedules. Inability to speak English, or to speak it sufficiently for employment, has served to make immigrants and in-migrants disadvantaged. To be "culturally disadvantaged" would seem to include the language problem (but not necessarily), lacking those skills needed in the society, and falling short of a life style (competitive spirit, hustle and bustle, prolonging of gratification, the Protestant ethic of hard work) generally associated with successful Americans.

The term "culturally disadvantaged" has not received favorable acceptance in very recent years by all cultural anthropologists, sociologists, and educators. And ethnic and racial groups, themselves, reject the concept. American Indians, Hispanic Americans, and, increasingly, Afro-Americans have been heard from regarding this view. Much more is likely to be said (and educational programs influenced) concerning subcultures in America and their relationship to the American way.

New York City has served as a haven for immigrants throughout its 300-year history. In its colonial period (1609 to 1783), Dutch, Walloons, Jews, French Huguenots, West African and West Indian Negroes, English, Scots, and Irish made up its diverse population. As for schooling provided for its children, with the exception of the school established by the Dutch Reformed Church and the Dutch West India Company in 1638 (now known as the Collegiate School), the "voluntary principle" associated with English educational policy and practice prevailed. The family, private tutoring, charity schools, proprietary schools, the apprenticeship system, and education provided by religious denominations served to instruct the young in the vernacular.

The Free School Society of New York City (renamed the "Public School Society" in 1826), chartered by the state in 1805, was concerned with the schooling of poor children who were not provided for by any religious society or by any of the existing charity schools. Although this charitable organization was only quasi-public in nature, it provided what was really the beginning of free, common school education on a large scale in the city. Its first school, opened in May, 1806, using the Lancastrian monitorial system of instruction, undoubtedly included among its early urchin-pupils, youngsters who were recent immigrants or whose parents were immigrants.[3] New York immigration, at this time, was made up heavily of English-speaking people.

Henry Bradshaw Fearon, an Englishman who came to America in 1817 to gather information for a book intended for British emigrants, paid some attention to the schools of New York City. The Free School Society's schools, with their Lancastrian methodology, were spoken of as being for "the lower orders," and Fearon felt that the monitorial system of instruction had not spread as widely here as in England due, perhaps, to its being less wanted by the common people themselves.[4]

The work of these schools, greatly expanded from their 1806 beginnings, and until they became a part of the public schools of the New York City Board of Education in 1853, provided schooling for many children of the poor and recently-arrived. Although the Scriptures were read daily in these schools, the trustees of the society represented most of the religious groups prominent in the city and those in charge of the schools were instructed to avoid inculcation of the tenets of any particular religious sect. But these schools remained Protestant Christian in orientation, even though their rolls showed Roman Catholic children. It was the alleged permeation of Protestant Christian thought in these charity schools, and later in the public schools, that in part led the Roman Catholic Church towards opening its own schools in the 1840s.

At about the time of the early period of the Free School Society, the Economical School gave instruction to children of refugees from the West Indies, and the Manumission Society (whose work had begun in 1785) schooled hundreds of children of New York City's Negroes. This latter group joined with the Free School Society (then known as the Public School Society) in 1834. Accordingly, separate colored schools were built into the

---

[3] *An Account of the Free-School Society of New York* (New York: Collins and Company, 1814).

[4] Henry Bradshaw Fearon, *Sketches of America: A Narrative of a Journey of Five Thousand Miles Through the Eastern and Western States of America* (London, 1819), p. 38.

system of schools handed over to the Board of Education in New York by the Public School Society in 1853.

In spite of these efforts to extend common schooling to those who could not afford to pay for it, not all city children by any means were receiving instruction. Compulsory school laws and child labor laws were many years away. And poor and immigrant families did not all make use of those limited facilities that were available, some because they could see little value in education and others because they needed the services of their young.

The opening of the West saw immigrants following. How did immigrants settling in the interior of the nation fare so far as education was concerned? The territory and later state of Minnesota, a popular Midwestern agricultural land, where many people of Irish, German, and Scandinavian blood settled, might epitomize a typical frontier settlement in the middle 19th century. Beginning about the 1850s, there were Yankees from New England, Irish, Germans, Norwegians, Swedes, and Czechs residing there. After statehood in 1858, the Homestead Act of 1862, the end of Indian troubles, and the end of the Civil War, many more of these people, essentially small farmers, came to Minnesota. By 1890, the population of the state had reached 467,000, 215,000 of whom were Scandinavians.[5] The diverse population of Minnesota in that year can be shown by the presence of 39 foreign newspapers in that agricultural state.[6]

An immigrants' guidebook to the territory issued in 1856 boasted not only of the area's agricultural advantages, but made a strong point of stressing the provisions there for education, the prevalence of churches, and the "general intelligence of the people." By an Act of Congress, grants of land were made available in every township for the support of common schools. The guidebook informed its readers that, with regard to the villages, "nearly all have good district schools." A comparison was even made with New England's schools, generally accepted as among the best in the country: Minnesota's schools were only second to them, and "but a short time will elapse before they will be fully equal or superior. . . . never in the history of the West in so new a country as Minnesota, has so much attention been paid to the subject of education, or so deep an interest manifested in it."[7]

In the towns of Minnesota, Roman Catholic and Lutheran parishes often had their own parochial schools. As might be expected, they were highly ethnic in composition and no doubt often carried on the language pattern and other mores of the particular group for another generation. But there were those who spoke for more rapid Americanization. Georg Sverdrup, a Norwegian-

---

[5] Theodore Blegen, *Building Minnesota* (Boston: Heath, 1938), p. 370.

[6] Ibid., p. 374.

[7] *The Immigrants' Guide to Minnesota in 1856. By an Old Resident* (St. Anthony: W.W. Wales, 1856), p. 87.

Lutheran church leader in Minnesota in the 1870s, advocated public education for children of the newcomers: "Our children must grow into the language and history of this country."[8] There were ethnic associations and institutions, aside from the churches, that aided the immigrant in adjusting to the land. These were similar to the ones he would have found in the Eastern cities. The Czechs in Minnesota established the *sokol*, a Bohemian social, athletic, and educational organization, for their fellow countrymen. One Czech immigrant, Antonin Jurka, was teaching English to Czech children in the St. Paul public schools in the early 1870s.[9] With the exception of provisions such as those mentioned above, schooling available to the rural immigrant child was the same as that for the native-born.

There is little doubt that the prevalence of common schools in Minnesota and its advanced educational policy were important factors in helping its many foreign pioneer settlers to come into the mainstream of American life as quickly as most of them did. Of course, these immigrants prospered more in a land of good soil on independent farms, and in an absence of exploitation, than was the situation with so many others in the factory system of the East. Certainly, the Germans, Irish, and Scandinavians (perhaps the Finns less so) amalgamated into American life more rapidly than did some of the immigrants coming to America from Southern and Eastern Europe in the late 19th and early 20th centuries.

The development of industry through the factory system in New England attracted Europeans from a variety of backgrounds in the 19th century. The public schools in the cities and larger New England towns began to be aware of the presence of foreign children in the 1850s. Beginning in the 1840s, the Irish predominated as an immigrant group.

The report on schools for the year 1849–1850, in Cambridge, Mass., stated that in one common school "nearly all the children attending are of foreign parentage." That there was some difficulty in reaching them with instruction is reflected in the comment that, "while many of them are, intelligent and studious, and acquire a good standing as scholars, the results of instruction on another portion are less satisfactory."[10] At the annual examination, the school cited above ranked the lowest in reading and spelling accomplishment.

True to the 19th century attitude associating education and virtue, the School Committee of Cambridge concluded that, if all the children of its foreign population attended school (there were no means for compelling at-

---

[8] Theodore Blegen, *Minnesota: A History of the State* (Minneapolis: University of Minnesota Press, 1963), p. 414.

[9] Ibid., p. 370.

[10] *The City of Cambridge: Report of the School Committee for the Municipal Year Ending April 1, 1850* (Cambridge: Metcalf, 1850), p. 11.

tendance), they would become virtuous youth and respectable citizens. Their absence would tend to direct their lives toward idleness and vagrancy.[11]

In Manchester, N.H., the School Committee took cognizance of the preponderance of Irish children in three of their primary schools. "Could they have equal advantages with our native children, and improve as they do in these schools, they would not be excelled by any," reported the committee.[12] Again, there was the concern with schooling as the route to goodness.

No arrangements seem to have been made in the mid-19th century in the schools of New England industrial towns and cities to provide any special tutelage for these youngsters of immigrants. The common school emphasis, aside from instruction in the three R's, was on improvement of moral character. This had supplanted, to some degree, the strong religious emphasis in the schools during the 17th, 18th, and early 19th centuries.

The influx of foreigners from other than the British Isles and Northern Europe, after 1882, shifted the school emphasis somewhat to that of loyalty to the Republic. People began to realize that free, public elementary schooling was essential for the newcomers as well as for the natives. There was fear regarding these strangers coming to America. They represented economic competition for many older Americans; they came from lands that were not democracies; they did not speak English; most were non-Protestant Christians—and many were not Christians at all; and they came from countries not having a heritage of free, public education. In some instances their loyalty was called into question. Cubberley, in referring to Massachusetts at this time, wrote of the "avalanches of foreign-born peoples who have corrupted her politics, diluted her citizenship, and often destroyed the charm of her villages."[13] The Americanization function of the public school began to be realized in the latter decades of the 19th century.

New York City bore the brunt of the influx of immigrants during the late 19th and early 20th centuries. The New York City system of public schools had come into existence in 1842 and had absorbed the charity schools of the Public School Society in 1853. There was no child labor law until 1886, nor a compulsory education law until 1894, and even then the enacted legislation was directed to factory labor of children under 13, and only required school attendance of youngsters from eight to 12 years (children over 12 and under 14 could go to work if they had attended school for 80 days during the year).

It was not the public schools of New York City, however, that geared themselves in philosophy or practice to handle the influx effectively. Indeed, it

[11] Ibid., p. 39.

[12] *Report of The School Committee of the City of Manchester, for the Year 1854-5* (Manchester: Abbott, Jenks, 1855), p. 8.

[13] Cubberley, op. cit., p. 479.

appears from a study of curriculum, textbooks used, sources of teachers, school regulations, evidence from students then in attendance, and other contemporary sources that the public schools of the city went on about their business in about the same manner as they had earlier in the century. Many of the children of immigrants and the poor were outside of the reach of public education. An 1868 source related that "there are forty thousand vagrant and destitute children in this section of the great city [The Five Points, Fourth, and Sixth Wards]. These are chiefly of foreign parentage. They do not attend the public schools, for they have not the clothes necessary to enable them to do so, and are too full of vermin to render them safe companions for other children."[14] Although the schools were public and free, the pupils (or their parents) were required to maintain habits of cleanliness and neatness. And for many this was hopeless.

Almost three decades later, another observer of the New York situation wrote that "Fifteen thousand homeless, hungry, cold, and naked children wander today in our streets, and as yet no agency has been found that meets their need, and the hands that would rescue are powerless. The city money jingles in Tammany pockets, and the taxpayers heap up fortunes for Tammany politicians, while these thousands of little ones are outcasts and soon will be criminals."[15]

But an agency had come into being that began to do something about the plight of poor and immigrant children in New York City, and before long it was more potent and of greater influence with regard to these youngsters than the public schools. It was the Children's Aid Society, a charitable organization founded in 1853, for the industrial education of young "street arabs" who attended no schools, that helped to meet this need. The mission of the society also embraced providing lodging houses for uncared-for children, providing foster homes for them in rural areas, and in transporting unwanted and surplus city children by the hundreds off to the American West.

This mass movement of excess and unwanted poor and immigrant youngsters to the new territories and states of the West has received very little attention from social and educational historians. This episode was, in a sense, a throwback to an earlier British practice of increasing the population of Canada, Australia, and South Africa by removing thereto thousands of children from the crowded cities of Britain. From 1853 to 1882, the Children's Aid Society sent 62,287 boys and girls from New York City westward.[16]

[14] Edward Winslow Martin, *The Secrets of the Great City* (New York: Jones Brothers, 1868), p. 191.
[15] Helen Campbell, *Darkness and Daylight; or Lights and Shadows of New York Life* (Hartford: Hartford Publishing Co., 1896), p. 168.
[16] George C. Needham, *Street Arabs and Gutter Snipes* (Boston: D. L. Guernsey, 1884), pp. 327–328.

Farmers, always in need of help, adopted them, and many a city urchin grew up along with the West and prospered. Letters came back to the Society from some of the transplanted youth, and these tended to support the emigration undertaking. "Once a New York pauper, now a Western farmer. . . . when I was twenty-four I married, and two years afterward I bought myself a farm of eighty acres. . . . have been out West seven years . . . was not contented, and I had four different homes before I made up my mind to settle down. . . . I like this country well, and I like my new home that I am in, and the people are very kind to me. . . ." wrote the boys and girls.[17] Cases on the Society's records showed that some of these redundant city children had received schooling through college, had married well, and had generally prospered in the upwardly mobile social and economic life of the West.

The Children's Aid Society also was helpful especially in aiding in the education of recently-arrived Italian and German children. Three of the Society's 22 industrial schools were designated to serve Italian young people. Here instruction was given in carpentry, cooking, and sewing. By the 1890s, thousands of Italian-American youngsters were benefiting from these programs. "Nothing has done more to make the Italian immigrant contented with New York than the industrial schools which are thronged with children," wrote Helen Campbell in commenting upon Italian life in the city.[18] The story was told of one pair who had landed at Castle Garden (point of disembarkation) at six in the morning and were found in line the same morning at the Children's Aid Society's industrial school—and they announced that seven others would be there that afternoon.

Immigrant self-help organizations—almost every ethnic group had at least one—were vital in the process of adjusting to the harshness of the ghettos and to the new world in general. The Italian colony in New York had nearly 80 benevolent societies, several weekly papers, Italian banks, and a chamber of commerce by 1891.[19] Some ethnic groups attempted schooling on their own, but here the Roman Catholic Church was most successful with its large Irish population.

The public schools of Brooklyn, Queens, and Staten Island joined with those of Manhattan, in 1898, to make up the consolidated New York City school system, when those areas came together to make up greater New York. William H. Maxwell, who had been superintendent of schools in Brooklyn, became superintendent of the new enlarged system. It was under his leadership (1898 to 1914) that the public schools gave attention to the crying need of its immigrant population.

Before the time of Maxwell, there were practically no provisions made for

[17] Ibid., pp. 314, 328, 331, 337.
[18] Campbell, op. cit., p. 406.
[19] Ibid., p. 410.

the non-English speaking child in the public schools. Morris Cohen (1880–1947), later to be an eminent professor and philosopher, arrived in America as an immigrant boy in 1892, and has left an autobiographical account of his experiences in the public schools of Manhattan and Brownsville, in Brooklyn, from the fall of 1892 until the spring of 1895.[20] He found no arrangements for the older or more advanced immigrant student. Young Cohen was precocious, a voracious reader, and he brought with him a heritage of Hebrew studies and a love of learning. And he was fortunate in meeting up with a few teachers who took a personal interest in him, encouraging him at the age of 15 to take the entrance examinations to the City College. But Morris Cohen was the exception among the throng of immigrant youth.

An extensive Federal investigation in 1908 and a subsequent massive report (42 volumes) in 1911 on the problems associated with immigration paid considerable attention to education. Among a mass of data, it reported that children of foreign-born parents left school at an earlier age; that only 4.7% of the high school enrollment was made up of students from foreign parentage; and that retardation of children of foreign parents was greater than that of those from native parents.[21] On the matter of retardation, the differences were not great, and they practically disappeared in the second generation. The backwardness of children from foreign descent appeared to be the result of language difficulties and of various conditions of home life.[22] John Haaren, an associate superintendent of schools in New York City, warned against assuming that all immigrant children were culturally deprived. He pointed out that immigrants brought their particular contribution to enrich American civilization, and some of these additions might serve to soften the materialism so characteristic of life here.[23]

Before the advent of Maxwell as New York City's superintendent of schools, immigrant students were put into regular, lower-grade classes. Here, difficulty for the teacher, generally unable to speak the foreign tongue, as well as for the overage student was brought about. Maxwell, between 1904 and 1905, instituted "C" classes for non-English speaking students, "D" classes for slow students about to reach age 14, and "E" classes for late entrants who had the potential of doing several grades' work in a short time.[24] These endeavors

[20] Morris Raphael Cohen, *A Dreamer's Journey* (Boston: Beacon Press, 1949), pp. 70–84.

[21] U.S. Congress, *Report of the Immigration Commission* (Washington: Government Printing Office, 1911), Vol. II.

[22] Roland P. Falkner, "Immigration and Education," in Paul Monroe, ed., *A Cyclopedia of Education*, Vol. III (New York: Macmillan, 1912), pp. 390–396.

[23] U.S. Bureau of Education. *Education of the Immigrant* (Washington: Government Printing Office, 1913), p. 19.

[24] Selma C. Berrol, "William Henry Maxwell and a New Educational New York," *History of Education Quarterly*, **8**: 222, Summer, 1968.

marked the first, large-scale public school effort toward Americanizing recently arrived children and the children of immigrants. There was some homogeneity (ethnic segregation) in these classes due essentially to the language factor. One district superintendent, in referring to the separation, wrote that "the Jewish child is more ambitious than the Italian child" and that he found parent cooperation better from the former.[25]

Adult education in the Americanization of immigrants was undertaken by a number of agencies. The International Ladies Garment Workers' Union (providing students and encouragement) in conjunction with the New York City Board of Education (providing buildings and teachers) established 19 English classes between 1918 and 1919.[26] Attrition was high in the evening schools; the long hours of labor, fatigue, the necessity of changing clothes, lack of social life for the students, and the working-shift arrangement (causing attendance in alternate weeks) were factors limiting the success of this institution. But the desire for citizenship and to improve themselves economically kept many an immigrant at the task of getting an education.

At the outset of the 20th century, there was little or no research available on teaching English as a second language, on citizenship education, or on teaching the so-called culturally disadvantaged. There were no national funds available and few states offered a subsidy to towns and cities faced with the problems of immigrant education. But, by 1921, most states that had a substantial foreign-born population had provided facilities for Americanization classes. The greatest accomplishment attributed to the American public school has been the Americanization of hundreds of thousands of newcomers to this country in the late 19th and early 20th centuries.

In the 1960s, when the problems of economically disadvantaged in-migrants, mainly Negroes and Puerto Ricans, flocking to the cities have challenged every level of educational institutions, reference often is made to the American schools' experience with the immigrant. Irving Kristol has written that, had a conference been held 100 years ago on "The Crisis in Our Cities," it would have described conditions not too different from those in black and Puerto Rican ghettos today.[27] It is, however, fair to say from all evidence that conditions in the city slums were much worse a century ago.

Negroes are different from immigrants—indeed they are among the oldest of Americans. However, the literature about immigrant groups in the 19th and early 20th centuries—in terms of their disadvantaged status—has its counterpart in some of the writings by and about blacks today. Recognizing the racial factor, but not letting it block out everything else, it is Kristol's

---

[25] U.S. Bureau of Education, *Education of the Immigrant,* op. cit., p. 24.

[26] Frank V. Thompson, *Schooling of the Immigrant* (New York: Harper, 1920), p. 107.

[27] Irving Kristol, "The Negro Today Is Like the Immigrant Yesterday," *New York Times Magazine,* September 11, 1966, p. 50.

thesis that the tragedy of the recent, urban Negro is not that he is black or poor, but that he has come rather late into a highly technical and organized society. Writing as an assimilationist (he did not deal with the Black Power or the separatist movement), his prognosis is, on the whole, a sanguine one: that Negroes in large numbers are "making it" by virtue of their own efforts, and they are entitled to assistance from the society that has made them into the new immigrants.

27

The Children of Immigrants in the Schools

Francesco Cordasco

Introduction

American concern with immigration is not illustrated better than by the Immigration Commission, which the Congress convened on Feb. 20, 1907.* This Commission, chaired by Sen. William P. Dillingham, published its massive *Reports* in 1911 and afforded a kaleidoscope of immigrant life in American society of such dimension that its deliberations became one of the great social documents of all time. If its conclusions are controversial (and the subsequent restrictive quotas derived from its judgments), the data it assembled are invaluable nonetheless in piecing together the intricate mosaic of

---

* *Extract from Act of Congress of February 20, 1907*, creating and defining the duties of the Immigration Commission:

"That a commission is hereby created, consisting of three Senators, to be appointed by the President of the Senate, and three Members of the House of Representatives, to be appointed by the Speaker of the House of Representatives, and three persons to be appointed by the President of the United States. Said commission shall make full inquiry, examination, and investigation, by subcommittee or otherwise, into the subject of immigration. For the purpose of said inquiry, examination, and investigation said commission is authorized to send for persons and papers, make all necessary travel, either in the United States or any foreign country, and, through the chairman of the commission, or any member thereof, to administer oaths and to examine witnesses and papers respecting all matters pertaining to the subject, and to employ necessary clerical and other assistance. Said commission shall report to Congress the conclusions reached by it, and make such recommendations as in its judgment may seem proper. Such sums of money as may be necessary for the said inquiry, examination, and investigation are hereby appropriated and authorized to be paid out of the 'immigrant fund' on the certificate of the chairman of said commission, including all expenses of the commissioners, and a reasonable compensation, to be fixed by the President of the United States, for those members of the commission who are not Members of Congress. . . ."

late 19th- and early 20th-century American life and in furnishing a basis from which American national character and history are to be understood. The *Reports* furnished a statistical review of immigration (1819–1910); studied emigration conditions in Europe; studied immigrants in industry; studied the urban immigrant; surveyed the occupations of first and second generation immigrants and the fecundity of immigrant women; studied the children of immigrants in the schools; studied immigrants as charity seekers; surveyed immigration and crime; studied steerage conditions, the importation and harboring of women for immoral purposes, and immigrant banks (all incongruously gathered in one volume); mapped changes in bodily form of the descendants of immigrants; surveyed federal and state immigration legislation; reviewed the immigration situation in other countries; and collected statements and recommendations submitted by societies and organizations interested in the subject of immigration.† An impressive document, it influenced American policy for decades. Any one of its *Reports* supplies both a point of reference and a watershed of influence which help explain subsequent American history. This is particularly apparent in its *Report on the Children of Immigrants in Schools* (Vols. 29–33), which is a vast repository of data on the educational history of the children of the poor and the schools.

The Migrations

Since the keeping of records, which were begun in 1819, it has been estimated that some 43,000,000 human beings made their way into the United States of America, truly one of the greatest peaceful human migrations in the whole history of mankind. Of these, at least 40,000,000 were of European origin and the remainder of widely scattered origins. The bulk of the migration in the period before 1819 (i.e., 1607–1819) came from northern and western Europe, and of this a preponderance came from the British Isles; the remainder was from other parts of Europe and also included an estimated 300,000 blacks, mostly brought in as slaves. The period between 1819–1882 often is referred to as the era of the "old migrations" in which some 10,000,000 immigrants arrived, with the majority again originating in northern and western Europe. During 1882–1921 ("the new migration"), the period of the greatest sustained migration, the migrants were largely of southern and eastern European origin (some 20,000,000) out of an estimated 23,500,000. Since 1921, with the imposition of quotas, immigration was reduced drastically, and

† United States Immigration Commission, *Report of the Immigration Commission,* 41 vols. (Washington: Government Printing Office, 1911). Vol. 42 (*Index of Reports of the Immigration Commission,* S. Doc. No. 785, 61st Congress, 3rd Session) never was published.

an effort was made to maintain the basic population composition as it existed in 1890 just prior to the great influx of southern and eastern Europeans. Since 1921, and especially after further reductions in 1929, average immigration annually has been about 200,000.[1]

The immigrants of the "new migrations" (1882–1921) differed in language and customs from earlier American residents, and they arrived during those decades when the American "common school" had largely evolved into its framework of "a genuine part of that [American] life, standing as a principal positive commitment of the American people."[2] The children of the immigrants of this later period presented particular challenges to the American school. With reference to the period between 1880–1920 (particularly, the late 19th and early 20th centuries), this essay presents an overview of the American school in form and function as it presented itself to the immigrant child, and of the response of the American school to the immigrant child.[3]

The American School in Form and Function

The immigrant child was the child of his own immigrant subcommunity within the American city in which his parents had settled. In this immigrant subcommunity (or "ghetto" which carries with it a pejorative connotation), the child was securely related to an organized social life that largely duplicated the customs and mores which his parents had transplanted to America. It was the school which introduced him to a different world, and it was the school which saw its role essentially as one of enforced assimilation. Cubberley, the educational historian, makes this vividly clear:

Everywhere these people [immigrants] tend to settle in groups or settlements and to set up their own national manners, customs and observances. Our task is

---

[1] A vast literature exists on immigration. See Richard C. Haskett, et al., "An Introductory Bibliography for the History of American Immigration," in *A Report on World Population Migrations* (Washington: George Washington University Press, 1956), pp. 85–295. Particular reference should be made to Jeremiah W. Jenks and W. Jett Lauck, *The Immigration Problem* (New York: Funk and Wagnalls, 1917); and to the *Reports of the United States Immigration Commission,* 41 vols. (Washington: Government Printing Office, 1911).

[2] Lawrence A. Cremin, *The American Common School: An Historic Conception* (New York: Bureau of Publications, Teachers College, Columbia University, 1951), p. 219.

[3] This essay limits itself to the experience in New York City, and largely to the period between 1890 and 1915. It is the writer's view that the experiences of the immigrant child in other American cities during this period would be essentially the same, and that differences would be in terms of the size of the immigrant subcommunity, its spatial distribution within the greater urban context, and in responses by the schools.

to *break up* their groups and settlements, to assimilate or amalgamate these people as a part of the American race, and to implant in their children, so far as can be done, the Anglo-Saxon conception of righteousness, law, order and popular government, and to awaken in them reverence for our democratic institutions and for those things which we as people hold to be of abiding worth.[4]

By 1911, 57.5% of the children in the public schools of 37 of the largest American cities were of foreign-born parentage; in the parochial schools of 24 of these 37 cities, the children of foreign-born parents constituted 63.5% of the total registration.[5] "To the immigrant child the public elementary school was the first step away from his past, a means by which he could learn to assume the characteristics necessary for the long climb upward."[6] And, by 1911, almost 50% of the students in secondary schools were of foreign-born parentage.[7] In American cities, the major educational challenge and responsibility was the immigrant child.

The situation in New York City was not atypical. Serious deficiencies existed in the adequacy of available school facilities. In 1890, some 10,000 children in New York City, who were within the legal ages for school attendance, were without actual school accommodations, and this figure was undoubtedly conservative.[8] The passage of the Compulsory Education Act in 1895, stipulating that all children attend school between the ages of eight and 16 (with certain exceptions as to employment, etc.), exacerbated the situation in New York City, and, because of the lack of accommodations, the Act was, to all intents, inoperative.[9] The expansion of secondary education (three new high schools were opened in 1897) imposed the need for vast curriculum changes in the upper grades of the elementary school, with a concomitant awareness of the need for the expansion of mutual training schools. When the Consolidation Act (Jan. 1, 1898) created a greater New York, bringing together the boroughs, the schools in the Manhattan and Bronx boroughs were divided into

[4] Ellwood P. Cubberley, *Changing Conceptions of Education* (Boston: Houghton Mifflin, 1909), p. 16. See also Leonard P. Ayres, *Laggards in Our Schools* (New York: Russell Sage Foundation, 1909) ; and, as a point of dissent, Jane Addams, "The Public School and the Immigrant Child," *National Education Association Journal*, **46**: 99–102, June 1908.

[5] The United States Immigration Commission, op. cit., *Abstracts of the Immigration Commission Reports. The Children of Immigrants in Schools*, vol. II, pp. 1–15.

[6] Alan M. Thomas, "American Education and the Immigrant," *Teachers College Record*, **55**: 253–267, April 1954.

[7] See footnote 5, supra.

[8] New York City Department of Education, *Annual Reports of the City Superintendent of Schools to the Board of Education, 1898–1915*. See also New York City Commission on the Congestion of Population, *Report of the Committee, 1911*.

[9] The biennial school census in 1895 showed that there were 166,000 non-attendant children in the city who were entitled to enter school. See New York City Board of Education, *Report of Finance Committee on School Systems*, 1896, pp. 4–5.

primary and grammar departments, with separate classes for boys and girls and with the elementary schools consisting of seven grades. In the other boroughs the elementary school was organized into eight grades. The first New York City superintendent of schools, William H. Maxwell, addressed himself to the major problems of the expansion of facilities, the opening of more kindergartens, the uniformity of an eight-year elementary school, and the establishment of manual training schools. To the problems of urbanization and mounting school enrollments (some 20,000 to 40,000 new students had to be accommodated each year) was added the increasing patterns of heavy immigration.[10]

It was against the background of these problems that the immigrant child presented himself to the New York City public schools. By 1900, about 80% of the New York City population was either foreign-born or of foreign parentage, and, by 1910, a significant shift in the birthplace of the majority of the immigrants from the north to the south of Europe had occurred. For the schools, the non-English-speaking child presented still another dimension to overwhelming problems.[11] *The Third Biennial School Census* in 1906 showed that 17% of the entire public school enrollment was foreign-born (113,740) and, although there was some controversy about the accuracy of the figures (particularly, that the figures did not reflect cases of truancy and the number of children working illegally), the enormity of the problems presented to the schools was dramatically underscored.[12] The children of the more recent immigrants constituted the bulk of elementary and intermediate enrollments, while the children of earlier immigrants were generally in higher grades.[13] More symptomatic than any other factor of the general malaise of

[10] For the population growth in New York City between 1890–1910, see U.S. Census Bureau, *Thirteenth Census of the United States, 1910, Supplement for New York City*, pp. 569–571; and, for growth in school population, see New York City Department of Education, *Annual Reports of the City Superintendent of Schools*, 1899, et seq.

[11] See H. H. Wheaton, *Recent Progress in the Education of Immigrants*, Department of the Interior, Bureau of Education (Washington: Government Printing Office, 1915), in which it is noted that, in 1910, there were in New York City 421,951 persons 10 years of age or over who could not speak English and over 245,000 in the same category who were illiterate.

[12] New York City Department of Education, *Annual Report of the City Superintendent of Schools, 1906–1907*. See also John D. Haney, *Registration of City School Children* (New York: Teachers College, Columbia University, 1910).

[13] See, generally, the United States Immigration Commission, *The Children of Immigrants in Schools*, vols. 29–33, op. cit. For New York City, see vol. 32, pp. 603–765. "On the other hand, there are several races which have an unusually high portion of their children in the schools. These are the Greeks, the North and South Italians, the Poles, the Roumanians, the Spaniards, and the Syrians. This may be due to the recent immigration of these races and the preponderance among their children of those of early ages, as well as to the fact that where the children are themselves born abroad and are ignorant of the English language they are frequently forced to begin their

the schools was the pervasive phenomenon of the overage pupil who was classed under the rubric "retardation" with all of its negative connotations. The Immigration Commission of 1911 found that the percentage of retardation for the New York City elementary school pupils was 36.4, with the maximum retardation (48.8%) in the fifth grade.[14] The Commission observed:

> . . . thus in the third grade the pupils range in age from 5 to 18 years. In similar manner pupils of the age of 14 years are found in every grade from the first of the elementary schools to the last of the high schools. It will, however, be noted that in spite of this divergence the great body of the pupils of a given grade are of certain definite ages, the older and younger pupils being in each case much less numerically represented. It may, therefore, be assumed that there is an appropriate age for each grade. This assumption is the cardinal point in current educational discussion in regard to retardation. If it were assumed that there is a normal age for each grade, then the pupils can be divided into two classes—those who are of normal age or less and those who are above the normal age. The latter, or overage pupils, are designated as "retarded."[15]

Although the Immigration Commission concluded that the "races" which had most recently arrived in the United States (and in which a foreign language was used in the home) had a higher percentage of retardation, it cautioned against deriving from these data less mental ability, and rather ascribed the retardation to environmental and external circumstances that would be corrected within a generation.

That the educational system was inadequate to the problems presented is unquestioned. In the main, there was a slow shift from concern with the

work in the public schools of the United States at a point considerably below that which corresponds to their age." (Ibid., p. 613); in its conclusions, the Immigration Commission noted: "Of the pupils who are children of foreign-born fathers, three races—the Portuguese, Slovak, and South Italian—show less than one percent in the high school." Abstracts of *Reports of the Immigration Commission*, vol. I, p. 43.

[14] United States Immigration Commission, *The Children of Immigrants in Schools*, op. cit., vol. 32, p. 609.

[15] Ibid, pp. 608–609. The Commission further noted: "Again certain races may be noted which have a less proportion of retarded children than has the group of native parentage. They are the Danish, the Finnish, the German Hebrew, the Roumanian Hebrew, the Magyar, the Norwegian, the Roumanian, the Russian, and the Swedish. It cannot fail to attract attention that many of these races are those of comparatively recent immigration. On the other hand, there are some races with a conspicuously high degree of retardation among the children. These are the French Canadian, the Greek, the Italian, the Spanish, the Spanish-American, and the Syrian." (Ibid., p. 614.) General reference should be made to Leonard P. Ayres, *Laggards in Our Schools* (New York: Russell Sage Foundation, 1909), which, in an effort to determine the causes of retardation, conducted studies in 29 cities and which includes a detailed study of 20,000 children in 15 Manhattan schools. Ayres concluded that slow progress (not late entrance) was the greatest factor in retardation.

problems of physical facilities, of congestion, to the more important concern of the needs of immigrant children, with the problems of their maladjustment, "retardation," with the particular needs of ethnic groups, with the preservation of the multicultures which the children brought to the schools, and to the articulation of a learning situation which was fashioned out of new curricula and understandings.[16]

The Response of the American School to the Immigrant Child

In the effort to respond to the immigrant child, it is important to note at the outset that no overall programs were developed to aid any particular immigrant group. Although there was little agreement as to what Americanization was, the schools were committed to Americanize (and to Anglicize) their charges. Ellwood P. Cubberley's *Changing Conceptions of Education* (1909), which Lawrence A. Cremin characterizes as "a typical progressive tract of the era,"[17] saw the new immigrants as "illiterate, docile, lacking in self-reliance and initiative, and not possessing the Anglo teutonic conceptions of law, order, and government . . . ," and the school's role was (in Cubberley's view) "to assimilate and amalgamate."

What efforts were made to respond to the needs of immigrant children were improvised, most often directly in answer to specific problems; almost never was any attempt made to give the school and its program a community orientation. The children literally left at the door of the school their language, their cultural identities, and their immigrant subcommunity origins.[18] A child's

[16] See, generally, Lawrence A. Cremin, *The Transformation of the School* (New York: Knopf, 1961), pp. 66–75; and, particularly, Leonard Covello, "A High School and Its Immigrant Community: A Challenge and an Opportunity," *Journal of Educational Sociology*, 9: 331–346, February 1936.

[17] Cremin, *The Transformation of the School*, op. cit., p. 68. "To Americanize, in this view, was to divest the immigrant of his ethnic character and to inculcate the dominant Anglo-Saxon morality." (Ibid.) See also Frank V. Thompson, *Schooling of the Immigrant* (New York: Harper, 1920), for a more eclectic view; and, for the more pragmatic efforts of the settlement houses and other non-school agencies, see Robert A. Woods, et al., *The Poor in Great Cities: Their Problems and What Is Being Done to Solve Them* (New York: Scribner, 1895); and Morris I. Berger, *The Settlement, the Immigrant and the Public School* (unpublished Ph.D. dissertation, Columbia University, 1956).

[18] See the autobiography of Leonard Covello, *The Heart Is the Teacher* (New York: McGraw-Hill, 1958). It is significant to note that Covello, as an immigrant boy in East Harlem, was more influenced by the work of the evangelist Anna C. Ruddy, who had devoted years to social work in the East Harlem Italian Community, than by the public schools. See Anna C. Ruddy [pseudonym, Christian McLeod], *The Heart of the*

parents had virtually no role in the school;[19] and the New York City experience was not atypical in its leaving the immigrant child to the discretion of the individual superintendent, a principal, or a teacher. In New York City, no city-wide system or policy was developed to meet the special needs presented by the immigrant child. Instead, largely left to the management of district superintendents, constructs and programs evolved along the broad lines of individual promotion, English instruction for foreigners, the provision of special classes, and, in some instances, of special schools.

Julia Richman, district superintendent in New York City School Districts 2 and 3, was particularly responsive to the needs of immigrant children. She experimented with a new system of individual promotion (in essence, graded patterns of instruction geared to individual needs), and her writings show a growing awareness of the need for community liaison and support.[20] As early as 1903, other district superintendents (in Division I, embracing Manhattan

Stranger (New York: Fleming H. Revell, 1908); see also Selma Berrol, "Immigrants at School: New York City, 1900–1910," *Urban Education*, 4: 220–230, October, 1969.

[19] See Leonard Covello, *The Social Background of the Italo-American Child: A Study of the Southern Italian Family Mores and Their Effect on the School Situation in Italy and America*, edited and with an introduction by F. Cordasco (Leiden, The Netherlands: E. J. Brill, 1967). As late as 1938, Phyllis H. Williams, in a study under the aegis of the Institute of Human Relations, Yale University, observed: "Current theories of child training in American schools stress the pupil's role as an individual rather than as a group member. Teachers frequently expect the American-born child of Italian stock to manifest purely American traits, to have sloughed off almost all of the culturally determined personality traits that characterize his parents. When they attribute any variation to ethnic differences, they usually do so in the case of a vice rather than a virtue—in a typically ethnocentric fashion." Phyllis H. Williams, *South Italian Folkways in Europe and America: A Handbook for Social Workers, Visiting Nurses, School Teachers, and Physicians* (New Haven: Yale University Press, 1938; reissued with an introductory note by F. Cordasco, New York: Russell & Russell, 1969), p. 132. The persistence of an ethnocentric rejection of the use of native languages in the instruction of non-English-speaking children can be studied in the recent history (1966–1967) of the enactment of Title VII (Bilingual Education Act) of the Elementary and Secondary Education Act. See F. Cordasco, "The Bilingual Education Act," *Phi Delta Kappan*, 51: 75, October 1969; and F. Cordasco, "The Challenge of the Non-English-Speaking Child in American Schools," *School & Society*, 96: 198–201, March 30, 1968, which is an adaptation of testimony before the Committee on Education and Labor of the U.S. House of Representatives in support of the proposed Title VII (June 29, 1967). See further Mario Fantini and Gerald Weinstein, *The Disadvantaged: Challenge to Education* (New York: Harper, 1968); and a critique-review by F. Cordasco, "Educational Pelagianism: The Schools and the Poor," *Teachers College Record*, 69: 705–709, April 1968.

[20] All of Julia Richman's writings are important. See particularly the following: "A Successful Experiment in Promoting Pupils," *Educational Review*, 18: 23–29, June 1899; "The Incorrigible Child," *Educational Review*, 31: 484–506, May 1906: "The Social Needs of the Public School," *Forum*, 43: 161–169, February 1910; "What Can Be Done in the Graded School for the Backward Child," *The Survey*, 13: 129–131, November 1904.

south of 14th Street) were experimenting with a syllabus of instruction for teaching English to children who did not know the language.[21] Certain super- intendents instituted special classes for immigrant children (extending from one month to a whole year) for basic instruction in English which would bring them to grade level.[22] And the most ambitious of the constructs devised was the large-scale introduction of special classes by Julia Richman through- out the school districts under her governance. Her efforts are worthy of special note.

In 1903, Julia Richman conducted an investigation in her school districts to determine why so many children who applied to leave school were not at the fifth-grade level (legally, children could leave school by age 14); and she maintained that the clearest indication of the failure of the schools was in the fact that large numbers of children desiring to leave school for employ- ment at age 14 were not at fifth-grade level. Students who were 14 and had completed Grade 5A or its equivalent were eligible for work certification. Miss Richman found that pupils who were not progressing could be classified as follows: foreign-born children longer than one year in the city were unwisely classified and too slowly promoted; children who were turned away from school or kept for years on waiting lists in the days when principals had that privilege; children "run out of school" for misconduct when records were kept less carefully than at present; children excluded because of con- tagion in the days when medical personnel and nurses were not able to con- trol this situation; children who had been neglected in classes where substitutes were placed in charge of afternoon part-time classes; disorderly children; truants; defectives (mental or physical); and children whose individual needs were overlooked when promotions were made.[23] On the basis of these findings, Julia Richman received permission from the Board of Superintendents to allow her to form special classes for these children in which a simplified and individualized course of study was to be used. Only the absolute essentials demanded by the compulsory attendance law were to be taught.

The omission of paper folding, construction of paper boxes, the knotting of cord, sight reading in music, illustrative drawing and many other requirements of our present course (even though they have a distinct educational value to the normal

---

[21] See Joseph S. Wade, "The Teaching of English to Foreigners in the First Two Years of Elementary School," *School Work*, **2**: 285–292, November 1903.

[22] Basically, this technique was extensively used in meeting the English language needs of Puerto Rican children following the heavy migrations to American cities after World War II. See F. Cordasco and E. Bucchioni, *Puerto Rican Children in Mainland Schools: A Sourcebook for Teachers* (New York: Scarecrow Press, 1968).

[23] Julia Richman, "What Can Be Done in the Graded School for the Backward Child," loc. cit., pp. 129–130.

child of English speaking parents) will make it possible to cover the work of two or more grades in one term. This will bring these children nearer to the completion of the requirements of the law by their 14th birthday.[24]

By Sept. 30, 1904, some 18 special classes had been instituted in School Districts 2 and 3; and a significant reversal was made in the earlier practice of placing the immigrant child, whatever his age, in the lowest or next lowest grade. And, by the end of the 1904–1905 school year, some 250 special classes (principally for non-English-speaking children) were in operation.[25] As children acquired a competency in English, they were transferred to appropriate grades. Generally, an overall improvement was noted, with continuing difficulties only with those students who were highly transient and for whom the continuity of instruction was interrupted. Yet, even these difficulties were minimized by special efforts and adaptations.[26] Further refinements of the special class concept led to the definition of three categories of placement: Grade C, for foreign-born children who did not speak English; Grade D, for those pupils who were approaching age 14, could not finish elementary school, and wished to obtain work certificates; and Grade E, for those pupils who hoped to graduate but needed special help to enter the seventh grade.[27] There is little doubt that the special classes were an effective force in meeting the needs of the immigrant child; and a not inconsiderable number of native-born children received needed help as well.[28]

Although the special classes gave principals and teachers considerable latitude in dealing with the problems of immigrant children, no effort was made to change the basic course of study in the regular classes to which these children eventually moved. Out of mounting criticism that the New York City school curriculum was inflexible, and not geared to the wide variety of

[24] Ibid., p. 130.

[25] New York City Department of Education, *Annual Report of the City Superintendent of Schools, 1904–1905.*

[26] Ibid., Appendix A, p. 137. Since the special classes were largely for non-English-speaking immigrant children, lay observers of the public schools continued to call for restriction of immigration as a solution to school problems. Cf., Adele Marie Shaw, "The True Character of New York Public Schools," *World's Work,* 7: 4204–4221, December 1903. More sympathetic to public school efforts (and often the catalyst which brought them into being) was The Public Education Association of New York City which had been formed in 1894. See the invaluable study by Sol Cohen, *Progressives and Urban School Reform: The Public Education Association of New York City, 1895–1954* (New York: Bureau of Publications, Teachers College, Columbia University, 1964).

[27] New York City Department of Education, *Annual Report of the City Superintendent of Schools, 1905–1906.*

[28] See the results of an investigation of special classes which was conducted in 1909–1910. New York City Department of Education, *Annual Report of the City Superintendent of Schools, 1911–1912.* See also, *Education of the Immigrant,* U.S. Bureau of Education, Bulletin, 1913, No. 51 (Washington: Government Printing Office, 1913).

needs exhibited by children, came recommendations for industrial education, for vast curricular reforms (largely unmet), and the creation of schools for incorrigible boys[29] (the forerunner of the present day "600" schools). The emphasis on industrial education was a continuing reiteration of the need for manual education; a private manual training school had been established in New York City in 1887, and the city's Baron de Hirsch School (1891) trained boys for the mechanical and building trades.[30] And the emphasis on manual and trade education (no matter how inadequately met) may have been the surest symptom of a school system which found the children of immigrants uneducable along traditional lines.[31]

That the public schools in New York City were unable or unwilling to meet the challenge of immigrant children is readily apparent in the paucity of the concepts and programs which were fashioned; in the few educational reformers (e.g., Julia Richman) who responded constructively to the multitude of challenges; particularly in the continuing criticism of the schools by a host of lay reformers; and in the variety of nonschool agencies which were created to meet the very real problems which the schools ignored. Most of the social reformers directed their criticisms to the schools; and of these, Jacob A. Riis, Robert Hunter, and John Spargo are but a few whose writings are valuable chronicles of the deficiencies of the schools.[32] Despite its intricate involvements, The Public Education Association of New York City formulated a conception of the public school as "a legatee institution" whose responsibility (as the PEA saw it) was the entire problem of child life.[33] And central in the community mosaic of the urban Settlement House was provision for all those identities which poor youth sought and were denied in the schools.[34]

[29] See Isaac Russell, "Is Our Public School Behind The Times? James Creelman's Remedy For Existing Evils," *The Craftsman*, **20**: 141–143, May 1911; Paul Hanus, *School Efficiency: A Constructive Study Applied to New York City* (New York: World Book Co., 1913); for the "incorrigible" child, see Julia Richman, "The Incorrigible Child," *Educational Review*, **31**: 484–506, May 1906.

[30] See Cremin, *The Transformation of the School*, op. cit., pp. 24–57.

[31] Cohen has cogently advanced the thesis that the industrial education movement was an attempt to block the social advance of immigrant children. See S. Cohen, "The Industrial Education Movement, 1906–1917," *American Quarterly*, **20**: 95–110, Spring 1968.

[32] Jacob A. Riis, *The Children of the Poor* (New York: Scribner, 1892); Robert Hunter, *Poverty* [particularly the chapter entitled, "The Child"] (New York: Macmillan, 1904); John Spargo, *The Bitter Cry of the Children* (New York: Macmillan, 1907). See also F. Cordasco, ed., *Jacob Riis Revisited: Poverty and the Slum in Another Era* (New York: Doubleday, 1968).

[33] Cohen, loc. cit.

[34] On the Settlement House movement, see Berger, op. cit., and Robert A. Woods and Albert J. Kennedy, *The Settlement Horizon* (New York: Macmillan, 1922). On the

The schools reflected the attitudes prevalent at the time of the great immigrations, which, in essence, held that the immigrant was a one-generation problem. Assimilation was an educational process, and if immigrant children got a "good" education, the parents would be assimilated with them. In the process, parents and community were neglected, if not ignored. There is some doubt that the school acted as the main devise through which the child was assimilated, and if so, it did its job poorly; certainly, the schools did not ameliorate the plight of the immigrant parent. If anything, they provided little opportunity to the immigrant parent to obtain information as to what the aims and objectives of the schools were, and, in this respect, the schools and the parent were in continuing conflict. If New York City was typical, the urban schools provided no systemwide policy which dealt with the educational needs of immigrant children; and where programs were fashioned to meet these needs, there was no attempt made to differentiate between immigrant groups (e.g., the experience of Italian and Jewish children in New York City strongly documents this failure); instead, children were lumped under the rubrics, "native-born" or "foreign-born." If one discounts the multiplicity of disfunctional programs, rampant discrimination, authoritarian prejudice, it is still difficult to attribute the general patterns of failure to immigrant children or their parents. The blame for the failure lies almost wholly within the school and the dominant society which shaped its programs and articulated its cultural ideals.

Leonard Covello, who spent a half-century in the New York City schools as a teacher and an administrator, himself an immigrant child in its schools, observed: "Of no little importance was the fact that the Americanization programs were directed only toward people of foreign stock, without giving any consideration to the necessity of involving *all* Americans, regardless of the time of their arrival in the United States. But, above all, the earlier Americanization policies, by and large, denied or neglected the strength of, and the values in, the foreign culture of immigrant groups. The concept of Americanization was based upon the assumption that foreigners and foreign ideas and ways were a threat to American political, economic, social stability, and security. The infiltration of foreign culture, it was feared, would eventually bring about a deterioration of the American 'way of life.' Programs were designed, therefore, to suppress or eliminate all that was conceived of as 'foreign' and to impose upon the immigrant a cultural uniformity with an American pattern."[35]

educational and social aspirations of ethnic subcommunities, see Timothy L. Smith, "Immigrant Social Aspirations and American Education, 1880–1930," *American Quarterly*, **21**: 523–543, Fall 1969.

[35] Covello, *The Social Background of the Italo-American Child*, op. cit., p. 411.

28

Education for the Needs
of Cuban Refugees

J. Michael Davis

Thousands of Cubans have been forced to flee their homeland because of political upheaval in recent years. Over 320,000 immigrants from Cuba have officially registered at the Cuban Refugee Emergency Center in Miami, Florida, during the past decade.[1] Many have been resettled throughout the United States with friends and relatives, with nearly half the Cuban refugee population in this country residing in the greater Miami area.[2] A recent survey noted that the current population of Cuban exiles represents 26% of the residents of the city of Miami.[3] This number represents a dramatic contrast to the 20,000 population figure of Cubans in the Miami area before 1960.[4] Their arrival has changed the complexion of all facets of life in the South Florida area.

The first stage of the Cuban refugee movement began shortly after Fidel Castro's accession to power in 1959 and continued until commercial flights were suspended in 1962. The second stage of the exodus was the period between the Cuban missile crisis in 1962 and the beginning of the authorized flights in 1965. During this time, refugees arrived in the United States only by third countries or clandestinely in small boats.[5] The third stage was repre-

[1] U.S. Cuban Refugee Program, *Resettlement Re-Cap* (Miami, Fla.: Cuban Refugee Emergency Center, 1969).

[2] Clyde C. Wooten and Edward Sofen, *Psycho-Social Dynamics in Miami.* A study conducted by the University of Miami for the U.S. Department of Housing and Urban Development (Coral Gables, Fla.: University of Miami, 1969).

[3] Ibid.

[4] U.S. Department of Health, Education, and Welfare, *The Cuban Immigration 1959–1966 and Its Impact on Miami-Dade County, Florida.* Prepared by the Research Institute for Cuba and the Caribbean Center for Advanced International Studies (Coral Gables: University of Miami, 1967).

[5] Barney W. Stoutamire and Herbert W. Wey, "Cuban Teachers Train for Service," *Florida Education,* **46**: 20–23, November 1968.

sented by the recent air flights from Cuba. Ten flights a week brought 4,000 Cuban refugees from Cuba each month in search of freedom to the United States,[6] until the flights were suspended late in 1971.

Cubans who had specialized training in education, English, law, accounting, science, engineering, pharmacy, and philosophy and literature came on these flights, but were unable to resume their careers upon entry into the United States. Many found employment in the United States as private school teachers, tutors, teachers aides, factory workers, garment makers, hairdressers, taxi drivers, sales clerks, secretaries, translators, and waitresses.

The influx of Cuban refugees in such large numbers was not expected, and most of the children and the adults spoke little or no English. They created special problems for the community and the school system. Miami community leaders were sympathetic towards these homeless persons and were determined to demonstrate to them in a practical way how a democratic society could adjust to meet their needs.

American and Cuban cultures made up of numerous subgroups with different backgrounds, interests, and customs came together. During the first years, the local residents and newly arrived exiles went through an unique orientation period. Schools, churches, agencies, and the total community felt the influence of the migration and resettlement of Cuban refugees. Neighborhood compositions changed, as well as church congregations and school memberships. The local labor market experienced profound changes as an ever-increasing number of employable people entered the labor force at different levels.

A good example of this change can be illustrated by the growth in school enrollment of Cuban children. At the conclusion of the 1967–1968 school year, there were 24,360 Cuban refugee pupils enrolled in the Dade County public schools.[7] This represented 11.27% of the total pupil membership in the Dade County schools. It has been estimated that between 30,000 and 35,000 Cuban children are currently attending schools in the South Florida area. Dade County school officials contend that the number of Cuban refugee pupils almost certainly will continue to increase.

Programs were implemented to begin meeting the unique educational needs that become evident throughout the area. A brief review of a few programs indicate how the community and its educational systems began to meet this challenge of resolving present and potential difficulties.

During the early 1960s, an agreement was concluded between the Dade

---

[6] J. Michael Davis, "The Relationship of Selection Factors in the Cuban Teacher Retraining Program to the Effective Classroom Performance of Cuban Teachers" (unpublished Ed.D. dissertation, University of Miami, 1969).

[7] Dade County Public Schools, *Cuban Refugee Report—Number Seven* (Miami, Fla.: Dade County Administrative Research, 1969), p. 3.

County School Board and the United States Department of Health, Education, and Welfare. This subsequent "agreement" served to supplement previous federal assistance to the school system in order to provide for the educational needs of the ever-increasing number of Cuban students (children and adults).

Arrangements were completed so that free public education was furnished to the Cubans to the same extent and manner as it was to the children who were permanent residents of the country.[8] The government underwrote public education costs which included facilities, equipment, materials, supplies, transportation, and other related services for Cuban refugees in the Dade County area.

Non-English-speaking students were scheduled into special courses of study depending on their ability to speak and understand English, not on intelligence or academic achievement. Pupils concentrated on English instruction and then began taking additional subjects in the curriculum in which achievement was measured in terms of performance rather than verbal ability. As language proficiency was acquired, more of the regular program was included in their daily schedule.[9]

Another program developed exclusively for the refugee children was a tuition-free summer school. The summer program made it possible for newly arrived refugees to participate in an English program before school commenced in September.[10]

With the assistance of foundation money, a unique bilingual education program was implemented and has since been expanded. English was the medium of instruction for all pupils for half a day and Spanish during the other half in a select number of elementary and junior high schools. The staffs were composed of native Spanish-speaking teachers and native English-speaking teachers.

Extensive adult vocational training and educational programs were started to provide for the needs of refugees who wished to improve themselves. English instruction on different levels of competency was provided to adults in evening and day school centers throughout the county. Specific training in marketable skills was provided at special adult training centers (e.g., secretarial, upholstery, child care, welding, commercial sewing, and clerical).

In addition to providing instruction to the pupils, in-service training programs were offered in order to certify teachers and assist Cuban teacher aides. Workshops were designed to improve instruction in teaching Spanish as a vernacular language.

Bilingual Cuban teacher aides were recruited from among the refugee teachers living in Dade County. The aides assisted American teachers and

[8] Ibid.
[9] Wooten and Sofen, op. cit., pp. 314–323.
[10] Dade County Public Schools, loc. cit.

administrators by performing vital services in the school offices and participating in the execution of the instructional program in the classrooms. Their
performance has proven to be exceptional and their contributions to the
educational process have been extremely helpful.

During the early 1960s, the demand for bilingual teachers who could com-
municate effectively with the large number of Spanish-speaking children
became acute. A large number of teachers had to be employed to teach these
pupils.[11] To help meet this need, the University of Miami initiated the Cuban
Teacher Retraining Program in 1963 with a grant from the U.S. Office of
Education utilizing funds allocated from the Cuban Refugee Program appropriations.[12] The purposes of the program were to help meet the demands for
bilingual teachers in the Dade County School System and to assist displaced
Cuban refugee professionals in the resumption of their teaching careers.
During the past seven years the Cuban Teacher Program has served to place
over 300 Cuban refugees in useful and responsible positions in approximately
90 schools.

Exiles interested in becoming full-time students for undergraduate or
graduate degrees could participate in the college student loan program for
Cubans. Allocations were made to institutions of higher education under the
National Defense Education Loan Program. Funds were distributed by colleges and universities in South Florida to those Cuban students who were
eligible.

Numerous programs could have been mentioned, but this brief review of a
few education programs illustrates how a community has begun to meet particular problems resulting from the Cuban exodus. All educational needs
have not been resolved, but an excellent start has been made by public and
private education. Important lessons have been learned by educators, residents, and refugees.

Surveys, observations, and program evaluations continue to highlight
the fact that the influx of Cubans to South Florida has provided the area with
an invaluable asset. This community asset is due in large measure to the
high motivation and exemplary performance of the exiles. Another instrumental factor was the cooperative efforts of the Cuban Refugee Program, the
U.S. Department of Health, Education, and Welfare, the Dade County School
Board, and the University of Miami.

[11] Mabel W. Richardson, "An Evaluation of Certain Aspects of the Academic Achievement of Elementary Pupils in a Bilingual Program" (unpublished Ed.D. dissertation,
University of Miami, 1968).

[12] Herbert W. Wey, *The Professional Preparation and Placement of Cuban Refugee
Teachers—1968 Annual Report* (Coral Gables, Fla.: University of Miami, 1968),
pp. 6–19.

Part 6

The Rural Poor
and America's
Undereducated Adult

Appalachia
Education in a Depressed Area

Franklin Parker

The dimensions of poverty in the United States received marked attention in the 1960s. Crucial inner-city problems were examined and alleviatory programs were started. But less was known about the great feeders of urban slums—the poor rural areas where automation had squeezed people out of farming, mining, and manufacturing. Migrating to the cities for work and finding themselves untrained and ill-suited for urban life, they swelled the ranks of the jobless and swamped the welfare rolls. Then came some understanding in the Presidential campaign of 1960 when John F. Kennedy's important West Virginia primary victory brought that state's poverty to his attention, and through wide media coverage the nation's attention focused on poverty in the wider Appalachian region.

Appalachia Discovered[1]

America discovered Appalachia—or rather rediscovered it, for it often has been exploited and as often forgotten—as a place apart, different from the rest of the nation. Almost one-tenth of the nation, some 18,000,000 people, live here in 397 counties (see map). The Appalachian mountain ranges cut through 13 states, from parts of New York in the North to sections of Alabama and Georgia in the South. This underdeveloped area of rugged topography has the nation's greatest concentration of deprived people. The region's approximately 175,000 square miles are frequently traversed by hilly ridges and twisting streams running through many valleys. It is up-and-

[1] For a general description see Thomas R. Ford, ed., *The Southern Appalachian Region: A Survey* (Lexington: University of Kentucky Press, 1967). See also *Appalachia Bibliography* (Morgantown: West Virginia University Library, 1968), 2 vols.

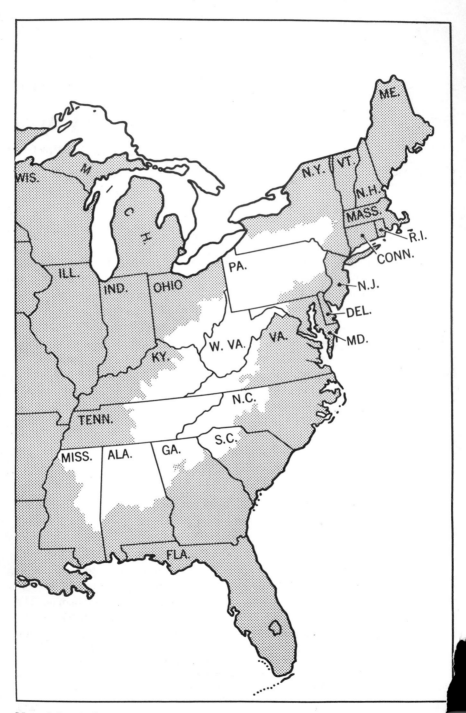

Map of Appalachia.

down hill-and-hollow country, sandwiched between the prosperous Atlantic seaboard and the industrial Midwest, with Atlanta's burgeoning business complex at its base. Because of lack of roads, long isolation, exploitation, and neglect, it has been overlooked and outdistanced by the rest of the country.

Unfulfilled Potential

Receiving as it does more rain than the national average, containing some of the nation's richest mineral deposits including two-thirds of the country's coal, having eye-filling mountain landscapes and three-fifths of its land richly forested—Appalachia ought to be a prosperous area. Yet locked into the diverse checkerboard pattern of its rural and urban subregions is a hard-core poverty that makes it the nation's most underdeveloped region. Rural Appalachia lags behind rural America and urban Appalachia lags behind urban America. As the 1960 census showed and the 1970 census sustained proportionately, Appalachia's people are underpaid, underemployed, under-educated, and undermotivated to change.

Income Gap[2]

In every category and by every measure Appalachia lags behind the rest of the nation. While 30.7% of its families annually earned $3000 or less, 20.5% of the rest of American families earned this amount. While 60.6% of its families earned from $3000 to $10,000, 63.9% of the rest of American families were in this income range. And while 8.7% of its families earned over $10,000, 15.6% or almost double this number of American families earned this amount.

[2] For income, education, and other statistics based on the 1960 census see Garth L. Mangum, "Manpower Development in Appalachian Regional Programs," in Frederick A. Zeller and Robert W. Miller, eds., *Manpower Development in Appalachia: An Approach to Unemployment* (New York: Frederick A. Praeger, 1968), pp. 45–61; and Carlton E. Beck, et al., eds., *West Virginia Youth in Crisis; Proceedings of the West Virginia Youth Awareness Conference Held at Mont Chateau Lodge, Morgantown, West Virginia, June 20–21, 1968* (Morgantown: West Virginia University, 1968). A 1966 survey showed that in some Appalachian school districts teachers' annual salaries were below $4000; see Appalachian Regional Commission, *Annual Report 1967* (Washington, D.C.: The Commission, 1968), p. 31. In 1968, West Virginia's average annual public school expenditure per child was $484 as compared with the national average of $623; elementary school teachers earned $5670 and secondary school teachers earned $5950 as compared with the national earnings of $7077 and $7569 respectively. In 1967 West Virginia's average annual income per capita was $2334 (ranking 46th among the 50 states) as compared with the national per capita income of $3159. See *Pocket Data Book USA 1969* (Washington, D.C.: Department of Commerce, Bureau of the Census, 1969).

The income gap is seen also in comparing the national per capita income of $1901 with Appalachia's per capita income of $1405, ranging from $1680 in western Pennsylvania counties to $841 in Kentucky counties lying within Appalachia. The unemployed constituted 7.1% of Appalachia's labor force as compared to about four percent in the rest of the United States. This job deficit would be even greater except that many unemployed former residents have gone elsewhere for jobs. Thus Appalachia's unemployed and underemployed are on welfare and, with nothing else to do, sit on rural front porches or crowd the streets of poor towns.

Education Gap

Appalachia has not produced enough educated people and lacks the tax base to provide adequate education. For every 100 persons over age 25, 11.6 persons in Appalachia had less than a fifth-grade education as compared to eight persons in the rest of the United States; 32.3 persons in Appalachia finished high school as compared to 41.8 persons in the rest of the United States; and 5.2 persons in Appalachia had four our more years of college as compared to 7.9 in the rest of the United States. Of the 10 states in the nation with the lowest percentage of 16- and 17-year-olds in school, eight were Appalachian states. While the national average salary for elementary and secondary school teachers was $6200, in Appalachia it was $4800. The national average school expenditure per pupil in 1961–1962 was $518, compared to $337 in Appalachia. While the national military rejection rate for mental reasons in 1964 was 27.6%, comparative figures in Appalachian states were 51% in North Carolina, 41% in Kentucky, and 36% in West Virginia. Most Appalachian states ranked below the national norms in National Merit Scholarship test scores.

In other categories—retail sales, bank savings, value and quality of housing—Appalachia has fallen behind the rest of the United States. The picture is one of poverty, a condition which has existed for several generations and is illustrated in federal food programs and other welfare assistance which in Appalachia are 45% above the rest of the nation. The result is a record of inefficiency, of lost hope, of the American dream unfulfilled, and of a region thwarted by historic neglect.

The Mountain People

Appalachia was settled mainly by poor immigrants from England, Scotland, Wales, and Ireland, many of them indentured servants who moved to the back country and the mountains. Finding the highland slopes and narrow valleys reminiscent of their ancestral lands, many of these independent people stayed where they were. Cherishing the freedom of their harsh environment, those who stayed and their descendants became the mountain people. Change came slowly, and the mountain people liked it that way. By mid-19th century, wrote Harry Caudill, the mountaineer had developed "as he is to an astonishing degree even to this day. . . . The illiterate son of illiterate ancestors, cast loose in an immense wilderness without basic mechanical or agricultural skills, without the refining, comforting and disciplining influence of an organized religious order, in a vast land wholly unrestrained by social organization or effective laws, compelled to acquire skills quickly in order to survive, and with a Stone Age savage as his principal teacher."[3]

What he gained in independence, he paid for in isolation, clannishness, superstition, and backwardness. His was a slower pace of change, and he fell behind the rest of the United States in growth of population, transportation, communication, roads, schools, and political sophistication.

Exploitation

First, the Appalachian forests were exploited by outside timber companies and large profit from that rich resource left the region. Not used to bargaining in a money economy, many a mountaineer sold great trees up to eight feet in diameter for less than a dollar apiece. He was often hired to cut his own logs at a low salary which seemed to him to be a fortune since it enabled him to buy factory-made goods he had never before owned. With the mere pittance he received he thought himself prosperous, and not until later did he realize that he had been cheated.

Then, coal became an important power fuel and the Appalachian coal mines attracted entrepreneurs from outside the region. The mountaineer often did not know he had coal on his land nor understand its worth. Often unable to read the contracts he signed, he unknowingly sold his land to the companies which bought up large tracts and whole valleys. Mining transformed mountain communities into coal camps and company towns. During World War I, the coal mines boomed and afterwards declined, causing many to lose their jobs. Union strife and the Depression put many on relief—half the populations in some areas. Coal boomed again during World War II and the Korean War. But automation, which came quickly to help coal compete with oil and gas, displaced two-thirds of the men.

3 Harry M. Caudill, *Night Comes to the Cumberlands: A Biography of a Depressed Area* (Boston: Little, Brown, 1963), p. 31; see also Jack E. Weller, *Yesterday's People: Life in Contemporary Appalachia* (Lexington: University of Kentucky Press, 1965).

The coal economy has been a boom and bust economy, which alternately has fed and starved, supported and let down its people. Large numbers found themselves without jobs or skills and with little education. After generations of disuse too many became physically and psychologically unemployable. Many left, but others with little experience of living outside the hills and no desire to leave the only homes they knew accepted welfare with few qualms.

Aside from some few flourishing cities and thriving coal communities, most of Appalachia is locked in poverty, the victim of exploitation and the inadequacy of a one-product economy. Appalachian poverty is self-perpetuating because the poorest communities are poorest in the services needed to eliminate it. Michael Harrington offered this gloomy estimate: "It seems likely that the Appalachians will continue going down, that its lovely mountains and hills will house a culture of poverty and despair, and that it will become a reservation for the old, the apathetic, and the misfits."[4]

Attitudes Toward Education

Resistance to book learning has been traditional among Appalachian people. Although parents now see increasingly the value of education for their children, traditional fear persists that it will separate children from their families and destroy the common level of the family and community reference group. Often the homes have few if any books and children needing help in homework find little encouragement. The adult Appalachian world is not one of ideas but of being and belonging. Dreary-lived mountaineers and miners seldom see much of the outside world with its mobility, complexity, aspirations, and careers. This localism is perpetuated by mountain-taught teachers, and by politically bound school systems where teachers are hired on a personal rather than a professional basis. Public education came late to Appalachia, has been overly inbred, and all too often has reflected narrow local interests and low aspirations. These long existing adverse conditions and backward attitudes put the region behind the rest of the nation until, in the 1960s, a new thrust emerged aimed at reversing Appalachia's downward trend.

Appalachian Regional Commission[5]

On May 8, 1960, a group of Appalachian governors met in Annapolis, Md., to seek a way out of the dilemma. They faced up to the sharp decline in coal

[4] Michael Harrington, *The Other America: Poverty in the United States* (New York: Macmillan, 1962), p. 43.

[5] See Appalachian Regional Commission, op. cit., *Annual Reports* for 1965, 1966, 1967, 1968, and 1969.

mining and agricultural employment, isolation caused by the terrain and poor roads, and the severe deficits in education, health, and other essential public facilities. They knew Appalachia to be rich in natural resources, with a large potential labor force needing training, and with possible communication routes to surrounding industrial centers. To develop this potential, they formed a Conference of Appalachian Governors and met with President John F. Kennedy at the White House in May, 1961. He recognized the need, directed the Area Redevelopment Administration to assist them, and at their request for a new state-federal agency, he established the President's Appalachian Regional Commission on April 9, 1963. Exactly a year later the Commission sent its report to President Lyndon B. Johnson, who packaged the proposals into a bill and signed it into law on March 9, 1965.

Thus was established the Appalachian Regional Commission (ARC), an ambitious new kind of independent state-federal agency. Because the Appalachian governors themselves initiated ARC, they have had a keen interest in supporting it. ARC has aimed at careful problem assessment and long-range program planning so that when funds became available they were put to use effectively in stipulated amounts according to plan.

ARC Development Strategy

ARC recognized Appalachia as an island in the midst of affluence which has been largely bypassed by national transportation routes. This bypassing reinforced early patterns of settlement which had dispersed Appalachia's millions into hollows and onto ridges in very many small communities and mining camps isolated from the mainstream of American economic growth. Interstate highway corridors to open Appalachia to national commerce and access roads for local people to get to jobs, schools, and hospitals became ARC's top priority. Rather than diffuse its limited resources on many communities, ARC identified established growth centers which had significant potential for future growth. Strengthening these growth centers became ARC's second priority. The third priority was to strike a balance of investment in education, health, and other services in order to live up the numerous surrounding rural areas.

Subregional Needs

ARC noted that Appalachia has four subregions, each with specific problems and strengths. Southern Appalachia (parts of Mississippi, Alabama, South Carolina, Tennessee, North Carolina, and Virginia) had moved from an agricultural economy to manufacturing and services; its prime need was high school and post-high school vocational education to provide skilled labor. Northern Appalachia (southern New York, Pennsylvania, Maryland, northern West Virginia, and southern Ohio) was in transition from a coal and steel economy to new manufacturing and services; its prime need was for post-high school and adult occupational training to aid in this transition. The Appalachian highlands (mountainous parts of Georgia, South Carolina, Tennessee, North Carolina, Kentucky, Virginia, West Virginia, Pennsylvania, and Maryland) were sparsely settled but rich in scenic beauty; its prime need was recreational development to attract tourists. Central Appalachia (eastern Kentucky, southern West Virginia, southwestern Virginia, and northern Tennessee) was made up of small communities with pronounced outmigration; its prime needs were growth centers, transportation, education, and health services.

ARC Program Allocations

ARC's federal fund authorization for highways was $1,015,000,000 for the six-year period, 1965–1971, and a nonhighway federal fund authorization was $420,000,000 for the four-year period, 1965–1969. Some indication of ARC's concerns can be seen from the types of programs listed in Chart 1.

ARC has received supplementary grants. From 1965 to 1968, ARC allocated $109,000,000 from these grants for programs listed in Chart 2.[6]

Some Criticism

ARC's priority funding for highway corridors and the extension of existing growth centers has been criticized as inadequate by some. They note that aid in these two categories will ultimately help already established business concerns and give rise to new business interests to benefit mainly outsiders and those relatively few enterprising people who are already successful. Such priorities will not effectively reach the poorer masses for some time, perhaps a decade, and even then may benefit them only to a limited extent. Critics point out that the highway building pace is necessarily slow and very costly, that it offers little or no immediate help to those in poverty, and that the same large funding might be used better for immediate educational and medical aid to the far greater number of smaller communities outside the growth centers. Critics also point out that once ARC was established and funded, political boondoggling inevitably took place when Congressmen from areas peripheral to Appalachia had their districts included in the program in order to benefit from the "money-for-Appalachia" appropriations.

[6] Charts 1 and 2 are from Appalachian Regional Commission, *Annual Report 1968,* op. cit., pp. 7 and 72.

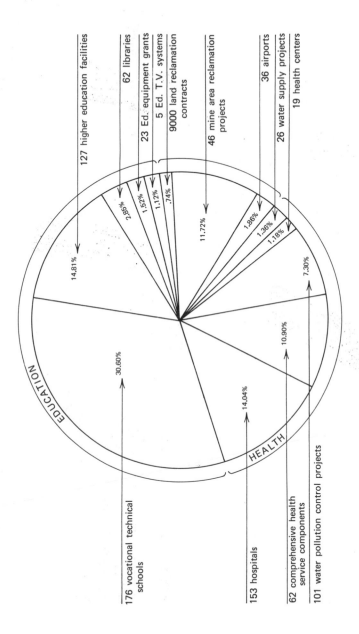

Chart 1. Appalachian Investments, 1965–1968 (includes all Appalachian programs except highways).

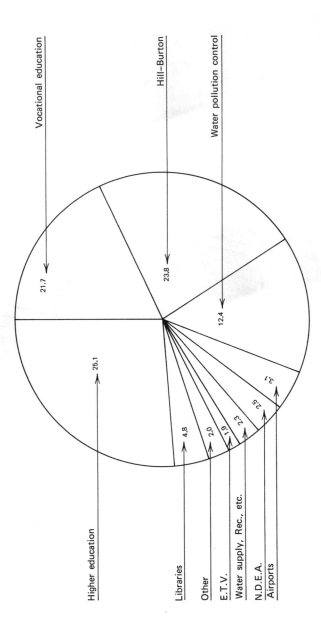

Chart 2. Section 214—Supplemental Grants (approvals by type of program), fiscal years 1965–1968. Total funds—$109,000,000.

ARC's Educational Assessment

On November 10, 1966, ARC established an Education Advisory Committee, currently chaired by Frank Rose, former president of the University of Alabama. An assessment by the committee uncovered these deficiencies in Appalachian education. The dropout rate between the first and the 12th grades averaged 65% and in some areas as high as 71%, compared with an estimated national average dropout rate of 36.2%.[7] The dropout rate is especially critical in rural schools. The Appalachian population is 52.7% rural compared to 30.1% for the nation. The retardation rate for youths in Appalachian schools is also higher than the national average. In 1960, those Appalachian youths in school between ages eight and 13 designated as educationally retarded included 11.2% of the farm youth, 11% of the nonfarm rural youth, and 6.9% of the urban youth. The dropout rate and the retardation problem are the result of sparse rural populations, geographic isolation, the low educational attainment of parents, and the meager tax base of most small communities. In two Appalachian states over 25% of the population is functionally illiterate. Some school districts with scattered settlements must spend over 50% of their budgets for transporting students between home and school. Nationally, out of every ten pupils in grade one, six will graduate from high school, 2+ will go to college, and 1+ will finish college. In Appalachia, out of every ten pupils in grade one, 4— will graduate from high school, 1+ will go to college, and fewer than one will finish college. Teacher turnover is high, 14.2% as compared to the national average of 8.2 percent. Some Appalachian states subsidize the education of their teachers up to $6000 for four years; by the end of their first four years of service, 65% of the younger teachers leave for higher pay outside the region.

One would expect Appalachia to be allocated a greater proportion of federal aid to education to offset the region's obvious shortcomings. But the opposite is true. Appalachia receives less than its pro rata share because of lack of knowledge of the availability of funds and of eligibility requirements as well as insufficient know-how in making out grant proposals.

ARC's Educational Priorities[8]

Recognizing that the high dropout rate was Appalachia's key educational deficiency, ARC's Education Advisory Committee set several priorities for

[7] It was reduced to about 55% in 1968 but was still about 30% higher than the national average. See speech by Frank Rose to the Educational Advisory Committee, December, 1969, in the files of the Appalachian Regional Commission, Washington, D.C.

[8] See Appalachian Regional Commission, *Preliminary Report of the Education Advisory Committee* (Washington, D.C.: The Commission, 1967) ; and Appalachian Regional

key investments. The first of these was early childhood education. The Commission found that as of 1967 fewer than 15% of the 600,000 Appalachian four-to-five year olds were enrolled in early childhood programs, mainly in Project Headstart funded by the Office of Economic Opportunity. While all of the Appalachian states except Alabama have legislation permitting kindergarten programs in local schools, only five states—Maryland, New York, Ohio, Pennsylvania, and Virginia—have funded such programs. Tennessee has had kindergarten demonstration programs but has not passed legislation for a state program of preschool education. Legislation introduced for such programs in Georgia, North Carolina, and West Virginia was defeated. In two other states the necessary legislation was passed but funds were insufficient to establish kindergartens in each school district.

A second Commission priority is to further career exploration and orientation programs in the upper elementary school and junior high school years. Chairman Rose expressed the rationale for this priority as follows: "Only if this is provided can our young people make rational and informed choices about their education and life needs. Only if this is done, can the intellectual snobbery of our schools which 'pushes out' many of its students be cured. Only if this is done, can the region's massive investment in training facilities be fully utilized and the region produce a labor force adapted to regional and national job demands. I might mention that 80% of today's jobs require less than a college degree, and the nation and region will founder in the future, not from a lack of college graduates, but from a lack of skilled technicians to support them."[9]

In connection with its third priority, job training in vocational high schools, the Commission made this assessment of Appalachia's needs in 1968. Over 60% of enrollment in high school programs leading to occupations was expected to provide workers in only 5% of the region's jobs in 1975. Almost half of the region's 1975 jobs are anticipated to be in trades and industries for which only 8% of the 1968 enrollees were being trained. Appalachia has 13% of the national enrollment in high school vocational education programs but receives only 7.3% of the federal funds available for such programs, indicating the greater effort which the Appalachian states are making to support vocational programs compared to the rest of the nation. Besides this federal fund imbalance, the educational appropriations by the Appalachian states are not well proportioned to prepare youths for future jobs. Also, unlike the national pattern of increasingly supporting postsecondary and adult vocational programs, Appalachia's vocational enrollment is focused on the high school level. Appalachian high schools account for 72% of the region's total

Commission, *Education Advisory Committee Interim Report* (Washington, D.C.: The Commission, 1968).

[9] Rose, loc. cit.

vocational enrollment, with relatively small enrollment in postsecondary and adult vocational programs. Another difficulty is that while Appalachian colleges and universities prepare teachers in vocational agriculture, home economics, and industrial arts, they do not prepare teachers for such modern occupations as auto mechanics and computer science.

Education Development Centers

To advance the three priorities of early childhood education, career information and work experience, and vocational training, ARC's Education Advisory Committee recommended in December, 1969, the establishment of education development centers. The first recommendation was to establish a Human Resources Council in each Appalachian state as a planning center where key education and welfare agency heads and planning officers would develop five-year programs on contract with the state governor's planning office. A second recommendation was to establish a model agency in each Appalachian state that would divide its resources on developing programs in the three priority areas (60%) and on cooperative purchasing of materials and services by district school systems (40%). It was hoped that each state's model agency would have a cooperating college or university for technical assistance and the training of needed educational manpower. A third recommendation was to establish one Appalachian Regional Agency to develop model career information and work experience programs. The final recommendation was to establish two Higher Education Centers to prepare teachers and paraprofessional aides needed to implement the three priorities and also to develop a college student exchange permitting non-Appalachian college students to work under supervision in Appalachia and Appalachian college students to gain experiences outside of Appalachia.

National Assessment[10]

One interesting question is about the value to Appalachia of national assessment, now being conducted under the auspices of the Education Commission of the States. A questionnaire on the subject was answered in 1969 by 29 Appalachian educators. One respondent felt that "We already know more about the difficulties in Appalachian education than we can correct. . . . The question is how to get the money and the manpower to overcome the problems." Said another: "National assessment should be one more indicator to plot just where we are in terms of a national scale. Surely this should help us

[10] *Appalachian Advance*, **3**: 6–9, April 1969.

assess our schools as against a larger norm. Too long have we compared our-selves with ourselves and find we come out pretty well in the comparison." In general, the respondents saw benefit in a better quantification of previous studies of educational deficiencies in Appalachia. Some believe that national assessment might result in a more equitable distribution to Appalachia of sorely needed federal funds. Perhaps even more important, it could make the Appalachian public and taxpayer more aware of local needs and thus more willing to support school bond levies and other revenue measures.

Appalachian Youth in Chicago Schools[11]

Some 40,000 Appalachian migrants live in a 120-block area of the Uptown section in Chicago. Of the population of Nicholas Senn High School, 29% are from Appalachia. How well do they perform in school? While there is no appreciable differences between their IQ's and those of city-born children, the Appalachian youngsters perform less well. They lack basic skills, especially in reading, and these deficiencies are compounded by constant moving and change of schools. In one Chicago school with a high Appalachian enrollment, 600 children moved in 1968, one-third to other parts of the city, one-third to other cities, and one-third back to Appalachia. Absenteeism is at least 10% higher than it is for the average Chicago student. Most of the Appalachian children, says a principal, "are woefully unhappy here." Counselors attribute their lack of participation in school activities (except for mountain music) to a feeling of insecurity. In Chicago's work-study programs and vocational schools, writes a school principal, "After we get a lot of these Appalachian children into a job, they can't keep it. Employers blame their slovenly habits and attitudes. The kids just don't see the importance of being neat on the job and for being on time." He added that while there is little hostility shown by other students and teachers, mountain children are sensitive to aspersions regarding their background and speech peculiarities. He concluded, "The Negro after years of being a second class citizen has come to the point where he is saying and believing it's good to be black. This is the attitude the Ap-palachian should have of himself."

Help for the Hollows

Some private institutions and agencies have labored long to uplift Appa-lachia. A notable effort has been that of Berea College near Lexington, Ky.

---

[11] "The Appalachian Child in Chicago Schools," *Appalachian Advance*, **3**: 6–13, Octo-ber 1968.

Founded in 1855 by John G. Fee, a northern abolitionist, Berea College has increasingly extended its resources toward mountain youth as a multiracial, religious (but nondenominational), work-study school. Soon after the Civil War other schools and colleges were established, aided largely by missionary efforts, and brought Appalachian needs and problems to the attention of northern and western church groups. Notable, too, is the Council of the Southern Mountains in Berea, Ky., founded in 1913 by John C. Campbell to help mountain people help themselves.

Other than through the Department of Agriculture's Extension Service, the federal government, which depended on young Appalachian men in time of war, did little for the region until the founding of such Depression-inspired agencies as the Civilian Conservation Corps, the Works Progress Administration, and the Tennessee Valley Authority. Recent federal assistance has been provided under such legislation as the Manpower Development and Training Act, the Economic Opportunity Act, and the Appalachian Regional Development Act. Also noteworthy in its experimental enrichment programs is the work of the Appalachian Educational Laboratory in Charleston, W. Va., funded along with other such laboratories under Title IV of the Elementary and Secondary Education Act of 1965. Appalachia is fertile ground for the multiplicity of programs now operable, such as the Job Corps, Volunteers in Service to America, and Community Action Programs.

While it is too soon to evaluate properly the efforts to improve Appalachia, critics are not sanguine about the results so far. Some believe that crash programs are often mounted on problems that do not lend themselves to crash solutions and that when results are disappointing the programs are abandoned. Too often there is disunity, duplication, and delay, as cited by one writer about the Appalachian Regional Commission and the Office of Economic Opportunity: "They are both spending millions in the same hollows and small towns of Appalachia. Yet they barely speak to each other."[12] Adds another writer, citing vested outside interests: "If Appalachia hasn't changed, it may be in part because too many are dependent on it as it now is."[13] The late Perley F. Ayer, a dedicated chairman of the Council of the Southern Mountains, may have been right when he said sadly that the reason help has never really come to the hollows is because "America doesn't have its heart in it."

[12] *Louisville Courier Journal*, July 28, 1968.

[13] Peter Schrag, "Appalachia: Again the Forgotten Land," *Saturday Review*, **51**: 14–18, January 27, 1968.

Education for the Migrant and Other Deprived Children in Rural Schools

Kenneth T. Henson

Are equal educational opportunities provided for children in our rural schools today? It is generally recognized that, in this country, public schools were established to provide for all people, yet it also is obvious that these same schools have catered toward the needs and desires of middle-class people —the children of families with average income and common social backgrounds.

During the developmental period of the public schools in this country, each child had similar educational advantages and disadvantages. Most rural children were farmers' children. A lack of adequate transportation forced each child to attend a school within walking distance from his home. Although this distance frequently extended for a few miles, the community was not compact and a family located several miles from the school was considered to be in residence in the community.

Today, some of the children in rural schools are hundreds of miles from home—in a setting which is completely foreign and different from their native culture. They may face two or more of these unfamiliar situations during the school year.

Other pupils who have resided in the community since birth are so poverty-stricken that they find the school atmosphere equally strange and different from their home environment. Ironically, most of these children are of farming families—those for whom the schools were developed.

AUTHOR'S NOTE: The writer served as research assistant and curriculum consultant to *The Survey to Identify Children of Migrant Workers and Certain Former Migrant Workers in Alabama*, 1969. The project was concerned with the educational needs of migrant children in Alabama.

These children of migrant farmers and poor resident farmers share similar problems which decelerate and actually limit their educational growth. Many of these problems are obvious to rural teachers; some are not. In either instance, most problems, since they are shared by less than a majority of the student body, are generally not provided for by the schools. The following pages are an attempt to identify some of the most critical problems and suggest some possible solutions.

The Migrant Child

Children who continually move from school to school, as their parents follow their jobs, experience educational needs which often are not provided for by the schools. Recent concern for these children has resulted in the development of special education programs. Most programs have been developed at the state level. Some of the leading states in this effort are California, Arizona, Texas, New York, Florida, and Indiana.

By definition, migrant children, regardless of ethnic origin, share needs which are unique to migrants throughout the nation. Their school year is shorter than that of the resident student, because they usually arrive at school two or three weeks after the school year has begun and they usually leave school in the spring before the regular school year is over, spending a few weeks in transit. Furthermore, their higher rate of absenteeism reduces the amount of time spent in school. Many school days are sacrificed to work in the fields or to attend to younger family members, freeing both parents to engage in their occupation. Therefore, one of the more obvious educational needs of migrant children is more time for education.

Each time a family moves, the children are forced to transfer from one school to another. The curriculum for each individual is disrupted. The student experiences some parts of the curriculum two or more times; other parts are completely omitted. The continuity is destroyed and, therefore, much of the understanding which depends on the continuous development of the learning process never is developed adequately. These disadvantages are obvious and they help to explain the below-average performance level of many migrant children; however, other damaging effects develop which are not so obvious and yet are perhaps more detrimental to the educational development of a child.

Prolonged exposure to experiences such as those discussed can affect permanently the character of the child. For example, because a child operating under these limitations frequently performs less adequately than the resident pupils, and because migrant children are usually fewer in number than their resident counterparts, they often are perceived as "poor" students. Since success in the school setting usually depends on one's ability to compete with others, the migrant child often learns to perceive himself in this image. Once the child develops this attitude toward himself, learning becomes almost impossible.

The child who sees himself as a failure in the school setting is not likely to possess positive feelings toward school. The migrant child is certainly no exception, for there even are other factors which contribute to his negative feelings toward school. For example, the migrant family often has little regard for schools and education. The parents' level of formal education is usually very low. The family income depends not on education, but on manual labor; therefore, the value of education is less obvious to these people.

Although the migrant travels extensively, he does not experience many of the benefits commonly derived from travel. Migrants commonly travel in groups, and they must emphasize economy.

The closeness of the group is maintained after the destination is reached. The migrants settle together—isolated from the resident population. Little contact is made with the resident community and, therefore, few experiences are shared with the people of the different areas. Often the migrant does not speak the language of the surrounding community. Also, the migrant's economy is altogether different from that of the residents. His economy is based on cash transaction only. His lack of close association with any of the various cultures would prevent the establishment of a credit basis. His low economic status further precludes extensive association with the community.

All of these disadvantages make the migrant a truly deprived person. The child often does not achieve in school because of an accumulation of these preventative circumstances; he decides that he is not capable of learning, and rationalizes by accepting the idea that education is really not necessary.

An obvious purpose of our schools is to provide for the educational needs of the children. Our curricula supposedly have been designed toward this end. Obviously, the curriculum plan undergoes continuous modification. Each time a need develops, the curriculum must be adjusted to satisfy it. What specific changes are needed to provide for the needs of migrant students?

To prevent the migrant student from associating with the resident students would deprive him of the advantages of intercultural experiences; yet, to force the migrant into a competitive classroom with the resident students will contribute to all of his negative attitudes toward the school. Perhaps the most effective alternative is to develop special classes for the migrant in those areas in which he is most incompetent, leaving him in the general integrated classes throughout the major part of each day. As he removes his deficiencies and develops the necessary skills, he gradually can be transferred to the general program.

The concept of competition among students should be abolished. Each migrant student should compete only with himself. Grades should be determined by individual progress, based only on the migrant student's own performance.

Each teacher of migrant children should be selected according to his ability to relate to children and his desire to help low-achievers. He must be able to restore lost self-confidence and create confidence where it never before has existed.

The teaching of migrant children requires patience. Progress is always slow with low-achieving individuals, and it is especially slow with children who do not recognize their abilities. The migrant child needs encouragement. He must be rewarded for each successful endeavor. Furthermore, he must be taught to accept a certain degree of failure and to learn from his failing experiences.

The attitude of the resident students toward the migrant student often is very damaging to him. This is not necessary. The resident student should be taught to understand and accept the difference in the two cultures.

Class discussions should be devoted to increasing understanding of the resident students toward the "unique" migrant. The importance of the migrant worker to the economy should be explained. The study of the historical and cultural background of the migrants could assist in the development of understanding toward them.

The migrant students also should learn to understand the resident pupils and to adjust to the school climate. An orientation period in which each migrant child is assigned a "buddy" to introduce him to other resident students can be helpful. Field trips which take the migrant child into the community can help him develop a needed sense of belonging.

Any educational program for migrant students faces all of these problems. Before the decision is made to develop a program in a community which has migrant students, the institution and the financing agency should answer "yes" to each of the following questions: Does this institution have teachers qualified for this task? If so, do these teachers want to participate in a migrant program? Is adequate space available for additional classes for teaching the needed skills and will materials and equipment necessary for teaching the low-achiever be made available? Will inservice training be provided for teachers, including competent consultants who can explain the special needs of the migrant child, and will energy be devoted to evaluate continually the progress of this program?

The Resident Child

The recent development of several educational programs has shown that educators realize that many of our educational materials have been developed to meet the needs of the middle-class student. New materials adjusted to the standards of less fortunate children have assisted some schools in coping with this problem. However, many of these programs have been limited to densely populated urban areas. Others have been limited to specific ethnic groups.

Poverty is not limited to either race or geographic area. Each rural school is responsible for providing for the needs of students residing in the community, some of whose living standards are so different, so far behind those of the majority of the community residents, that the school climate is alien to these children.

Children from poor farming families, both black and white, are so unfamiliar with many school materials that they can benefit little or not at all from them. Recently developed basic reading programs have assisted by providing special materials and specially trained teachers to correct reading problems which are common among lower-class students. Teachers in each discipline can assist these efforts by using a variety of reading materials. The textbook should not be the major curriculum determinant. The text, if used at all, should be heavily supplemented with newspapers, magazines, and materials developed by the students—each of which is more meaningful to the students. A high degree of student activity, both oral and physical, is needed among these students.

The poverty-stricken resident student often is forced to compete with middle-class children who perform higher on academic examinations because the content is based on middle-class values. Frequently, the poorer student has not had the previous experiences required to perform at the level of his contemporaries. The less fortunate farm children still are required occasionally to sacrifice school days to work in the fields. Because of the typically low level of formal education of the parents and the long working day, little help is given at home with school work and often little encouragement is provided to produce continuing success in school work.

The final responsibility for providing an atmosphere in which each student can progress belongs to the classroom teacher. Each teacher must learn to be patient with these students and tolerate a below-average rate of progress. He must show concern for each student in his class and express recognition for his efforts, rather than disgust or dissatisfaction with his failures.

The teacher of slow achievers must remember that academic progress, as measured by the schools, is always comparative. A small accomplishment by the slow achiever can be a tremendous breakthrough for that child. The degree of success is not as important as the fact that a child succeeds rather than fails. This is equally true in all schools, whether they be rural or otherwise. The teacher must search continually for new experiences which will make success possible for each child. Once the child really begins to grow, more attention can be given to the rate of growth and the degree of success experienced.

Finally, the school, the community, and the child, himself, must remember that academic growth is not the only responsibility of the schools. The teachers must emphasize continually the importance of acceptable moral and social behavior. In essence, the teacher should strive for one over-all objective —to provide a situation which will encourage and enable the less fortunate children to move gradually into a self-sustaining role in society.

31

Rural Education
and the Disadvantaged Child

Robert L. Bailey

That there are large differences in individual incomes in every community is too well known to need proof. It is not as well known, however, that there are very substantial differences in per capita personal income between different states in the United States and, in particular, that there are significant differences between urban and rural families. It is the broad social and educational problem associated with these differences in an individual state and a particular rural region that falls within the province of this chapter. Such economic differences between regions and racial groups tend to differentiate the way in which people live and to determine to a significant degree the expenditures on a community function such as education.

The 994 school districts in Oklahoma had a total enrollment of 598,400 students in the fall of 1966.[1] Of this total enrollment, over 65% lived in the urban area, which includes an estimated 100 school districts. This left only 109,440 students spread among the other 894 rural school districts. In 1965, Oklahoma ranked 36th among all the states in per capita personal income, with an average of $2289.[2] Because of this low economic ability level of the population outside the urban areas, coupled with low student population as compared with the urban school population, the education potential is one of general disadvantage.

Much of the school population in rural Oklahoma has ethnic group representation. The first Oklahoma district to desegregate—Poteau—acted voluntarily on June 7, 1955.[3] In 1966–1967, all districts were in federal compli-

---

[1] National Education Association, *Estimates of School Statistics, 1966–1967* (Washington, D.C.: National Education Association, 1966), p. 23.

[2] National Education Association, *Ranking of the States, 1967* (Washington, D.C.: National Education Association, 1967), p. 35.

[3] Southern Education Reporting Service, *Statistical Summary* (Nashville, Tenn.: Southern Education Reporting Service, 1967), p. 26.

ance: one under court order, 92 by signing HEW 441B, and all others under HEW 441. Unfortunately, in the rural areas, more than 400 Negro teachers have lost their jobs over the last 11-year period.[4] While the financial situation of the rural school has supported the elimination of the dual school system, it has not provided the rural student with the advantages of multiethnic teachers. Too often, the rural student has to attend a school with a single self-contained class at each grade level and almost no opportunities to select electives in science, mathematics, and foreign languages.

No doubt, the rural Oklahoma school makes a disadvantaged child out of its student, but there is presently an effort to counteract this trend. The people of the Wewoka rural school district have decided to do something about their problem of the disadvantaged child.

Team teaching, central area schools, and complete school integration are becoming realities in the Wewoka schools. The self-contained classrooms at the elementary level, the neighborhood schools, and racial segregation are being replaced. These advances are the result of preplanning and participation by the patrons of the Wewoka School District, the faculty and administration of the Wewoka schools, and the Consultative Center of the Southwest Center for Human Relations, University of Oklahoma.

Three things motivated the administrative authorities toward this program. First, the administration knew that the elementary school buildings needed replacement. The three buildings were built in the 1920s and were showing definite signs of deterioration. After consulting with their architects, the Board of Education decided that constructing one building to house all elementary children would be most efficient. Second, the Wewoka School District already had desegregated the schools at the junior and senior high levels in 1960. With a new central area elementary school, the school district would achieve complete desegregation of both the students and faculty in full compliance with Title IV of the Civil Rights Act of 1964. Third, the faculty, seeking a way to make most effective use of their special skills, felt that varied grouping would improve the quality of education for each student. Team teaching seemed a sound way to correct some of the inherent deficiencies in the traditional self-contained classroom.

With the need realized and the plan and cost calculated, the Wewoka Board of Education decided on September, 1967, as the tentative date of operation. The first move came early in the spring of 1966. The Wewoka citizens voted $312,000 in school district bonds to construct one building for all the elementary grades in the Wewoka system. The flexible floor plan of this new building was designed to allow for various types of groupings, not

---

[4] Commission on Professional Rights and Responsibilities, *Task Force Survey of Teacher Displacement in Seventeen States* (Washington: National Education Association, 1965), p. 35.

merely the self-contained classroom. With the building scheduled for completion in the summer of 1967, the next logical step was to prepare members of the professional staff for their new role of helping the disadvantaged child. The building schedule allowed the administration and elementary teacher one full school year for in-service preparation.

The ethnic student population of the Wewoka district is 25% Negro, 5% Indian, and the remainder Caucasian. About 25% of the elementary school staff is Negro. Each grade level had four groups of students, except for kindergarten, which had two day-time sessions. Despite the handicap of still being in the three separate buildings, one with predominately Negro staff and students, the following plan was set in motion. The kindergarten completely desegregated its students, and a team of one Caucasian and one Negro formed this group. One three-room wing of the elementary school was arranged as to allow for temporary team-teaching groupings. Three out of the four elementary first-grade classes were grouped in this wing. One-third of this group was Negro. The first-grade teaching team was composed of one Negro and two Caucasians. With this accomplished, complete integration and team teaching was possible. But even so, nothing noticeable was accomplished until an in-service training program in team teaching was provided.

The Wewoka administration asked the Consultative Center, University of Oklahoma, to participate in an in-service team-teaching program. A team with experience in the team-teaching process was formed, including Robert Bailey, staff coordinator, Consultative Center; Robert Ohm, Education Department; Bettye Jewel, chairman, Intermediate Division Laboratory School; Edith Steanson, chairman, Primary Division Laboratory School; and James Elliott, Bartlesville elementary school.

In-service training sessions were divided into three segments. The fall segment provided for three separate meetings of two hours each in three successive weeks. The objectives of these sessions were general familiarization with team teaching and working with disadvantaged students, organization of the Wewoka faculty into working units, and completing a successful simulated example of team teaching.

The initial presentation was one of orientation. It dealt with the rationale and concept of team teaching. It explained the various types of team teaching and the various levels on which it might be accomplished. Much time was left for questions and answers so that the teachers might rid themselves of apprehensions and misunderstandings. At the same time, all elementary teachers were divided into seven different teams according to grade levels (K–6). Each team normally had four members, one Negro and three Caucasians. No leaders were chosen, and no assignments were made at that time.

The second session considered the composition and individual skills of each team. Student and ability grouping was discussed. In the last part of the session, individual meetings of the teams were held and previously mentioned subjects examined.

In the third session, a specific example of a successful teaching situation was presented. The example used was not to be taken as a perfect plan for the Wewoka situation. Afterwards, the individual teams were asked to group their reading students according to different ability levels. In addition, each group was asked to consider an adequate method of teaching reading skills and to seek alternate or additional methods which might be possible with these new considerations: composite and individual skills of the teaching team; the knowledge which was then available or could be obtained about the students in the classes; and the flexibility in organization possible in the new building. The teams were to meet and discuss these items and two of the seven teams were to give an oral presentation at session four.

At the fourth session, presentations were given by two of the teams. The first team already was trying out team teaching and had had a chance to test their ideas. The second presentation was more theoretical, because this team had not had an opportunity yet to do any team teaching. General consensus was that team teaching took more time and effort, but that the greater flexibility and individual attention given the students through team teaching was worth the effort.

The fifth session was devoted to a panel presentation on the human relations aspects of complete staff and student integration and working with the disadvantaged child. The topics considered were prejudice and its manifestations, the equality of opportunity concept, use of multiracial materials, and the grouping of minority and low socioeconomic students.

At the sixth session, the individual teams met to structure the planning for the time between this session and the beginning of school in the fall. Items covered were goal setting, time schedule, and directional patterns within the individual teams and as a group. Each team selected a recorder and was given an additional assignment for planning a late spring session which would be attended by the Consultative Center team.

The scope of the plan and the methods used by the school administration must be considered a pioneer effort in the Southwest region. This is an area where, until recently, the dual school system existed. The success of the Wewoka program will encourage more rural school districts to include in their planning and programs the minority and disadvantaged student problems.

32

The Undereducated Adult

Leonard Nadler

At the turn of the century, the adult in the United States who could not read or write might still be upwardly mobile and could achieve economic success. In our world of today, the inability to read and write makes one a disadvantaged person. Without the ability to engage in communication with the society which surrounds him, the undereducated adult cannot possibly avail himself of the advantages of our affluent society.

A factor which contributes to our lack of success in helping the undereducated adult is the proliferation of words we have amassed in our attempts to describe this group. Just what is an "undereducated adult"? How is he different from an "adult illiterate"? And how does "functional illiterate" relate to "adult basic education"? In essence, all these terms represent overlapping dimensions as we struggle to sort out the problem in our efforts to work towards a viable solution.

Some base line might be provided by using the definition suggested for functional illiterates: "Persons who have less than eight years of formal schooling [who therefore] lack, by and large, the background for effective performance as employees and citizens."[1]

Substantially, this same definition now is being used when working with the term, "Adult Basic Education." One report defines A.B.E. as "instruction for those adults whose educational attainment is below the eighth grade. Their inability to speak, read, or write the English language constitutes a substantial impairment to getting or retaining employment commensurate with overall capability."[2]

[1] *Poverty in the United States*, Report of the Committee on Education and Labor, House of Representatives, 88th Congress, Second Session (Washington: U.S. Government Printing Office, 1964), p. 216.

[2] *Abstract of a Conceptual Model of an Adult Basic Education Evaluation System*, produced for the Adult Education Branch, U.S. Office of Education, by Management Technology Inc., June 1967, p. 23.

In most definitions, at least two components are included. One is the level of education attainment, usually either prior to dropping out of school, or as measured in subsequent tests. A second element is employability. Linking the two, we find that lack of at least an eighth-grade education is a severe disadvantage on the labor market. However, the reader should be cautious about overgeneralizing from this. Education is certainly not the only factor affecting low employability.

To explore the problem further, it is helpful to have some understanding of people involved. For a long time we have prided ourselves on the accomplishments of our educational system, and well we might. However, with our success we have been producing some citizens with a failure experience in education.

According to the 1960 census, there were 22,000,000 persons over the age of 25 who had completed less than eight years of schooling. This is a staggering blow to our educational ego. Yet, since the census of 1960, there are other adjustments which must be considered and all of them tend to increase the number of adults without sufficient education.

The cutoff point of 25 years of age in the census figures is an arbitrary line. Obviously, the figure of 22,000,000 adult illiterates will climb considerably when we lower the description of adult from 25 years of age to 18 years of age. Additionally, the impact of the rising birth rate in the late 1940s will tend to raise the figure. There is also recent evidence that some population statistics may be understated in that adult male minorities (principally Negroes) are not represented adequately in the statistics. It may be assumed that such adult males would swell the illiterate population.

What happens to an adult who is illiterate? Is there any doubt that he is disadvantaged? One report notes that "The close relationship between low levels of educational attainment and high unemployment is well known and has been demonstrated in numerous studies. Less generally known is the substantial impact that inadequate education has on reduced labor force participation. While the correlation between limited education and low levels of utilization are not perfect, it is clear that the most educated are most fully utilized, and those with the least education suffer from the highest unemployment and participate least in the job market."[3]

The disadvantaged adult also must face the problem of not being able to participate in the noneconomic aspects of our society. His political life is extremely limited and he has no appreciation of how to use the machinery of democracy to improve his situation. Is it any surprise that he takes to the streets and engages in other behavior which is commonly termed antisocial?

Meanwhile, all around him, the affluent society is growing. The gap be-

---

[3] *Unused Manpower: The Nation's Loss*, Manpower Research Bulletin Number 10, September 1966 (Washington: U.S. Government Printing Office, 1966), p. 17.

comes wider. In previous generations, mobility across a much narrower gap always was a possibility. Even today, it is not beyond the reach of most. But more and more the bridge across the gap is education. Still, we should not be lulled into a false sense of importance. Education alone cannot do the job. The holding power of the school is not exclusively a function of education. The National Manpower Council has said that, "when there is little evidence that further education or training will lead to promotion, permit free job mobility, or result in social acceptance, immediate earnings . . . may seem preferable to another year or two in school."[4]

As educators, however, we must look to those activities that we can effect and which can approach the problem of adult illiteracy in the United States at this time. While concentrating in our own areas, we should not be blind to what others are doing. The problem is much too large for any one group to be able to meet the need without reliance on others.

The Economic Opportunity Act of 1964 was an attempt to coordinate the varied efforts of our government in trying to meet a myriad of problems, and chief among them was adult illiteracy. An analysis of the original Act rapidly will disclose that most of its various titles were designed to focus on adult illiteracy and employability. Particularly, if the concept of adult is changed to include youth over 16 years of age who are permanently out of school, then the massive Job Corps effort certainly becomes part of the movement to eradicate adult illiteracy.

Today, the number of pieces of federal legislation focusing on individual and environmental problems is reproduced in a telephone-booklike document. It lists 459 different programs concerned with the overall problem and of these there are 17 which directly are related to adult illiteracy.[5] A more detailed reading of this valuable volume will disclose many other programs which relate to other adult training and education programs which could likewise have implications for adult illiteracy.

Up to this point, we have not mentioned any of the nongovernmental activities in this area. Educators sometimes are too prone to think of education as only existing within our school buildings. There is a great deal going on outside, particularly in the realm of adult education.

There are many voluntary agencies which are involved in some aspects of combatting adult illiteracy, and not the least of these are our religious institutions. Many corporations also are providing for the upgrading of the literacy

[4] Henry David, *Manpower Policies for a Democratic Society* (New York: Columbia University Press, 1965), p. 63.

[5] *Catalog of Federal Assistance Programs*, a description of the Federal Government's domestic assistance programs to assist the American people in furthering their social and economic progress. Produced by the Office of Economic Opportunity (Washington: U.S. Government Printing Office, 1967), pp. 42–43.

skills of their employees. The emerging concept of social responsibility among our business organizations has not been given sufficient attention. Labor unions are devoting some of their resources to reduce the illiteracy rate.

Even some of the efforts conducted within our traditional educational framework do not find their way into the statistics. Little is said of the teacher who coached the parents of her pupils, as well as the pupils. In the Head Start program, it has been found that although the primary focus is on children, there is a valuable by-product in the interest of the parents to improve their own education. "Parents involvement" has become a significant part of the Head Start program.

Statistically, there is woefully little to report. From its inception in early 1965 until June, 1967, the Adult Basic Education activities of the Office of Education only have touched some 500,000 persons. The Job Corps program has not involved more than about 103,000 young adults. Statistics on related programs are likewise pitifully small when compared to the millions of adult illiterates who we counted in 1960 and those who have been produced by our society since then.

Problems have plagued our efforts to combat adult illiteracy effectively. Some have been of our own making as we approached the problem in a Quixotic posture. Adult illiteracy was not born in one generation. It has been with us for a long time. The attack on the problem has proceeded as if the rapid injection of funds and good intentions would be sufficient.

Some of our earlier mistakes have been partially remedied. For example, the initial legislation on A.B.E. did not provide funds rapidly enough for teacher-training. The Ford Foundation came forward and funded three training institutes in the summer of 1965.[6] In subsequent summers, federal funds were provided and additional institutes were conducted. These institutes are highly controversial in their method of organization and execution. The preoccupation of the organizers of the institutes with hardware becomes apparent in their preliminary evaluation report in which they state: "The participants generally agreed (74%) that instructors used or demonstrated educational technology as often as was appropriate for their presentations. However, over one-half of the participants reported that most of the instructors did not utilize any *equipment media*" (emphasis mine).[7] The development of teachers in A.B.E. is crucial and it may presently be concentrated in the hands

[6] One product of these institutes is now available in *A Guide for Teacher Trainers in Adult Basic Education*, published in Washington by the National Association for Public School Adult Education.

[7] *Abstract of the Evaluation Report, National Adult Basic Education Teacher Training Program, Summer 1966*, prepared under a grant from Adult Education Branch, Division of Adult Education Programs, U.S. Office of Education, by the National University Extension Association, November 1967, p. 8.

of too few individuals who do not represent the forces in the adult education community who should be involved.

There are other aspects of the A.B.E. program which are to be applauded for the imagination and innovativeness displayed. The A.B.E. operation in the Office of Education has encouraged special projects covering a wide range of activities.[8] In Washington, D.C., a program under the United Planning Organization is concentrating on the linkage between the Neighborhood Youth Corps program and the job market. In this program, the youth are being paid to learn. This is in contrast to the Opportunities Industrialization Center in Philadelphia. Under that program, funded by the Office of Economic Opportunity, no pay is given for training. The Rev. Leon Sullivan, the dynamic innovator and director of this project, has said that "I want to be sure the people are not going to train just so they can get $40 or $70 a week."[9] Both Rev. Sullivan and the UPO may be correct in their divergent approaches as we lack adequate data regarding the most effective techniques of reaching the adult illiterate.

The support of the OIC by the Office of Education is not in its job training aspects but in another of its programs under the title of "Adult Armchair Education Program," which provides for small groups of undereducated adults to gather informally in neighborhood homes for basic instruction. There are currently 21 such groups functioning in Philadelphia. This has promise of being an exciting adult basic education program involving several elements of the community.

The reports of special projects goes far beyond those cited here and may prove to be one of the more effective uses of federal funds and influences in combatting adult illiteracy. It is regrettable that all the work done at this time does not yet give a feeling of being on the road to success. The directions are far from clear and merely providing additional funds is not sufficient if we are to make an impact on the eradication of illiteracy in the United States at this time.

There have been some unique successes, and we should be endeavoring to build on these. We have to find ways of unchaining ourselves from the past but not at the price of charging over a precipice. Experimentation and innovation are important, but these elements alone cannot insure any modicum of success. The remainder of this essay will try to identify some areas which can contribute to reducing, if not eliminating, the problem.

Authorizing legislation by Congress and the states can go far to legitimizing the goals involved in A.B.E. For example, we need legislation which will

[8] The examples cited here are from Progress Report No. 3, Compilation of Reports submitted by Special Projects Directors. This duplicated paper was provided to the author by the U.S. Office of Education.

[9] "Teaching People to Hold Jobs," *U.S. News and World Report*, January 1, 1968, p. 59.

provide a high school education as a minimum for all adults in the U.S. A bill to this effect was introduced by Sen. Hartke in the 90th Congress (First Session), but was defeated. Hopefully, such a bill will become the law of the land if we are to proceed further.

After the authorization, our legislatures still must pass the necessary appropriations. At the present time we have several examples (e.g., Teachers Corps., International Education) of authorization without the necessary appropriation. Money alone will not solve the problem. Without sufficient funding, good intentions will not suffice.

Adult illiteracy is a result, not a cause. It is the result of many influences in our society, but the one which is easiest to identify is the dropout from the regular school system. Most of the illiterate adults did not complete the full cycle of education which is presumably available to them. Reducing school dropouts will not lessen the present problem of the more than 25,000,000 functionally illiterate adults. It will reduce the pressure, however, by slowing the flow of illiterates (i.e., dropouts) and allowing us to concentrate on those we now have.

The problem of school dropouts is outside the purview of this essay. However, there is a project currently in operation wherein we find adult education impacting on the problem of secondary school dropouts. This is an interesting phenomenon in which several cities are involved, but it does not appear to have aroused sufficiently the educational community.

The work being done in the Job Corps, with the young adult who has dropped out of school, can be expected to be significant. The annual per pupil expenditure is about 10 times higher than the national average, and maybe it must be if we are to produce high impact. But, if the Job Corps is successful, where the traditional school system has not been, should we therefore criticize and tear down the school system? Would it not be more meaningful to take the results of the work in the Job Corps and integrate it into our school systems which so desperately need inputs but cannot afford the cost of experimentation. Actually, this is what is being done under Project Interchange.[10] Teachers from school systems producing large numbers of dropouts are working for a year in Job Corps camps. At the end of this period, the teachers return to their school systems and try to share the newer experiences of the Job Corps with their respective school systems. It is still too soon to relate much in terms of specific changes. But the channel is open, and this approach is reducing the gap between experimentation and utilization. Hopefully, it will have some influence on practices which have produced

---

[10] This Project is administered by the Adult Education Services of the NEA under contract with the Office of Economic Opportunity. For 1967–1968, the administrator was Carl Minich, who was on leave from his position as Director of Adult Education for the Amherst (New York) Public School System.

dropouts, and thereby we may see a reduction in the number of dropouts and potential adult illiterates.

Teaching adults is unlike other forms of educational endeavors in a myriad of ways. To apply traditional norms and certification would be deadly. However, this does not relieve us of the responsibility for a carefully developed and multifaceted plan to upgrade the quality of educational leadership available to the adult illiterate.

Experience has shown that there are few teachers of adults who start out with adult education as a career. Indeed, the teaching of the illiterate adult is still mainly a part-time function and can be expected to remain so for the foreseeable future. Therefore, pre-service education of teachers of adults would not return the investment which might be required.

Emphasis on in-service education requires more than the traditional concern. Public school education has not been strong in in-service education except where it has been related to increments or retentions of certification. In-service education for adult educators has a completely different focus. There is much similarity and precedent in the work that has been done by government and industry in providing in-service education for its employees. We need to gain from the experience of those who have been engaged in in-service education outside of the public school arena. It is not being suggested that we turn this function over to those outside forces, but the tendency is to ignore them and to enlist their aid in using the vast storehouse of experience and materials which already exists.

Our activities in teacher training have extended from the Laubach "each one teach one" to the highly formalized summer institutes. We have little research and not very much pooled experience to indicate how best we can provide adequate in-service training for teachers of illiterate adults. Part of this stems from our confusion as to who should be the teachers and our attempts to provide a common training experience for all of them. There is a vast difference between the day school teacher who is supplementing her pay by teaching illiterate adults at night, and the volunteer who is doing the job to meet some commendable ego needs. Flexibility is necessary if we are to adequately develop and utilize our instructional human resources.

The problem of what to do with educational technology is obviously not one exclusively in the area of adult education. There are few reliable educators who would suggest we ignore the newer developments, but there is a resentment born of harassment. As cited earlier, there are those who evaluate a teacher on the basis of how much equipment (or media) he uses. Until we have sufficient research to indicate that there is a direct correlation between media usage and good teaching, it is unfair to force good teachers out of the way to make room for the hardware.

We need to learn how and where to use the contributions of educational technology. But the impact on the classroom destroys the possibility of innovation. We know how to modify behavior, and for a professional it is not done by backing him into a corner where he must either fight or be labelled a saboteur. Rather, we must provide opportunities for experimentation and adaptation.

Given the mass of adult illiterates who must be reached, it is doubtful if this can be done in any meaningful time frame without utilizing more advanced forms of communication and instruction. But, these adults have had lives filled with failure. We should not expose them to another opportunity which might breed failure in the name of experimentation. We must be sure that what we offer them will reach their objectives, as well as those of the producer of the equipment. Possibly more money at this time on experimentation is necessary. Meanwhile, we continue with the more traditional programs until we can identify, through reliable research, those aspects of the newer educational technology which are truly meaningful and contribute to the problem without incurring additional problems.

Adult illiteracy is not a phenomenon in the United States alone. Worldwide we have one of the lowest illiteracy rates, though we must be careful how this is stated in the absence of clear agreement on what illiteracy is and how one tests for it. Suffice it to say that, in the United States today, less than an eighth-grade education can be a strong contributing force to reducing one's economic level and opportunity for social mobility. If we are to remain true to our concepts of providing opportunity for all, then adult illiteracy must be reduced far below the current figure of 25,000,000.

The facilities and the will to accomplish this tremendous task have been strongly evidenced. We have made some false starts, but not enough has been accomplished within the past few years. It has been years of learning by the educators. It has been a time of finding out what our colleagues have been doing. In the very near future, we should be able to make considerable strides in the task of reducing the number of adult illiterates in the United States.

Part 7

The Middle Class
as
Culturally Deprived

33

Education and Society
in Disadvantaged Suburbia

William E. Kuschman

A large segment of America's disadvantaged children live in the suburbs where, according to legend and the popular western song, ". . . seldom is heard a discouraging word and the skies are not cloudy all day." Contrary to popular belief, "cultural disadvantage" and the resultant crippling effect upon learning are not restricted to "pockets of poverty." Debilitation of a child's self-concept can be as devastating in middle-class suburbia as in the minority ghettoes.

An admission of the above is not a vote against poverty. Neither is it a reflection of opposite to present efforts on behalf of children from low socio-economic circumstances. Such programs are needed urgently and long over-due. Proper perspective, however, calls for balanced concern and a healthy resistance to positions of polarity which tend to obscure practical issues. An analogy may be useful here.

In the present fight against segregation, North and South, the fact that northern resistance is more subtle makes the problem no less real to those bearing the brunt of northern discrimination. The effects of tension-producing agents upon suburban children, while more subtle and harder to identify, make them no less important than the more obviously seen effects of abject poverty upon children in the slums and ghettoes.

The big house, green lawn, and tree-shaded patio are the armor that allegedly shields the suburban child from "real life"—somewhat on the order of a brick-and-mortar Salk vaccine. But the difference between being destroyed by the big city club and the suburban laser beam is of little importance to those suffering the consequences. Commonly cited indices* of "cul-

SOURCE. Reprinted from *School & Society*, November 12, 1966, by permission of the author and publisher.

* Baltimore City Public Schools, "Research Design for Evaluating Project Help," *The*

tural deprivation" include such concerns as median value of homes and poor homes per 1,000 housing units; separated and divorced per 1,000 population; and a lack of long-range perspective, or the inability to prolong gratification. There are others, but these should amply serve as items of comparison between deprivations suffered by children in slums and suburbs.

The slum child is known to come from physical home conditions ranging from a status of mere existence to almost tolerable. The suburbs? Johnny Suburban may live in the cleanest, classiest, and highest mortgaged house in the village—a house with all the plumbing conveniences that two and one-half baths can provide—yet a home which has what is loosely referred to as "wall-to-wall" indebtedness.

Who is the "poor" child? Who is to say that the pressures are greater for one child than the other? The tensions impressed upon the slum child are enormous but have the questionable virtue of visibility—they can be seen and, therefore, society is presently disposed to treat them. Who knows of the end-of-the-month pressures felt by the suburban child whose parents quarrel over the lack of money to meet bills accumulated in keeping up the front? Such parents are forced by the unwritten code of the suburbs to maintain a smiling countenance and to instill in their children the need to "play the game."

The suburban child may not experience the tensions caused by drunken "uncles" visiting mother, but he knows whether or not the luxuries he "enjoys" can be paid for at the end of the month. In addition, the fact that both of his parents are "in the home" may be of no more comfort to him than the fact that the child of the slums may have "no known father."

Youngsters from "problem" areas suffer the consequences of parental separation about five times as often as those in "non-problem" areas. The implication of such a statement is that children of divorced parents are subjected to school-learning handicaps not present in families that stay together. Skirting the moral-religious side of the argument, this thesis calls for thorough investigation by school personnel and other community service agents.

In the suburbs, it is not "nice" to show overtly that one is unhappy. The impression of a solid, happy state of familial bliss must be maintained at all costs. In typically defined disadvantaged neighborhoods, close proximity of family-to-family living, as fragmented as the family unit may be, makes the concealment of feelings almost impossible. It is commonly known when all is not well, all the way down to the level of the street. Under these circumstances, even the most cursory investigation reveals the problem for what it is and, again, attempts can be made to ameliorate negative effects upon the child's feelings toward himself and others.

Research Council of the Great Cities Program for School Improvement, Baltimore, March 15, 1963.

In suburbia, few people know that all is not right between husband and wife. The children know it, of course, but, being good little suburbanites, they keep it to themselves. They bottle it up except as it leaks out in ways which make people wonder how children who have everything can be so "ornery" and unappreciative. The resulting treatment for "spoiled brats" adds to an already tense situation.

Finally, it would appear that neither children nor adults of low socio-economic straits have a corner on inability to prolong gratification. The financially over-extended suburbanite who cannot prolong gratification seems no rarer a bird than his low-income cousin. The difference, again, seems to be one of obviousness versus subtlety, rather than a difference of kind.

The consequences to the child of the low-wage earner who falls prey to the unscrupulous salesmen of time-payment merchandise are pitifully dramatic and make the headlines. The consequences to the child of the suburban family which never seems to be able to keep up with the Joneses may be known to no one outside the immediate family and creditors who, attuned to the niceties of suburbia, are "properly discreet," but equally ruthless.

The suburban child who has been conditioned to expect everything and who is unable to finish a task in school without an immediate extrinsic reward is likely to be personally blamed for his "overindulgence." For this child, overindulgence is as much an unhealthy aspect of his environmental conditioning as is the inability of the child from the low-income family to finish a task because he has learned, of necessity, to live from day to day and to worry about tomorrow if and when it comes. The end products seem disturbingly similar and dissimilarly disturbing to a society which is inherently committed to helping the "underdog."

34

The Culturally Deprived
Middle Class

William H. Boyer

American educators are beginning to show new concern for the education of lower-class children. Carefully avoiding a Marxist interpretation of social class, they are defining the communicational gulf between middle-class and lower-class children as a "subcultural" difference. They are treating the education of the lower class as "cross-cultural" education not unlike an American teaching a Filipino or a Russian teaching an Egyptian. Sociology, anthropology, and social psychology are being used to understand subcultural differences. The materials and methods of instruction are being fitted to the psychological world of the lower-class child. Yet, it is not sufficient merely to utilize new means, for educators also must have appropriate ends or goals for which the means become instrumental. This is where the hang-up occurs.

Most middle-class American teachers continue to do what comes naturally, using an ethnocentric view that assumes the superiority of their own middle-class values. The new approaches to the teaching of lower-class children consist primarily of increasing the effectiveness of the means of achieving *unrevised* goals.

The American Middle Class as a Model

How virtuous is the American middle class, how enlightened and humane is it to offer the best examples of modern man and to serve as an educational model for American youth? Middle-class values include emphasis on verbal ability, perseverance, and the willingness to deter gratification. These can be valuable attributes if they are balanced by other characteristics. Yet, many other middle-class characteristics are less valuable, and some are major obstacles to social and political progress.

The report of the President's Commission on Civil Disorder (1968) correctly identifies white racism as a major cause of Negro slums and urban riots. Most white middle-class Americans hold an official creed of equal justice and opportunity, but private profit and in-group exclusion are more often the dominant motives for actual deeds. For example, the dominantly middle-class real estate establishment effectively has created a system of housing exclusion mainly in the service of white middle-class clients, which has helped perpetuate the ghetto and has hindered the social progress of America.

In addition to acerbating race conflict, many middle-class Americans have resisted creating humane programs of medical care. The aged also have been neglected callously. The burgeoning affluence that has been so rewarding to the middle class has not produced any noticeable increase in their willingness to share with the less fortunate. The enormous increase in gross national product has provided no relative improvement in the economic status of the lower class in the last two decades. Neglected minorities almost always have obtained their minor achievements through organized power and persistent effort. Middle classes have offered the rhetoric of altruism but, in practice, acquisition usually has been "in" and sharing has been "out."

As a result, the American middle class has a major responsibility for having created one of the most backward of modern nations in relation to planning for the general welfare. A negative conception of "freedom" still pervades much middle-class thought, stressing freedom from government instead of cooperative planning. When a crisis becomes sufficiently acute, frantic stop-gap measures are instituted, aimed more at the symptoms than the causes. Planning occurs in specific industries, but integrated social-political-economic-educational planning is still largely suspect. Latent Calvinism produces many middle-class devils, and those who try to change the old ideology are seen often as satanic influences, un-American heretics, or outright enemies.

This modal middle-class outlook aids in the perpetuation of air pollution, water pollution, the profitable desecration of natural beauty, and the creation of alienation and desperate millions who are only beginning to protest a plight they are increasingly less willing to tolerate.

If the conventional middle-class outlook is an imperfect model for domestic policy, its international outlook is even less desirable. Compulsive anticommunism and a boundless reliance on military technology has contributed to the cold war and is helping to make it increasingly hot. Unilateral military excursions into countries propounding the "wrong" ideology has hindered United Nations authority and has increased the prospects for solving international conflict through atomic annihilation instead of through international law.

No class in American society shares a larger responsibility than the middle class for perpetuating the techno-fanatic tradition. While millions have struggled to exist and many have starved, the race to the moon has commanded vast intellectual and economic resources. The techno-fanatic tradition is not concerned with whether something ought to be done, but only with the question of whether it is technologically possible. And it assumes that all problems can be solved by technology, that values and institutions need no reconstruction.

There are admirable characteristics in all social classes and subcultures, but their ethnocentric tendencies usually make them inadequately aware of their limitations. The American middle class is immensely powerful but no less blinded to its limitations. Characteristics that may have been valuable at an earlier period now may be obsolete or even catastrophic. When schools confuse education with salesmanship and sell students the middle-class package of values, they are likely to be selling an indiscriminate tangle of sense and nonsense, progress and regress, humanitarianism and barbarism. Such education equates style with morality and offers confusion instead of clarification.

Three Different Goals

What are the viable choices for goals? There are at least three. Education can be a continuation of the usual indoctrination of middle-class values, a way of creating two-way communication between the middle class and the lower class, or a commitment to a social philosophy which is different than the value system of any single subculture.

Indoctrination of Middle-Class Values. The first choice is the most common, though it is an aim more often implied than stated. It intends to impose the middle-class beliefs shared by most educators. This goal assumes the superiority of middle-class values over lower-class values. It sanctions indoctrination with respect to values and prescribes the "right" values. As an ethnocentric system it assumes that "our way is the right way."

Alternative values are examined or tested within their own frame of reference. No basis for independent choice is offered. Middle-class values become matters of faith and are allowed to be imposed on students with a claim of objectivity. The usual rationalization for this is that middle-class values are claimed to be representative of the American way of life and schools have been used historically to shape Americans. But in reality many Americans do not share middle-class values. And this melting-pot objective of creating a personality stereotype abandons the democratic method, substituting in-group domination for individual choice and responsibility.

Typically in such education, the conventional notions of proper attitudes, beliefs, speech, hair style, and dress are dictated. The beliefs are usually those which support the ethos and the power of a given class, emphasizing a particular economic, political, and religious outlook. Regardless of the new means being employed, most American education still is oriented toward these established goals.

Interaction Between Social Classes. A second choice of goals provides a *two*-way communication between social classes. The objective is for middle-class students and teachers to develop cross-cultural interaction with lower-class students. This involves widening of social experience without fostering "right" beliefs. The procedure requires a humility from middle-class educators that is difficult for a group enjoying in-group advantages. It assumes that the middle class can learn from the lower class and that middle-class values need to be examined.

This approach to education advances communication between social classes. Still, such communication is not sufficient. Something must be communicated, something must be taught. The new goals also need to encompass a social philosophy appropriate to the central issues of our age.

Mutual Participation Toward Intelligent Social Change. A third choice includes a social philosophy. Rather than assuming that the beliefs of one or the other particular social class are necessarily right, the focus is on developing understanding useful in solving the common problems of our age. Such education tries to help students clarify the alternatives and to aid them in examining the consequences of choices. It works toward understanding the causes of social class conflict. It develops direct cooperation between children of different social classes which may transcend both middle-class and lower-class mores.

This third choice uses the natural sciences, social sciences, and humanities. But these fields are used selectively and are problem-centered rather than being purely descriptive. Schools are no longer places to console students about the state of the world and to absolve them from the responsibility for participating in change. In this kind of education, new concepts of "success" are compared with the usual middle-class standards of other-directed respectability. Current myths of economics, history, and foreign policy are analyzed critically, and the realities of the American way of life are confronted honestly. This education discards many of the instruments currently used to convince educators that lower-class children are inferior. Devices such as I.Q. tests are abandoned as sorting devices to favor middle-class children.

Social change would be more just and less agonizing if schools did not serve as allies of any one class or value system. With a reexamination of middle- and lower-class goals, students would be more self-conscious about their beliefs and possibly less certain about the compulsive patterns which characterize their class mores and their class conceptions.

Conclusions

In spite of the recent concern for more effective means of educating lower-class children, American education still flounders because it has not reassessed its goals. To continue to indoctrinate class beliefs is unworthy of a society that claims to be intellectually open, and it stultifies examination in the most important area—goals and purposes. Those who have advanced to the point of genuine dialogue between social classes have helped halt the self-righteous ethnocentrism of American education and have helped create an environment more congenial to all students.

However, a choice is needed which goes beyond dialogue and aids students in understanding the world in such a way that they can participate effectively in cooperative social change. A society that excludes some groups from the central social, political, and economic structure invites change by violence, for isolated and discontented minorities are forced to use desperate unilateral means to achieve their improvement. Schools have a major responsibility for developing a society that is not only aware of the symptoms but also capable of identifying the causes of dislocation. And such knowledge would need to be treated as an instrument of action rather than as social class adornment and as an excuse for escape.

Dominant classes, as for example the affluent upper classes, often treat equality of opportunity as a threat because they assume that it demands redistribution of existing wealth. It may be to a limited degree, but if the top is kept open on economic growth and if individual opportunity is maximized, everyone profits by the education of everyone else. Aside from the over-all economic advantage, the present ghettoized experience of both lower and middle classes is unnecessarily limiting to the enrichment of everyone's life.

To be at the bottom in American society is restrictive, frustrating, and degrading, but being part of that ever growing American middle class often involves the kind of tedious and meaningless life that also would be enriched by breaking down the cultural isolation. Middle-class life may be comfortable, but it is often insensitive to human values, boring, status compulsive, and anxiety-ridden in its search for personal wealth and other-directed respectability. Expanded communication and cooperation with lower classes could give middle-class life more meaning and also could provide a more effective basis for aiding in the nonviolent solution of increasingly critical social problems. In addition, it may reveal to the middle class that anyone can be culturally deprived.

35

Project Slow Down: The Middle-Class Answer to Project Head Start

Robert Fisher

We have been waging a losing struggle to compensate poor children. We never will be able to equalize educational opportunities for the poor, no matter how young we start the children in school. The middle-class competition is simply too tough. The middle-class parents always are going to maintain their own head start on the Head Starters who are poor. Poor people are too handicapped in the great race toward respectability.

As usual in education, we have been concentrating on the wrong group. Instead of "uplifting" the poor by jacking up the children with Head Start programs, why not concentrate our energies upon the well-to-do through a new Project Slow Down?

The purpose of Project Slow Down is to take some of the steam out of advantaged, middle-class children. Before outlining the essential features of this new program, let us briefly examine what has been wrong with the old tactics. Why have Head Start and other programs for disadvantaged preschool children failed, despite their popularity and despite favorable publicity? First, Head Start is too little and too late. How can we, in the summer before kindergarten, or even in the year before kindergarten, make up for the advantages which middle-class children have enjoyed since birth? Second, even if we should start earlier than Head Start, offering a publicly subsidized preschool education for the poor, the middle-class parents are not standing still. They are sending their children to better-equipped private nursery schools. And after school the parents keep up the good work. Third, we follow through on Head Start to counteract the loss of initial gains in

SOURCE. Reprinted from *School & Society*, October 1970, by permission of the author and publisher.

traditional kindergarten and first-grade programs. But let us not fool our-selves, the parents and the children of the middle classes also are following through with increased determination. Finally, we try to teach the poor to copy the middle classes. We compensate for restrictive linguistic development. We model programs for the poor after the pressure tactics which seem so effective with the well-to-do. But all we do is to equalize the anxiety levels of the poor to match the middle class, when the academic preschool for the poor pressures the poor kids into middle-class motivational patterns.

We have tried everything: new techniques, new materials, concrete objects to manipulate, the old Montessori methods, talking typewriters, language games. We even can force poor parents to come to school to get educated themselves.

But it is all going to be in vain. We live in a racist, affluent, pressurized society; the suburban WASPs already have the head start and the financial ability to follow through. Many middle-class parents even enjoy this new competition provided by the poor. "If those poor kids are getting government help, we'll show them what free enterprise and individual initiative can do by educating our own children better!"

We have been working on the wrong group. We have been trying to help poor kids acquire middle-class values, middle-class motivation, middle-class language patterns, middle-class learning styles, middle-class competitive values; but the poor never will be able to compete on even terms with middle-class mothers and fathers.

A predictable reaction has developed in suburbia. "If the socialistic gov-ernment is wasting the taxpayers' dollars on nursery schools for the poor children, we will expand nursery school provisions for our own children. We can teach the kids how to read at home by the age of two, if necessary."

Now we are witnessing increased pushing, pressuring, cajoling, rewarding, and threatening of middle-class infants. Middle-class preschoolers have in front of them some excellent examples of status-seeking—their middle-class mothers with a college education. How can the mothers of the "disadvan-taged" possibly take on such competition and hope to win?

Instead, we propose a new "very subversive" program. We leave it to others, perhaps skillful politicians, perhaps dyed-in-the-wool communists, to disguise the project. Someone else needs to come up with a more deceptive title, with some convincingly false promises. We might employ that old Nazi technique, the Big Lie. We tell the parents that this new program is guaran-teed to get their kids into an Ivy League college! All parents have to do is to enroll their kids in Project Slow Down.

Many intriguing possibilities exist for Project Slow Down. The most ob-vious way to implement the program is, of course, through the use of drugs. What we can do is to tranquilize the children, and we might as well tranquilize the parents for good measure. We could accomplish this secretly by infiltrating the suburban water supply, much like fluoridation, and nobody even would be aware of what is going on.

But let us start with a more modest proposition. We will establish new nursery schools. These schools will have very high status. We will charge the parents plenty to get their youngsters into the schools, and we will offer opportunities to guarantee the children places by making it possible to register them at birh. We will begin these schools at the age of two or three, when early intervention might still make a difference.

We deliberately will allow these middle-class children to behave like two-year-olds and three-year-olds. They will be allowed to play and dress up and fight and listen to stories, to build things with blocks, to sleep, eat, urinate, and explore their bodies at will.

The same kind of education will continue through the ages of four and five. We will have more dramatic play, more creative art, more large-muscle activities. There will be singing and dancing and having fun. The only things forbidden will be rules, teacher expectations, rewards, and punishments. Above all, there will be *no* reading readiness.

While we are at it, we will begin the subtle process of indoctrination: "Love is good." "The body is clean." "Be spontaneous." "Do what you want to do." "No one needs to get ahead." "Reading is a waste of time." "Have fun." "Teacher-pleasers are finks." "People who try to get good grades are drags." "Be yourself." "Do your thing." "Dream, sing, dance, and gaze at the stars."

Most important of all, we will tell the children not to listen to their parents. Do we want to produce another generation of cigarette clutchers, martini swillers, pill swallowers, and headache sufferers who are running to their psychiatrists while keeping up with the Joneses? We will help the youngsters to reject the culture of their parents. We will point out what the rat race has done for Mama and Papa.

We do not have to lay it on "too thick." The children see for themselves. All we need to do is to sharpen their power of observation. They will see. After all, they *live* with their parents. They already know, anyway. By the age of five, and often at an earlier age, they know that parents are people who "don't let you do what you want to do." But, in our Slow Down school, "It is OK to do what you want to do."

All we have to do is to copy some of those reformers who are pushing preschools for the disadvantaged. They find no contradiction in implying to poor kids that their "disadvantaged" parents speak the wrong language, live the wrong family life, observe the wrong habits, practice the wrong morals, and do not belong in respectable society. We just will make the same insinuations to middle-class children about the middle-class culture.

We need to keep up a steady stream of brainwashing. "Slow down! Slow down! Reject the culture of your parents. Laugh at their authority. Have fun now. Forget about the future. Take it easy."

After all, nature is working for us. Kids in Samoa concentrate on having fun; why not kids in suburbia?

Eventually the children will slow down. They will refuse to get on the treadmill. They will not compete or please teachers or do homework or learn modern math or fear the wrath of their striving Mamas and Papas.

What we intend to do is to allow the middle-class youngsters some of the advantages that "disadvantaged" children take for granted. Then we no longer will have to try to enrich the lives of the "disadvantaged." We no longer will have to make all of the children of the poor into middle-class strivers.

We can forget Project Head Start. We can stop trying to graft middle-class respectability and status-striving upon the children of the poor.

Let us ask a serious question: What is so wonderful about our uptight, middle-class way of life? Compared to our affluent society, nine-tenths of the world is impoverished. Culturally "disadvantaged" babies are born every second. In some cultures, it is not even a sin to be poor. True, children need enough to eat, a smallpox vaccination, the love of their parents, and a healthy self-concept. But, if we are to look at the two problems which most threaten life on this earth, they are neither the population explosion nor the threat of riots in American streets. They are atomic annihilation in a worldwide war and the sickness of authoritarian conformity. Comparing the life styles of the "advantaged" suburbanite with the "disadvantaged" poor, which produces the greatest source of explosive anxiety which might actualize these threats?

Part **8**

The Culturally Disadvantaged
Reader

36

Reading Progress
for the Culturally Disadvantaged

Howard Ozmon

Among the terms applied to the disadvantaged in our society are *culturally deprived, socially disadvantaged, inner-city child, slum dweller, minority pupil, ghetto youth, educationally deficient, in-migrant, undereducated,* and *underachiever.*[1] This group exhibits the most severe scholastic retardation, the highest dropout rate (exceeding 50%), and the least participation in higher education (probably under five percent).[2] Whipple refers to the children who come from culturally disadvantaged or impoverished homes as "children without"—without enough space, food, warmth, clothing, toys, or books.[3]

Although reading difficulties are not the cause for a child being culturally deprived, they do become a major factor in his remaining in that category. The development of reading skills opens the way to successes in terms of academic achievement, which in turn opens the way to success in the social system. It has long been recognized that there is a close correlation between socioeconomic class level and reading level. Wittick points out that the mean average for children reading below grade level was only three percent for the upper class and six percent for the middle class, while it was 10% for the upper working class and as high as 33% for the lower class.[4]

[1] A. Harry Passow and David L. Elliott, "The Nature and Needs of the Educationally Disadvantaged," in A. Harry Passow, ed., *Developing Programs for the Educationally Disadvantaged* (New York: Teachers College Press, 1968), p. 3.

[2] Ibid., p. 4.

[3] Gertrude Whipple, "Inspiring Culturally Disadvantaged Children to Read," in J. Allen Figurel, ed., *Reading and Inquiry* (Newark: International Reading Association, 1965), **10**: 253.

[4] Mildred L. Wittick, "Culturally Disadvantaged Children and Reading Achievement," *Combining Research Results and Good Practice* (Newark: International Reading Association, 1966), **2** (Part 2): 29–34.

In recent years, there has been great recognition of this correlation between reading achievement and achievement in other educational and social areas, and we have seen the development of such programs as Project Read, CRAFT, STAR, and others designed to help solve the reading problems of disadvantaged youngsters in the early grades. Although there are also a number of programs providing remedial reading instruction for high school students, and, though such programs are necessary and highly important, it still appears that the place for emphasis in trying to correct the reading problem of the culturally disadvantaged is in the elementary and preschool programs. Harris points out that, by the time a severely disadvantaged child reaches junior high school, his grade score in reading is likely to be two or three years below the national norms.[5] This problem began not in the high school, but earlier, and probably it became intensified between grades one and five.[6]

Thus, our greatest efforts should be directed toward the earliest levels of schooling, if not within the early home environment itself. According to Bloom, Davis, and Hess, studies repeatedly show that the home is the single most important influence upon the intellectual and emotional development of children, particularly in the preschool years: "The ways in which parents spend their time with their children at meals, in play, and at other times during the day have been found to be the central factors in developing skills which prepare children for school. The objects in the home, the amount of parental interest in learning, and the amount of practice and encouragement the child is given in conversation and general learning have been found to be significant influences on language and cognitive development, development of interest in learning, attention span and motivation of the child."[7]

One of our fundamental premises should be that a child's reading difficulties are not innate or inherited, but caused. In the case of the culturally disadvantaged child, they are caused by a variety of factors, such as the low cultural level of the parents and the environment, the lack of intellectual stimulation found in the home, and the feelings of depression and hostility engendered by slum life. We still live in a society characterized by lingering feelings of Social Darwinism, where to be poor is a disgrace and, perhaps, even immoral. The child born to culturally disadvantaged parents begins life with vast hurdles to overcome, the greatest of which is probably the little understood fact that society looks with disdain upon his efforts to rise above his class level and may even penalize him when he attempts to do so. Such

[5] Albert J. Harris, "Beginning Reading Instruction for Educationally Disadvantaged Children," in Passow, op. cit., pp. 187–188.

[6] Ibid., p. 188.

[7] B. S. Bloom, A. Davis, and R. Hess, *Compensatory Education for Cultural Deprivation* (New York: Holt, Rinehart & Winston, 1965), p. 69.

penalization exists everywhere in terms of the resistance toward Negroes who desire to enter professional fields, and even may come from the parents who have internalized an attitude of submission and defeatism. When the child from this background attends ghetto schools, one often finds this kind of resentment displayed by teachers of the child's own minority group who managed to pull themselves up by their own bootstraps and resent the child who cannot do the same. This attitude automatically provides for a "programmed deprivation" where the child is undermined without understanding why. "Programmed deprivation" also exists in the fact that, generally, the schools which the culturally disadvantaged child attends will be the worst schools with the worst teachers. Such schools usually are staffed with people who are resigned to the belief that one cannot do much with such children. In these schools, teachers are "tried out" or they see their task largely in terms of "policing" or "baby sitting."

The view that children have a limit of expectancy, particularly when that limit is low, is a very damaging educational belief. A number of recent studies point to the fact that a teacher's expectations of a child's potential seriously affect what he does accomplish. Thus, if a teacher expects very little from a child, this attitude may be conveyed to him in very subtle, yet tangible, ways. He will tend, consequently, to produce little, or else his accomplishments will be belittled in order to reinforce the preconceived view that the teacher has. Rosenthal mentions a study where one group of students were given rats chosen at random and told that they were intelligent, good problem-solvers, and had been bred for brightness in running a maze. A second group were given another random selection of rats and told that they were slow, not too intelligent, and would be poor at running a maze. The results were that the group, told that their rats were capable of great accomplishment, found this to be true, whereas the group that was told that their rats were incapable of much performance found this also to be true. Rosenthal then conducted an experiment where one teacher was given a random selection of children labelled as "spurters," while a second teacher was given another random sample and told that they were not likely to perform well academically. The results were the same as with the rats, with the first teacher finding that the children revealed "spurts" of achievement, while the second teacher found her class to be dull and slow, as labelled.[8] Thus, a growing evidence indicates that there is a "self-fulfilling prophecy" in the sense that people's expectations have a great deal to do with actual accomplishment. Accordingly, when teachers expect very little from children, as is often the case with culturally disadvantaged children, then, they do very little in reading as well as in anything else.

[8] Robert Rosenthal and Leonore F. Jacobson, "Teacher Expectations for the Disadvantaged," *Scientific American*, **218**: 19–23, April 1968.

Thus, to attack the reading problems of the culturally disadvantaged really means to deal with the nature of cultural deprivation itself, as well as our attitudes about it. We have just begun to awaken to the enormity of the task that lies before us, and there is, at the present time, a tremendous upsurge of interest in the need to eradicate poverty and racial and social injustice in this country. These are the fundamental causes of cultural deprivation. But, unfortunately, a great deal of damage already has been done, and our attempts are much like trying to bolt the barn door after the horse has escaped. When former President Johnson appointed a National Advisory Commission on Civil Disorders, he was really asking for an inquiry into the meaning and effects of cultural deprivation.[9] When the commission reported that white racism was the underlying cause and that we were moving rapidly toward two cultures, one black and one white, in effect it was talking about two cultures, one advantaged and one disadvantaged.

In recent years, we have been making a concerted effort to eradicate the causes that separate people both racially and economically, and we have seen the passage of a number of acts to aid education for the underprivileged, such as the Vocational Education Act of 1963, the Civil Rights Act of 1964, the Economic Opportunity Act of 1964, as well as parts of the National Defense Act of 1965, the Elementary and Secondary Education Act of 1964, and the Higher Education Act of 1965. But these attempts, regardless of the amount of Federal money expended, cannot be effective without a corresponding concern on the part of the citizenry, a concern directed toward acculturating our culturally disadvantaged people into the mainstream of American culture. This concern must manifest itself in an attitude change, not merely as an external economic concern.

The problem of reading for the culturally disadvantaged, therefore, needs to be attacked on long-range and short-range fronts. The long-range approach will seek to eliminate the vicious cycle of poverty and ignorance that exists in all of our cities and in many of our rural areas as well. This problem must be met in providing decent housing, medical care, and a good education for all of our citizens, regardless of race, origin, or the causes of their poverty. We cannot afford to lose the valuable resource of manpower that is today's children in the slums, and we cannot continue to penalize slum children because they were born in a slum environment of slum parents who, in turn, were born of the same kind of parents in the same condition, and so on ad infinitum. This unfortunate chain reaction must be stopped, and educators must take their part. I would hope that no teacher would say that his concern with reading comes before his concern with his fellow man, or with children, particularly the disadvantaged child. Educators at all levels must work

---

[9] Cf., Otto Kerner, Chairman, *Report of the National Advisory Commission on Civil Disorders* (Washington: U.S. Government Printing Office, 1968).

against the forces which condemn a child to a life in the slums in inferior conditions and schools. This implies participation in programs that work to eliminate poverty, bias, and injustices of all kinds. If a teacher is really interested in improving the reading level of the culturally disadvantaged, then he also must become a social worker, a crusader, and a humanitarian, as well as one who helps a child to read books—often, unfortunately, books in which the child is not interested because they reflect a middle-class world to which he is still a stranger.

In the short-range approach, teachers must recognize that too much already has happened to the people who live in our slums and that the causes are too long-standing for us to expect a change overnight. In the intervening years, as we work for the abolition of the whole problem of cultural deprivation, we also must try to counter the problems as they exist by looking for better ways to teach reading to the disadvantaged, as well as the work and the courage needed to put them into operation. At present, many research projects deal with teaching children in slum areas how to read. This is all to the good, but we must endeavor to remember that we are still dealing with the symptoms of poverty and not with causes, and that our efforts, at best, are probably only going to assist a few and not the many that really need our help.

The problem of cultural deprivation is now widely recognized, and there is a growing attempt to understand and combat it, especially in the area of reading. Harris points out that, during 1960–1963, no papers in the International Reading Association programs were concerned specifically with the reading problems of the disadvantaged. In the 1964 program, however, there were 13 papers in this area, and the number is steadily growing.[10] We do need more study of this kind, especially of new kinds of reading programs for the culturally disadvantaged. We also need to alert the general public to the enormity and complexity of our problem, and, in the years ahead, to lend our intelligence, our special talents, and our hearts toward helping our culturally deprived citizens to become intelligent, happy, and productive members of our society.

[10] Harris, op. cit., p. 187.

37

Enrichment for
Culturally Disadvantaged Readers

Nicholas P. Criscuolo

An essential goal in our country is the development of a literate society. New programs and materials in reading constantly are being devised to achieve this aim. Colleges are attempting to improve their pre-service training for teachers, and school systems are offering practical in-service work in order to help teachers provide effective reading instruction in the classroom.

Teachers work with pupils coming from all levels of our society. Great concern of late, however, has been generated concerning youngsters coming from the lowest stratum. These children have been termed culturally disadvantaged. In the educational setting, this term refers to those pupils with a particular set of educationally associated problems which tend to restrict their intellectual and social growth.

Culturally disadvantaged children usually reside in the slums and poorer sections of cities, certain rural areas, migrant labor camps, and Indian reservations.[1] In racial and ethnic terms, a majority of these children are Negro and Puerto Rican. To this group, Havighurst[2] also adds Mexicans with a rural background, whites from the rural and mountain South, and European immigrants with a rural background.

Families of culturally disadvantaged children have flocked to the Northern industrial cities in the last several years. The Negro population density in major Northern cities is four times that of whites[3] and there are indications

SOURCE. Reprinted from *School & Society*, March 30, 1968, by permission of the author and publisher.

[1] Joe L. Frost and Glenn Hawkes, eds., *The Disadvantaged Child* (Boston: Houghton Mifflin, 1966).

[2] Robert J. Havighurst, "Who Are the Disadvantaged?" *Education*, **85**: 455–457, April 1965.

[3] Clemmont Vontress, "Our Demoralizing Slum Schools," *Phi Delta Kappan*, **45**: 77–81, November 1963.

that, in the near future, one out of two public school pupils in the large cities will be culturally disadvantaged.

Since we must give these children a sound, basic education, what can we do to shape an effective reading program? Most school systems use a basal reading program. These basal texts are designed to develop reading skills sequentially. Critics, such as Flesch[4] and Klineberg,[5] have questioned the content of basal readers. Lack of multi-ethnic content, the critics say, makes it difficult for culturally disadvantaged pupils to identify with, and relate to, the characters and situations depicted in the typical basal reader.

Two reading approaches used in a basal reading program are enrichment and acceleration. Enrichment involves using a variety of materials, activities, and resources to extend and reinforce reading skills. Suggestions for enrichment activities, such as dramatization of stories read, puppet construction, and the use of related filmstrips and records, are offered in the manuals which accompany basal texts. Enrichment obviously takes time, and some teachers do not take the time to do them. Acceleration involves developing the basic reading skills, but spending less time at one basal reading level before moving to the next level. Due to the time factor, little attention is given to the use of a variety of materials and activities to enrich what is read.

Both approaches have been identified almost exclusively with gifted readers, who usually come from a high socio-economic background.[6] It seems a justifiable hypothesis, however, that both approaches, particularly enrichment, might also serve the needs of children who are not classified as gifted, or who do not come from a high socio-economic background.

In order to test this hypothesis, the author initiated a study with 87 third graders enrolled in two public schools in New Haven during the year 1965–1966.[7] The duration of the study was six months, and the Houghton Mifflin Reading for Meaning Series (1963 edition) was used. School A represented the lower-middle social class and School B the lower-lower. Warner's Index of Status Characteristics was applied to measure objectively each socio-economic level.[8]

The teachers who were assigned randomly to use the acceleration approach were instructed to complete the activities suggested in the teacher's guide of each basal text up to and including the workbook assignment, as well as

[4] Rudolf Flesch, *Why Johnny Can't Read* (New York: Harper, 1955).

[5] Otto Klineberg, "Life Is Fun in a Smiling, Fair-Skinned World," *Saturday Review of Literature,* **56:** 75–77, February 16, 1963.

[6] Mary C. Austin and Coleman Morrison, *The First R* (New York: Macmillan, 1963).

[7] Nicholas P. Criscuolo, *A Comparison of the Enrichment and Acceleration Approaches with Children of Different Socio-Economic Backgrounds and Their Effect on Reading Achievement,* unpublished Ph.D. dissertation (Storrs: University of Connecticut, 1967).

[8] W. Lloyd Warner, Marchia Meeker, and Kenneth Eells, *Social Class in America* (New York: Harper and Row, 1960).

Section 3 (Developing Reading Skills). The teachers selected to use the enrichment approach were instructed to spend additional time on each teaching unit, doing the Optional Related Activities and Suggestions for Broadening Reading for each story. The enrichment groups spent the entire six months of the study on one reader, whereas the accelerated groups moved into the next highest reading level after three months.

Scores from Forms A and B on the Metropolitan Reading Test (World Book Company, 1959) served as the pre- and post-standardized test measurements. Two-way analysis of variance, which permits the simultaneous investigation of the two variables in this study (reading approach and social class status), was the statistical procedure used.

Analysis of the data revealed that the enrichment approach had produced the greatest growth in general reading achievement. The difference was significant at the five percent level of confidence for the word knowledge sub-test and the one percent level of confidence for the reading sub-test of the Metropolitan Reading Test. Findings also revealed that the enrichment approach achieved the most growth in word knowledge, but not reading, for the children of the lower-lower social class.

The enrichment groups grew an average of 6.1 months, while the accelerated groups grew an average of 3.2 months. Since enrichment involved doing all the activities suggested in the basal reader, it can be concluded that, the more intensively a teacher uses the basal reader, the better the results will be. Inasmuch as enrichment was offered in the context of a basal reading program, it seems that criticisms regarding the use of basal readers with culturally disadvantaged children are not justified completely.

One implication which can be drawn from this study is that enrichment should not be reserved for the academically able or one particular social class. Regarding culturally disadvantaged children, it is hoped that programs and new techniques will continue to be developed for use with them, but educators should be aware that the enrichment activities outlined in the teachers' manuals of basal readers provide a veritable "gold mine." As we search and explore for something new, let us not overlook what we already have.

Part 9

The Teacher
and Federal Programs
for the Disadvantaged

38

The Case
of the Disadvantaged Teacher

Philip I. Freedman and Nathan Kravetz

In Metropolis, U.S.A., the scene of the struggle for educational improvement of the "culturally disadvantaged" child, a startling phenomenon has emerged. Out of the turbulence generated by the charges and countercharges on this issue, there appears to have developed a consensus on one question. In a rare display of harmony, the proponents of busing, the advocates of pairing, the racial balancers, and the various integrationists have united and declared at least one truth to be self-evident—that the teacher is one of the villains of the piece.

To most observers, this is understandable. Frustrated by decrepit buildings, inadequate materials and texts, irritated by the pressures of poverty and segregation, and exhausted by the battle for mobility in a restrictive environment, parents in the ghetto seek a target for their bitterness.

"Teacher prejudice" is a commonly offered explanation for lower mean achievement scores among Negro and Puerto Rican youngsters.[1] The accusers have amassed a variety of "proofs," ranging from conceptions of what a teacher should be to odious comparisons with ostensibly ideal situations which demonstrate desirable practice. Numerous anecdotes attesting to the teachers' lack of motivation and hostility towards minority groups are cited, and pronouncements from professors, social workers, and psychologists are flaunted, excoriating the teacher for giving up too easily under adverse conditions and for not giving his all for *"the* child."

The evidence, though admittedly empirical, assumption-laden, and subjec-

SOURCE. Reprinted from *School & Society*, March 30, 1968, by permission of the author and publisher.

[1] *The New York Times*, September 12, 1966, p. 33; and *The New York Times*, September 13, 1966, p. 38.

tive, is impressive. And yet, a closer, calmer examination of reality might temper some heat, and even cast light upon a frustrating problem.

There is no doubt that among teachers, too, may be found examples of the varieties of human difference. We find the indolent, the awkward, the uninterested, the callous, the mercenary, and even, alas, the unfit. No profession is completely free of such problems among its members. No screening yet has been devised to guarantee the purity and altruism of public servants.

But, while it is just to demand of those beginning a teaching career qualities of dedication, sympathy, and sensitivity, it also is appropriate to ask the question of all whose work affects the education of children: Are you doing all you can to facilitate and enhance the task of the teacher?

For, when the denunciations are thundered—the teacher is not paying attention to the individual child; the teacher is making too fast a getaway in the "three o'clock Olympics"; he is not showing sufficient initiative in adapting materials to special situations; he is not willing to meet with the parents —it becomes clear that the teacher, were he a combination of Socrates, Einstein, Florence Nightingale, and the angel Gabriel, could not meet all these demands.

One need only glance at the teacher's circumstances to appreciate the conditions—both psychological and physical—under which he labors, and to understand how even the most skillful and most experienced can grow frustrated. There is entirely too little time and assistance, personal and material, to accomplish what must be done.

Consider first the position of the teacher *vis-à-vis* the school administration and structure. He hears exhortations from his supervisors to show initiative and daring. The same message is pronounced to laymen and non-teaching professionals by educational orators. Should he attempt to implement some of these suggestions, however, he soon receives another message, somewhat muted, but no less clear than the previous one, that he be careful about rocking the boat, and that, if he persists, he ultimately will bear the wrath of the Admiralty in whatever forms may be current.

Thus, the enterprising teacher is caught in a nutcracker, whose two arms consist of an overt call to act and do, and another, subtler call to refrain from acting and to refrain from doing. If observers of the educational scene wonder that so many teachers who begin their careers full of enthusiasm, aspiration, and altruism, lapse into apathy within a few years, they might do well to examine the impact upon teachers of discordant communiques from above.

Consider next the teacher, as he hears the theme, "you must pay attention to *the* child," sung by a mixed chorus of social workers and psychologists. It should occur to people who usually work with children on a one-to-one basis that the teacher has numerous "*the* childs" in his class, and that each "*the* child" has as much claim to the teacher's time and energy as any of his classmates.

The point of the foregoing is that the pupil-teacher ratio in most school systems is unrealistic. To the anticipated rejoinder that it is not a question of money, the counter-rejoinder is offered that money, while not *the* answer, is a prerequisite to an acceptable answer. Teacher refusal to exert maximum efforts because conditions are not ideal certainly is not an acceptable position. However, the attempt to coerce teachers through slogans (*e.g.,* "You should be able to teach in a telephone booth") neither is appropriate nor realistic.

Perhaps the most unhappy aspect of the teachers' plight relates to the stand taken by a number of minority group spokesmen and their sociologist allies. For them, the teacher, being of the middle class, can do no right, and whatever approach the teacher takes is to be regarded as wrong and, even worse, as reflective of a wrong-thinking person, or, at the very least, of a distorted attitude.

Thus, it follows that teachers who feel that the underprivileged child is like any other child and should receive no special consideration are insensitive, unfeeling dolts, whereas teachers who affirm that the underprivileged child is different and must be approached in a unique way are offensive patronizers. In short, the teacher is the villain of the play, "Why Minority Children Don't Succeed"; he is damned if he does either one thing or another. Unless the teacher straightens up and flies right, or is replaced, says this outlook, most learning problems of the underpriviliged child will persist. Nor is the up-wardly mobile Negro teacher the answer, since he is as much a middle-class target as his white colleague.

This position serves as an outlet for adult frustration, but does little for their children. While it may be a safety valve for some, it increases anger and despair in another minority group, the teachers, who see a supreme irony in the attacks on them: the victims of racial visibility and vulnerability aiming their hatred not at overpowering and pervasive social and community forces, but at people who also are visible and vulnerable. Just as stereotypes have developed of other exposed minorities, teachers find themselves univer-sally denounced on the basis of specific incidents; evidence favorable or supportive is dismissed as incidental or accidental; and their alleged unde-sirable practices are attributed to smallness of spirit, to intrinsic limitations, or to heredity.

The rejection of false witness against teachers is not intended as a white-wash of all teachers, nor is it an endorsement of the status quo. There are teachers who are prejudiced, small, narrow, and simply incompetent, and it is in order to ask teacher organizations, which recently have exercised a meas-ure of power, to assume the professional responsibility which is a concomi-tant of this power. But logic, morality, and common sense dictate that any approach to the problem of minority children's underachievement be a multi-dimensional one, and that each participant sector review its efforts towards a solution.

Colleges and universities must ask themselves if their highly-publicized projects, centers, and institutes are contributing to broad solutions of the problems, or if they merely are holding actions with little effect. Organized minority groups must decide whether vituperation will accomplish their aims, or whether it merely affords the luxury of retaliation. Expectations of teachers must be pegged at reasonable levels, and not at heights which flout reality. Unrealistic, poorly defined demands upon teachers mask the shirking of responsibility by non-teachers and obscure the operation of community forces which are out of control. The result is a mounting destructive skepticism among teachers. Surely, there is too much intelligence and desire for true achievement in the Metropolis for its members to seize upon panaceas in place of serious thought and action. Can we not dispense with clichés and slogans, tortured logic, and scapegoating, and get on with the education which truly will serve our children and their families?

39

Cultural Diffraction
in the Social System
of the Low-Income School

Daniel U. Levine

Much has been said about the supposed ineffectiveness of the middle-class teacher who works with educationally disadvantaged youth whose experiences and values are different from her own. According to this view, the teacher who insists on adherence to such middle-class values as punctuality, completion of all tasks undertaken, and self-initiative in carrying out homework does little but alienate the low-income child for whom these expectations are totally foreign to his own values. The inference is that, rather than attempting to hold disadvantaged youth to such expectations, teachers somehow should arrange educational experiences in accordance with the values of their students.

Undoubtedly, there is some degree of truth in this position, particularly in its recognition that the values of the middle-class teacher can interfere with her ability to perceive how disadvantaged children are reacting to overly rigid expectations. In its over-all thrust, however, this argument is misconceived. The negative effect of cultural differences in the social system of the low-income school is traceable, not so much to the differences *per se* between teachers and students, as to the behavioral variations these differences generate among the faculty.

To understand why this is so, it is necessary to reject the simplistic view that the values of low-income groups are totally in opposition to the middle-class orientation of education in American schools. That the poor do not share precisely the same attitudes as the middle class has been demonstrated amply in such empirical studies as the one in which Schneiderman found that: "The

SOURCE. Reprinted from *School & Society*, March 30, 1968, by permission of the author and publisher.

points of significant differentiation of the culture of poverty . . . include (1) an inclination to . . . live in harmony with what is seen as natural or given in life, as opposed to the view of man as master . . . of his social and physical world . . . (2) an inclination to . . . free expression of what is conceived as given in human personality . . . in contrast with the . . . go-getting attitudes so valued in American life; and (3) an inclination to emphasize present time and present concerns over the requirements of either past or future in contrast to . . . concern for future planning."[1]

Note, however, that the term Schneiderman uses to describe the lower-class value orientation is "inclination." This is precisely the right term, because it acknowledges that the prototypical low-income individual is inclined, though not unambiguously committed, to the work-success ethic which, despite erosion, is still characteristic of American culture. He hardly could do otherwise, since many of the formative institutions in his environment have as a major goal the inculcation of the society's norms. To say, then, that a low-income citizen is present-time oriented and hedonistic is to say that he is ambivalent on the work-success ethic, as compared with his middle-class counterpart. Torn between the norms of the wider society and the contradictory forces in the debilitating environment of the slums, the working class aptly has been characterized by Rodman as caught in a "value stretch" which reduces the potency of the middle-class value system in molding conformity to "respectable" norms.[2]

What does this mean in terms of the performance of the disadvantaged child in the social system of the school? Primarily, it means that ambivalence in the child's orientation is reflected in the way he fulfills the role of student and in his interactions with other participants in the system. On the one hand, he tends to accept the demands and expectations of the teacher as legitimate, at least to the extent that, in general, he outwardly acquiesces when instructed in what he should do and even when berated for not doing it. Though he often fails in trying to carry out his intentions, he does aspire to do well in his work and often he almost pitifully resolves to do better, even after an unbroken record of years of failure to act on this resolution. Unfortunately, however, he has developed only fragments of the intellectual skills and the personal self-discipline which would enable him to satisfy the demands of the school. As a result of this ambivalent socialization, he does not postpone gratification compulsively to concentrate on abstract tasks, which, in any case, he has not been prepared to master, and he has not internalized the values of the school fully to the degree that they could be said to govern

---

[1] Leonard Schneiderman, "Value Orientation Preferences of Chronic Relief Recipients," *Social Work*, 9: 13–18, July 1964.

[2] Hyman Rodman, "On Understanding Lower-Class Behavior," *Social and Economic Studies*, 7: 441–450, December 1959.

his behavior. Thus, he is less successful in disciplining himself to the tasks of the school than are children not so "stretched" in opposing directions by conflicting value orientations. In the school, he is the marginal man.

From this point of view, the ineffectiveness of the school in teaching disadvantaged youth derives not so much from its commitment to values which are foreign to them as from its failure to provide the type of environment which would reinforce their groping and half-hearted attempts to live up to these goals. The consequences are easily discerned. In the face of conflicting tendencies, students make more or less superficial attempts to live up to expectations, but fall far short. The exasperated teacher either may lower the level of expectations set for students and/or admonish them to overcome the personal "defects" responsible for their failure. To protect their egos from further attack, students withdraw psychologically or become ever more resistant to the demands of teachers. They learn to play off the behavior of one teacher against that of another, by protesting against the threat in one classroom of requirements which "other teachers don't make us do" or which unfairly are "forced on us only because we are poor [or Negro—or Mexican—or what have you]." Thus does the disadvantaged child adroitly turn the lack of uniformity in the behavior of teachers to his own advantage as he perceives it in the short run.

In considering the meaning for the school of his seminal research on child development, Bloom concluded that, in any educational institution, "a highly consistent environment is likely to produce marked effects on the students while a highly inconsistent environment is likely to have only a negligible effect on the students' development both in the cognitive as well as affective domain."[3] The truth of this observation particularly is evident in the slum school, where the inconsistencies between the behaviors of various teachers and between the orientations of teachers and students are greatest. In the middle-income school there is likely to be a strain toward consistency merely because students are conditioned to comply with the requests of their teachers. Consider, for example, the key field of the language arts. Most middle-class youngsters realize that reading and writing are an integral part of the work that must be attended to in all their classes, because their parents always have emphasized the importance of "good" language and often take pains to provide models of good usage. The disadvantaged child, however, is not predisposed to push toward a high level of linguistic performance in all school activities. If he is a poor reader, as so often happens, he understandably is relieved when leaving the English class where, as Fader has pointed out, "his previous experience has assured him that only English teachers demand constant proof of his literacy; he can hardly avoid learning the lesson that read-

---

[3] Benjamin S. Bloom, "Stability and Change in Human Characteristics: Implications for School Reorganization," *Educational Administration Quarterly*, **2**: 47, Winter 1966.

ing and writing are special functions reserved for special occasions, in this case the English class, and that they have no unavoidable, normative relationships to the rest of the world."[4]

Before a person is able to perform satisfactorily in any role, he "must know what is expected of him . . . , must be able to meet the role requirements and must desire to practice the behavior and pursue the appropriate ends."[5] The inner-city school, in which teacher behaviors and expectations differ from one classroom to another, fails on all three counts to provide a social situation in which the disadvantaged child can learn to perform well in the role of student. Because he is less certain to understand what is expected of him, less proficient in carrying out the tasks which define the role, and less committed to expending serious efforts to reach distant academic goals than is the middle-class pupil, the disadvantaged student needs to be reinforced continually in mastering limited, clearly defined aspects of the role of student. Thus, the major problem faced by his teacher is "not to overcome a hostile set of values, but to help pupils whose values are confused and underdeveloped to clarify their values and to work effectively toward the realization of them."[6] Such clarification cannot be achieved as long as inconsistency in the instructional practices in the low-income school magnifies the confusion in the value system of disadvantaged youth and, therefore, makes it all but impossible to acquire competence in the role of student.

One of the reasons why the inconsistency between the values of the teacher and the disadvantaged student has received more attention than the more crucial inconsistency in instructional practices among the faculty is that outsiders have a hard time appreciating how very pervasive this latter inconsistency so often becomes in low-income schools. Any social system, if it is to operate effectively, must be integrated in the sense that its participants are reinforcing each other's contributions, rather than working at cross purposes. Much of this coordination is a result of shared expectations that allow participants to predict each other's actions and responses, thus giving the system a "common culture" which generates continuing commitment to the goals of the system. If the teachers in a low-income school do not work together in a concerted effort to achieve the teacher-induced consistency which might substitute for the consistency supplied almost automatically by the congruence of teacher and student orientations in the middle-income school, their students will not acquire the middle-class habits needed for success in the system.

[4] Daniel N. Fader, *Hooked on Books* (New York: Berkeley, 1966), p. 19.

[5] Orville G. Brim and Stanton Wheeler, *Socialization After Childhood: Two Essays* (New York: Wiley, 1966), p. 25.

[6] Robert J. Havighurst, "Overcoming Value Differences," in Robert D. Strom, ed., *The Inner-City Classroom: Teacher Behaviors* (Columbus, Ohio: Charles E. Merrill, 1966), p. 56.

Moreover, neither students nor teachers will feel the personal satisfaction which comes as a result of participating in a common culture. Such a situation, of course, engenders continual, and often open, bickering between students, between student and teacher, between teachers, and between teacher and administrator. From this point of view, the low-income school is a social system on the verge of disintegration.

To illustrate the constant erosion of norms in the low-income school, let us consider the apparently innocuous tendency of teachers to use different grading policies. Almost all teachers follow policies which, to some degree, are different from those of their colleagues in the same school. In most schools, a degree of uniformity and coherence is present, if only because students generally understand what is expected of them, thereby making it likely that deviance will be singled out and punished. In the low-income school, however, common understandings of this sort seldom are developed adequately. Nowhere in American education does an observer encounter so bewildering a confusion of grading norms as in a high school in a slum neighborhood. In many such schools, a resemblance between the grading practices utilized in any two classrooms seems entirely coincidental. More often than not, these practices appear to be designed with one major purpose in mind: somehow to avoid giving failing grades to students. Sometimes, passing grades are awarded to all students as a simple act of charity. In other classrooms, teachers withhold failing grades because they do not want to penalize students for environmental conditions which make it hard to study. Other teachers, though not many, insist that students work as hard and perform as well as the child who receives an equivalent grade in a middle-income school. In between these two extremes is a continuum on which teachers are distributed according to their willingness to reward or not reward students who long since may have stopped trying to accomplish tasks on which they had experienced nothing but failure.

Teachers trying (as most do) to justify passing grades for their disadvantaged students embrace one or more of a variety of procedures. In some classrooms, good attendance becomes the main criterion for a passing grade. In others, a passing grade represents a good conduct award. Many teachers adopt purely subjective standards. Some exclude library work altogether and limit assignments to exercises in the text. Others give only short, occasional assignments. The same examination may be given over and over until most students pass it. Meanwhile, the minimum grade constantly is lowered, until it coincides with whatever score the teacher finds most students customarily achieve. Some teachers give long, daily quizzes, solely to accumulate passing scores on simple questions. Others spend much of their time pleading for assignments due weeks before. Visitors to some schools will find that a majority of the teachers use class periods for student "homework" assignments, this being the only way to ensure that many students will attempt to complete them. All these practices, it must be emphasized, are understandable in the context of the problems encountered in the low-income school. What is understandable, however, is not necessarily constructive. For how can the disadvantaged child learn to live up to even minimal standards of academic behavior when he moves from one classroom in which there are no standards to another in which standards shift with each passing week, then to one in which teachers constantly threaten to utilize standards but only infrequently do so, and to other classrooms in which the definitions of standards vary widely between individual teachers?

Once the low-income school is seen primarily in these terms as a social system which will function ineffectively until it counteracts pupils' unpreparedness and resistance by providing and, therefore, reinforcing consistent learning experiences in all its constituent classrooms, the burden of responsibility for the effectiveness of the system immediately is placed on the shoulders of the person who coordinates the organization's activities: the building principal. For it is only the principal who is in a position to persuade or cajole or convince a faculty somehow of the need to identify and accept a common modus operandi. The school, after all, is a complex organization in which teachers hardly can be expected to commit themselves more or less automatically to similar policies, no matter how facilely the "paper organization" assumes that all staff members are carrying out similar policies. No individual teacher can expect that a consistent set of learning experiences she strives to provide for her pupils will be replicated somehow in other classrooms, or that her best efforts can have very much effect unless as part of a schoolwide attack on the learning problems of the disadvantaged student.

Educators long have paid lip-service to the importance of the principal's leadership, but, until recently, few noted that outstanding leadership by the principal is even more crucial in the low-income school than in other schools.[7] Consider again, for example, the matter of grading practices among teachers in the low-income school. For faculty in such a school to put into practice a unified set of policies which also are educationally sound will require almost Herculean labors of the principal. Somehow, for example, he will have to convince teachers of the need to modify approaches which may be a cherished part of their respective, educational philosophies, and this is only the first step. Even if a faculty agrees on the need for a set of relatively standard policies with regard to grading, there remains the greater problem

---

[7] For examples, see Robert Herriott and Nancy St. John, *Social Class and the Urban School* (New York: Wiley, 1966), pp. 135–142; and Carl L. Byerly, "A School Curriculum for Prevention and Remediation of Deviancy," in William Wattenberg, ed., *Social Deviancy Among Youth*, Sixty-Fifth Yearbook, National Society for the Study of Education, Part 1 (Chicago: University of Chicago Press, 1966), p. 231.

of deciding exactly what they should be. On the one hand, these policies must avoid any aspect of a simple "sink or swim" philosophy which hardly could benefit the educationally-handicapped student. On the other hand, they must be founded on the principle that no rewards are given unless efforts are expended, if the disadvantaged student is to learn to discipline himself in undertaking and carrying out activities directed at non-immediate goals. Obviously, it will not be easy to work out such policies, and the principal will have to make sure that faculty members not only understand them, .but are following them conscientiously. But, until administrators and teachers define and implement a set of coordinated professional practices in all the classrooms of the inner-city school, the outlook for improving the performance of disadvantaged youth will remain bleak.

40

Disadvantaged Teachers
in Disadvantaged Schools

Richard M. Bossone

"We educate one another; and we cannot do this if half of us consider the other half not good enough to talk to." Shaw, in his penetrating wit, usually speaks wisely not only to his own age, but also to generations that follow him. Unfortunately, our age, which is beset by strong racial and social-class conflicts, is not taking his wisdom to heart. This is especially true where our public schools are concerned.

Social changes usually have great consequences for educators. However, the growth in the number of culturally deprived or disadvantaged students— that is, those who come from low socioeconomic groups burdened with socially disruptive factors and an improper background for formal academic learning—is one change that many educators tend to ignore or superficially acknowledge with the hope that it will not create undue problems. That this is often the case is borne out by James Squire, executive secretary, National Council of English Teachers, who, in a national study of high school English programs, stated that "no one can travel to 168 high schools in the country without sensing an appalling fact: despite the overwhelming acceptance of the tracking program in America's high schools today, teachers and administrators are giving little attention to the lower tracks."[1] Squire found the lack of interest, effort, and time devoted to curricula planning for the slow and average to be "shocking and shameful."

Shocking and shameful, indeed, because teachers and administrators, in many instances, willfully have given the problem of what to do with lower tracks a backseat to the more glamorous problem of providing challenging programs for the college-bound students. In a society where a universal education from early childhood through college is rapidly becoming a right,

[1] James R. Squire, "National Study of High School English Programs: A School for All Seasons," *English Journal*, **55**: 289–290, March 1966.

not a privilege, this approach, as well as the failure and dropout rates, only reveal that our present educational system is either indifferent to the problem or else incapable of dealing with diversity. Our schools are caught in the dilemma of believing in a meaningful education for all, but not knowing how to provide for it. As a result, we simply accept, neglect, and finally reject approximately 70% of the students (at least in large urban centers) who do not fit into an antiquated system which caters only to those who have strong academic potential or can be placed in upper tracks. For the majority, then, our educational system is proving to be ineffective, inefficient, and degrading.

With the 1954 Supreme Court decision relating to the desegregation of public schools and the recent commitment of Congress and the President to the "Great Society" and to an unprecedented war upon poverty, education for diverse learners has become an urgent necessity. Yet, those who control our educational system have not seized the opportunity to introduce needed reforms and innovation which might benefit all students—especially the culturally deprived minorities who are becoming the urban majority. But, with all the current emphasis upon the disadvantaged learner or the culturally deprived student evidenced in workshops, institutes, and research studies supported by federal legislation, one might easily be duped into thinking progress is being made at last. But is it? A more careful analysis of the situation reveals that there is a prevalence of talk and a lack of achievement; more specifically, there is a profusion of descriptions about the nature of the culturally deprived student, which admittedly can be helpful in understanding him, but a lack of instructional prescriptions which are suitable. Teachers who flock to the federally supported institutes and workshops with breathless idealism generally leave with a better understanding of such students, but they still do not know what to do with them in the classroom.

We must go beyond a mere understanding of the culturally deprived student; we must reform an outdated educational system nurtured mainly by "disadvantaged" teachers and administrators who tend to impose an irrelevant curriculum upon the majority of students. We must improve teacher training in this area enormously just to be mediocre, or teachers will continue to work on the assumption that they should teach their students as they themselves were taught in the university; they will continue naively to hope that courses loosely labeled remedial, usually born of frustration and failure, will do the job.

Teachers need a real acceptance of, and more knowledge about, the intelligent handling of culturally deprived students. This acceptance and knowledge only can be gained by teachers if they are trained not only to question their own attitudes toward such students, but also if they are trained to put ideas of diagnosis and treatment into practice. Most teacher training programs totally ignore the teachers' attitudes and the causes of their own intolerance.

As a result, most teachers confronted by these students are emotionally handicapped and unprepared to cope with what they call an impossible and exhausting scene, which in turn engenders frustration, resentment, boredom, or worse. Ironically, then, most teachers become as disadvantaged as the students, working in an educational setting which they find meaningless.

We cannot assume that teacher training programs alone can insure the new education that is needed for the culturally deprived student, but, certainly, a training program that is more realistically geared is a step in the right direction. A teacher faced with the arduous task of working with lower-track students is under the strain of his own insecurities and uncertainties, and educators in teacher training programs have a responsibility to help lessen them. For instance, the professional training of future secondary English teachers in urban centers might involve the following courses which would help facilitate the teacher's understanding, acceptance, and instruction of the culturally deprived student: a course in educational psychology with clinical applications to explore and clarify psychological and sociological character-istics of culturally deprived students and ways of counseling and motivating them to seek further education; a course in cultural anthropology to make clear the distinction between the culturally deprived and the uncultured; a course in urban sociology to elucidate the forces in urban society, its structure, its various class cultures, and particularly the mores, values, and attitudes of the students in urban centers who are culturally deprived; a course in corrective and remedial teaching to explicate concrete and practical methods for diagnosing and alleviating learning problems of these students; and a course in methods of teaching English to convey to the future teacher the structure of the English language, the patterns of language learning, the teaching of reading and literature appropriate for these students, and the significance of mass media and technological changes.

In addition, a teacher training program should be planned as a gradual progression from observation to participation. For instance, teacher candi-dates might engage in observation of the culturally deprived students while taking the first three courses listed above, serve as a teaching assistant while taking the last two, and then engage in student teaching or a classroom intern-ship closely supervised by a teacher who has been successful in working with such students. This could be done more easily if there were an end to the schism between higher education and the public schools; such a new approach could lead to the establishment of clinical schools based on a symbiotic rela-tionship between school and college to insure theoretical applications in real settings.

Having more qualified teachers who understand the students is only the first step toward educational reform. Also necessary is reform in the curricu-lum, which is a responsibility of qualified teachers, the closest agents to the learners, and not the sole responsibility of administrators who may be ignorant of the teacher's instructional problems.

Education must place more emphasis upon affective and less upon cognitive objectives—that is, there must be more attention given to the concerns of the learner and not just the concerns of the academic discipline. If teachers, administrators, and consultants are to design a curriculum that is more relevant, they must ascertain, after diagnosis is made, what concepts and skills can assist the learner with his human imperatives: his need to maintain his physical well-being and a job, his need to get along with others, and his need to live with himself.

Instruction in the coming years must be adapted to the abilities of the learner. The new educational technology will have to be refined and developed further in order to make individualized instruction a reality. Programs will have to be developed that arrange content in a more logical or meaningful sequence of increasing complexity in order to insure a student's continuous progress toward mastery at his optimum rate.

Public educational institutions, especially the secondary schools, traditionally have been designed for the middle classes whose background, concerns, and goals determined the aims and curriculum of education. Now our "Great Society" is faced with the idea of educating everybody to the limit of his capacities—including that vast majority from alien class cultures who were considered too unimportant in the past to be taken seriously. The present educational system will have to change its attitudes toward these pupils; the schools must provide a better education which relieves the "unhappiness, anxiety, boredom and frustration" that David Stafford Clark says are "more frequent causes of apparent dullness or backwardness at school than is sheer lack of intelligence."[2] The unhappy alternative is a growing number of "educopathic students" who will be disaffected learners, unfit for the tasks of a complex society.

These suggestions are only possible beginnings to solving a complex problem. However, they are representative of the most crucial factors in reforming our educational system because teachers in an instructional situation are the heart of any school and its program, and education can be only as good as its teachers. Furthermore, if our urban society wishes to avoid additional racial and social strife, it cannot afford to have an ignorant citizenry being taught in disadvantaged schools by disadvantaged teachers who fail to understand the significance of Shaw's words.

[2] David Stafford Clark, *Psychiatry Today* (Baltimore: Penguin Books, 1951), p. 61.

41

Reaching the Disadvantaged

Allan C. Ornstein

Instead of educating the disadvantaged, schools merely mirror a world that these youth have learned to reject. As the curriculum of the school is geared to a middle-class system, teachers must reject those students who do not fit into the mold. These students, in turn, reject the teachers, thereby continuing the cycle.

Children who grow up in poverty, embittered by discrimination, refuse to believe in a possibility of their succeeding in a middle-class world. They realize that this world will accept only the few who are really exceptional.[1] By building a barrier between themselves and the world beyond their ghetto, these youth feel that they are protecting themselves, and therefore distrust even the teachers who arrive with good words and encouragement.

Because the disadvantaged do not depend on the middle-class world, they either exploit it through welfare or reject it completely. This rejection is recognizable in the dropout statistics and in the disadvantaged youths' constant display of and defense of their values. Having themselves to depend on, they have faith only in their group.

Having middle-class values, most teachers only find reward in working with those students whose values are the same. Upon encountering disadvantaged youth whose values are different, teachers measure progress on a middle-class scale. These teachers often perceive these youth as not having a culture, rather than having a culture that is different. (Gans, Harrington, Lewis, and Riessman have postulated the existence of a "culture of deprivation" having a working system of its own.) Teachers then encourage the child to succeed

SOURCE. Reprinted from *School & Society*, March 30, 1968, by permission of the author and publisher.

[1] Richard Hammer, "Report from a Spanish Harlem 'Fortress,'" in Harry L. Miller and Marjorie B. Smiley, eds., *Education in the Metropolis* (New York: Free Press, 1967), pp. 239–248.

on their terms, therefore teaching the child that his values are wrong.[2] To win their favor and receive the rewards of school that come with middle-class conformity, the child must give up his individuality and his style of life.[3] This much sacrifice cannot justify the loss of identity. Thus, teachers are seen as condescending caretakers, who lack understanding or insight into his problems, yet want to make him one of them.[4] When they fail with him, he can be blamed for not caring.

By applying labels to groups—a source of comfort rooted in the work of behavioral and social scientists—and so being able to group many children as "disadvantaged," teachers begin to see the children in terms of group characteristics rather than individual characteristics. In turn, a stereotyped "deprivation theory" is fostered: these children are unteachable because they come from deprived homes and neighborhoods. The result is the self-fulfilling prophecy: children who are considered uneducable soon believe they are so and become just that.[5] Teachers, then, misinterpret their own difficulties and blame the students for the failure of the school as they gradually shift their function from teaching to custodial care and discipline.[6]

The clash between the culture of the disadvantaged and the middle class is reflected in terms of "us" and "them," with the school representing the outside world and preventing these children from expressing their values. Henceforth, out of frustration, some rebel in school, just as their society turns to violence in the streets. However, most of the children, as well as their society, merely withdraw into their own group and make their own laws so that no outsider can tell them what to do.

Just as the school intimidates its disadvantaged children, it threatens their society. The school is built around the desire to siphon off the "bright ones,"[7] which alienates them from the group and changes their loyalty to a desire for individual success. This makes them ashamed of their culture and heritage by absorbing them into the "ideal" middle-class world. Those who are absorbed usually reject the group (including their families) and adopt new ideas. They rarely return to the old neighborhood to supply leadership. For

[2] Albert Cohen, *Delinquent Boys* (New York: Free Press, 1960). Also, Nathaniel Hickerson, *Education for Alienation* (Englewood Cliffs, N.J.: Prentice-Hall, 1966).

[3] Herbert J. Gans, *The Urban Villagers* (New York: Free Press, 1955).

[4] Cohen, op. cit. Also, William F. Whyte, *Street Corner Society* (Chicago: University of Chicago Press, 1943).

[5] Kenneth B. Clark, *Dark Ghetto* (New York: Harper & Row, 1965).

[6] Miriam L. Goldberg, "Adapting Teacher Style to Pupil Differences: Teachers for Disadvantaged Children," in John C. Gowan and George D. Demos, eds., *The Disadvantaged and Potential Dropout* (Springfield, Ill.: Charles Thomas, 1966), pp. 240–262.

[7] Dan Dodson, "Education and the Powerless," in A. Harry Passow, et al., *Education of the Disadvantaged* (New York: Holt, Rinehart and Winston, 1967), pp. 61–73.

these reasons, mobility into the middle-class often is opposed[8] within the Negro ghetto because it is synonymous with the outside world. The climb from poverty to the middle class is an individual venture, accompanied by isolation and hostility from the group.

How do we reach the disadvantaged? Relying on compensatory education, without changing the basic middle-class philosophy of the school, is wasteful in terms of money, time, and energy. The meager effects of billion-dollar programs seem to indicate that money alone is not enough, and the taxpayers may become disgusted. These programs usually are staffed by "moonlighting" teachers, whose middle-class attitudes are the reasons the school have failed in the first place.

True, compensatory education is needed, but the beginning of the solution is to do away with the strict middle-class standards of the school. They are effective with middle-class children and reinforce what they learn at home, but these standards do more harm than good with the disadvantaged. The school must accept the disadvantaged on their own terms and work to achieve its goal by serving as an ego-supporting, meaningful institution which encourages diversity. This would enable the disadvantaged to become their best possible selves by utilizing their culture, not by trying to change it.

Students behave according to what they perceive is their role. If they are expected to be stupid or inferior, they will behave accordingly, but will ultimately rebel. The school must bury these stereotypes. Students should be encouraged to take the initiative and influence their own school activities, rather than remain passive. Instead of the school authorities dictating what students can do, the students should have the opportunity to organize, take action, and govern their own behavior and fortune in school.

A student government might be organized in which everyone would have the right to vote, hold office, and voice his opinions. No one is isolated or rejected,[9] for there are no middle-class restrictions put on non-conformists. Each class elects its own officers and representatives. The formal governmental structure is organized like a pyramid, with class councils at the bottom, grade councils in the middle, and a school council at the apex.

The students govern themselves by their own values, help shape policy, and take an active role in solving school problems. By effectively organizing under democratic procedures, they enhance their values and life styles. Similarly, learning school politics can be used to make gains through their neighborhood programs. Their school organization and their new-found power serve as a springboard for learning about local social and political issues in the classroom. Hopefully, this new learning will encourage the students to become future leaders, offering them a way of improving their environment

[8] Gans, op. cit.

[9] Earl C. Kelley, *In Defense of Youth* (Englewood Cliffs, N.J.: Prentice-Hall, 1963).

and status without "selling out" or moving away from their family and friends.

If the neighborhood lacks a poverty program, the school must use its resources and organize one. The school must become a part of the neighborhood; otherwise, it will be left out and lose even more status within the home and neighborhood.

Closely allied with the poverty program is the Negro protest, which will continue to grow in depth and intensity. Rarely does one find a magazine.or newspaper that does not have an article on the black-white conflict. How can we not teach this in class?[10] Here is the chance for students to voice their own opinions, being exposed to all sides before making decisions. Here is the chance for the school to have real meaning for the disadvantaged.

The black struggle for equality does not challenge our way of life; rather, it demands that other ways of life be recognized. Teaching the civil rights movement is a lesson in liberty and citizenship. It is a movement toward, not against, the mainstream of American culture.[11] Teaching about the civil rights movement would improve the image of the Negro and produce positive attitude changes toward school and society.

Teachers, therefore, should refuse to use racially biased materials. Their unions must use pressure tactics to bring about reform, and they must provide orientation sessions for new teachers, insisting that school libraries be stocked with accurate, fair material. Students must be taught to exercise initiative where biased materials are used.[12] They must be encouraged to bring civil rights material to school to supplement the regular materials. They need to understand what color and race mean by learning about black heroes and Afro-American history and culture. Recognizing that there are more colored people than white people in the world, they need to realize their potential power, not only in the world but locally, as more Negroes migrate to the city. They need to compare the basic principles of the Ku Klux Klan and the John Birch Society with those of SNCC, the Black Muslims, and the NAACP.[13] Not only should they read about Anderson, Carver, and King, but, more so, James Baldwin, Malcolm X, and H. Rap Brown, even if discussion makes the white teacher feel uncomfortable or guilty. The reason for the riots should be investigated, thus teaching the disadvantaged how to take socially

[10] Thomas F. Pettigrew, *A Profile of the Negro American* (Princeton, N.J.: Van Nostrand, 1964). Also, Lawana Trout, "Involvement Through Slanted Language," in Peter G. Kontos and James J. Murphy, eds., *Teaching Urban Youth: A Source Book for Urban Teachers* (New York: Wiley, 1967), pp. 23–44.

[11] William C. Kvaraceus, et al., *Negro Self-Concept: Implications for School and Citizenship* (New York: McGraw-Hill, 1965).

[12] Ibid.

[13] Trout, loc. cit. Also, C. Ornstein, "Basic Understanding for Teaching the Disadvantaged," Kappa Delta Pi, December, 1967.

acceptable grass-roots action in solving their own legal and social problems. This would involve them with learning and participating in what they have learned. They need to organize demonstrations, marches, and sit-ins in order to handle real experiences. The fusion of reality with learning is the best way of getting the students excited, making school make sense, and developing the students' intrinsic motivation. This would make the task of education much easier.

Of course there is danger, but there is more danger in ignoring what is happening beyond the classroom as Negro youth develop their own irrational stategy. The race riots attest to this. Schools must teach not only the basic American values and skills, but also pride in one's race and culture.

It does little good to belabor the teacher for his middle-class values. Teachers need only to be made aware of the differences in cultural values without viewing one as right or better. Instead of reshaping the disadvantaged child, teachers should accept his culture and improve him within the scheme of his own values. Indeed, teachers should maintain their system of values, but, at the same time, respect and enhance the child's own values in order to reach him. All children need to be respected, to exercise their own values, and to develop their own thinking in context with their life style and culture.

Teachers should present a purposeful, relaxed, but structured classroom atmosphere. Classes should be organized around small groups of students working together. The work the students do should be more on a problem-solving, discovery basis, with students learning from each other, rather than on a teacher-directed lesson.[14] There should be opportunities for small groups to work at home, planning panel discussions and committee reports. This will serve as a prelude to helping them organize neighborhood activities. This type of creative teaching is needed for all students, but it is needed more for the disadvantaged since teachers often are reluctant to experiment with them. Teachers must stop stereotyping the disadvantaged as problems and pathetic learners. Actually, the fostering of creative teaching should increase control in the classroom through added rapport and interest in the lesson.

If teachers are to accomplish these things (and no extra money is needed), their own self-images and ego-strengths need to be reinforced positively. Wholesale and generalized criticism of teachers of the disadvantaged is unjust and does harm to many competent and concerned teachers.[15] These teachers

[14] Hilda Taba and Deborah Elkins, *Teaching Strategies for the Culturally Disadvantaged* (Chicago: Rand McNally, 1966). Also, Allan C. Ornstein "Techniques and Fundamentals for Teaching the Disadvantaged," *Journal of Negro Education*, **36**: 136–145, Spring 1967.

[15] Allan C. Ornstein, "Preparing and Recruiting Teachers for Slum Schools," *Journal of Secondary Education*, December 1967.

are working to overcome problems which primarily are the result of the operation of the school system and other institutions within our middle-class society. While the hostility and frustration of parents and neighborhood, coupled with criticism by college professors, are understandable, their attacks drive good teachers out and disillusion new teachers who are about to be assigned.

T-groups, although usually unstructured, should be organized during teacher-administrative periods in context with the mutual examination of teachers' attitudes, values, and strategies. Teachers need to observe each other, clarify their problems and gripes, and organize within the school so action can be taken. Students', parents', and teachers' groups should recognize publicly effective teachers. This way a better teacher-student-parent relationship could develop, and teachers would be accepted and admired, becoming influential objects of emulation.

42

Recruiting and Training Teachers for Spanish-Speaking Children in the Southwest

Herschel T. Manuel

The recruitment and training of teachers for Spanish-speaking children is part of the general problem of providing an adequate and competent staff for public and private schools. Year after year, new teachers must be found to fill positions left vacant or to expand the teaching staff, new personnel must be trained, and retraining must be provided for teachers in service and for former teachers who re-enter the profession.

The continuing problem of providing qualified teachers now is aggravated by the imbalance of supply and demand. The number of qualified teachers is far short of present needs. For example, a recent issue of the Texas State Teachers Association's *Texas Schools* carries a statement that Texas is faced with its worst teacher shortage in 25 years. The shortage over the nation appears to be greatest in the elementary school. The Oct. 9, 1966, issue of the *NEA Reporter* reports an estimated shortage of between 37,700 and 66,500 beginning teachers in elementary schools. This shortage may be expected to increase as education is extended downward, unless heroic efforts are made to improve the situation. There is evidence that the education of five-year-olds soon will be accepted generally as the responsibility of public education, and that in increasing numbers four-year-olds (at least the disadvantaged) will be included. Persons of good-will well may pray, "God speed the day."

Therefore, at first, we may consider, at least briefly, the problem of recruiting and training teachers in general. Although the profession of teaching attracts many able men and women toward a career in teaching, the

SOURCE. Reprinted from *School & Society*, March 30, 1968, by permission of the author and publisher. Based on address in Symposium, Committee on Civil and Human Rights of Educators, National Education Association, Tucson, Ariz., October 30, 1966.

supply of fully qualified and experienced teachers is likely to remain for some years below the number needed. For many, teaching is only a temporary occupation preliminary to the rearing of children (in the case of women) or to other employment.

The shortage of qualified personnel suggests two remedial measures: the provision of help in the schoolroom for routine jobs and for such instructional activities as can be carried on by untrained or partially trained assistants under supervision—all this to allow the fully qualified personnel to render their best service; and the making of teaching a more attractive profession. We dare not depend too much on the desire to help others as the incentive which will draw able young people toward teaching; the modern world offers many different opportunities to be of service.

One easily can think of four ways to make teaching more attractive: by providing improved working conditions, with standard physical plant, equipment, teaching materials, and the like; by assuring a reasonable working load (for example, in the number of pupils to be taught), and by providing assistants both at the clerical level and the professional level (counselors, for example); by improving the public concept of the profession of teaching, and, in some cases, the teacher's own self-concept as a teacher; and by adjusting salaries to make them more nearly competitive with salaries in other areas.

Turning now to the problem of providing qualified teachers for Spanish-speaking children, we may observe first that the supply of these teachers is influenced by the same factors as those which influence the supply of teachers in general. The basic qualifications of the good teacher of Spanish-speaking children are precisely those of other good teachers—superior native ability, mastery of subject matter, understanding of human nature, broad general education, satisfactory teaching skills, well-adjusted personality, dedication to the work, and the like. In other words, the problem is part of the general problem of staffing schools, and differs only because of the special needs which the teacher of Spanish-speaking children must meet.

What are these special needs? How does the learning of Spanish-speaking children differ from that of other children?

In discussing Spanish-speaking chidren, we must be ever mindful that we are dealing with an extremely varied population and with schools which differ widely. Like other children, these children vary in native ability from feebleminded to genius, in living standards from very low to superior culture, and in economic status from extreme poverty to wealth. In language, many are comfortably bilingual when they enter school, many know Spanish only, many have a limited knowledge of English, and some (strange as it may seem) speak English only. The schools in which they are enrolled vary in financial resources, in the proportion of Spanish-speaking and other children enrolled, in the background and preparation of the children who attend, and in the level at which instruction is offered. "The Spanish-speaking child" turns out to be a number of very different children, and the school which he attends, a number of very different schools.

The stimulating report of the NEA Tucson survey, *The Invisible Minority*, contains a statement which we may lift from its setting and generalize: ". . . different schools present different problems . . . and thus tend to require somewhat different solutions" (p. 26). Let us recall too that not all is discouraging. Large numbers of Spanish-speaking children have understanding and capable teachers, make normal or superior progress, and are happy in their school work. Through the years, we have been moving forward.

However, we must accelerate our progress. We still see too many children retarded in their school work, too many with low academic achievement, too many dropping out of school, and too many with serious personality problems. We must improve the educational process and recruit and train teachers to carry it forward effectively.

The problem of providing qualified teachers for Spanish-speaking children —aside from the problem of schools in general—appears to be more a matter of training than of recruitment. Even the provision of teachers for the disadvantaged appears less difficult than one might expect. Additional remuneration probably is unnecessary—as one of my correspondents (an assistant superintendent) points out, a monetary bonus might attract "persons interested more in money than in children." He finds that geographical location is a factor in placing qualified teachers. Teachers prefer assignments close to their residence, which may be far from the schools in which most of the disadvantaged children are enrolled. Another correspondent, a director of personnel, takes a similar view of additional remuneration as an incentive: "We have no additional remuneration for the teachers of the disadvantaged, but . . . I find no more problem in staffing in this area than I do in the area where the children are not disadvantaged—incentives are certainly not material."

Although teachers, in general, have retarded children in their classes, teachers of Spanish-speaking children need special help in this area because of the large proportion of the children who are retarded and because of the special difficulties which contribute to their slow progress. Retardation in any group is in part a result of native endowment. In part, however, the retardation of Spanish-speaking children is a result of the disadvantages which many suffer. The level of achievement reached by any child at any age level is determined by his inherited capacity and the conditions under which he develops. The cultural poverty of the disadvantaged home lacks the stimulus to normal intellectual growth, and quite naturally the reduced rate of growth increases the gap between his achievement and that of others of equal potential who develop under more favorable conditions.

There are two ways to reduce the retardation which results from the disadvantages of the home: to remove the disadvantages and to compensate for them outside the home. Removing the disadvantages of the home is a socioeconomic problem of the community as a whole. In this process, the school can play an important part through adult education, but for the foreseeable future large numbers of children will continue to enter the school from disadvantaged homes. The task of the school is to compensate as far as possible for the cultural deficiencies of the home. At best it can compensate only in part, and what it can do is limited by the time in the child's life when it is given the opportunity.

Children whose home language is Spanish, advantaged and disadvantaged alike, are handicapped by having to learn a second language and to do most of their school work in that language. They have other difficulties also which, for the moment, we may group together as cultural conflicts.

These special difficulties of Spanish-speaking children are compelling reasons why formal education should be extended downward. Earlier entrance into school will enable a larger number to make normal progress with English-speaking children beginning in the first grade, and for this blessed event we should prepare. Earlier school enrollment will change the situation radically for many children. It will require the development of materials and methods adapted to children of the lower ages. It also will require extensive revisions of the materials and methods which have been developed for Spanish-speaking children who have entered school without these earlier learning experiences. Its impact will be felt throughout the elementary school.

When we come to specifics in the training of teachers of Spanish-speaking children, we inevitably are confronted with problems of policy and philosophy. We and the teachers we train should have a clear concept of the goals toward which we are striving. Perhaps we all can agree that one objective is the development to the maximum of the capacities of every child; but we may be ill-prepared to follow it through. It means the transfer of attention from groups to individual children. It means the preparation of teachers for an individualization of teaching which schools in general have never mastered.

A second objective depends upon our concept of the position which Spanish-speaking people should have in the larger group. One point of view stresses strong group ties and places emphasis on group relations. Another— the one which I hold—advocates the weakening of divisions on ancestral lines and the preparation of all children for full membership in the larger community. It states that every child should be prepared to participate freely and effectively in the business, industry, commerce, government, and community life in general, with equal rights and responsibilities working for the common good.

In this point of view, the central problem is not one of subgroup identity and power and of the relation of minority to majority; it is the problem of building a united community. It is not to make all children Anglos; it is to make children of every origin members of the new community which we are building together in the Southwest.

To be sure, every child well may be proud of the great achievements of his ancestors, but the major goal of education is to help him find his identity in the community as a whole. Exaggeration of group differences and of past conflicts only can be divisive. A child properly may say, "I am of Mexican, English, German, or other ancestry"—or, as in my case, he may be blissfully ignorant of the national origin of his ancestors—but he should be able to say with a feeling of reality, "I am an American. This is *my* community. This is *my* state. This is *my* country." Then, in cooperation with others, "This is *our* country. We all share its opportunities and responsibilities."

This point of view has an immediate application to the teaching of language, making efficiency in the use of English the primary language problem in the education of Spanish-speaking children. But this does not mean that Spanish should be neglected. On the contrary, the Spanish-speaking child has a built-in language resource which is valuable both in advancing his own education and in contributing to the public welfare. The teaching of Spanish should begin with the first enrollment and continue through the grades. It should be a functional kind of Spanish, not devoted exclusively to mechanics of the language or to literature, but directed toward the mastery which can be acquired only by teaching "content" in various subject-matter areas. If teaching Spanish means a longer day and additional personnel, schools must be prepared to pay that price.

If it were possible, all teachers in schools of the Southwest in which both Spanish-speaking and English-speaking pupils are enrolled should be bilingual. If children of other home languages are enrolled, they should know those languages also. But this degree of language competence for all teachers obviously is impossible if other requirements of a teacher's preparation are to be met. In many cases, we shall have to compromise by providing teachers of Spanish who are expert in that language and acquainted in some degree with English, and teachers of English who are expert in that language and acquainted in some degree with Spanish. Naturally, we shall find most of our experts among native speakers of the language in question, but not exclusively. The provision of competent teaching in both languages often will require a form of team teaching in which one teacher primarily is responsible for Spanish and another for English.

Although we know a great deal about the teaching of language, we still are uncertain as to the best way of teaching both languages together. As a matter of fact, there probably is no single best way for all situations. We need additional experimentation, such as my distinguished colleagues, Profs. Theodore Andersson and Thomas D. Horn, and a number of others elsewhere, are developing. But experimentation as contrasted with mere experience in this area is difficult, expensive, and time-consuming. It requires careful supervision with scientific controls and painstaking measurement of results. We must not be too impatient, seeking quick answers, or rush to embrace the new simply because it is new.

A major unsolved problem in dealing with young children whose home language is Spanish is that of providing sufficient contact with and participation in spoken English. In 1938, the U.S. Office of Education published a bulletin by J. L. Meriam entitled, *Learning English Incidentally: A Study of Bilingual Children.* That intriguing title expresses how young children should learn much of their language—incidentally as a by-product of the activities in which they engage and of their communication in these activities. But we need ways to increase such activities and turn them toward language development. Assistants who can work with children other than those being instructed at the moment by the teacher offer a partial solution. Tapes, television, and other mechanical assistance may provide a partial answer. But in all of these there must be careful systematic work toward some goal. Just having children play or look at pictures and listen to tapes can be a kind of merry-go-round, rather than something that carries a child forward.

Somewhere in the training of teachers for schools in the Southwest, attention must be given to the characteristics of disadvantaged people in general and to the cultural traits of the Spanish-speaking population. Again, however, individual differences must be emphasized. It would be a grave error to substitute for the study of the child himself a study of his group, but a knowledge of the conditions that frequently are found helps the teacher and counselor to discover the traits and the difficulties of individual children and to understand their behavior.

What about the conflict of cultures? Of course, we should know and appreciate the culture of our neighbors and the contributions which they have made to our common life. At the same time, we need not be concerned greatly with preserving any aspect of a culture on the basis that it is hereditary. We should see ourselves as inheritors of the culture of many people and of all the ages. It is our privilege to choose freely from the past and to develop a way of life that best fits our present and future needs in a changing world.

We rightly are concerned with action. We are seeking not simply an understanding of the situation, but ways of moving forward. The problems obviously are difficult and complex, requiring action by many different people in different areas. Partly by way of summary and partly for emphasis, I make the following seven recommendations for action:

1. Work toward a reduction of the teacher shortage in general—by raising salaries to make them competitive with the salaries of other occupations; by providing good working conditions in school plant, equipment, educational materials, and the like; by assigning teachers a reasonable working load with clerical and professional help to enable them to do a thorough professional job; and by improving the concept of the teacher as a member of a learned profession. (The primary responsibility for these general measures rests upon legislators, executives, and the public in general, for they alone can give the schools the support which they need.)

2. Promote programs in which school systems cooperate with colleges and universities in the training and retraining of teachers who will have both the general qualifications of good teachers and the special qualifications required for effective teaching of Spanish-speaking children.

3. Continue and extend experimentation, with careful scientific controls and measurement of results, to improve policies, materials, and methods of teaching disadvantaged children, children whose home language is Spanish, children of different cultural background, children who enter school at varying ages, children of different native endowment, children of different levels of achievement in Spanish and English, and children who are taught in groups with varying proportions of children whose home language is Spanish or English.

4. Continue emphasis on English in preparation for full participation in the community at large, giving earlier and more extensive experiences with English in interesting activities—experimenting to find more effective ways of using tapes and other mechanical aids; experimenting also to extend experiences in the use of English through paid and volunteer English-speaking assistants, working under careful supervision.

5. Develop the home language of the Spanish-speaking child, beginning with the child's first enrollment in school. The schools have been right in assuming that the major language problem of the Spanish-speaking child is the mastery of English, but they have not been right in neglecting his native language. Spanish should be taught in all grades of the elementary school. Whether the six-year-old who knows no English should read first in Spanish is a question on which we need careful experimentation.

6. Extend education downward to include the five-year-old and, at least for disadvantaged children, the four-year-old—possibly even the three-year-old. Appropriate early experience with English will increase the possibility of normal progress with English-speaking children. Early enrollment will compensate in part—but only in part—for the deficiencies of the home. Until we

can break the chains of poverty which enslave children, the achievement of many will continue to lag behind the possibilities which were theirs when they were new-born.

7. Finally, cultivate in the school and in the community the concept of a united community in which every person participates freely and effectively for the common good, with equal rights and responsibilities for all.

The building of a united community dedicated to the welfare of all should be a major goal of civic and religious organizations, of parent-teacher associations, of educators, and of all people of good will. Here we find the key to the solution of group tensions and cultural conflicts. Here we find the motivation for dealing effectively with the special problems of this symposium. The building of such a community is part of the most difficult and most urgent problem of the human race—that of learning to live together—a problem still only partially solved nearly 2,000 years since the command, "Thou shalt love thy neighbor as thyself."

43

Teacher Competencies for Work with Culturally Different Children and Youth

Edward G. Olsen

Teachers and tutors of the culturally disadvantaged need certain special competencies if they are to be really successful in their efforts. These competencies are of three kinds: *feelings*—attitudes, concerns, commitments; *knowledge*—understandings, insights, perspectives; and *skills*—performance abilities. Within each of these general categories, specific kinds of needed competencies must be identified, recognized as professional objectives, stated in behavioral terms, and consciously pursued in the training program—whether through formal instruction, in-service workshop, individual self-improvement, or some other approach in professional preparation and upgrading. Such a list of personally sought competencies then may be used by the student to estimate and continuously appraise his own learning needs, and also may be used by his instructor or supervisor to help him evaluate his progress in developing new abilities, finding varied resources for advance, and deepening his satisfaction in the process.

At California State College in Hayward, a significant experiment in teacher education for the deprived had been conducted. Called "Operation Fair Chance," this project has completed its second and terminal year. It was a search for more effective procedures in preparing usually middle-class college graduates without professional training to become successful teachers of culturally different children and youth. Its unique feature was the abolition of all formal courses in Education and the substitution for them of extensive community and school field experiences in disadvantaged neighborhoods and their schools. Problem-centered seminars served to conceptualize those experiences.*

* For a description of Operation Fair Chance's first-year program, see Edward G. Olsen, "Teacher Education for the Deprived: A New Pattern," *School & Society*, **95**: 232–234, April 1, 1967.

During the project's first year, the staff and teacher-candidates decided that a listing of specific and functional objectives would be a helpful—even an essential—checklist against which to evaluate the project program itself as well as to assess developmental progress of the prospective teachers. Over a period of some months, an Operation Fair Chance Objectives and Self-Appraisal Check List was produced in tentative form. This was done through a series of stages: appointment of a staff *ad hoc* committee to do preliminary thinking; selection of an Objectives Committee consisting of three staff members and eight teacher-candidates; formulation of a model objectives suggestion instrument by the director of Operation Fair Chance; distribution of this model to all candidates and staff members with the request that they respond with lists of affective, cognitive, and skills objectives, some testing ideas, and also with suggestions for "content vehicles"; collation of replies received; submission of this collation to committee members with the request that they individually examine critically the rough draft, strike out items, clauses, phrases, etc., they thought not needed and add others they believed should be included; editing of the replies received and further collation; committee analysis of the result, leading to general approval of progress made and referral of the whole project to the Operation Fair Chance director to complete; and revision of the document by the director, as presented below, and subject to much improvement through experimentation and refinement.

Operation Fair Chance: Candidate's Self-Appraisal Check List

OFC's five major General Objectives are stated in turn, each one with constituent behavioral objectives grouped as *feelings, knowledge,* and *skills.* Opposite each item is a 5-point scale for evaluation-of-competence use. To save space here, the scale check lines are omitted after the first illustrative category.

OFC General Objective #1: The Effective Teacher will "improve (his) understanding and acceptance of children whose backgrounds and behavior patterns are drastically different from his own."

(Candidate's FEELINGS)   *Extent of Empathy Developed*

	MUCH		SOME		NONE
1. Care about disadvantaged groups and individuals	___	___	___	___	___

2. Sensitivity to conflicts between own values and those of the disadvantaged area in which one works   _____ _____ _____ _____ _____

3. Commitment to social and political action beyond contractual responsibilities of traditional teachers   _____ _____ _____ _____ _____

4. Preference for working with children and in communities identified as disadvantaged   _____ _____ _____ _____ _____

(Candidate's KNOWLEDGE)   *Degree of Understanding Achieved*

1. All people are motivated by similar needs and desires, but their behavior patterns are culturally molded by social class, racial and religious outlooks, etc. (In what specific ways?)

2. Social trends, community tensions, family situations, and peer influences profoundly affect the child's behavior in school and out (With what results?)

3. For the culturally different child, schooling is usually a negative, even hostile, experience (Why and how?)

4. Compensatory education is of little avail so long as exploitative social conditions such as slums and discrimination endure (Implications?)

5. Value-systems and personal aspirations of lower-class children and middle-class teachers differ widely (How?)

6. People disadvantaged by poverty or prejudice or both may legitimately organize themselves as power groups to force social changes (Who? Why? How?)

7. Legislation, demonstrations, community organization, and education are all valid strategies to secure needed social change (Why? When?)

(Candidate's SKILLS)   *Range of Abilities Attained*

1. Identify one's own basic attitudes toward culturally different people

2. Become sharply aware of minority group feelings, attitudes, outlooks, fears, aspirations, frustrations—and resultant behaviors

3. Interpret children's behavior as form of nonverbal communication

4. Comprehend lower-class and racial vocabularies and equivalent standard English meanings

5. Work with parents in ways which demonstrate sensitivity to parental roles characteristic of specific groups

6. Convey at all times an uncompromising commitment to the essential worth and dignity of all human beings

OFC General Objective #2: The Effective Teacher will "improve (his) ability to generate in such youngsters a real motivation to learn through greater creativity and skill in the design and use of novel and specialized teaching tools, methods and techniques."

(Candidate's FEELINGS)

1. Strong preference for the new, the untried, the radically different approaches —to be sought and tested on their own merits, along with fresh evaluation of accepted procedures

2. Zeal for learning that is contagious. Enthusiasm for each new learning opportunity as a key to open, expand, and enrich life experiences of children and youth

3. Intense concern to develop genuine (two-way) communication with disadvantaged people of all ages and backgrounds

(Candidate's KNOWLEDGE)

1. Awareness of learning experience backgrounds of the disadvantaged, their attitudes toward middle-class preoccupations, life-styles, community and school authority figures, etc.

2. Understanding of ways in which deprived and middle-class children differ in cognition, abstraction, verbal skills and nonverbal communication, reading, creativity, vocational concerns, motivation, etc.

3. Comprehension of particular ways in which disadvantaged children respond to different motivational techniques, and of how to relate desired learnings to their emotional motivational needs

(Candidate's SKILLS)

1. Convey to children the feeling that they are worthwhile people with potential

2. Demonstrate sensitivity to problems faced by students, and concerned awareness of realistic alternative solutions or approaches to solutions

3. Tailor the curriculum to the child's real world of family and community experiences. Through relevant affective and cognitive learnings help him to im-

prove the quality of his living as an individual and a member of family, peer, and community groups

4. Structure possible successes for each child, using expressive, creative material and providing opportunity for him to change his activities before the need to do so becomes too apparent

OFC General Objective #3: The Effective Teacher will "create and maintain learning situations which will lead students to realistic vocational objectives, effective preparation for an occupation, pride in workmanship, and confidence in their ability to succed in the vocations of their choice."

(Candidate's FEELINGS)

1. Genuine respect for all types of legitimate work, mental or physical; also for parents as people, even though unemployed
2. Sensitivity to vocational perplexities of children
3. Optimism and enjoyment in helping children learn to work together and to help each other in academic and out-of-school situations
4. Concern to build world-of-work concepts and expectations into the curriculum as a basic strand permeating every subject field through all grade levels from primary grades through college

(Candidate's KNOWLEDGE)

1. Comprehend basic trends and social issues in the world of work, including automation and cybernation, job discriminations and unemployment rates, proposed economic remedies of all types
2. Be aware of the variety of jobs which are closing down, expanding, not yet created. Think imaginatively about the problems of leisure as well as those of work in the discernible future.
3. Understand kinds of preparation necessary for vocational careers in many fields; know sources of continued valid information about them; be alert to ways of introducing such helps to students at all school levels
4. Recognize specific kinds of differences in vocational objectives of middle-class and culturally deprived children
5. Know varied approaches to vocational learning and motivational experiences such as field trips, interviews, films, tapes, service projects, work experience programs

(Candidate's SKILLS)

1. Show equal pleasure and respect in meeting all parents, and in any job discussion with children

2. Structure learning situations so children may know they are really achieving—by collecting all work done, displaying much of it (not just art items), and praising them for jobs completed

3. Relate vocational awareness to basic education, demonstrating ability to help children explore vocational and programmed material and also to stimulate and deepen their interests in vocational areas

4. Plan with children so that they will become familiar with many "families" of vocations and will start thinking realistically about their lives after school years are over

5. Secure cooperation of parents, including development of functional adult orientation and service courses and informal programs for them

6. Teach goals for success in the world of work: finishing the task at hand, mutual respect for the skills of others; pride in work well done and in one's own contributions to class projects

OFC General Objective #4: The Effective Teacher will "increase his utilization of the possible contributions of all agencies in the community which usually become involved with such youngsters during their lifetime."

(Candidate's FEELINGS)

1. Deep concern to achieve widespread interrelation between school and community to meet the educational needs of all children, youth, and adults

2. Readiness to develop cooperative school-community planning with parents, community workers, and public and private agency officials

3. Willingness to trust the community's varied agencies so that, working together, they and the school can better relate to the fundamental life needs of the children

4. Eagerness to support and implement the life-centered school philosophy and practice

(Candidate's KNOWLEDGE)

1. Comprehend "community" as essentially a spirit and practice of "common-unity" requiring continued "communication" between all segments of its people

2. Understand basic elements and interactions in any community generally, and in the immediate community specifically: the people; their dominant and minority-group values and aspirations; the economy and political system; health and welfare conditions; recreational facilities; kinds and extent and effects of racial and religious discrimination, etc.

3. Familiarity with the roles, functions, and operations of existing community agencies, public and private, especially in relation to present and potential needs of the people and their children

4. Know which children's families receive welfare aid, which children come from fatherless homes and/or those held together by tired, lonely, overworked mothers; which are under stress and distress because of such home conditions

5. Be aware of how clothing, medical and dental care may be secured, and where and how parents may find help in increasing language skills, seeking legal aid, finding sources of job referrals, etc.

6. Acquaintance with poverty program officials and minority group leaders as persons, and considerable knowledge of their group histories, customs, contributions, and community problems as they see them

(Candidate's SKILLS)

1. Survey the community to discover needs, problems, and resources in such fields as job appointments, recreational and health facilities, housing conditions, public safety, civil rights, police procedures, etc.

2. Study community agencies to learn their organizational patterns, philosophies, programs, and procedures as these actually operate

3. Effectively use a variety of community resources in teaching, in curriculum development, and in counseling, whether formally or informally

4. Confer successfully with community persons who deal with school children, to the end that cooperative planning for better education and welfare may progress

5. Demonstrate ability to work with youth authorities, police and fire departments, neighborhood groups, recreation centers, city planners, welfare workers, public and private counseling services, etc.

OFC General Objective #5: The Effective Teacher will "increase the receptivity and capability of the participating school system to implement and activate the new learning of teachers."

(Candidate's FEELINGS)

1. Sensitivity to the philosophy and the mood of a school system, with determination to utilize the channels through which change may take place

2. Emotional ability to relate well to the teachers and principal in the participating school district

3. Attitudes of innovation: not satisfied with existing program, feels strong

enough to stand and be counted on important issues, demonstrates sensitivity to the power structure and to what is possible as well as desirable, listens intently to others at all times

4. Maintains strong concern that all changes contemplated or made be evaluated in terms of what they achieve to help the children, both in their academic progress and in the ways they feel about school

(Candidate's KNOWLEDGE)

1. Recognition that children and all learners are interested and really involved only in those elements of the program to which they can relate psychologically

2. Awareness that children may be psychological dropouts by third grade and that symptoms and signs of that development can be discerned through preceding years

3. Knowledge of promising practices in teaching such children at varied maturity levels, including experimental programs currently under way and attitudes of the local school district administrators toward such research and development

(Candidate's SKILLS)

1. Abilty to move with tact and diplomacy in suggesting experimental changes, and to work cooperatively with others rather than as an impatient "loner"

2. Competence in analyzing areas where improvement is most needed, and in proposing modifications or alternate policies and procedures

3. Flexibility in purposes and approaches combined with tenacity

Positive feelings, functional knowledge, and working skills—all are or should be dynamically interrelated as essential professional competencies developed in at least minimum degree by anyone who aspires to teach culturally different children and youth. With the deprived—as with all children —"you gotta reach them before you can teach them." Such a tentative check list as this one may help all of us evaluate our true response to that dual challenge.

44

Excellence in Training Programs
for Teachers
of Disadvantaged Youth

A. Bruce Gaarder

This is an attempt to identify in broad terms the marks or signs of the promise of excellence in proposals to conduct training programs for teachers of disadvantaged children. The same marks will indicate the realization of excellence in ongoing or completed programs. The intention is not to point out the only road to Rome, but rather to make it easier to recognize Rome itself.

In a successful proposal for a recent teacher-training institute made by a midwestern university, the introductory statement (concerned with Mexican-American school children, the "target group") contained two candid references to the rejection of these children and their parents by the dominant majority in that area: ". . . the total community which, in spite of himself, will not accept him as a bona fide citizen with all its attributes." And (we must consider) "the lack of his complete and total acceptability by 'American' society." Leaving aside the "unacceptability" of such syntax from a university professor, the point is clear and leads directly to my thesis: acceptance is the reward of conformity, but, to the extent that conformity is not possible or is not desirable, acceptance comes only with the power to demand respect and one's fair share of things.

That teacher training program is most successful which does most to facilitate the acquisition of power, to increase this kind of power in children, teachers, parents, and other members of the so-called disadvantaged groups. Power in this context means many things: knowledge, specific skills, prestige, authority, experience, confidence, money, self-sufficiency, and many more.

AUTHOR'S NOTE: This chapter is not represented to be a statement of the official position of the U.S. Office of Education.

"Facilitation of the acquisition of power" must be translated first into teacher-training talk. In a training program it is recognizable in three overlapping emphases.

Maximum Involvement of the Disadvantaged Group. A quick examination of some federal aid-to-education programs focused on disadvantaged youth lends credence to the suspicion that, whatever else may result from them, they have been a bountiful source of new careers off the poor. The roster of persons on the letterhead of the Arizona Bilingual Council includes no Indian and no person with a Spanish surname. It is unlikely that any federally-supported teacher training program has been as pure and free from ethnic influence as that. Nevertheless, a cursory examination of aid-to-education programs and their budgets for disadvantaged youth shows most of the money by far goes to middle-class people several stages removed from the disadvantaged state. This is neither for nor against the argument that "it takes one to teach one." The point seems to be that, although it is virtually impossible to know the effect on the pupils of most teacher training programs (indeed, the effect might sometimes be nil or even negative), it is almost certain that the teacher participants, the faculty, the director, and the contracting institution benefit in many ways—ways that increase their power as suggested above. The participants get a period of subsidized schooling, increased knowledge, skill, experience, college credit, prestige, etc., and increased chances for advancement. Likewise the director. The institution benefits, often in prestige, always financially. It follows, then, that whenever a choice is at all possible, these increases in power should go to members of the disadvantaged group.

The next point concerns the sheer disproportion in American schools of the number of teacher representatives of the disadvantaged groups. Most disadvantaged children (even in segregated schools) have middle-class, majority group teachers. The disproportion is especially acute at the supervisory and administrative levels. Bearing in mind the rather obvious help to disadvantaged children from the presence of authority figures of their own kind, and bearing in mind that teaching, supervising, and running schools are also good sources of livelihood, respectability, and self-sufficiency, training programs should, to the maximum extent possible, be designed to increase the number of these people and, thus, their power.

The third point of involvement is at the level of the school board and the community of parents and other adults. This point will be discussed more fully below and in another context. Here it is appropriate merely to recall that the school alone does not educate the child, that it is the major formal system for that purpose but is heavily outweighed in overall influence by all of the other educative forces in the child's life. Stated succinctly, the schools traditionally have taken too much credit for their part in the education of children and currently are receiving and accepting too much blame when children do not become educated. The parents and the entire sub-society of the particular disadvantaged group must come to understand the limitations of formal school systems. There is no better way to put this matter in perspective than by placing in that subsociety's hands the overall determination of fiscal, administrative, and pedagogical policy in their children's schools. This seemingly negative objective may in fact represent another kind of power: sober, illusion-free realization of the extent to which the responsibility and blame cannot be shifted to third parties. More of this anon.

Finally, there is the new role for "paraprofessionals" or teacher aides. Here again the jobs and the chance should go to members of the disadvantaged group, for all the reasons noted above. There is only one caution: The use of such persons, whether as a bridge or link between two cultures (*e.g.*, American Indian and American middle class) or simply to share any part of the load of the regular, certified teacher, can be harmful if the relationship between teacher and aide is such as to show the latter to the child in a subservient role of inferiority.

The Mutually Supportive Relationship. Whichever segment of a society controls the schools will find usually, to its quiet gratification, that somehow, in what can seem only the natural course of events, its children are the most successful performers, the highest achievers in those schools. If a different segment controlled the schools, its children would stand out above the rest.

The premise here is a simple one: Formal schooling is most effective when there is a strong, mutually supportive relationship in every sense between the school and the particular community and encompassing sub-society of pupils and their parents. This notion becomes clear through reference to two extreme, opposite cases: on the one hand such fine learning-teaching systems as Phillips Exeter Academy, the Choate School, and Groton, in tightly interlocking combination with the subsocieties which support and are supported by them; on the other hand, reservation schools for American Indian children, oriented, managed, and taught almost exclusively by middle- and lowerclass representatives of the alien, dominant, "conquering" majority—with the avowed purpose of alienating the children and rescuing them from the baleful influence of their parents. It is altogether likely that if one of the three schools mentioned above were moved to Spanish Harlem—every brick and book, all the ivy and aura, the complete staff and governing board—but without its regular student body, it would become a problem school within six weeks.

In an essay on Indian education—not without relevance here—the point is made thus: ". . . the only road to development of a people is that of self-development, including the right to make its own decisions and its own mistakes, educate its own children in its own way, write its own poems and stories, revere its own gods and heroes, choose its leaders and depose them— in short, to be human in its own way and demand respect for that way.

"If it is true that society as a whole—in this case each separate tribal society with its own history, language, and system of beliefs and behavior— is inescapably the major shaper and educator of a child (as compared to the much lesser effect of the school) educational policy should seek to strengthen and develop and ennoble the social structure as a whole. The opposite strategy, efforts to weaken or bypass the Indian social structure and lessen its influence on the child, inevitably deprives him of his main source of growth and strength."[1]

The premise of mutually supportive relationship suggests that insofar as choices are possible, they should be made in favor of maintaining and strengthening in every way the sub-society from which the pupils spring and facilitating for its members the acquisition of power over themselves and their lot; the community and its encompassing sub-society should have responsibility and control (policy, fiscal, administrative, pedagogical) over their children's education, and a majority of the teachers, principals, and other authority figures should be of the children's kind; every time the op- portunity comes (in the curriculum, for example) to choose between an emphasis on the value system, the history, the language, etc., of the child and the alternative of converting him swiftly and cleanly to the value system, history, and language of the dominant "mainstream," the former should be preferred for the sake of the power that comes from self-realization; since there will be and always should be a mixture of teachers and other authority figures, including members of the dominant, "advantaged" mainstream, the latter should be sensitized by every means to the ethos of the disadvantaged; and, in the case of disadvantaged groups who have a mother tongue other than English, the community should give this tongue a powerful role in the schools through bilingual education.[2]

---

[1] A. Bruce Gaarder, "Education of American Indian Children," in James E. Alatis, ed., *Monograph Series on Languages and Linguistics* (Washington, D.C.: Georgetown Uni- versity School of Languages and Linguistics, 1968), pp. 83–96.

[2] In teacher-training programs, besides the obvious need to select participants who are mother-tongue speakers of the other language and prepare them to use it as a medium of instruction, there is at least one other way to use the language as a power facilitator. In an institute designed, for example, to give history teachers a less ethnocentric view of Mexican-American relations, if the teacher participants were Mexican-American speakers of Spanish and Anglo-Americans with competence in Spanish, a course in Mexican-American history taught in Spanish to all the participants by a historian from Mexico would give prestige to Spanish (hence, power to its native speakers), and, in- stead of the usual attempt to de-ethnicize the Mexican-Americans, in some measure would turn the tables and ethnicize the Anglos.

Remediation and Compensation. The question here is a delicate one: remediation and compensation for what? For the shortcomings, inadequacies, deficiencies, mistakes, and failures of the children and their parents? Or for the shortcomings, inadequacies, deficiencies, mistakes, and failures of the teachers, the school, and the larger system which these reflect? The writer is fully aware that there are semantic traps and that a slum child or an American Indian child probably has been shortchanged by the system and has some compensation coming to him. That is the simplistic premise of today's remedial and compensatory school programs. The view taken here subsumes the simplistic premise and rests on the more fundamental one that there is nothing wrong with children. With a child, yes; with an entire sub-society of children, no. Therefore, while bearing fully in mind that this is no either-or dichotomy, the premise calls for massive modification and adaptation of the educative system to make it fit the child.

Some specific propositions flow from this premise. One is the importance of "relevance." Another is the need to enhance the child's self-concept. Here, indeed, "it takes one to teach one." The notion that a middle-class white lady can give a group of Negro teenagers a sense of pride in their heritage is basically ludicrous. Pride, like patriotism and love, comes through emotion, not from the most sympathetic statement of fact. Germans do not teach it to Frenchmen. Here the need is for exemplary human models of their own kind to set the children aglow and dreaming of what they might be: heroes, artists, athletes; poets, plumbers, doctors; sergeants, statesmen, spell-binders.

A third proposition deals with the question of nonstandard English. A man wise in these matters has stated the matter in terms of "linguistic repertories" and "social roles." On one side is the list or ladder of the roles (jobs, positions) people fill in society. Here the simplistic theory has been that if the child speaker of a nonstandard variant of English can be taught to speak in a way corresponding to a given societal role, he then will have easy (easier?) access to that role. Joshua Fishman has made the disconcerting suggestion that if the child truly had access to that role and knew it, there might be little need to "teach" him the corresponding language. In other words, if the child were fully aware of the role and had full confidence (along with his parents) that it is within the realm of his expectations, the teaching problem would tend to disappear. In still other words, in a major sense "language disability" is not the malaise. It is only the major schoolroom symptom.

This is not to say that the schools should cease trying to improve the child's language. Rather, the intention here is to suggest that much less reliance should be placed on the efforts of "reading specialists" and linguistic research, however well-meaning and expert both might be.

The fourth proposition concerns preschool education. The idea back of this misnomer is not challenged here as long as the preschooling efforts are designed in accordance with the other recommendations explicit or implied in this essay.

The final proposition focuses on the differences among black people, Spanish speakers, and American Indians. Many proposals attempt to combine in the same program—with the same objectives, courses, and professors—efforts to improve teaching for children of two or all three of these groups. This may be in some degree unavoidable to the extent that the children are mixed in the same schools and classes. Nevertheless, it is a bad practice, because, although they have difficulties in common, there are essential and conflicting differences in their present and past cultural roots and patterns, in their own view of themselves, in their school problems, and in their potential as adults.

These children's language problems arise from entirely different causes, are widely divergent linguistically, and call for different kinds of help. The Spanish speakers, by definition, have a mother tongue other than English, and, therefore, a special learning potential and career potential if they can have the advantage of bilingual schooling.[3] The black child's potential is certainly no less great, but the reconsideration of his past history which he needs and demands will require totally different treatment in the schools.

Bilingual schooling is no less important for Indian children, but, since the languages are not the same, the programs cannot possibly be combined and the same teachers cannot serve two distinct groups. Each of the three—the blacks, the Spanish speakers, and the American Indians—has a different ethos, family system, and history. Their need for inspiring adult human models to emulate is the same, but one group's models would be meaningless to the others. They need teachers of their own kind. Understanding one group helps in no way except theoretically to understand the other. Finally, although the three groups carry the burden of being visible minorities, it is in widely differing degree. To throw all or any two of them together increases the burdens of each. Few teachers could learn to cope with all three together.

There is an instructive parallel between social welfare approaches to poverty and current, massive compensatory education programs. Rein has described the situation for social welfare. He sees that ". . . two broad theories of the conditions which create poverty—and by implication the strategies required to provide change—can be identified." One is that poverty results from economic conditions and that it "can best be understood in terms of the organization of our economic system and our value system. . . ." The other view "stresses the contribution of personal characteristics, sometimes defined

---

[3] See A. Bruce Gaarder, testimony before U.S. Senate Special Subcommittee on Bilingual Education on S. 428, Part 1, May 18, 1967 (Washington: U.S. Government Printing Office, 1967), pp. 46–57.

morally or psychologically—illegitimacy, marital breakdown, low motivation, lack of skills and resourcefulness." It is "the view that poverty is a reflection largely of individual pathology." Rein reflects as follows on the two approaches: "It is characteristic of our society, as Cloward has stated, to define human problems as resulting from personal rather than from institutional inadequacies. Such definitions deflect criticism from the social order and focus it upon the presumed moral, social, or psychological defects of the people implicated in various problems. To the extent that such definitions are successfully imposed, a pressure for the maintenance of existing systems of social arrangements is set in motion. Hence, such definitions are essentially conservative. They tend to preserve the institutional status quo."[4]

What Rein says about poverty and social welfare theories applies to educational malaise and compensatory programs. The result in both cases of accepting the theory of "individual pathology" is an ever-increasing battery of specialists concentrating their therapy on the supposed ills of individuals. In the schools they are called counselors, school psychologists, psychiatrists, language specialists, reading specialists, school social workers, etc.

The writer does not impugn the motives or deprecate the skills of these specialists. The fact remains, however, that they are middle- or higher-class people, far removed from the disadvantaged state, and theirs are highly desirable new careers off the poor. The intention here is to show that there is another, sounder point of view and to invite attention to it.

[4] Martin Rein, "Poverty, Social Services, and Social Change," in William C. Kvaraceus, et al., eds., *Poverty, Education, and Human Relations* (Boston: Allyn and Bacon, 1967), pp. 42–43.

45

Is Anyone Indicted
by the Success of Upward Bound?

Lawrence A. Wenzel

The U.S. Office of Economic Opportunity began its Upward Bound operations in 1965, and, by the summer of 1967, there were more than 22,000 students involved in 248 projects. Students in these projects are admitted if they meet the family income requirements, based upon a sliding scale ranging from $1500 for two in the family to $4000 for six in the family, and if they are recommended by an appropriate person as having college ability. They must have sophomore standing. The students spend eight weeks on a college campus during the summer studying in "enrichment" programs, and during the academic year they are assisted with counseling, some tutoring, and medical attention.

During Upward Bound's short period of existence, it has enjoyed huge success. Admissions to college from it average about 85%, and in those programs designed as high risk (students with low grades or dropouts) the average is greater than 70%.

In an attempt to gain insight into some of the sociological factors related to Upward Bound students, the writer interviewed 50 high-risk students at the California State College at Chico. Nearly all of the high-risk students had poor experience in their high schools, and they identified themselves as losers prior to their entry into Upward Bound. The root cause for their poor experience is poverty, and it has several manifestations. Between the low family income and poor school performance there is usually a culturally barren home environment, low status in the community, and discrimination from a great variety of sources both on and off campus. When the 50 Upward Bound students were asked, "Why haven't you been more successful in high school?," 40% said they had poor attitudes regarding school and study habits; 20% said that they had poor home conditions for study; 20% said that their failure was related to poor treatment by teachers; 12% said they were poorly

.iuenced by their gang; and the remaining 8% gave a variety of other reasons for their failure, including a language problem, fatigue, and having to work.

In an effort to get an explicit statement about their problems in school, the same 50 were asked, "What 'bugs' you most about your high school?" Criticisms of some of their teachers were involved in 50% of the responses; 40% complained of inadequate relations with their fellow students involving bullying, social class discrimination, and suffering from anonymity; 8% had no complaints; and 2% complained about an administrator.

The Upward Bound projects have managed to break the pattern of being losers for a great majority of the participants. Of the 50 high-risk students who were asked, "Has Upward Bound helped you?" and "How?," 95% said that Upward Bound had helped them. The breakdown revealed an equal percentage (32%) between those who had improved their relations with others and improved motivation regarding school; 24% claimed great self-knowledge was gained through the Upward Bound experience; 12% said they had learned something of what college was about. These explanations of changes in the Upward Bound student's outlook from being "down and out" to "in and up" are consequences and are not intended to provide any causal explanations.

Speculation regarding the causes of change in student behavior would have to include the Hawthorne effect very prominently. As in the Western Electric plant, the Upward Bound students have enjoyed being important in the eyes of significant others. Teachers, counselors, or administrators have expressed a degree of confidence in Upward Bound youngsters by recommending them as college potential. Certainly, the youngster recognizes that he is important to some by these recommendations. The people working in Upward Bound projects carry through with encouragement on a class and personal basis. The high contact rate between students and teachers and tutor counselors provides an arrangement for optimum encouragement.

The substance and method in the curriculum of Upward Bound projects frequently break the routinized approach to education that is common in high schools in which Upward Bound students have experienced failure. Because of the absence of rigidity, the Upward Bound teacher may move swiftly to attend to passing student interests. The teachers are not strongly influenced by a traditional method of presentation; experimentation with method has a high premium placed on it. The programs are very often rich, varied, and exciting; they are designed to take the blinders off the youngster—to make him more alive to his environment. At least a portion of the Upward Bound success may be attributed to imaginative teaching and to imaginative experiences. But of the 248 projects, there no doubt is some failure to establish exciting programs; yet, all of the programs have sent at least 70% to college.

A major portion of the success of Upward Bound must be attributed to the effect of identifying the loser as a potential winner.

The rediscovery of poverty as the cause of many of our problems brought Upward Bound into existence, but the Upward Bound student's failure in schools is not solely a direct manifestation of raw poverty involving hunger and anxiety. Instead, discrimination, intentional or not, against the low status-poverty group by teachers and fellow students results in people who bow out of the system. There are few or no honors in the system for them; on the contrary, they frequently experience a good deal of contempt because of low family status in the community. This is why Upward Bound is needed—to give back to a small percentage of the students some of the dignity that has been taken from them because of their parents' low status.

Who is indicted by the success of Upward Bound? Any teacher or student is indicted whose judgment is based fundamentally on social class considerations. Upward Bound's success is another reminder for the educational establishment to guard against discrimination based upon social class considerations.

46

Freedom from Ignorance:
U.S.O.E. Programs
for Assisting Needy Students

Thomas E. Harris

A fifth freedom, freedom from ignorance, was added to President Roosevelt's famous four freedoms by President Johnson on Feb. 5, 1968, when he transmitted his education message to the Congress. According to the president, freedom from ignorance means that "every man, everywhere, should be free to develop his talents to their full potential . . . unhampered by arbitrary barriers of race or birth or income."

The President established one of the goals of the fifth freedom as increasing the number of high school graduates going on to college from more than 50% in the fall of 1967 to two-thirds by 1976. This meant providing financial assistance to about 1,500,000 students in the academic year of 1968–1969. In trying to achieve this goal, the U.S. Office of Education's Division of Student Financial Aid administers six student financial aid programs, National Defense Student Loan, College Work-Study, Educational Opportunity Grants, Guaranteed Loans, Vocational Student Loans, and Cuban Student Loans.

Under these programs, more than 900,000 students in America's colleges and universities received funds to help pay the costs of higher education during the 1966–1967 school year. This was the largest group of students so far to benefit from the Office of Education's student financial aid programs since the first program was initiated over a decade ago. Overall, about one out of six students attending college received some form of financial aid.

Oldest of these programs, the well-known National Defense Student Loan program, began in 1958 shortly after the shock of the launching of the

EDITORS' NOTE: This chapter does not represent the opinions or policies of the U.S. Office of Education.

Soviet Sputnik spacecraft. During the first 10 years of operation, more than 1,300,000 students borrowed more than $1,000,000,000 in NDSL funds to finance their education. During the academic year of 1966–1967, nearly 395,000 students obtained loans under Title II of the National Defense Education Act. Loans under NDEA require no particular field of study by the student, although those students who choose teaching can obtain a loan cancellation at the rate of 10% for each year of teaching up to a maximum of 50% of their loan. The cancellation rate increases to 15% for teachers who elect to serve in certain schools in low-income areas or to teach handicapped children. The entire loan may be cancelled under this provision. More than $10,000,000 were provided by the Office of Education to pay for these two types of teacher cancellations in the 1966–1967 school year.

Undergraduates can borrow up to $1000 each school year to a maximum of $5000. Repayment is not required until nine months after graduation, at which time the student borrower pays an interest charge of three percent. No interest is charged while the student is enrolled. Due to the increased cost of postbachelor's degree study, graduate students are able to borrow up to $2500 each school year, or a total of $10,000 for both graduate and undergraduate study. Principal repayment may extend for 10 years for both graduate and undergraduate loans under NDEA. Repayment may be deferred for students who continue their education, enter the armed services after college, join the Peace Corps, or become a Volunteer in Service to America (VISTA). The latter program is part of the Office of Economic Opportunity's war on poverty effort.

The second largest college-based program is the College Work-Study Program, which encourages the traditional ethic of working one's way through college. Originally developed as an adjunct of the war on poverty, the College Work-Study Program (CWSP) provided more than $134,000,000 to 1,540 higher education institutions in 1966–1967 for student salary payments. Nearly 300,000 students received wages under this plan, which allows a student to work an average of 15 hours weekly while attending classes fulltime. Students may continue to work during the summer on a 40-hour or full-time work schedule per week.

The original impetus for CWSP was to aid in the elimination of poverty by assisting needy students to increase their formal educational achievement. Work under CWSP may be in any area that can be construed as benefiting the public or the institution where the student is enrolled. No work may be paid for under this program for employment by profit-making firms. In 1966–1967, more than 80% of the students employed came from families in the $7500-or-under annual income bracket.

The third of the institutionally based financial aid programs is Educational Opportunity Grants (EOG). High school graduates of exceptional financial need who are financially unable to meet the costs of education can receive grants from $200 to $800 each year. Each of these grants must be matched by an equal amount by the institution, state programs, or other approved organizations.

From fiscal year 1967 funds, 1,614 institutions granted a total of about $108,700,000 to more than 220,000 students. The average grant was estimated at $425 for the school year; $200 more were given to about 63,000 of the 220,000 students who ranked in the upper half of their class in the preceding year. There are no fixed academic levels of achievement required of recipients of Opportunity Grants. They must be full-time students in good standing and have a demonstrated need determined by an institution's financial aid officer.

David Johnson, director, Educational Opportunity Grants Branch, USOE Division of Student Financial Aid, has said: "The goal of the EOG program is quite simple. We hope to be able to help those students who need financial aid [to] obtain a post-secondary education. We also know that without this grants program many of these students could not possibly aspire to any formal education beyond the secondary school. We now are helping more than 300,000 young people get at least some of the education they would otherwise be deprived of."

In terms of dollar volume, the largest student aid program is provided by the nation's private lending institutions through the Guaranteed Student Loan program. Two of these programs were established under Title IV B of the Higher Education Act of 1965 for college students and the National Vocational Student Loan Insurance Act of 1965 for students attending eligible business, trade, technical, or other vocational schools.

Under these programs, students borrow directly from their banks, credit unions, savings and loan associations, or other eligible lender. There is no needs test applied in this program; however, the educational institution must certify that the student is enrolled or accepted, is in good academic standing, and that the student's estimates of college expenses are reasonable.

Students whose adjusted family income is $15,000 or less who obtain a guaranteed loan may be eligible for payment of federal interest benefits of up to six percent simple interest while they are in school. Once repayment commences, the federal government will pay three percent simple interest on the unpaid principal balance. Students who do not qualify for federal interest benefits may borrow, but they must pay all of the interest.

Banks, insurance companies, credit unions, and savings and loan associations made loans of private capital in excess of $247,000,000 to students during 1966–1967. Since a student may obtain more than one loan during a school year, a precise count of students participating in these programs is difficult to obtain. However, it is known that nearly 329,000 loan applications were approved during academic year 1966–1967 under the Higher Education Act. Eleven hundred loans were approved for students in vocational education programs for about $741,000.

The sixth of these programs is directed toward aiding a smaller segment of the population—Cuban refugee students. The Cuban Loan program benefitted 3,700 students in 1966–1967 with loans totalling $3,144,000. The great majority of these students are studying in Florida. Cuban students, however, are enrolled in educational institutions in all but six states.

These six programs do not operate independently and they are not mutually exclusive with respect to the individual student. That is to say, an institution's financial aid officer has the option to tailor or "package" a program that best meets the needs of each student by using one or a combination of the institutionally-based programs. The student may supplement CWSP, EOG or NDSL funds through borrowing under the Guaranteed Loan program.

For example, should a student receive a grant under EOG of $400 matched by the institution's equal contribution of $400, he still may borrow under NDSL or take a job under CWSP to make up the difference to meet his total college costs. The student, of course, must have a demonstrated need for financial aid.

In determining whether a student can receive financial assistance, one of the critical ingredients is sufficient lead time. Students planning to attend college in September of a given year should contact the institution of their choice by November of the previous year or 10 months ahead of registration.

During the 1967–1968 school year, the National Defense Student Loan program was funded at the same amount of Federal funds ($190,000,000) approved by the Congress for 1966–1967. Since the NDSL operates as a revolving fund where loan repayments again are made available for loans, a total of $242,900,000 was estimated to be loaned during the 1967–1968 school year. This total includes, in addition to loan repayments, carryover amounts collected too late in the school year 1966–1967 to be reloaned, loans made in the summer of 1967, and balances available at institutions. The number of students aided was estimated at about 405,000, with an average loan of $600. In fiscal year 1969, $185,878,000 were appropriated for NDSL to provide loans for 442,000 students. Budget estimates for fiscal year 1971 showed a substantially lower appropriation request of $141,900,000 for this program, with a decline in students aided to 383,600.

College Work-Study remained at approximately the 1967 level for fiscal year 1968 ($134,300,000). In the CWSP, fiscal-year funds are used the following calendar year, causing an overlap of six months beyond the official termination each June 30 for fiscal-year expenditures. In 1969, the CWSP appropriation was increased to $143,400,000. There was an additional increase to $156,600,000 in 1970; the 1971 budget estimate was $160,000,000.

Students working under CWSP were estimated at 375,000 for academic years 1969–1970 and 1970–1971.

The Educational Opportunity Grants budget was $145,900,000 in 1969, although the funds were not disbursed until academic year 1969–1970. The average grant amount was $525, with the total students aided at about 347,000. By fiscal year 1971, the Office of Education projected a need for $185,-600,000 for 309,200 EOG recipients.

Some 500,000 guaranteed loans were estimated for 1967–1968 for higher education and 60,000 for vocational students. In an effort to induce more lenders to participate, amendments have been made to the Higher Education Act providing for a special allowance to be paid lenders when such payments are essential to the program. Rapid changes in the money market and continuing increases in the rates of interest charged by lenders made this provision necessary. By 1971, Office of Education officials estimated more than one million (1,087,200) students will be signing with lenders for guaranteed loans for college and vocational training. The cost of this program in 1971 in Federal funds were projected at $149,840,000.

The Cuban Loan program maintained the 1967 level of loan activity through 1969. Students aided under this program were about 3,800 to 4,000, with the majority of Cuban students beginning or continuing studies in Florida.

The Office of Education began administering the Upward Bound program in 1968 following a transfer of this activity from the Office of Economic Opportunity. OE educators have calculated that approximately 24,000 young people are benefiting from Upward Bound activities each year.

It should be emphasized that the U.S. Office of Education does not make loans or grants and does not assign jobs. All funds disbursed to students are administered by colleges, universities, and lending institutions.

Part 10

The Disadvantaged in International Perspective

47

Education of the Poor
from Ancient Times to 1800
in International Perspective[1]

William W. Brickman

A vast abundance of literature has appeared in recent years, and no doubt will continue to be published in the years to come, on the problems of educating the poor. Generally, such writings tend to avoid the term poor, but use the circumlocutions of economically deprived, financially disadvantaged, fiscally handicapped, monetarily underprivileged, and the like. Much has been written about the culturally depressed, the urban underprivileged, the inner-city indigent, or simply the different. What all these terms amount to is an expression of social, governmental, and humanitarian concern with respect to persons who have not shared in the benefits of the contemporary affluent society. The accent is on the role of educational institutions in remedying prevailing injustices and in propelling children and young persons into a situation which will reflect the highest ideals of human rights and equality. At least, this seems the sum total of the underlying ideology of the many writings on anti-poverty education.

What is missing to a large extent from the plenitude of printed matter on the poverty problem in education is an awareness of the historical dimension and of the experience of various nations, other than one's own, in meeting the issue. The educational struggle against poverty did not begin with the program for the Great Society by President Lyndon B. Johnson or with the reforms by the Labour Party in Great Britain or even with the Russian Revolution. It may be that the functionalists and the activists do not regard the historical development as relevant to the immediate, practical task of

[1] A portion of this essay has appeared under the title, "Notes on the Education of the Poor in Historical and International Perspective," *McGill Journal of Education*, **3**: 141–150, Fall 1968.

aiding the poor. However, it is hard to understand why the scholars in education, particularly those who are associated in teaching and research in the area called educational foundations, have seldom called attention to the antecedents in time of the campaign to eradicate poverty via education.

One must hasten to add that the standard histories of education do contain data on past efforts to educate the poor, but these items of information are frequently buried in masses of other detail. There does not appear any systematic analysis of the attempts at antipoverty education in past eras in various parts of the world. The second edition (1966) of Brubacher's useful historical analysis of education problems omits the education of the poor as an identifiable problem. To find any historical information in his book concerning this question, it is necessary to look into the chapter on economic influences on education and the one on elementary education.[2]

A thoroughgoing presentation of antipoverty education in its international and historical dimensions can be the subject of a substantial book. What will be attempted in this essay is an overview suggestive of further and deeper study leading to a more definitive analysis of the historical factors in the drive against poverty in the educational experience of mankind from ancient times onward.

To trace the history of education in relation to poverty in antiquity is not at all an easy assignment. One might begin with examples from such developments as poor relief and social legislation. The Bible contains numerous references to the obligations by the individual and the community toward the needy of all kinds, such as the propertyless Levite, the stranger, the orphan, and the widow.[3] Concerning "thy brother" who becomes impoverished, the Bible warns that "as a stranger and a settler shall he live with thee."[4] This equates three types of disadvantaged whose welfare became the responsibility of the community and had to be aided as brothers. It might be assumed that the responsibility was not merely to prevent starvation or any form of misery, but also to rehabilitate the individual and to enable him to recover economically. Such a process might involve adult vocational training. This is the interpretation of Moses Maimonides (1135–1204) in the legal compendium and commentary published about 1180. The physician-philosopher-rabbi specifies eight levels of charity, the highest of which is to give the poor a grant or loan, to invite him as a partner, or to find him work so that he would become self-supporting.[5] Like the Bible, the Talmud, upon

[2] John S. Brubacher, *A History of the Problems of Education,* second edition (New York: McGraw-Hill, 1966), pp. 88–89, 367–370.

[3] *Deuteronomy,* **14:** 29, **16:** 11.

[4] *Leviticus,* **25:** 35. See also **25:** 36–37.

[5] Moses Maimonides, *Mishneh Torah, Sefer Zeraim, Hilchot Matnot Aniyim,* Chapter X, 7–14. Vol. V of edition published by El Ha-Mekorot, Jerusalem, 5716 (1956), pp. 273–274.

which it is based, is replete with admonitions regarding the necessity of aiding the poor to the fullest possible extent and to help avoid the status of poverty and dependence. Thus, according to Rabbi Judah, "He who does not teach his son a trade . . . is as though he taught him to be a robber."[6] Here is the recognition of the link between deprivation and delinquency.

In Tractate *Taanith* (folio 24a) of the Babylonian Talmud there is an interesting passage. An unnamed Jewish religious functionary is quoted as saying: "I am an elementary teacher and I instruct the children of the poor as those of the rich, and I do not charge a fee from anyone unable to pay."

Another Talmudic passage praises the High Priest, Joshua ben Gamala, who ordained about 64 A.D. the establishment of schools in every town and province for children of six or seven. This ordinance was promulgated after Joshua observed that orphan children, in contrast to those with fathers, were not receiving an education. In order that all children get as much attention as possible, Raba stated that a teacher preferably should have no more than 25 pupils and that if he should have 40 children, the town should pay for an assistant.[7]

In another section of the Talmud is an interesting account of provision for the underprivileged. Rabbi Hiyya narrated how he helped feed orphans with the meat of deer caught with nets woven from flax he had sown. From the deerskin he prepared scrolls which he brought to a town which lacked a school for young children. He then wrote on the skins the five books of Moses (the Pentateuch) for five children, and taught the six sections of the Mishnah to six children. "I said to each one, 'Teach your section to your friend.' "[8] This procedure earned him the approval of Rabbi Judah the Prince, the editor of the Mishnah (the basis for the Talmudic discussions and disputations). This slogan of Rabbi Hiyya is an ancient precedent for the twentieth-century formula "Each one, teach one!" by which the Reverend Dr. Frank C. Laubach, the American missionary, succeeded in bringing literacy to underdeveloped countries.

Finally, it is pertinent to quote the well-known statement that one should take care not to neglect the children of the poor, for the learning (Torah), goes forth from them.[9] In other words, the disadvantaged pupils have educational capabilities which the community cannot afford to leave undeveloped. The Talmudic era, then, made provisions for the education of the poor children because they were entitled to it by reason of being children and because education would enable them to rise above poverty.

Urban problems reared their head in ancient Greece. In Book IV of the

[6] Babylonian Talmud, Tractate *Kiddushin*, 29a. Translation by the present writer.
[7] Babylonian Talmud, Tractate *Baba Batra*, 21a.
[8] Babylonian Talmud, Tractate *Ketuvot*, 103b.
[9] Babylonian Talmud, Tractate *Nedarim*, 81a.

Republic, Plato maintains that ". . . any city, however small, is in fact divided into two, one the city of the poor, the other of the rich; these are at war with one another. . . ."[10] He goes on to say that "if you . . . give the wealth or power or persons of the one to the others, you will always have a great many friends and not many enemies."[11] But the optimum solution to the problem in the ideal state, according to Plato, is to elevate "into the rank of guardians the offspring of the lower classes, when naturally superior. The intention was, that, in the case of the citizens generally, each individual should be put to the use for which nature intended him, one to one work, and then every man would do his own business, and be one and not many; and so the whole city would be one and not many."[12]

It is interesting to note that Spartans who were too poverty-stricken to contribute their share to the *pheiditia,* their eating clubs, were deprived of citizenship. As a result, their children could not be educated in the state schools.[13] Such instances may not have been frequent, but they illustrate the lack of concern by the Spartan state for the education of the underprivileged. Significantly, Xenophon, who glorified the Spartan way of life, also applauded the expulsion of children of poor parents from the schools. However, one should not overlook the practice whereby wealthy Spartans could pay for the education of disadvantaged boys chosen by them.[14]

The ancient classical culture rested, in a large measure, on slavery. The slaves were poor, defenseless, and hence disadvantaged in numerous ways. Throughout Greek and Roman literature, one finds references to the instruction of nonfreeborn slaves, not in the liberal arts, but in the vocational arts. In point of actual fact, however, "many individual cases are known, and these are symptomatic, where a respectable or good education was achieved by those who were born or reared as slaves."[15]

The lot of the slaves was improved during the cosmopolitan context of the Hellenistic period, and more educational opportunities were available to them. Educated slaves were not rare in Rome. "By apprenticeship methods and by education formal and informal, slaves were constantly being prepared for skilled trades, for business enterprises, for clerical occupations, for some forms of entertainment, and even for the professions of teaching and medicine."[16] In many instances, education followed by efficient performance led to freedom. Even the rescript of Emperor Domitian, 93–94 A.D., against the

[10] Scott Buchanan, ed., *The Portable Plato* (New York: Viking, 1948), pp. 417–418.
[11] Ibid., p. 418.
[12] Ibid., pp. 418–419.
[13] Kenneth J. Freeman, *Schools of Hellas* (London: Macmillan, 1912), pp. 13–14.
[14] Ibid., p. 15.
[15] Clarence A. Forbes, "The Education and Training of Slaves in Antiquity," *Transactions and Proceedings of the American Philological Association,* Vol. **86**, 1955, p. 322.
[16] Ibid., p. 328.

medical training of slaves did not close the door.[17] In sum, "scores of thousands of slaves were educated in a wide variety of lower and higher occupations" in Roman times.[18]

In imperial Rome, at a time when the socioeconomic situation was deteriorating, Emperor Trajan (98–117 A.D.) took steps to improve the situation by paying attention to the needs of the poor. Accordingly, he opened schools for needy boys and girls, illegitimate as well as legitimate.[19]

Another example from a later period in antiquity may be taken from the writing of the Greek Church Fathers. Gregory Nazianzen's *Peri Philoptochías* (Concerning the Love of the Poor), which was based upon the practical charitable work by St. Basil in Caesarea and was dedicated to the importance of the principle of Christian charity, provided inspiration to the French social reformers in the early 16th century in their efforts to ameliorate the condition of the poor and thereby to raise the level of society.[20] One indication of this campaign was the appearance of translations of Gregory's Sermon Fourteen in German, French, English, and Italian. Of the ten recorded vernacular editions published between 1530 and 1615, seven were in French. And indeed it was the welfare organization of the municipality of Lyon, the Aumône-Générale, which utilized a French version of Gregory's sermon to raise funds to improve the status of the poor in the community. The organization, which was founded in 1534 by a group of Protestant and Catholic businessmen and lawyers, was influenced by two local humanists, Jean de Vauzelles, Prior of Montrottier, and a Dominican friar, Santo Pagnini. The latter two were interested in the Aumône-Générale for a number of reasons: "a humanist sensitivity to noise, disorder, and ugliness in the city; a strong appreciation for what education could do to divert the young from begging; and Erasmian conviction of the value of lay piety and that 'Charity is certainly much more agreeable to God than fasts, prayers, abstinence or austerity of life.' "[21] It is interesting that the people of Lyon were able to draw upon a sermon some 1,200 years old, and couched in the traditional terminology of loving and aiding the poor, in the campaign to eliminate death by starvation, the need

[17] Ibid., pp. 348–353, 359.

[18] Ibid., p. 360.

[19] Pliny the Younger, *Panegyric of Trajan*, 26–28; Dio Cassius, *History of Rome*, lviii, 6. Cited in H. I. Marrou, *A History of Education in Antiquity* (New York: Sheed & Ward, 1956), p. 303.

[20] Natalie Z. Davis, "Gregory Nazianzen in the Service of Humanist Social Reform," *Renaissance Quarterly*, **21**: 455–464, Winter 1967; and "Poor Relief, Humanism, and Heresy: The Case of Lyon," in William M. Bowsky, ed., "Studies in Medieval and Renaissance History," Vol. V (Lincoln: University of Nebraska Press, 1968), pp. 217–269.

[21] Ibid., p. 456. The quotation is from Vauzelles and the Erasmian reference is to the *Enchiridion Militis Christiani*.

for begging, and the presence of potential young hoodlums on the streets. It was unfortunate that, for all the assiduous activity, this goal remained unfulfilled.[22]

During the long Byzantine era there were efforts at various times to provide education for poor children, especially during the reign (1081–1118) of Emperor Alexius I Comnenos (1048–1118). This monarch undertook an "extensive program" of philanthropic activity involving aid to the poor, the aged, and the physically handicapped.[23] According to the account by his daughter, the learned Anna Comnena (1083–1148), after his victorious campaign against the Turks, he made provisions for the resultant orphans: "The children who had lost their parents and were afflicted with the bitter evil of orphanhood he distributed among his relations and others who, as he knew, led a well-conducted life, or sent them to the abbots of the holy monasteries with orders to bring them up, not as slaves, but as free children and allow them a thorough education and instruction in the Holy Writings. Some he also admitted into the orphanage which he had established himself and which he had converted more or less into a school for those anxious to learn, and told the governors of it to give these orphans a good general education."[24] This educational program was conducted in the Orphanage, situated near St. Paul's Cathedral in Constantinople. As described by Anna Comnena, "On entering you would find the sanctuaries and monasteries to your left; and on the right of the large sanctuary stood the grammar school for orphans collected from every race, in which a master presided and the boys stood round him, some puzzled over grammatical questions, and others writing what are called grammatical analyses. There could be seen a Latin being trained, and a Scythian studying Greek, and a Roman handling Greek texts and an illiterate Greek speaking Greek correctly."[25] According to a biographer of Anna, "Even if the Orphanage School of Alexius I was a revival and not an entirely new foundation as Anna represents it, it would seem to have filled a great need."[26]

Apart from this Orphanage School, there were other provisions for the education of these disadvantaged children during the reign of Alexius I. Orphans were cared for in monasteries, churches, and diocesan headquarters. At the monastery of Gregory Pacourianos, a priest was assigned to organize their education, with six children to be trained as priests.[27]

22 Ibid., p. 459.

23 Demetrios J. Constantinos, "Byzantine Philanthropy and Social Welfare" (New Brunswick, N.J.: Rutgers University Press, 1968), p. 244.

24 "The Alexiad of the Princess Anna Comnena," Book XV, translated by Elizabeth A. S. Dawes (London: Kegan Paul, Trench, Trubner, 1928), p. 409.

25 Ibid., p. 411.

26 Georgina Buckler, "Anna Comnena: A Study" (London: Oxford University Press, 1929), p. 182.

27 Constantinos, op. cit., pp. 247–248.

An examination of many secondary writings on the history of education in ancient and medieval times has yielded very little that will illuminate the development of antipoverty education. This might be understandable in societies where there was a great gulf between the rich and the poor, the noble and the lowly, the learned and the ignorant. One does not expect, as a rule, to find examples of education of serfs in a medieval West European manor. Nor can one anticipate the education of poor peasants in Eastern Europe when the upper and priestly classes revealed many who were illiterate and untutored. There were exceptions in the Middle Ages, however. According to Herman, a local English historian of the late 11th century, the Danish conqueror of England, King Canute, made provisions for the education of poor boys: "Nor must we pass over in silence what this good king did by way of charity, namely, whenever he went to any famous monastery or borough he sent there at his own expense boys to be taught for the clerical or monastic order, not only those whom he found among the freemen but also the cleverer of the poor, and with his own hand in kingly munificence he also in his progress made some free."[28] An historian of the following century, Abbot Sampson, outdid Herman in his tribute to Canute in describing him as "establishing public schools throughout the cities and boroughs and appointing masters to them, and sending to them to be taught not only noble boys of good promise, but also the freed sons of slaves, charging the cost to the royal purse."[29] Another example of educational aid to the poor was provided by Bishop Ireton in 1285 when he appropriated church funds for the education of 12 poor scholars in the school adjoining his cathedral in Carlisle.[30] The English chantry schools of the 14th and later centuries, maintained by foundations which arranged for the singing of masses and for other religious services for the souls of the departed, admitted children of poor parents to the classes taught by the priests in their spare time without charge.[31] As a general rule, however, such provisions for the poor were few and were made primarily to select brighter lads for the Church. The education of the children of the lower and poorer classes in Germany and elsewhere in Europe was in a state of neglect.[32]

[28] Quoted in A. F. Leach, "The Schools of Medieval England" (London: Methuen, 1915), pp. 91–92.

[29] Quoted in ibid., p. 92.

[30] James Wilson, "Medieval Education in Carlisle," *Scottish Educational Journal*, **11**: 42, October 1913.

[31] Arthur F. Leach, "Chantry Schools," in Paul Monroe, ed., *A Cyclopedia of Education*, Vol. I (New York: Macmillan, 1911), p. 568. See also Arthur F. Leach, *English Schools at the Reformation* (London: Constable, 1896) for a more detailed treatment of chantry schools. For a representative foundation grant for a medieval chantry school, with its provision for the teaching of poor boys, see document 73 in Ellwood P. Cubberley, *Readings in the History of Education* (Boston: Houghton Mifflin, 1920), pp. 105–106.

[32] Cf., O. Pache, "Armenschulen," in W. Rein, ed., *Encyklopädisches Handbuch der Pädagogik*, second edition, Vol. I (Langensalza: Beyer, 1903), p. 273.

At this point, it is perhaps fitting to take note of a non-European culture, that of China. Unlike India, China never had a rigid caste system, although there were indications of differentiation among social classes, such as the nobility or Superior Men (scholars, officials) and the common, uneducated people. In spite of the fact that ancient China gave first priority to the education of the princes and the upper class, attention was also given to the educational needs of the underprivileged. The obligation upon the higher echelons of the population to educate the lower is stressed in the *Book of History* (Shu Ching) and in the sayings of Mencius (*c. 372–c. 289*). The *Book of Rituals* (Li Chi) states that, "if the Superior Man wishes to transform the people and perfect their social life, he must begin with education."[33] The phraseology, "transform the people" and "perfect their social life," according to Galt, "are among the phrases of the Classics most quoted in memorials and edicts on education throughout all the later dynasties. They represent a fundamental doctrine in the Chinese theory of education."[34]

A relation between the economic status of the common people and their education was pointed up by Mencius in his statement that "there is a way for humanity, and if the people, with plenty to eat and plenty to wear, merely live in creature comfort without education they are much like the birds and beasts."[35] In other words, to uplift the masses it was not only important to feed and clothe them, but also to educate them so that they would contribute toward a stable society. The *Kuo Yü* (Discourses of the States), possibly written by Kuan Chung in the seventh century B.C., warns that, if local public officials do not report the presence of "some talented ones with capacity for scholarship" among the common people and indicate that they are candidates for education, "this delinquency is a punishable offence."[36] Here we have a case of the obligation upon the authorities to identify the gifted children of the low economic level and to inform the imperial government so that suitable arrangements could be made to develop their talents. This requirement is repeated time and again in all later periods of Chinese history. This policy was well summed up by the statement of Confucius (*c. 551–c. 479 B.C.*): "In education there are no distinctions of class."[37] As Galt put it, ". . . educational theory and practice had a place for the talented student who, by study and exertion, might rise from lowly origins to high rank among scholars. To this extent China's educational theory has always been democratic and it is a point of excellence."[38] It is also pertinent to observe that, in the long history

[33] Quoted in Howard S. Galt, *A History of Chinese Educational Institutions: Vol. I, To the End of the Five Dynasties (A.D. 960)* (London: Probsthain, 1951), p. 120.
[34] Ibid.
[35] Quoted in ibid., p. 121.
[36] Quoted in ibid., p. 123.
[37] Quoted in ibid., p. 124.
[38] Ibid.

of selection by the examination system for the imperial Chinese civil service, poor youngsters with ability did not lack patrons to finance their studies and their upward climb.

Coming back to Europe, we find interest in educating the poor in the 14th century and in Renaissance circles. It is strange the Humanism did not give birth to humanitarianism. Too many of the humanistic scholars were concerned with the writings of ancient times and too few with educational needs of the lower rungs of the academic ladder. There were instances of economic and educational aid to the poor in the early period of the Renaissance, in that phase of it known as the Christian Renaissance.

The highly influential religious community of the Brethren of the Common Life, founded in Deventer, Holland, by Geert Groote (1340–84) and Floris, or Florent Radewijnsz (1350–1400), which devoted itself to education, also included the instruction and welfare of poor boys. At first, Groote provided food for the needy pupils of the Deventer cathedral school, as well as opportunities to copy books.[39] Over the centuries, the Brothers taught the poor boys and those of more affluent background, whether in their own or other schools, without discrimination.[40] They maintained a *domus pauperum* for impoverished pupils in Gouda, Utrecht, Groningen, Nijmejen, and other Dutch towns.[41] In this way, they were able to furnish the necessities of life and an education to boys who otherwise would have been condemned to poverty and ignorance for the rest of their lives.

The opening in 1386 of Winchester College, the "Mother of Schools" and the pioneering public school in Britain marked a mild milestone in the development of educational facilities for the poor. Back in 1378, by virtue of a Papal Bull, William of Wykeham, Bishop of Winchester and Chancellor of England, had obtained recognition for his repeated efforts to provide aid to poor scholars. In the Foundation Deed for the College, written by Wykeham in 1382, the educator-cleric first called attention to the fact that he had "lately erected and founded a perpetual college [All Souls' College] of seventy poor scholars, clerks, to study theology, canon and civil law, and arts in the University of Oxford."[42] He then pointed out the need for a preparatory

[39] H. Douma, "De ontwikkeling van het lager onderwijs in Nederland" (Zutphen: Thieme, 1922), p. 22.

[40] G. R. Potter, "Education in the Fourteenth and Fifteenth Centuries," in *Cambridge Medieval History*, Vol. **VIII** (Cambridge: University Press, 1936), p. 711; Albert Hyma, "The Christian Renaissance: A History of the 'Devotio Moderna,'" second edition (Hamden, Conn.: Archon Books, 1965), p. 124; and Albert Hyma, "The Brethren of the Common Life" (Grand Rapids, Mich.: Eerdmans, 1950).

[41] R. R. Post, "Scholen en onderwijs in Nederland gedurende de Middeleeuwen" (Utrecht: Het Spectrum, 1954), p. 171.

[42] Quoted in A. F. Leach, *A History of Winchester College* (London: Duckworth, 1899), p. 65.

school where "many poor scholars . . . suffering from want of money and poverty" would become proficient in grammar.[43] "For such poor and needy scholars, clerks, now and hereafter, in order that they may stay and be busy at school (*litterarum studio*), and more freely and liberally profit in the faculty and science of grammar, and become, as is desirable, more fit for the sciences or liberal arts; to increase the roll of all the sciences, faculties, and liberal arts, and enlarge, as far as in us lies, the number of those studying and becoming proficient in them; we propose, by the help of God, out of the means and goods given us by God, to hold out helping hands, and give the assistance of charity in the form underwritten."[44] The outcome was the establishment of a college near Winchester, consisting of "seventy poor and needy scholars, clerks, living college-wise in the same, studying and becoming proficient in grammaticals, or the art and science of grammar."[45]

One Renaissance educator with an advanced social conscience was Vittorino da Feltre (1376–1446), a person who is generally recognized not only as the leading schoolmaster of his era, but also one of the most successful pedagogues in the history of education. A renowned scholar in mathematics and Latin, Vittorino maintained a school at his home in Padua, where he charged high tuition rates for the sons of the wealthy, but nothing for the poor who were sent to him on the personal recommendation of friends. His objective was "to equalise the treatment of the whole household, repressing indulgence on the one hand, and lifting the burden of poverty on the other, and thus to all alike 'libris, domo, victu, vestituque optime consulebat.' "[46] This provision of books, lodging, food, and clothing for all pupils, rich and poor, once again revealed the uniqueness of Vittorino as a man and as an educator. He apparently continued this custom at his school in Venice, where again parents offered "large fees to secure the admission of their sons" to his home.[47]

It was at Casa Giocosa, at the school set up on the estate of Gonzaga, Duke of Mantua, that Vittorino achieved his lasting fame and influence, in

[43] Ibid.

[44] Quoted in ibid., pp. 65–66.

[45] Quoted in ibid., p. 66. It is important to point out that "poor and needy" referred to the economically disadvantaged of the middle and upper classes, rather than to the "gutter children" or to boys of working classes. See ibid., pp. 97, 102–103. Cf., I. L. Kandel, *History of Secondary Education* (Boston: Houghton Mifflin, 1930), pp. 78–79. It is also instructive to note the expressions "poor and needy boys of good character" and "poor lads, or servitors" in the mid-15th century statutes of Eton College. See the document in the appendix of H. C. Maxwell Lyte, *A History of Eton College* (London: Macmillan, 1911), p. 581. Significantly, "No boy of servile or illegitimate birth, and no one suffering from a bodily or canonical defect which would incapacitate him from taking holy orders shall be admitted." Ibid., p. 582.

[46] William H. Woodward, *Vittorino da Feltre and Other Humanist Educators* (Cambridge: University Press, 1897), p. 19.

[47] Ibid., p. 22.

his own time and in the history of education since. Once more, "Vittorino, moreover, mindful of his own early struggles, and true to the scholar's instinct of the equality of genius, continued to receive free of all charges promising boys commended to him by trusted friends. These he treated absolutely on the same footing with the rest of the boys, and in some cases he undertook the entire cost of their maintenance, clothing, and books for ten years or more."[48] Furthermore, Vittorino ". . . provided an income for the parents [of the poor pupils] secured upon the State's treasury."[49] It is indeed remarkable that historical works in the field of education have infrequently picked up these points, not merely in praise of Vittorino, but also in recognition of practices that appear to be far in advance of much of contemporary thinking about the education of the poor.[50] Also noteworthy is the fact that Vittorino's Casa Giocosa equalized the education of rich and poor, male and female, and Italian and non-Italian.

The history of education during the Renaissance and later periods yields more examples of the thinking relative to poverty provisions made for the education of the impoverished and the orphaned. One thinks, in the first instance, of the treatise by Juan Luís Vives, De subventione pauperum (1526). This great educator, in dedicating his work to his adopted city, Bruges, exhorted the municipal fathers ". . . to take thought and to strive that one man should aid another; that none should be oppressed, none weighed down by loss unjustly incurred; that the stronger should stand by the weaker; that by charity daily increasing, harmony should prevail in the intercourse of the citizens and their assemblies, and should endure for ever."[51] Later in this treatise, Vives goes on to show that it is not enough to ameliorate the condition of the poor by the giving of alms or by other measures, but society must rather attack the problem of poverty at its roots and, with all resources at its

---

[48] Ibid., p. 30.

[49] Cited in ibid., p. 31, from Bartholomaeus Platina, Commentariolus Platinae de vita Victorini Feltrensis, in Tommaso Agostino Vairani, Cremonensium Monumenta Romae extentia (Rome, 1778).

[50] There may be some excuse that Woodward's work on Vittorino, long out of print, has been unavailable, but most larger, municipal, and higher institutional libraries no doubt have had copies for some time. In 1963, there appeared a reprint in the valuable series, "Classics in Education," under the general editorship of Lawrence A. Cremin and published by Teachers College Press, New York, N.Y. The reprint edition is a facsimile, but it omits the frontispiece illustration of the likeness of Vittorino. However, it adds a much-needed index, which, oddly it would seem for the 1960s, lacks the entry "poor," "poverty," or any reasonable synonym for lack of economic privilege. Also of interest is the fact that the author of the foreword to the reprint edition, Prof. Edgar F. Rice, Jr., Department of History, Cornell University, makes no reference to Vittorino's pluralistic philosophy or to his educational activities in behalf of the poor.

[51] "The De Subventione Pauperum of Juan Luis Vives," in F. R. Salter, ed., Some Early Tracts on Poor Relief (London: Methuen, 1926), p. 5.

command, must remove its underlying causes. In particular, Vives, one of the outstanding European educators of the 16th century, urged the establishment of public schools where "abandoned children" "shall receive education and training, together with maintenance."[52] Their teachers should be "men who have received a good liberal education, who shall infuse their manners into the rough school. For there is no greater danger for boys than a base and squalid and uncultured bringing-up. In selecting teachers of a suitable kind let the magistrates not spare expense. They will secure for the city over which they rule at small cost."[53] Girls, like the boys, should be given opportunities to learn the basic subjects, Christian piety and "the right way of thinking," as well as household arts, and to develop those qualities which would ensure "the safeguarding of their chastity." At a subsequent time, "let those boys who are quickest at learning be kept on in the school, to become the masters of others, and afterwards to enter a seminary of priests. Let the others move on into workshops, according to their individual bents."[54] Many ideas, which are innovative in the mid-20th century, are packed into the concise paragraphs by this 16th-century educator against poverty and degradation.

The student of the problem of historical context and international status of anti-poverty education may have to devote more attention to the 16th century than might be apparent at first sight. It is easy to overlook efforts by the well-known and the lesser known toward a solution of the problem. Few educational writers, for instance, refer to Martin Luther's *Ordnung eines gemeinen Kastens* (1523), in which the religious reformer proposed to the citizens of the small Saxon town of Leisneck (Leisnig) procedures for combatting vagrancy and poverty. He recommended that a compulsory tax be laid upon all members of the parish for the relief of the poor. One paragraph dealt with the allocation of funds to maintain orphans and poor children.

"Poor children who are left orphans shall be supplied with the means for moral and physical support, through the guardians in our towns and villages, from the common chest, until they can earn their bread and work for themselves. If among such orphans or children of poor people are found young boys, who would be clever in school and who are capable of understanding the liberal arts and literature, they should, along with the other poor men, be sustained and looked after by the guardians from the common chest. And other boys should be sent to work to manual labour and suitable trades. The young women among those bereaved orphans, daughters of the same poor people, shall be endowed for marriage with reasonable help through the ten guardians from the common chest."[55]

[52] Ibid., p. 18.
[53] Ibid.
[54] Ibid., p. 19.
[55] "Luther's *Ordinance for a Common Chest*," in Salter, op. cit., p. 93.

Here is an interesting proposal involving the identification, selection, and subsidization by the public of the academically talented. Presumably, such disadvantaged boys would obtain opportunities to pursue more advanced education or to serve the community in accordance with their abilities and educational background. The other group, made up of nonacademic youngsters, would receive vocational training, which would benefit both themselves and their fellow citizens. This two-track plan is a forerunner of the customary European school system from the 19th to the mid-20th century, except that Luther's program seems to impose a solemn obligation on the community to discover and foster talent wherever it could be found. Significantly, this regulation was "the direct inspiration" of the chest ordinance of Württemberg (1536), as well as of ordinances in Catholic countries.[56]

In his better known letter to the German mayors and aldermen concerning the establishment and maintenance of Christian schools (1523), Luther again called attention to the educational needs of "the poor youth." Since communities spent much money annually on arms, roads, and dams for the "temporal peace and comfort" of the people, "why should they not also allocate as much for a skillful schoolmaster or two for the needy, poor youth?"[57] This very same plea, but with reference to luxuries, cosmetics, and mass athletic spectacles, has been repeatedly made in the current century.

In Reformation England, the problem of reducing poverty was approached by a ban on begging and the apprenticing of poor children. A statute in 1535 provided that "Children under fourteen years of age, and above five, that live in idleness, and be taken begging, may be put to service by governors of cities, towns, etc., to husbandry, or other crafts or labours."[58] An even stronger step for the apprenticeship of pauper children was embodied in the Elizabethan act for poor relief (1601). Under this law, each parish appointed overseers of the poor who were empowered, with the consent of the justices of the peace, to put to work "the children of all such whose parents shall not by the said church-wardens and overseers, or the greater part of them, be thought able to keep and maintain their children; ... and also for the putting out of such children to be apprentices, to be gathered out of the same parish, according to the ability of the same parish. . . ."[59] The lawful period of apprenticeship was until the age of 24 for males and 21 or "the time of her marriage" for females.

The poor law of 1601 furnished the foundation for the apprenticeship

[56] Salter, op. cit., p. 81.

[57] Martin Luther, *Pädagogische Schriften*, compiled by Hermann Lorenzen (Paderborn: Verlag Ferdinand Schöningh, 1957), p. 66. Translation by the present writer. The text of this letter is given in English in F. V. N. Painter, *Luther on Education* (Philadelphia: Lutheran Publication Society, 1890).

[58] Document in Grace Abbott, *The Child and the State*, Vol. I (Chicago: University of Chicago Press, 1938), p. 91.

[59] Document in ibid., pp. 97–98.

legislation in the English colonies of North America and for practices prevailing during a considerable part of the 19th century. The Virginia statute of 1642, was enacted for the prevention of "sloath and idlnesse wherewith . . . young children are easily corrupted, as also for the releife of such parents whose poverty extends not to give them breeding." It authorized justices of the peace to "bind out children to tradesmen or husbandmen to be brought up in some good and lawfull calling . . . [so that they] may much improve the honor and reputation of the country, and noe lesse their owne good and theire parents comfort."[60] Other colonies, such as Massachusetts, made provisions, with different terminology, but based on the English poor law, for apprenticeship and other forms of education of poor children.[61]

The development of English society and culture in the 16th and 17th centuries was aided by the charitable gifts and bequests by the gentry and the merchants. Through their substantial contributions, the London merchants "wished to banish ignorance and its handmaiden, poverty," and especially "to endow men with that dignity and self-sufficiency which the modern world seemed to require of its competent citizens."[62] To some extent, such a program was achieved, but centuries were to go by before this goal was attained.

Also impressive were the charitable activities of rural England. Increasingly, in the 17th century, donors in Norfolk County gave larger percentages of their charities for educational opportunities for disadvantaged boys. During the early Stuart period, a large sum "was dedicated to the almost violent expansion of the educational facilities of the county."[63] The benefactors of Yorkshire concentrated their attention "on the foundation of schools in all parts of the country for youths who were literally without any hope of gaining even the rudiments of knowledge."[64] Between 1480 and 1660, the total sum given to the establishment and endowment of schools in Yorkshire was nearly 20% of all giving, "substantially exceeding the amount given for any other single charitable purpose, including even the household relief of the poor."[65]

Of special interest in connection with the relief of the poor is the internationally known Christ's Hospital, founded in 1552 in London for the education of poor pupils. The impetus came as a result of a sermon on

[60] Document in Edgar W. Knight, ed., *A Documentary History of Education in the South before 1860*, Vol. I (Chapel Hill: University of North Carolina Press, 1949), p. 46.

[61] For a detailed analysis of the education of the poor and other disadvantaged in the colonial period, see Marcus W. Jernegan, *Laboring and Dependent Classes in Colonial America, 1607–1783* (Chicago: University of Chicago Press, 1931).

[62] W. K. Jordan, *The Charities of London, 1480–1660* (New York: Russell Sage Foundation, 1960), p. 267.

[63] W. K. Jordan, *The Charities of Rural England, 1480–1660* (New York: Russell Sage Foundation, 1961), pp. 150–151.

[64] Ibid., p. 300.

[65] Ibid.

charity preached by Bishop Nicholas Ridley before the young King Edward VI at Westminster Abbey. Bishop Ridley stated in a letter that "the fatherless children and other poor men's children" would be given food, clothing, lodging, and "learning and officers to attend upon them."[66] This expression of aim was put into operation and carried out during the following centuries. The policy was continued into the present. According to an official statement of the school, "No child is admissible whose parents or guardians are not, at the time of the child's admission, in the opinion of the Council of Almoners, in need of assistance towards the education and maintenance of such children."[67]

It is pertinent to mention the activities during the Elizabethan era in behalf of the secondary education of the poor. A grammar school was founded at Highgate "for the education of poor boys."[68] A benefactor of the Seven Oaks school in 1571 specified that his gift was for the "meyntenance of God's glory and the crudition and bringing up of Pore Scollers of Sevenoke in virtuous discipline, godly learninge, and good and civil manners."[69] There were numerous instances of schools for the poor and rich, with the poor being given the preference in some.[70]

For a variety of reasons, including population growth, the industrial revolution, social and political neglect, these efforts did not result in the permanent establishment of a poverty-free, well-informed society in England. This achievement still eludes government and citizenry everywhere.

The educational needs of the poor were taken care of at various times during the 16th and 17th centuries. There is some evidence of movements on a wide, significant scale. A school for impoverished boys and girls was opened in 1597 in Rome by Saint José de Calasanz (1556–1648), a Spanish priest. He established in 1622 with the approval of Pope Gregory XV, a religious teaching order, the Congregatio . . . scholarum piarium. The success of the initial effort in Rome to furnish educational opportunities to poor children led to the spread of free elementary and even secondary Piarist schools from Italy to Austria, Hungary, Bohemia, Moravia, Poland, Spain, France, Germany, and elsewhere.[71]

---

[66] Quoted in Edmund Blunden, *Christ's Hospital: A Retrospect* (London: Christophers, n.d.), p. 5.

[67] George A. T. Allan, *Christ's Hospital* (London: Ian Allan, 1949), pp. 113–114.

[68] Quoted in A. Monroe Stowe, *English Grammar Schools in the Reign of Queen Elizabeth* (New York: Teachers College, Columbia University, 1908), p. 21.

[69] Quoted in ibid., p. 22.

[70] Ibid., pp. 125–126. Examples of the education of the poor in 16th-century England are also given in Leach, *English Schools at the Reformation*, op. cit.

[71] "Piarists," in Paul Monroe, ed., *A Cyclopedia of Education*, Vol. **IV** (New York: Macmillan, 1913), pp. 717–718; Werner Marcel, "Calasanza, Josef von," in *Lexikon der Pädagogik*, Vol. **III** (Bern: Francke, 1952), pp. 76–78; W. E. Hubert, "Calasanza,

Another order dedicated to the teaching of the poor was the Congregation of the Brothers of the Christian Schools, founded in 1684 at Reims by St. Jean Baptiste de la Salle (1651–1719). The Christian Brothers gave free instruction and other aid to poor children.[72] The objective of the educational work of the schools of the Christian Brothers was pointed up in the Bull of Approbation issued in 1725 by Pope Benedict XIII, calling upon the brothers to ". . . make it their chief care to teach children, especially poor children, those things which pertain to a good and Christian life. . . ."[73] The movement spread throughout France, providing elementary education for the disadvantaged prior to the formation of a national system of education.

Another familiar campaign in behalf of the education of the poor was organized by August Hermann Francke (1663–1740) beginning in 1695 at Halle. This Lutheran pastor and scholar set up free schools and orphanages (Franckesche Stiftungen) for boys and girls. In addition, he furnished meals for poor students of the University of Halle in exchange for their instructional service in his schools.[74] The orphanages of Francke became the model for institutions all over Germany. The Bethesda Orphan House, near Savannah, Georgia, was established in 1739 by George Whitefield, at the suggestion of John Wesley, "somewhat on the pattern of the remarkable educational and charitable institution" of Francke.[75]

The closing decades of the 17th century were productive of other ventures to promote the education and welfare of the disadvantaged. The assiduous labors of the Reverend Thomas Gouge (1609–1681) and of Thomas Firmin (1632–1697) in behalf of religious and industrial education of the poor bore fruit in England and Wales. The former founded in 1674 a society for teaching English to poor Welsh children and for circulating Welsh Bibles and prayer books.[76] The latter philanthropist also contributed a book, *Proposals for Raising a College of Industry* (1681), helped in the distribution of Bibles and the establishment of schools in Wales, and provided industrial training for the children of the streets.[77] In colonial America, the Pennsylvania

Josef v., hl.," in Ernst M. Roloff, ed., *Lexikon der Pädagogik*, Vol. I (Freiburg i. Br.: Herder, 1913), pp. 617–620; and "Calasanz, San José de," in Lorenzo Luzuriaga, *Diccionario de Pedagogía*, second edition (Buenos Aires: Editorial Losada, 1960), p. 66.

[72] Edward A. Fitzpatrick, *La Salle: Patron of All Teachers* (Milwaukee, Wis.: Bruce, 1951), pp. 85–103, 207–208, 232, 297–298; and J. Leif and G. Rustin, *Histoire des institutions scolaires* (Paris: Delagrave, 1954), pp. 85–86.

[73] Quoted in Fitzpatrick, op. cit., p. 158.

[74] G. Kramer, ed., *A. H. Francke's pädagogische Schriften* (Langensalza: Beyer, 1855), pp. lxxxiii–lxxxiv. See also Francke's listing of his institutions in 1698, ibid., pp. 446–447.

[75] Knight, *A Documentary History of Education in the South before 1860*, Vol. I, op. cit., p. 235.

[76] S. J. Curtis, *History of Education in Great Britain*, seventh edition (London: University Tutorial Press, 1967), p. 203.

[77] "Firmin, Thomas," in Paul Monroe, ed., *A Cyclopedia of Education*, Vol. II (New

colony's General Assembly, under the leadership of Governor William Penn, passed in 1683 a law to help the poor improve their situation. Chapter CXII of this law stated that, in order that "poor as well as rich may be instructed in good and commendable learning, which is to be preferred before wealth . . . all persons . . . having children, and all the guardians and trustees of orphans, shall cause such to be instructed in reading and writing, so that they may be able to read the Scriptures and to write by the time they attain to twelve years of age; and that then they be taught some useful trade or skill, that the poor may work to live, and the rich if they become poor may not want. . . ."[78]

In response to the prevalent poverty of the later Stuart era, the political philosopher and educator, John Locke (1632–1704), as a commissioner of trade and plantations, presented in 1697 a detailed plan in an effort to reform the English poor law. Poverty originated, he argued "neither from scarcity of provisions nor from want of employment for the poor . . . [but rather from] the relaxation of discipline and corruption of manners. . . ."[79] The "true and proper relief of the poor," according to Locke, "consists in finding work for them, and to take care they do not live like drones upon the labour of others."[80] To get the poor the work, society must undertake a campaign against that old Devil Rum. "The first step . . . ought to be a restraint of their debauchery by a strict execution of the laws provided against it, more particularly by the suppression of superfluous brandy shops and unnecessary ale-houses, especially in country parishes not lying upon great roads."[81] Moreover, the existing laws against the "begging drones" should be enforced. But these measures are insufficient without a new law "for the more effectual restraining of idle vagabonds."[82] The provisions of the law proposed by Locke seem to reflect the harsh punishment experienced by him and his fellow pupils at the hands of Dr. Richard Busby at Westminster School. Thus, ". . . whoever shall counterfeit a pass shall lose his ears for the forgery the first time that he is found guilty thereof, and the second time that he shall be transported to the plantations, as in the case of felony."[83] With regard to the younger malefactors, ". . . if any boy or girl, under fourteen years of age, shall be found begging out of the parish where they dwell . . . they shall

York: Macmillan, 1911), p. 616; W. H. G. Armytage, *Four Hundred Years of English Education* (Cambridge: University Press, 1964), p. 42.

[78] James P. Wickersham, *A History of Education in Pennsylvania* (Lancaster, Pa.: Inquirer Publishing Co., 1886), p. 39.

[79] Document in H. R. Fox Bourne, *The Life of John Locke*, Vol. **II** (New York: Harper, 1876), p. 378.

[80] Ibid., p. 383.

[81] Ibid., p. 378.

[82] Ibid., p. 379.

[83] Ibid., p. 380.

be sent to the next working school, there to be soundly whipped and kept at work until evening, so that they may be dismissed in time enough to get to their place of abode that night."[84]

Locke argued that children of the laboring classes were idle, hence a "burden to the parish," and the community does not benefit in any way until they are 12 or 14 years of age. His "most effectual remedy" for this situation was to organize, under the proposed new law, "working schools . . . in every parish, to which the children of all such as demand relief of the parish, above three and under fourteen years of age, whilst they live at home with their parents, and are not otherwise employed for their livelihood by the allowance of the overseers of the poor, shall be obliged to come."[85] Locke suggested the opening of spinning or knitting schools, an idea which recalled the factory schools of Thomas Firmin and John Cary.[86] It was not acceptable for a variety of reasons, not the least significant of which was that it was regarded by the royal advisers as too sweeping in nature.[87]

The Society for Promoting Christian Knowledge, founded in 1698 in London by the Reverend Thomas Bray (1658–1730) and his associates, is well-known to students of the history of education, for its popularization of education in England, and, through the Society for the Propagation of the Gospel in Foreign Parts (1701), overseas. According to the plan formulated by Bray, and later put into operation, this Anglican Society was ". . . to set up Catechetical Schools, for the education of poor children in reading and writing, and more especially in the principles of the Christian Religion."[88] The impact of the S.P.C.K. was immediate. Thousands of pupils were taught and over 1,500 schools were opened or reformed by the Society. In fact, it was "the first national body in England to organise schools for children in the seven to eleven (and sometimes fourteen) age range."[89] If the qualitative achievement of the S.P.C.K. did not always match the quantitative extent of its educational program, it is only fair to take note of the fact that it was, in essence, an embryonic national school system.

Late in the 18th century, with the waning of the impact of the charity

[84] Ibid., p. 381.

[85] Ibid., p. 383.

[86] Ibid., pp. 376, 391; Curtis, op. cit., p. 196; George P. Macdonnell, "Cary, John," Dictionary of National Biography, Vol. III (London: Oxford University Press, 1937–1938), pp. 1153–1155.

[87] Ibid., pp. 392–393.

[88] Document in W. O. B. Allen and Edmund McClure, Two Hundred Years: The History of the Society for Promoting Christian Knowledge (London: S.P.C.K., 1898), p. 23. See also W. K. Lowther Clarke, A History of the S.P.C.K. (London: S.P.C.K., 1959); and M. G. Jones, The Charity School Movement: A Study of Eighteenth Century Puritanism in Action (Cambridge: University Press, 1938).

[89] Armytage, op. cit., p. 43.

schools and the factory schools, the education of the poor in England was given a new impetus by the Sunday School movement. Although John Wesley and Hannah Ball (1734–1792) had started Sunday schools in the 1730s in England, various Scottish towns also had opened such schools by mid-century, and the Austrian reformer Ferdinand Kindermann (1740–1801) inaugurated Sunday instruction for children in his church in Bohemia, it was Robert Raikes (1736–1811) who has been acknowledged the leading light of this type of school. Beginning with his first Sunday School in 1780 at Gloucester, he exercised considerable influence on the secular education of children who worked all week in factories. The impoverished of England were now afforded educational opportunities in place of the declining and even vanishing charity schools. The founding in 1785 by Raikes of the Society for the Establishment and Support of Sunday Schools throughout the Kingdom of Great Britain aided in the spread of the idea all over the country. This campaign proved so successful that it began to reach overseas. One early example was the organization of the First-Day or Sunday School Society in 1791 in Philadelphia for the poor.[90]

It should not be imagined that the Anglicans had the field of the education of the impoverished all to themselves. The dissenters organized a charity school in 1687 at Southwark.[91] A significant contribution to the promotion of poor schools was made by a nonconformist clergyman, and famous hymn writer, Isaac Watts (1674–1748), who was author of manuals and other books on education. His work on charity schools[92] kept the idea alive outside the circles of the Established Church. He and his fellow-believers felt that children would get a better education in schools free from the teaching of the partisans of Anglicanism.

The preceding pages have emphasized efforts at educating the poor in England, but this is not to imply that there was no activity along these lines elsewhere in Britain or in continental Europe. As far back as 1560, John Knox and his colleagues declared in *The First Book of Discipline* that children of the poor who were found "apt to letters and learning . . . must be charged to continue their study, so that the Commonwealth may have some comfort of them."[93] During the 18th century, there were provisions in various parts of Scotland to raise the level of the poor through education. Edinburgh had charity or free schools from 1699 onward for the teaching of reading and religion. In addition, the Edinburgh citizens provided instruction in charity

[90] Curtis, op. cit., pp. 197–200; Henry F. Cope and George A. Coe, "Sunday Schools," in Paul Monroe, ed., *A Cyclopedia of Education,* Vol. V (New York: Macmillan, 1913), pp. 452–454; and A. Gregory, *Robert Raikes* (London: Hodder and Stoughton, 1877).

[91] Curtis, op. cit., p. 194.

[92] Isaac Watts, *An Essay towards the Encouragement of Charity Schools,* 1728.

[93] Quoted by G. S. Osborne, *Scottish and English Schools* (London: Longmans, Green, 1966), p. 6.

workhouses in the Orphan Hospital.[94] Also worthy of mention are the Welsh Circulating Charity Schools of the 18th century, founded by Griffith Jones (1683–1761) for teaching the skill of reading the Welsh to children and adults.[95] According to one estimate, Jones "established 3,395 schools in Wales between 1737–1761 in which 158,288 persons of all ages learned to read the Bible in Welsh."[96] This was no mean achievement even for a more developed area than Wales.

The course of educational aid to the poor did not run smooth. The movement had many defenders, it is true, as, for example, the Reverend William Sharp of Oxford, who showed his flock in 1755 that "suitable provision for the education and employment of poor children" would yield them many advantages, whereas neglect of the poor children would result in "publick Nuisances . . . idle dishonest disorderly Behaviour . . . Vice and Violence. . . ."[97] One might regard Jonathan Swift's celebrated essay, "A Modest Proposal" (1729) which sardonically suggested how Irish society could get rid of poor children, as an implied argument for the education and welfare of those unfortunates. In his classic history (1776–1788), Gibbon called attention to the edict of Constantine the Great "directing immediate and sufficient relief to be given to those parents who should produce, before the magistrates, the children whom their poverty would not allow them to educate."[98] Gibbon praised this law, but he realized that it did not have a lasting effect.

Probably the leading opponent of the charity schools was the Dutch-born satirist, philosopher, and physician, Bernard de Mandeville (1670?–1733). In his 1723 edition of the *Fable of the Bees* he added "An Essay on Charity and Charity-Schools," in which he criticized severely these schools. He ridiculed the claims that charity and the charity schools benefit society. When charity is "too extensive . . . [it] seldom fails of promoting sloth and idleness, and is good for little in the commonwealth but to breed drones, and destroy industry. The more colleges and almhouses you build, the more you may."[99] Education is not a preventative of crime, he insisted; in fact, ". . . charity-schools, and every thing else that promotes idleness, and keep the poor from working, are more accessory to the growth of villany, than the want of reading

[94] Alexander Law, *Education in Edinburgh in the Eighteenth Century* (London: University of London Press, 1965), pp. 35–47.

[95] E. T. Davies, *Monmouthshire Schools and Education to 1870* (Newport: Starsons, 1957), pp. 54–61.

[96] Cope and Coe, op. cit., p. 453.

[97] Quoted in Betsy Rodgers, *Cloak of Charity* (London: Methuen, 1949), p. 12.

[98] Edward Gibbon, *The Decline and Fall of the Roman Empire*, edited by J. B. Bury, Vol. I (London: Methuen, 1930), p. 433.

[99] Bernard de Mandeville, *Fable of the Bees* (London: Bathurst, 1795), p. 164.

and writing, or even the grossest ignorance and stupidity."[100] After lengthy discussion, some of it repetitive, Mandeville offered his formula for the good society: "to make the society happy, and people easy under the meanest circumstances, it is requisite that great numbers of them should be ignorant, as well as poor. Knowledge both enlarges and multiplies our desires, and the fewer things a man wishes for, the more easily his necessities may be supplied."[101] He shuddered at the prospect of popular education. "Where deep ignorance is entirely routed and expelled, and low learning promiscuously scattered on all the people, self-love turns knowledge into cunning; and the more the people fix all their cares, concern, and application, on the time present, without regard of what is to come after them, or hardly ever thinking beyond the next generation."[102] His conclusion was that there was a ". . . necessity . . . for a certain portion of ignorance, in a well-ordered society. . . ."[103] A Marxist's field day.

It was not at all surprising that this essay was roundly denounced by clergy, declared a public nuisance by the Grand Jury, and burned by the royal hangman in France.[104] It is not easy to determine whether such a critique damaged the charity school movement to any marked extent. Certain it is that Mandeville was more than a destructive critic. He satirized the uniformity that characterized the attire of the boys and girls in these schools, and reacted against their lockstep march.[105] His suggestions of expanding secondary and higher education, naturally enough, were for the benefit of the elite. Yet, there is one remarkable passage which reveals a rather rare sensitivity to human relations. "When a man excels in any one study or part of learning, and is qualified to teach others, he ought to be procured, if money will purchase him, without regarding what party, or indeed what country or nation he is of, whether black or white. Universities should be public marts for all manner of literature, as your annual fairs, that are kept at Leipsic, Frankfurt, and other places in Germany, are for different wares and merchandises, where no difference is made between natives and foreigners, and which men resort to from all parts of the world with equal freedom and equal privilege."[106] This feeling for fellowman, akin to the Virgilian *Tros Tyriusque mihi nullo discrimine agetur*, may possibly have been limited to the nonpoor. Mandeville's arguments are also reminiscent of H. L. Mencken's railings against the *Booboisie* and the Boobus Americanus. One might have wondered

[100] Ibid., p. 167.
[101] Ibid., p. 179.
[102] Ibid., pp. 201–202.
[103] Ibid., p. 203.
[104] Armytage, op. cit., pp. 46–47.
[105] Mandeville, op. cit., p. 175.
[106] Ibid., pp. 183–184.

if the essay was not, after all, a satire in the Swiftian sense, were it not for the fact that it was one of several attacks on charity schools, such as Soame Jenyns' *Free Enquiry into the Nature and Origin of Evil* (1757).[107]

In the closing years of the 18th century, the Bell-Lancaster system of monitorial instruction was introduced into England. This method made possible the mass teaching of hundreds of pupils through the use of pupil teachers under the direction of a master teacher. Hence, the low cost encouraged the enrollment of many poor children.[108] The monitorial procedure became popular before long on both sides of the Atlantic, and, in both areas, paved the way during the 19th century toward the gradual development of a public educational system for all the children.

The education of the poor was also promoted in various continental countries during the 18th century. Several prominent German educators were concerned with the problems of the poor. Johann Julius Hecker (1707–1768) followed in the footsteps of Francke in aiding the poor and orphaned.[109] Baron Friedrich Eberhard von Rochow (1734–1805) educated the disadvantaged peasant children.[110] His schools enabled them to better their status through social mobility. To some extent, his work affected the growth of the Prussian state school system. On the other hand, the philanthropinum movement, founded by Johann Bernhard Basedow (1724–1790) and carried on by Christian Gotthilf Salzmann (1744–1811) and others, was primarily concerned with the educational needs of the middle and upper, rather than the lower class.[111] Since they obtained their basic ideas from Rousseau, it may be that they took seriously his statement that "le pauvre n'a pas besoin d'éducation" other than that forced upon him by his milieu.[112] And yet, another famous contemporary, Johann Heinrich Pestalozzi (1746–1827) drew upon the same doctrines of his fellow-Swiss educator but emphasized the education of the poor and orphaned. His aims and methods were continued by his disciple, Philipp Emanuel von Fellenberg (1771–1844), also of Switzerland, and his assistant, Johann Jakob Wehrli (1790–1855). The tradition of educating the poor was not only transmitted throughout the 19th century in Switzerland, but also to the rest of Europe and the other continents.

[107] Harold Silver, *The Concept of Popular Education* (London: MacGibbon & Kee, 1965), p. 23.

[108] David Salmon, *The Practical Aspects of Lancaster's Improvements and Bell's Experiment* (Cambridge: University Press, 1932).

[109] Frederick Eby and Charles F. Arrowood, *The Development of Modern Education* (New York: Prentice-Hall, 1934), p. 513.

[110] Alfred Rach, *Biographien zur deutschen Erziehungsgeschichte* (Weinheim: Verlag Julius Beltz, 1968), pp. 141–142.

[111] Eby and Arrowood, op. cit., p. 519.

[112] Jean-Jacques Rousseau, *Emile, ou de l'éducation* (Paris: Garnier, n.d.), p. 23.

Reference should also be made to the numerous instances of public aid to the education of the poor and other disadvantaged in 18th-century France before and after the Revolution.[113] An example of private enterprise was Jean-Frédéric Oberlin (1740–1826), a pastor who pioneered in the establishment in the vicinity of Strasbourg of schools for the education of very young, disadvantaged children.[114]

The efforts of Benjamin Franklin and his generation should not be overlooked. Franklin prevailed upon the trustees of the Academy at Philadelphia to "maintain a free school for the instruction of poor children."[115] To the members of the Common Council of Philadelphia he recommended in 1750 that they subsidize his academy to enable it to perform its functions, among them "that a Number of the poorer Sort will hereby be qualified"[116] as teachers. Thus, the economically underprivileged would be enabled to contribute their abilities to improve society. In 1752, he reported that 100 "poor children" were taught "reading, writing, and arithmetic, with the rudiments of religion"[117] in the Charity School, which interestingly, remained in operation until July 1, 1877. Franklin was also active in improving the status of the Negroes as first president of the Pennsylvania Society for Promoting the Abolition of Slavery, and the Relief of Free Negroes Unlawfully Held in Bondage. In his Address to the Public, Nov. 9, 1789, he stressed that the free Negro, "poor and friendless," should be guaranteed civil liberty, employment, education for their children, and other rights of citizens. Appended to this address was a plan for Improving the Condition of the Free Blacks which specified such activities as guidance, apprenticeship training, and educational opportunities. A Committee of Education ". . . shall superintend the school instruction of the children and youth of the free blacks . . . [either by influencing them] to attend regularly the schools already established in this city, or form others with this view . . . [so] that the pupils may receive such learning as is necessary for their future situation in life and especially a deep impression of the most important and generally acknowledged moral and religious principles."[118]

[113] Shelby T. McCloy, *Government Assistance in Eighteenth-Century France* (Durham, N.C.: Duke University Press, 1946), Chapters X, XVII.

[114] Thomas Sims, *Brief Memorials of Jean Frédéric Oberlin* (London: Nisbet, 1830); C. Leenhardt, *La vie de Jean-Frédéric Oberlin* (Paris, 1911); and Robert R. Rusk, *A History of Infant Education*, second edition (London: University of London Press, 1951), pp. 107–112.

[115] Quoted in Thomas Woody, ed., *Educational Views of Benjamin Franklin* (New York: McGraw-Hill, 1931), p. 236.

[116] Quoted in Saul Sack, *History of Higher Education in Pennsylvania*, Vol. II (Harrisburg: Pennsylvania Historical and Museum Commission, 1963), p. 511.

[117] Quoted in Woody, loc. cit.

[118] Document in ibid., p. 251.

Those who are interested in the historical development of anti-poverty education on an international scale will want to study in depth the 19th century, where, of necessity, the present account must stop. Special attention might be given to the work and writings of Jeremy Bentham, Robert Owen, Sir James Kay-Shuttleworth, Joseph Kay, and Charles Dickens in the 19th century; the impact of Jane Addams and Jacob A. Riis on the social welfare and education of the poor and the immigrants in the metropolitan centers of Chicago and New York around the turn of the century; the selfless devotion of Count Leo N. Tolstoi to the educational needs of the poor peasant children and the establishment of his school at Yasnaya Polyana; the settlement house work in the slums of Moscow at the beginning of the century under the leadership of the Stanislav T. Shatskii; the remarkable achievement of Anton S. Makarenko with the reeducation of the homeless and the delinquent children and young people (*bezprizorny*) in the 1920s in Soviet Russia; and more and still more.

The discerning reader will recognize that this essay is merely an outline of a vast area hitherto unexplored on the basis of source materials in any systematic manner. Considerable research still remains to be done. After the research should come analysis and reflection. The past yields many ideas which have to be pondered for possible experimentation today and action tomorrow.

Society, at present, in whatever country, is not so constituted as to be able to ignore the thought and practice of its predecessors. Let us hope that, once the past experience of many nations and of our own has been explored in breadth and depth, we will gain more ideas and more wisdom, not only in terms of knowledge for the sake of knowledge, but also in the form of suggestions toward the solution of one of the persistently plaguing problems facing humanity.

48

Poverty and Education
in Latin America

Richard R. Renner

North Americans usually are numbed by their first exposure to poverty in Latin America. People are so much poorer, so much worse off, that one wonders if education is really capable of making much difference. The Latins, too, are often perplexed. How they go about dealing with the problem of educating the poor casts our own difficulties in a different perspective.

Although poverty to most Latin Americans is as much a state of mind as it is of money, the economic data are dismal enough. Despite the fact that per capita income increased during the mid 1960s, the poor, who are a majority in most countries, have benefited little. Instead, the position of the lower income strata is deteriorating absolutely as well as relatively.[1] Severe poverty is widespread. Average per capita national income in the United States in 1966 was $3133; in Argentina, the most prosperous of the Latin American nations, the comparable figure was $663.00.[2] The grinding poverty in which some children exist even there is illustrated by a survey published in 1964 of 78 rural families in the Chaco which showed an average daily cash income of one-half cent per person.[3]

But poverty is not merely a matter of low income; comfort and health are also necessary for human development. In Mexico and Paraguay, for example, over half the population lives five or more persons to a room. Although the United States had one physician for every 650 inhabitants, Brazil

[1] Economic Commission for Latin America, *Education, Human Resources and Development in Latin America* (New York: United Nations, May 1968), p. 5.

[2] Comparable data from several other nations are: Mexico, $445; Brazil, $238; Bolivia, $144; Paraguay, $106; and Haiti, $81. Pan American Union, *América en cifras, 1967, Situación económica: balanga de pagos, productos e ingresos nacionales, y finanzas* (Washington: Organization of American States, 1968), p. 38.

[3] Victor Alba, *Nationalists without Nations: The Oligarchy Versus the People in Latin America* (New York: Praeger, 1968), p. 93.

had one for every 2,303 and Haiti one for every 15,156.[4] Although the poverty picture in Latin America is mixed, it seems clear that the poor are more truly disadvantaged than in the United States. For millions of families in such circumstances, food is more important than schooling.

At the bottom of the poverty hierarchy is the Indian—often called "the animal next to man." Only slightly above is the peasant or *campesino*. Both may be extremely short of worldly goods, but their prospects vary as the following contrast between Colombia and Ecuador illustrates. In Colombia, the *campesino* has to be taken into account as a voter, as a producer, and as a consumer. And during the *violencia* of the past generation he learned to use firearms and to feel free to go to the village when he wished. In fact, he has migrated to the cities in increasing numbers since the 1950s. In neighboring Ecuador, the Quechua-speaking Indian still subsists outside the market economy in a semifeudal condition. Both of these "Latins" may be equally poor, but in Colombia the peasant's demand for education is likely to be heeded by the political powers that be; in Ecuador, cultural and economic isolation result in a lack of political influence and a scarcity of schools in many areas. And within each of these countries, the situation varies enormously.

In the cities, migrants from rural areas take up residence in squatter slums or *barriadas*. One study of a newly established *barriada* in Lima found that, although they arrive with less formal schooling than the city dwellers, the migrant's educational level was higher than the general population of Peru. Many long-established squatters establish their makeshift shack "suburbs" on publicly owned land at the margin of the city in an effort to flee center city slums which are even worse.[5] Thus, some are upwardly mobile, despite their position of extreme poverty.

What is the nature of Latin American poverty? The Mexican author, Octavio Paz, supports a widely held stereotype of his countrymen when he recalls asking the mayor of a village near Mitla what the income of the local government was. "About 3000 pesos a year" was the reply. "We are very poor. But the Governor and the Federal Government always help us to meet our expenses." And how were the 3000 pesos spent? "Mostly on fiestas" was the reply. "We are a small village and we have two patron saints."[6]

Certainly this is only one example of the nature of Latin American poverty.

[4] Others include Argentina, 616; Mexico, 1,814; and Honduras, 5,547. Pan American Union, *América en cifras, 1967, Situación social: hogar, habitación, mejoramiento urbano, previsión social, asistencia médica, y de salud, y trabajo* (Washington: Organization of American States, 1969), p. 80.

[5] William Mangin, "Squatter Settlements," *Scientific American*, **217**: 21, October 1967.

[6] Octavio Paz, *The Labyrinth of Solitude: Life and Thought in Mexico* (New York: Grove Press, 1961), p. 48–49.

But even more pessimistic is a tendency for peasants to develop a culture of isolation, a state of mind which enables them to see even neighbors and close relatives in dire need without lifting a hand to help. The tradition of subservience to a *patrón* is so strong that many peasants seem incapable of redemption. Little wonder, then, that many doubt the poor's ability to profit from schooling. Such remarks as "Why teach them? They are really brutes, virtually incapable of learning," or "Those 'boys' who attend school get to be pretty slick talkers, but sooner or later they even forget how to sign their name," might have come from Southern poor whites instead of Peruvians. There is also the belief that "[schooling] corrupts the good Indian."[7] These widespread presumptions make the extension of education to the rural masses difficult.

At the same time, as the United Nations Economic Commission for Latin America points out, "Everyone supports the ideal of education for the masses; everyone believes that education should give extensive and widespread opportunities for social mobility and that it should be used as a fundamental tool of change. No groups will be found in Latin America . . . publicly opposing education for the poor or arguing that they should be educated just enough to maintain the structure of society and accept their life with resignation."[8] While this is true in principle, it is also true that during a literacy campaign in the early 1960s in Mexico, housewives refused to teach their servants to read and write on the grounds that servants had no need for literacy. An elderly owner of an industrial goods factory indicated that he preferred to hire workers that could neither read nor write because they are much easier to manage. At the same time, there are peasants in rural Guatemala who teach their neighbors to read simply because such services are appreciated.[9] Without literacy, the poor see themselves as buffeted by the forces which they are attempting to manipulate and influence, but which they can seldom hope to change. Literacy conveys a feeling of ability to dominate one of the important mysteries of the environment.

Latin America abounds with institutional efforts to help the illiterate poor. In Mexico, almost every radio and TV station broadcasts, as a public service, five 15-minute literacy lessons per week. In addition, there are some 15,000 adult education centers which offer day and night literacy classes. The

---

[7] Cipriano Angles, "El analfabetismo en el Perú," *Educación*, **178**: 19–20, 1965–1966.

[8] United Nations Economic Commission for Latin America, op. cit., p. 95. At the same time, only half of the 77,000,000 persons employable in 1965 had attained third grade or less, and many of these had no schooling at all. The percentage of illiterates over age 15, for example, include: Argentina, 8.5%; Mexico, 37.8%; Brazil, 39.4%; and Guatemala, 62.1%.

[9] Alexander Moore, "Las motivaciones de los maestros campesinos voluntarios en un pueblo guatemalteco," *Anuario Indigenista*, **29**: 234–235, December 1969.

government provides free teaching materials.[10] Literacy and fundamental education programs are sponsored by government, churches, and international agencies. The Misión Andina, established in Ecuador in 1954 with United Nations support, cooperates with the various Andean countries to achieve "the integration of the campesino." The Fundamental Education Movement of the Bishops' Conference of Brazil, since 1963 an official organ for a campaign against illiteracy, is concerned with similar problems. Brazil's National Council for the Protection of the Indians (CNPI) is concerned with providing literacy and basic education for the indigenous population.[11]

Mission churches have long been active in Latin American education. The Committee on World Literacy and Christian Literature, a department of the National Council of Churches of Christ, is working in 17 Latin American countries. Laubach Literacy Inc. is active in Mexico, Colombia, Ecuador, and Brazil. The Summer Institute of Linguistics, with headquarters in seven Latin American countries, provides technical skill and research on languages and cultures needed for Bible translation. It also converts the peoples with whom it works into functional literates. The Wycliffe Bible Translators collaborate closely with the Summer Institute.

Roman Catholic organizations also have made important contributions, but, because of the Church's ties with government in a number of countries, many of its programs are not easily distinguished from state efforts.[12] In Colombia, for example, the Catholic church not only supervises all public education in the national territories, but its Radio Sutatenza literacy program (Acción Cultural Popular) also receives a large subsidy from the national congress. The Regional Center of Fundamental Education for Latin America (CREFAL) was established by the Organization of American States and Unesco. Its main function is to serve as a clearinghouse and a research center for the Latin American Fundamental Education Press. There are also privately sponsored literacy programs including the National Association of Newspapermen in Ecuador, the Pacific Literacy Corps in Chile, and many semiautonomous adult extension programs sponsored by universities.

Perhaps the most dramatic out-of-school literacy effort was that undertaken by Castro Cuba in 1961. Not the typical token gesture, the program repre-

---

[10] Thomas V. Greer, "An Analysis of Mexican Literacy," *Journal of Inter-American Studies*, **11**: 473–474, July 1969.

[11] William F. Marquardt and Richard Cortright, "Review of Contemporary Research on Literacy and Adult Education in Latin America," *Latin American Research Review*, **3**: 55–56, Summer 1968. In a few areas of Brazil this Indian Protection Service was so corrupt that natives were murdered in order to free their land for development purposes. See Norman Lewis, "Brazil's Dead Indians: The Killing of an Unwanted Race," *Atlas*, **19**: 22–29, January 1970. Such murders also have occurred in other Latin American countries.

[12] Marquardt and Cortright, ibid., pp. 56–59.

sented a significant diversion of upper- and middle-class educational resources for the benefit of the poor. Illiteracy in Cuba was estimated at 40% in 1953, although the official census showed only 23.6%. Following the 1961 campaign, a census showed that only 3.9% of the population remained unable to read. Although Latin American literacy statistics should never be taken very seriously, Unesco seemed to agree that the Cuban effort had been highly successful.[13]

Cuba's approach was simple but determined. Schools were dismissed in mid-March, 1961, and teachers, older students, and worker-volunteer brigades taught illiterates until August. During this period, 34,722 of Cuba's 36,000 teachers and 233,608 individuals or members of literacy brigades directed their efforts in behalf of the nation's illiterates.[14]

Not everyone made literate in such campaigns remains literate for long, but the intellectual skills newly acquired confer dignity and a sense of the possibility of further personal development. A Mexican effort to combat backsliding among its newly literate consists of some 150 *Salas Populares de Lectura* in the small towns. These are mainly reading rooms containing books, magazines, newspapers, and maps, and often radio and television. Reading and writing classes are usually taught at the *Salas* as well.[15]

Inability to read and write is a phenomenon which is both social and structural; that is, it relates closely to other characteristics of the social structure so that when they improve, so does the tendency toward literacy. What this means is that literacy should be regarded as a good indicator of the extent to which individuals and groups are really integrated into the national culture.[16] Without literacy, the poor remain isolated from the benefits of the modern world.

While literacy programs are important gestures of aid to the disadvantaged, systematic schooling offers better prospects for the development of human potential. However, the Latin American nations have failed to offer their poor a high quality educational experience. Public elementary schools are usually looked upon as pauper institutions, to be avoided if one can afford something better. If the poor have access to schooling at all, its quality and status is likely to be quite low.

A 1969 estimate places the annual cost of elementary schooling in Latin America at only $42 per pupil. On the same basis, a general secondary

[13] "Una revolución en la educación: la campaña de alfabetización," *Universidad de la Habana*, **32**: 165–167, 158–159, January–March 1968.

[14] Ibid., p. 160.

[15] Greer, op. cit., p. 479.

[16] Ines Cristina Reca, et al., "El analfabetismo como fenómeno estructural y las perspectivas de una compaña nacional de alfabetizacion," in Pan American Union, *Investigaciones educativas en América, Reseña analítica no. 3* (Washington: Organization of American States, 1969), p. 41.

education costs $155, while vocational and normal schooling costs $210. University students represent an expense of $700.[17] Not only does elementary schooling, where the poor are most numerous, receive the smallest per capita assistance, but additional expenses must come out of parents' pockets. These include clean clothes, shoes, pencils, textbooks, notebooks, and transportation, most of which are essential if the child is to remain in good standing. In addition, a paradox of elementary education in most of Latin America is that real costs borne by the parents are relatively much higher than in affluent societies. What this means is that family standard of living is lowered when children between ages 8–11 forego earnings in order to attend school. In the United States, for example, children have little economic value and parents need not consider such a loss. In much of Latin America, the labor value of children increases at about age 10 and the poor family is under considerable pressure to withdraw him from school.[18] If one were to consider realistically the cost of bringing the disadvantaged child to a point where he can receive maximum benefit from the school as an instrument for equalizing social and economic opportunity, then present public expenditures must go far beyond schools and teachers. Supplementary services such as allowances for food and clothing, for loss of family income, and for extra social and economic aid to the child's family itself are needed. Thus, no matter how efficient a particular school may be, it may never have a chance to be fully effective unless these other aspects of the child's situation are also improved.

Some important efforts have been made, usually with the assistance of foreign aid programs, to introduce lunches and health services into the schools. For example, an agreement between the United States and Peru under the Alliance for Progress initiated in 1965 the distribution of a million daily rations worth 900 calories each to preschool and school-age children. Religious agencies have also collaborated in this program.[19] But no country has a general program to assist low income groups in this way. Even inducements in the form of food sometimes turn out to be a considerable expense. In one Guatemalan school district, for example, CARE donates powdered milk and wheat. The wheat is made into rolls at a local bakery and is distributed to all ten schools. But milk and sugar are also needed for the baking, thus raising the total cost to about $70 per month. To defray the added expense of preparing this "free" food, a child is charged 15¢ (U.S.)

[17] Economic and Social Council, Economic Commission for Latin America, *Social Development Policy for Latin America*, 13th Session (Lima: United Nations, April 1969), mimeographed, p. 214.

[18] Martin Carnoy, "Education in Latin America: An Empirical Approach," in William V. D'Antonio, editor, *Viewpoints on Education and Social Change in Latin America*, Occasional Papers No. 5 (Lawrence, Kansas: Center for Latin American Studies, 1965), p. 47.

[19] Angles, op. cit., p. 209.

per month. When there are many children per family, this becomes a sizeable sum, particularly where annual family income seldom exceeds $200 a year.[20]

While free breakfasts sometimes draw pupils into school, high rates of failure tend to drive them away again. The overall rate of pupil failure in first grade averages 26.8% and ranges from 50% in Brazil to 8% in Costa Rica.[21] In Argentina, for instance, 12.2% of elementary school children will repeat two or more years.[22] While this pattern has a tendency to maintain academic standards, the situation favors pupils whose families are affluent enough to keep them in school the additional time needed to pass the examinations. The large number of children who repeat each year also has the effect of denying schooling to less fortunate pupils in thousands of communities where schools are filled.

Under such conditions, considerable dropout is to be expected. In Mexico, for example, only 51.4% of pupils beginning urban elementary schools in 1960 were still enrolled in 1965; in rural areas, only 6.4% remained that long. Although a similar pattern prevails in most Latin American countries, retention rates have increased slightly in recent years.[23]

The causes of this dropout are not simply a product of firm academic standards. In Teotihuacan, a typical rural community near Mexico City, the fact that only 97 pupils completed six years of schooling out of an original 3,128 is attributed to poverty.[24] Yet there is also little doubt that many existing illiterates have spent several years in school and found it ineffectual and irrelevant. Indeed, some schools produce a sense of bewilderment and failure in disadvantaged children which retard their personal and social development.[25]

The benefits of schooling are less than obvious to many marginal communities in Latin America. In Bolivia, for instance, legislation requires primary instruction in Spanish, even if the teacher and pupils happen to be more fluent in their native Quechua or Aymara. Teachers are often poorly

[20] Oscar Horst and Avril McLelland, "The Development of an Educational System in a Rural Guatemalan Community," *Journal of Inter-American Studies*, **10**: 480, July 1968.

[21] Pan American Union, *Las normas de promoción y el problema de la reprobación escolar en América Latina* (Washington: Departament de Asuntos Educativos, 1968), p. 2.

[22] Organization for Economic Cooperation and Development, *Education, Human Resources and Development in Argentina* (Paris: OECD Publications, 1967), p. 59.

[23] Pan American Union, *América en cifras, 1967, Situación social*, op. cit., p. 89.

[24] Ramón E. Ruiz, *Mexico: The Challenge of Poverty and Illiteracy* (San Marino, Calif.: Huntington Library, 1963), p. 199–200.

[25] Adverse effects are lamented by Ivan Illich, "The Futility of Schooling in Latin America," *Saturday Review*, April 20, 1968, pp. 56–59 +, and illustrated by Gerardo and Alicia Reichel-Dolmatoff, *The People of Aritama: The Cultural Personality of a Colombian Mestizo Village* (Chicago: University of Chicago Press, 1961), pp. 115–125.

prepared,[26] and although they may be dedicated, their instructional ideals favor a classroom style which is formal, mechanical, and noncreative. Emphasis is placed upon precision, neatness, and artistic qualities such as those necessary in the preparation of a well-organized notebook. In such schools, an Indian child may become adept at Spanish (or Portuguese). What is more likely, however, is that the limited relevance of such alien instruction will lead children to drop out. It may also diminish the Indian pupil's sense of personal identity.

The shortage of classrooms is another reason for the dropout, for overcrowding makes for ineffective learning. In coastal Peru, for example, there are seats for only 53% of the elementary school children. Brazil alone needed about 142,500 classrooms between 1964 and 1970, if the goals of its national education plan were to be met. Inequitable distribution of this space is another problem; some communities have more classrooms than they need, while poorer and politically less influential constituencies have to turn children away.

A study of long-term truants or "dropouts" in an Argentine city illustrates still another aspect of the problem. Of 151 children located by researches, 32% had never attended school at all. A high proportion of the educational backgrounds of the mothers also showed a record of no schooling or early dropout. Nearly half the pupils who had repeated grades had done so three or more times.[27] Repeated failure in school and poor maternal example appear to be major causes for dropout in this community.

Perhaps the greatest factor limiting educational opportunity in Latin America is the sharp urban-rural distinction which prevails. In Costa Rica, for example, it is estimated that two-thirds of rural school dropout is due to the fact that the *escuela incompleta,* which runs for only three or four years of the six-year elementary cycle, makes it impossible for rural children in many communities to complete their primary schooling without moving into the larger towns.[28] In 1968, Colombia began to correct a similar situation by providing in-service training so that, hopefully, primary teachers would become competent to instruct all five grades and thus facilitate their pupil's access to secondary school.

[26] Typical is the case of Colombia, where three percent of urban teachers and 20% of rural teachers have not completed five years of elementary schooling.

[27] Tomás Amadeo Vasconi, et al., "Características socioeconómicos de un grupo de niños inconcurrentes y desertores en la enseñanza primaria de Paraná," in Pan American Union, *Investigaciones educativas en América, Reseña analítica no. 3* (Washington: Organization of American States, 1969), pp. 54, 56.

[28] Juan Porras Z., "La escuela incompleta en Costa Rica—estudio estadístico," in Pan American Union, *Investigaciones educativas en América, Reseña analítica no. 3,* op. cit., 1969), p. 39.

Disadvantaged populations in rural Latin America vary greatly. Some own their own land, some work for daily wages, and some are virtual serfs. Many "independent" *campesinos* cultivate land upon which they have no legal claim. Some produce surpluses which they sell on the national market, but many grow only subsistence crops for their family's consumption. Some peasants participate in highly developed indigenous cultures, but many others are economically and psychologically on the margin of human existence. Some are anxious for their children to emulate, understand, or imitate the elementary teacher's interpretation of national culture; others reject his efforts as morally deficient, shallow, discriminatory, or, at best, irrelevant. Where national educational systems have been extended to reach these lower-middle and lower classes, the schools have generally retained their urban-oriented, verbal, encyclopedic content without significant change. While these values are highly attractive to an actual or would-be elite, their relevance is much less clear to the person who must earn his living with his daily toil. And when such a curriculum is interpreted by poorly trained teachers, the defects of the old educational systems are sorely exaggerated.

Many countries have made efforts to develop elementary school programs of greater relevance to the peasant's condition. Unfortunately, such efforts have usually been imposed in a paternalistic manner, without any effort to seek an evaluation from the beneficiary of the schooling offered. Frequently, there is little campesino interest in an agricultural curriculum, mainly because of its poor quality. There is also a feeling that many vocational education programs are pandering to the peasant's inferior status. What the rural poor generally want from schooling is a mastery of the practical skills necessary to defend themselves from exploitation—skills which consist mainly of the ability to do arithmetic, calculations and reading. Only after these are attained do they become interested in education as a means of freeing their children from grueling farm work.[29] In addition, peasants are often resistant to the more vocational types of education, not because they are conservative and resistant to social change, but because the new methods may be inappropriate to local conditions, or the economic setting and land tenure, credit, and marketing arrangements do not offer them adequate incentives to adopt new methods.

A promising means of extending education in rural areas lies in the willingness of many local communities to make greater contributions of labor and materials for the construction and maintenance of schools. In Bolivia, as in other countries, peasant communities are eager to build their own school if the government will send them a teacher. In one case, after a pilot school was erected for them near Lake Titicaca, the *campesinos* built a series of

[29] Marshal Wolfe, "Educación, estructuras sociales, y desarrollo en América Latina," *América Latina*, **10**: 30, July–September 1967.

similar schools on their own initiative without supervision or support.[30] The growth of such locally oriented ventures depends to a great extent upon the infusion of new vigor into local governments. However, despite a Brazilian move toward decentralization in the 1960s. Latin America's strong tradition of administrative centralization makes prospects for this kind of a reform seem quite uncertain.

A more radical approach would simply allow peasants to build and staff their own schools without outside intervention. However, few governments are so unsophisticated politically that they would permit the lower classes to take educational matters into their own hands for long. Nevertheless, such freedom for local initiative might lead to the growth of schools where none now exist, even if they are of poor quality. Moreover, such schooling would confer a greater sense of personal worth to its more apt pupils, particularly if the teacher is beholden to peasant parents for her salary. Such freedom would mark the beginning of grass roots initiatives, even if such peasant schools were eventually absorbed into the state-controlled system. What makes such a proposal seem radical is the widespread assumption that lower-class initiative is virtually nonexistent or doomed to failure. The very notion that people without "culture," without a knowledge of the great truths of Greco-Roman civilization, with an insensitivity to philosophy, poetry, and logic—that such persons are capable of determining the curriculum even of an elementary school—is an idea which runs counter to much that is cherished by many of Latin America's most capable educators.

At present, practically any primary school worthy of the name feels an obligation to initiate the quest for these academically defined cultural truths. If a lower-class child is able to persist for the complete course, he will become accepted as a high-status, cultured, and fully human person. But few poor children are in a position to persist the 11 or 12 years required to complete the secondary school and obtain the *bachillerato* certificate. As a consequence, teachers do not avidly encourage lower-class children who have difficulty mastering the content of this long-range process. In its way, the traditional school is seeking to give the child the best of the human tradition if he is capable of profiting from it. If not, there are usually several others to take his place. That public elementary schools exist at all is evidence of the Latin Americans' concern for providing this humanizing opportunity to the poor. But they are not likely to share with much fervor the North American's faith that everyone can profit from a lengthy exposure to what schools teach.

The difficulty of the school's task in Latin America is magnified by demographic factors which have been overcome in the more urban nations. For

[30] Lambros Comitas, "Educación y estratificación social en Bolivia," *América Indígena*, **28**: 644, July 1968.

instance, one reason why so many children begin school two or three years late is the lack of roads. In rural Peru, for example, 30% of the children walk over two and one half miles to school daily each way.[31] Such distances are too great for young children to negotiate alone. The resulting heterogeneous age group found in first grade contributes to the failure of the less mature pupils. Fortunately, increased emphasis on road construction in recent years has contributed to a better educated population in many parts of Latin America. Migration to large cities has also accounted for some of the increases reflected in literacy statistics. Although schools in urban slums may be very unsatisfactory, they are at least more accessible than those in the countryside. Land reform has also stimulated interest in schooling. As peasants become masters of their economic destiny, education of all kinds comes to be valued more fully.

Although rural education is in the worst shape, urban elementary schools are not much better, with many on two or three sessions a day. It is not unusual for ten- or eleven-year-old children to work during the day and attend school at night. Under such circumstances, some students entering the first year of secondary school may not have even mastered the multiplication table, despite the great emphasis on selection.

Many methods are used to stretch scarce facilities. These include the rescheduling of periods to permit the use of three teachers to teach four primary classes, the introduction of coeducational primary classes in cases where pupil population is too low to justify the establishment of two schools, and the shortening of the school day in the early grades. With a view to discouraging early dropout, the idea of automatic promotion in the first three grades is increasingly appealing to Latin American educators. They see it as a means of retaining the child without the discouragement of early failure, until he has had several years to attain the fundamentals.[32]

There has been no lack of experimentation with vocational education in Latin America, but, in general, it has met with little acceptance, for it fails to confer the social status necessary to secure the more attractive jobs. In Brazil, for instance, one survey found only 6/10 of one percent of trade school students with fathers in professional occupations.[33] Despite the need for skilled labor, employers who need the technically trained outside the larger industrial cities tend to utilize untrained personnel because those with

[31] Angles, op. cit., pp. 195, 228.

[32] Jesús Vasquez-Marquez, "Deserción y repitencia en la escuela primaria," *Educación: Revista para el Magisterio*, **30**: 50, December 1968.

[33] Jaime Abreau, "Craft and Industrial Training in Brazil: A Socio-Historical Study," in Joseph A. Lauwerys and David G. Scanlon, eds., *The World Year Book of Education* (New York: Harcourt, Brace and World, 1968) p. 225.

formal technical schooling prefer white-collar work. In Bolivia, for example, only 55.3% of the *expertos* and 2.8% of the technicians who graduated from vocational schools were employed in their field of specialization in 1968.[34]

Generally, vocational skills developed in schools are not expected to yield many direct advantages. Persons with school-acquired competencies do not share the relatively open access to employment enjoyed by their peers in more industrialized societies. Friendship ties, family affiliation, and political connections are relatively more important in obtaining and keeping suitable employment than the mere possession of skills. Too often school-conferred status narrows rather than enlarges the range of manual tasks a highly trained technician may be expected to render. Thus, employers often feel it is better to employ a less able individual who is loyal, or at least cheap or docile, than a highly trained individual who may carry business secrets to a competitor. Consequently, on-the-job experience tends to be more useful to the poor than trade training.

One of the most persuasive arguments of United States educational reformers over a century ago was that free schools would convert dissolute leftist-leaning rabble into dependable workers. However, such arguments are seldom offered to persuade Latin American elites to support improved schooling for the poor. Such a pragmatic position tends to be viewed as a spiritual cheapening of the learning experience. The function of schooling is to purvey information about questions that matter. "True education" must be an end in itself, and its truth can be apprehended only by a logically organized and full examination of intrinsically worthwhile knowledge. The poor suffer by default from such a conception of education, for it is obviously hopeless for them to aspire to a complete understanding of *la cultura* when their next meal is in jeopardy. The school's "truths" are sources of moral authority, the right idea, the best way. To the Latin intellectual, the tragedy of the North American is that "he wants to use reality rather than know it."[35] For the North American, the tragedy is that the Latin wants to know reality rather than use it.

To most educated Latin Americans, this insensitivity blinds North Americans to what is really worthwhile in life. Material poverty is not actually an educational problem. The school's role is to select from the masses those who can profit most from its quest for truth, those who can learn to be most sensitive to what is good and beautiful, poetic and profound. The Uruguayan spokesman of the Latin American spirit, José Enrique Rodó, recognized this fundamental difference when he wrote that "Sensitivity, intelligence, customs—all are characterized in [North Americans] by a radical ineptitude for

---

[34] William E. Carter, *Bolivia: The Improbable Land* (Gainesville, Fla., 1970). Unpublished manuscript.

[35] Paz, op. cit., p. 22.

selection which, together with the mechanical order of their material activity and their political life makes for a profound disorder in everything pertaining to the mastery of the idealistic arts." But true education is not merely academic and logical, and a person who is really *educado* is much more. Rodó explains that North Americans "lack that superior gift of *amiability*—in the highest sense—of that extraordinary power of sympathy with which the races blessed with a providential trust of education learned how to make of their culture something similar to the beauty of the classic Hellene. . . ." So long as Rodó's "intelligence, sentiment, and idealism" continue to be more highly prized by Latin leaders than the North American qualities of "will and utility,"[36] it will be difficult to transform Latin American schooling into a practical agency for the economic betterment of the poor.

This chapter has emphasized the poor's relationships with elementary schooling because they seldom continue beyond this level. But the few who do find secondary schooling to be a major barrier, partly because only half of Latin American secondary school places are in tuition-free public institutions. Although many countries are now using international loans to plan and construct multipurpose public secondary schools, the introduction of such schools primarily aids the growing middle class. Of course, some disadvantaged youth do attain secondary education, but even there they have a strong tendency to drop out. In Montevideo, for example, children of day workers among first year *liceo* students amounted to only 3.3% of their school class; by the fourth year only 0.4% remained.[37]

At the same time, the total number of students in Latin America completing secondary education nearly doubled between 1957 and 1965. However, where educational levels are rising more rapidly than the number of jobs, the minimum amount of formal schooling demanded of job applicants also rises. This means that the person with only a few years of education is now at a greater disadvantage in seeking employment than he would have been a decade ago, despite the fact that he might be perfectly able to perform many jobs quite adequately. This "credentialism," or increased emphasis on a certain amount of formal schooling as a precondition to employment, is an important factor in making the poor more disadvantaged than ever before.[38]

At the university level, tuition is cheap, and in some countries, it is scaled according to ability to pay. Courses of study, such as those at the University of Buenos Aires, are stretched over many years, thus permitting impecunious students to work their way through. A 1958 survey there showed that 2.3% of the students had parents with no formal education—a crude index of the

---

[36] José Enrique Rodó, *Ariel* (Buenos Aires: Editorial Tor, 1947), pp. 115, 128, 134.
[37] Wolfe, op. cit., p. 24.
[38] Jorge Balán, "Migrant-Native Socio-economic Differences in Latin American Cities: A Structural Analysis," *Latin American Research Review*, 4: 10–11, Spring 1969.

mobility of the poor into the highest level of education in that city.[39] Actually, the participation of the poor varies greatly from one country and one university to another.

Finally, despite some grounds for optimism, the education of the Latin American poor is faced with a fundamental dilemma. On the one hand, schooling is expected to affirm a society's hierarchical symbols, occupational preferences, and work habits to new generations. At the same time, it is asked to initiate a change in prevailing values. Both, of course, are needed, but both are fundamentally contradictory. What is good education for the middle classes is not necessarily good for the poor who must cope with a different environment. At present, the long-standing tradition of lower-class docility is gradually responding to the increasing importunities of the mass media, to ever more ominous population pressures, and to increased urban-rural contacts. The result is a growing clamor for opportunity. Hopefully, the governments of Latin America will find a way to use the schools to convince the poor that they, too, have some real measure of control over their destiny.

[39] Organization for Economic Cooperation and Development, op. cit., p. 120.

49

The Canadian Government, Poverty, and Education

Mitchell Sharp

Traditionally, governments have approached the question of poverty from two aspects—economic growth and social security. There was once a theory that, given sufficient economic growth, poverty would be solved by every able-bodied man or woman being able to find work. For those who were not able to work, governments provided relief or other forms of assistance. Desirable as both objectives are, they will not in themselves solve poverty. While times of general prosperity, like the present, benefit most Canadians in very visible ways, there remains a substantial minority of poor as high in absolute numbers as during the great depression who do not share this affluence. To the extent that poverty is a relative term, they are poorer than ever. Prosperity tends to widen the gulf between rich and poor just as depression tended to be a leveler. That is one reason why poverty today is a top priority in government thinking and government action.

In the spring of 1965, the Canadian government announced a new organization to fight poverty and broaden opportunity. That was not the beginning of the Canadian War on Poverty. For years there have been many positive approaches aimed at helping the poor. Some, like the Agricultural and Rural Development Act, have been developed in such a way as to put Canada in the very forefront of bold programming for the elimination of human want. But there have been gaps. Even the best of projects must be constantly subject to review in the hope of improvement.

This was the thinking which prompted the federal government to establish the Special Program Committee of the Cabinet under the chairmanship of the Prime Minister. It is served by the Cabinet Secretariat which carries the role of coordination, stimulation, of information gathering, of information dissemination. Its job is to analyze the problems of poverty and to help develop and coordinate the federal government action which will be most effective in improving the situation of the poor and developing new opportunities to help them take a full part in Canadian life. We then might call this a third dimension in government policy—social opportunity to go with economic expansion and social security. The federal anti-poverty organization is partly to strengthen federal programs and partly to help link the projects of federal agencies with the vital programs of provincial governments, voluntary groups, our research institutions, and private citizens. This is not a federal war against poverty. It is a national war in which the federal government will discharge its full responsibility for leadership.

There are stark statistics which tell something of the problems we Canadians face in erasing the blot of poverty—statistics on education, on housing, on health. There is a lot of discussion today about priorities in action: whether we should tackle, first, undereducation, or poor health, or insecure income. The obvious answer is that none can be tackled alone. In naval terms, we must advance line abreast, not line astern. Fortunately, we do so against a background of national economic strength: of high national employment, of steadily advancing income, of reassuring prospects for continuing growth. This is well, for the investments in human resources required to maintain this economic strength is very great.

Take manpower training. As the Economic Council of Canada has pointed out, Canadians are seriously undereducated and undertrained to operate the kind of technological society we are developing today. To meet the needs of 20 years hence, when two-thirds of our present population will still be in the labor force, we are critically unprepared. Without a revolution in education and training, we just cannot continue to operate the industries on which our national well-being depends. I need hardly point out that we neither can, nor do we want to, depend on the immigration of skilled workers to maintain our pace. This is why, since 1961, over $820,000,000 has been approved by the federal government for new vocational training facilities. While this is a dramatic increase over a short period, the gap in our education facilities means that we must continue this expansion not only in the vocational training field, but in all other areas of education. With the enormous expansion of universities in Canada, we might well become complacent with higher education. We have no cause. One out of every 12 Canadians of university age is taking university education. In comparison, one-half the young Americans of appropriate age are going to a university. Another discouraging figure is that 30% of young Canadians between the ages of 14 and 24 have left school with only Grade 8 education with no apparent intention of returning. These are tomorrow's poor.

Despite the rapid expansion of vocational training facilities, the dropout rates among unemployed workers, 50% and higher, indicate that solving training needs requires more than schools. Canada needs new ways of teaching, attracting, and motivating many Canadians who are not able to adjust to our present educational systems. The school dropout rate indicates we are talking about more than a quarter of our young population. We cannot afford to write these people off. Ministers from the federal government and the provinces recently decided on bold new pilot projects which will test new approaches and methods in vocational training. Financed by the federal government and administered jointly with the provinces, we hope they will lead to drastically revised programs capable of giving skills to those people who had previously given up all thought of further schooling.

The average worker will hold about three jobs in his lifetime, each requiring specialized training. Advancing technology creates new wealth and new opportunities but it also destroys less skilled jobs. It is becoming harder for those left behind to catch up.

What of those who have the skills but who live in areas where no jobs are available? There are two choices. Governments may encourage industries to locate in areas where there is a dearth of employment opportunities. The federal government, through its Area Development Program, is doing just this. It has designated 92 Canada Manpower Centre areas and contiguous counties and census divisions where about 18% of the Canadian labor force lives. Within these areas, manufacturing and processing industries which establish new plants or substantially expand old ones will receive nonrepayable development grants. The direct financial aid to a plant opening or expanding in an underdeveloped area may reach $5,000,000.

The second choice is to move the worker to areas where his skills can be used. This is the purpose of the Manpower Mobility Program. Through this program, outright grants are provided to workers to move temporarily to explore employment possibilities; to individuals to move to attend approved occupational training; and to workers formerly unemployed or underemployed to move themselves, their dependents, and household effects when they have obtained continuing full-time employment in localities other than those in which they reside. The resettlement part of the aid may be as high as $1000 for a large family, and a worker who has had to sell his house or buy a new one can get a further $500 grant. In addition, a worker who has received an exploratory grant can get an allowance of up to $40.00 per week to support his dependents while he is looking for work. The object of this program is to combat the problems of distance so costly to our national life. It is to help make all Canada into one community of workers.

Even in this brief reference to measures to help members of the labor force who are chronically underemployed, I should mention the new Department of Manpower. This is, of course, a part of a broad government reorganization. The responsibility of the new department is to provide those manpower programs which the Economic Council has pointed out are so important in the effort to fight poverty and create opportunity. Even the name of the new department is an indication of priorities in national development.

Much of Canada's poverty is concentrated in rural areas. In 1966, Parliament approved the creation of a $50,000,000 fund for rural development under the Agricultural and Rural Development Act program. In 1967, the amount which may be spent under this Fund was increased to $350,000,000. This makes possible the redevelopment of rural areas which have serious adjustment problems and low income. The projects in such areas must conform to comprehensive development plans worked out by the provinces. A feature of the plans must be local participation under rural development committees, illustrating how government resources are being used for a truly national attack on poverty.

In this national movement for new opportunities, the Company of Young Canadians is going to take a place in the forefront. The Company is intended to give Canada's youth an opportunity for service. Because the emphasis will be on community development, the volunteers will play a large part in enabling the poor to help themselves by use of the resources available to them. It is a truism that the best possible government measures will be useful only if the people who need them are able to take advantage of them. While there will always be a place for conventional forms of charity, the cycle of poverty will not be broken until the poor themselves become involved in the solution of their own problems. To the extent that they manage their own affairs and obtain the self-respect that goes with this, they will become less and less a burden to society. Community development on a national scale must be an important element in an effective program. This is not just a matter of social conscience. It is designed also to reduce the waste of human resources for which all Canadians must pay.

So far I have been discussing social opportunity and economic growth programs. Even assuming that perfect world where all trainable people are matched with jobs using their talents to the full, we still will have many Canadians who, for one reason or another, will not be able to earn enough money to support themselves. In this group are the aged, the mentally or physically incapacitated, the deserted mothers. There are many support programs for these people. Old Age Security, Unemployment Insurance, the Family and Youth Allowances program, and, more recently, the Canada Pension Plan. All are part of a developing structure to provide a basic income and insurance against disaster. The new Canada Assistance Plan brings into a single program and administrative framework the varied welfare needs of all Canadians. The plan abolishes the means test for people receiving Old Age Assistance, or Blind or Disabled Persons Allowances. Benefits are geared to the needs of the applicant and his dependents. It is a big step forward in guaranteeing a certain level of human dignity for all Canadians.

Much work remains to be done in developing economic tools for a social purpose whether in training allowances, unemployment insurance, or levels of social assistance. I do not accept the proposition that people generally prefer to live on welfare, or that they would rather live on welfare than work. The man may well prefer to be independent and to work, but he simply cannot afford to do so. The relationship, then, of these measures to economic opportunity requires the deepest studies by governments and by research institutions.

Much has been said about Medicare, and I will not discuss this in detail here. Suffice it to say that it is the intention of the federal government to bring comprehensive health services into effect for all Canadians. Ill-health is a big factor in poverty. A sick man cannot work or improve his earning power. It is the poor who most often fall prey to serious health problems. Medicare will be a long step in the direction of increasing the health levels of all Canadians.

Closely linked to health is housing. Housing programs are available with massive federal support, but they are not being used as they were intended. We need more public understanding of housing and the means now available to meet it. This is an example of the need of local action to make government measures really successful. Nevertheless, the legislation is being constantly reexamined for improvements and within the last two years greater attention has been given to the problem of urban renewal.

I have been addressing myself to what government is doing. It is up to every Canadian to become a part of the struggle against poverty. The spread of knowledge will erode complacency. Then it is up to each of us to take a vital interest in designing new programs at every level of government. It is also up to each of us to make those programs work through a very personal engagement in the problems of the poor. We may help by working with poor people ourselves, or through our churches, home and school associations, or social organizations. This is what I mean by a national war on poverty.

50

The Education of the Poor
and Disadvantaged in Italy

Michael Anello

The term "disadvantaged" evokes in the contemporary mind a number of connotations. For the American scholar the term covers an array of meanings from lack of economic advantages to culturally deprived. Recently, the term has been given a broad interpretation; the disadvantaged include any child for whom the established educational process and the school curriculum is inadequate.[1] In the United States, the education of children from disadvantaged areas has become a national concern and the research in this area has grown voluminously.[2] In Europe, where there has been traditionally less research on young children, there is now evidence of greater interest in program development to lessen social and economic deprivation.

One country making slow but steady progress is Republic of Italy, which understands profoundly the meaning of poverty and which only recently has lifted itself to a productive and stable economy. The study of deprivation encompasses those children in Italian society who suffer some form of social, economic, physical, or mental restrictions. The disadvantaged child in Italy can be studied informally from several perspectives: the culturally deprived child, the economically handicapped child, the school dropout, the delinquents, and the physically and mentally handicapped. Through these areas, the educational and other governmental agencies are attempting to remedy the problems that plague this country. The problem of ethnic minorities, race relations, and desegregation, as known in other countries, has not been a significant question in Italy. The relationship of poverty, education, and social

[1] Mario D. Fantini and Gerald Weinstein, *The Disadvantaged: Challenge to Education* (New York: Harper & Row, 1968).

[2] Robert Havighurst, David Ausubel, Martin Deutsch, and Frank Riessman are a few who have contributed to the literature on the disadvantaged. See Joe L. Frost and Glenn R. Hawkes, *The Disadvantaged Child* (Boston: Houghton Mifflin, 1969).

and economic development is a triad of national concern. Education and political officials are addressing themselves to these problems by closely scrutinizing the present and traditional educational structure in Italy. Present reforms in the Ministry of Public Instruction encompass methods of coping with the problems of socially and economically disadvantaged children and ways of making the elementary and secondary schools more adaptable to the problems of these children.[3]

In this essay, we present the nature of poverty and deprivation in Italy and discuss the educational programs which could remedy these problems. There is no equivalent term in the Italian language for the word disadvantaged, but several terms have come into usage to describe youth who suffer some form of deprivation: *i minorati, gli incapaci*, and *i subnormali*.[4]

To give meaningful description to these terms or to deprivation in Italy, it is necessary first to explain that Italy is socially and economically divided in a way that many nations are not. A traveler in Italy can see quickly the vast difference between life in the north and life in the south. Writers in contemporary Italian society seldom fail to mention the Italy of two worlds—the one of the economic *miracolo*[5] and the other of poverty.[6] There is a sharp difference in standards of living; the industrial cities of the north have a standard of living which is similar to those of other Western European countries. Few who travel to Italy see the backward, small rural towns which are not on the tourist circuit. This is where the poverty lingers and is so widespread

[3] Substantial publications have been released in recent years dealing with social, economic, and educational legislation to improve Italian society. Primary among them is the five-year school development plan entitled *Il piano di sviluppo della scuola per il quinquennio dal 1966 al 1970* (Roma: Palombi, 1967). The plan outlines the role of the school in modern Italy stressing closer alliance between school and society. A book by Federico Orlando, *Guerra alla povertà* (Firenze: Sansoni, 1966), outlines Italy's war on poverty programs and provides a well-documented bibliography of social problems— health, education, welfare, immigration, unemployment, etc. The work of Giovannia Maria Bertin in *Scuola e società in Italia* (Bari: Laterza, 1964), deals with the transformation of Italian society from an agricultural to a technological and urban society. He calls for a restructuring of educational policy and expansion of educational opportunity.

[4] See "Bollettino della Società Italiana per l'assistenza medico-psico-pedagogica ai minorati dell'età evolutiva" (Roma: S.I.A.M.E., 1962); "L'assistenza ai minorati in età evolutia in Pulglia è Lucania" (Bari: Cressati, 1961); M. T. Rovegatti, *Fanciulli in difficoltà nella famiglia e nella scuola* (Roma: Garzanti, 1961).

[5] For a good English version of the growth and well-being of the economy, see *A Century of Economic and Social Development in Italy 1861–1961* (Roma: Istituto Centrale di Statistica, 1962), and *Italy, An Economic Profile* (Washington: Commercial Office of the Italian Embassy, 1967).

[6] For insight into southern life, see Edward Banfield, *The Moral Basis of a Backward Society* (Glencoe, Ill.: Free Press, 1958), and Carlo Levi, *Christ Stopped at Eboli* (New York: Farrar-Straus, 1947).

that, regardless of attempts to remedy the situation in these areas, the level of depravity remains high. The southern part of Italy, although helped by massive governmental aid, is still essentially a rural, poverty-stricken area. Peasants can be seen taking their day's work to the marketplace hopefully to make the day's earnings. Many of the young are still engaged in assisting their families to produce agricultural goods. Scores eventually leave the community to seek jobs in the northern part of Italy or in the neighboring countries, creating additional family problems and disadvantages.

Although there is some progress in the south, it is slow and it does not conform to the general prosperity taking place in the northern part of Italy where a solid middle class has taken advantage of innovations and technical progress.[7] A child born in the north can be expected to complete some form of high school education, occasionally obtain a university degree, gain a respectable job, own land and a house, have technical know-how, and raise his children with similar expectations. There are, of course, historical reasons for the rapid advances of the north which developed from a city civilization of lords and commoners, while in the south the rise of a small ruling class, who controlled the land, impeded social evolution and caused the development of a solidly poor population.

After World War II, it was still reported that the most depressed areas in Italy were those where ownership of land was still concentrated in the hands of relatively few.[8] Poverty breeds poverty; the south has had to struggle with illiteracy, high infant mortality, poor housing conditions, and a limited food supply. Agriculture in the south is a rather backward pattern. Service industries are mainly small trading activities which have been created in order to solve the problems of unemployment or underemployment.[9]

Characteristically, a nation's educationally disadvantaged have come from the rural areas, and Italy is a clear manifestation of this principle. Although school attendance has been improving,[10] and attempts are being made to improve school conditions in the southern part of Italy, there is still low

---

[7] The south suffers from a low income per head of population. A good example of this can be shown by looking at national income from the north and south. In 1955 the figures showed that 78.5% of the national income was received by the north and central parts of Italy. For the south, 21.5% of the national income was received. In 1959 the figures were 78.8% and 21.2%, respectively. Organization for European Economic Cooperation, *Economic Conditions in Member and Associated Countries of the O.E.E.C.: Italy* (Paris, February 1961).

[8] *New York Times*, November 20, 1949.

[9] "The Rebirth of the South of Italy and the Work of the *Cassa per il mezzorgiorni*," Poligrafica e Cartevalori, Napoli, 1963.

[10] In a ten-year period, 1955–1965, the number of diplomas awarded at the high school level has risen from 68,000 to 129,000. See *Bollettino Mensile di Statistica*, Istituto Centrale di Statistica, March–April, 1966.

motivation and a lack of goals among deprived students in southern schools. Performance is substandard.[11] Children come from homes where the adults have had little schooling. Characteristically, the poor have large families. Poverty, mistrust, and high mobility complicate school problems in this part of the country.

Culturally deprived youth, *i minorati*, are those living under economic and social conditions that are significantly below national standards. Notwithstanding the qualitative differences between *i minorati* of the south and those in the north there are notable factors which characterize these individuals. They have in common: inadequate housing, insufficient sanitary conditions, large families, low income, little or no schooling, and a mood of perpetual despair.

I minorati live in shacks either in the deep south or in northern poverty pockets. In the large cities of Rome, Milan, and Florence, conditions are similar to the conditions from which the poor originally had fled.

Among *i minorati* there has been increased mobility and emigration to other countries[12] in hope of seeking improved conditions, employment, and better education. In many instances mobility compounds the problems for the children of these families. Many who move to the north have language problems because of different dialects spoken in the south. Northern schools frequently have overcrowded classes and disenchanted teachers who teach large, disorganized classes.[13] The socially disadvantaged child who has migrated from the south becomes unhappy with the drudgery of school attendance and generally drops out. Although school legislation requires that children attend school up to the age of 14, this is seldom accomplished among the disadvantaged.

Related to the problem of school attendance is the problem of juvenile delinquency which has been growing in Italy.[14] Normally a child, after attending elementary school, is required to attend secondary school where a far stricter curriculum assists the student in completing his studies. This is one of the more positive aspects of the problem and it means that schools have a role of primary importance in the campaign against juvenile delin-

[11] During the writer's visit to several communities in the southern part of Italy, he was able to observe the lack of interest and motivation among children in ill-equipped schools. It is difficult to make scholarship central when life is hard and poverty omnipresent.

[12] According to one report in 1965, there are over 1,000,000 persons who have emigrated to other countries. Italian workers can be located in Belgium, France, West Germany, Holland, Luxembourg, Canada, and the United States. Orlando, op. cit., pp. 146–152.

[13] Carmelo Cappuccio, "Scuola Materne," *La Nazione*, January 3, 1966.

[14] "Education and the Campaign against Juvenile Delinquency," *Italy: Documents and Notes*, 1: 41, January–February, 1967.

quency. But compulsory schooling is not an answer in itself. School officials realize that additional programs must be implemented to assist the young who have withdrawn from school and others who want to complete some form of education. Courses for adults have been arranged for persons over 14 years of age who have not completed formal education and who lack sufficient basic knowledge. This movement in Italy is called the *scuola populare*. The specific aims of these schools are to reduce illiteracy, to enforce the principle that all children should be educated to the age of 14, and to institute a workable system of vocational training. Since 1958, the results have been extremely encouraging. For example, courses for adult illiterates number 44,000, and there are 821,000 in attendance; courses for semi-illiterates, 64,000, with 1,226,000 in attendance; general courses, 37,000, with an attendance of 701,000; special courses, 7,000, with an attendance of 158,000. In addition, 45 traveling libraries were established and 8,000 new courses in adult education were organized.[15]

More significantly, a new organization has been established to assist the poor in the rural communities. Italy's National Union for the Struggle Against Illiteracy, or UNLA, calls for a long-term program for the establishment of educational assistance programs for the educationally deprived of the south.

One of the primary tasks is to prepare education leaders who will voluntarily teach in these areas. UNLA has organized numerous seminars and in recent years has established training centers in key localities in the south. The existence of these cultural centers has had an immediate effect; there is a notable decline in illiteracy in these areas and there is evidence of a new, educated class emerging.

The content of the courses studied by the group leaders included instruction in audio-visual aids, art training, and leisure time activities. Some of the communities took the initiative to organize musical groups, sport activities, and Unesco clubs. Other trainees in the program were permitted to study economic, social, and political problems in southern Italy. A number of local officials took part in the program, outlining for the trainees specific problems of the community. The experience was beneficial, in that trainees became completely immersed in the problems of the community and were better able to assist the people of the community to help themselves.

The *scuola populare* has had a good impact in that it has provided basic educational programs for illiterates, job training for the untrained, and pro-

[15] See Marialla Tabellini, "Training for Adult Education and Rural Development in Southern Italy," *School and Society*, **93**: 395, October 30, 1965, and Michael Anello, "The Cure for Illiteracy: Adult Education in Italy," *Adult Leadership*, **15**: 159, November 1966.

grams to combat delinquency. However, it does not get to the root causes of poverty or provide better early childhood education.

Associated with the problem of the socially and culturally deprived and the delinquent youth in Italy is the problem of unemployment. Poor youth often fall into the ranks of the unemployed and further drain an economy which is in need of skilled and semiskilled technicians.

Italian industrial leaders demand trained and qualified personnel for numerous jobs at all levels. One study shows that, by 1975, Italian industrial concerns will demand a total of 8,350,000 employees, of which two-thirds must be qualified in some specific area.[16] Unemployment is one of Italy's most stubborn problems and quite obviously has a direct relationship to poverty and economic deprivation. In 1966, Italy's total labor force was 19,653,000 out of a population of 52,000,000 people. The unemployed numbered 769,000, primarily southern agricultural workers displaced by industrialization.[17] Although these figures do not depict extreme and serious conditions for the entire country, the south has had an unemployment problem of depression proportions.

It is probably superfluous to mention that, under these conditions, the stability of the family is in constant jeopardy. Orlando reports that, when it is necessary for the father of the household to seek employment either in other parts of Italy or in another country, there have been increasing instances where fathers did not return. He reports that half of the million workers who have emigrated not only have found jobs, but also have founded new families.[18] Although illegal, unilateral divorces have been reported and are on the increase. A national association has been formed to assist the rehabilitation of these families,[19] but here again poverty continues to breed poverty and the children of these families become more economically deprived than previously. The effects produce a society of chronic dependents who must draw heavily on the community's welfare services for survival.

Although the term *i minorati* has been applied to all who suffer some form of deprivation, the more specific terms used are *i subnormali* for those suffering some form of mental deficiency and *gli incapaci* for those children with some form of physical disability. Most of these children are placed in special classes provided by the Ministry of Public Instruction. The majority of them suffer no apparent neurological defects; they are mentally deficient

[16] Associazione per lo sviluppo dell'industria nel Mezzogiorno, *Il ruolo della scuola nello sviluppo economico Italiano* (Roma: SVIMEZ, 1960), p. 36.

[17] *Italy, An Economic Profile*, op. cit., p. 41.

[18] Orlando, op. cit., p. 152.

[19] Giuseppe Barilla, "Mezzo milione di mogli italiane sono colpite dall'emigrazione," *Il Messaggero*, November 21, 1965.

because their impoverished conditions restrict significant educational and cultural experiences.

It was Sante De Sanctis, a pioneer in neuropsychiatry, who focused attention on the study of idiot and mentally deficient children.[20] The mentally disadvantaged child is lacking in skills that are necessary for successful school achievement. Obviously the school environment fails to compensate, resulting in further troubles throughout the child's school career. De Sanctis offered suggestions for enriching the school environment, stimulating the need for special instruction, special services, and ways of increasing mental maturity. The Ministry of Public Instruction has increased its funds to support the schools for the *i subnormali* and the research in Italy in this area has gained significant momentum. Stimulated by a group of French, Dutch, Belgian, and German educators who founded an association for mentally handicapped children, Italian educators became aware of the need for professional recognition and in 1957 formed the Associazione Nazionale Educatori Gioventù Italiana Disadattat or ANEGID.[21] Today that association is well established, and it addresses itself to the delicate task of organizing education in community living for the mentally handicapped. Members of the ANEGID have received theoretical and practical training to enable them to understand the behavior of mentally handicapped children. These instructors are working in educational and re-educational centers and public assistance centers, carefully preparing education experiences for these handicapped students.

Giuseppe Montasano established a school for *gli incapaci,* the physically handicapped. This school is called *Scuola Magistrale Ortofrenico*; its instructors are specially trained for providing activities and educational materials for the physically handicapped.[22]

In the first decade of this century, a woman physician began working and trying her techniques with the underprivileged children in a slum area in Rome. These undisciplined and untrained children were among the economically and culturally deprived children in the Roman ghetto who were rejected by the traditional school system. Montessori's success far surpassed her expectation. These untrained, undisciplined children learned to read and write; they learned cleanliness and socially accepted manners; they became interested students; they received both sensory and motor training with the

---

[20] Giacomo Cives, "Documenti sulla storia delle scuole per minorati psichici in Italia," *Nuova Rivista Pedagogica*, No. 1, February 1966.

[21] The achievements of the National Association of Teachers of the Mentally Retarded have been encouraging and have stimulated cooperation of many other organizations, such as the Ministry of Health, Ministry of Public Instruction, Ministry of Justice, the Red Cross, and other governmental agencies. See "Educating Mentally Handicapped Children," *Italy: Documents and Notes,* **5**: 429, September–October, 1967.

[22] Cives, op. cit., p. 8.

didactic learning devices that Montessori provided. Many were not yet five years old. When, in 1909, Maria Montessori published her observations of the slum school of Rome in *The Scientific Pedagogy as Applied to Child Education in Children's Houses*, there began a worldwide interest in the Montessori method. For the Italians, Montessorianism placed emphasis on the educational needs of the culturally disadvantaged children in Italy. Although the Montessori method has received criticism, it has been a primary stimulus of improving childhood education in Italy.[23]

The Ministry of Public Instruction under the new five-year plan has emphasized a tremendous need for greater financial assistance in the areas of special education. Additional funds have been provided for the construction of new buildings for the physically and mentally handicapped children. Charitable trusts have been set up to provide for children of compulsory school age who are in need of financial assistance due to poverty and economic deprivation. This assistance includes transportation and book vouchers for needy pupils. It provides for school meals, boarding schools, school camps, and after-school activities. It was reported in 1965 that over 3,000,000 pupils of compulsory school age had benefited from the assistance programs provided by the Ministry. A total of 26,000 scholarships have been provided for needy pupils.[24] More significantly, over 100 accident prevention councils have been set up to assist in bringing the school and the family closer together. The councils take up such matters as school attendance, choice of career, selection of school, financial obligations, and the necessity for long-range economic planning.

Italian educational television is presenting educational courses for those who never advanced beyond elementary school. The Italian radio and television corporation, RAI, instituted in 1961 an emergency program referred to as *Telescuola*. *Telescuola* provides a variety of courses of a remedial nature at the elementary level; some courses provide the opportunity to learn a trade by viewing study courses that correspond to the first- and second-year curriculum of Italy's technical schools. The classes are given in two half-hour lessons daily along with 10-minute lectures in complementary subjects such as religion, music and singing, domestic science, writing, and physical training.

Telescuola has made a good impact, although some educators were concerned that there was little or no contact between student and teacher. In order to create a school atmosphere and to promote rapport between student

[23] See Maria Montessori, *The Montessori Method* (New York: Schocken Books, 1964), and E. Mortimer Standing, *Maria Montessori, Her Life and Work* (California: Academy Library Guild, 1957).

[24] *Rapporto sul movimento educativo nel 1966–1967*, Ministero della Pubblica Istruzione, July 1967, pp. 69–72.

and teacher, officials decided to develop *Telescuola* listening posts, called *Posti di Telescuola* staffed by group leaders holding senior secondary school diplomas. The function of these staff members is to travel to distant localities and offer assistance to students in *Telescuola* courses.

Since 1961, *Posti di Telescuola* have been formed in all parts of Italy and have had widespread influence. The number of students grouped in *Posti di Telescuola* and registered with *Telescuola* is 66,248. It is estimated that there are over 100,000 viewers who are following the courses. To develop an even more personal contact, the *Telescuola* authorities have sent to each group leader a register in which he keeps records of attendance and achievement scores. Each month this information is entered into the personal folders of the students to make complete records of the general progress made by each student. This gives *Telescuola* authorities an opportunity to note the effectiveness of the program and to make improvements. In communities of less than 3,000, where there are no secondary schools and no technical schools, *Telescuola* has won its greatest prestige in assisting *i minorati*.

The concerted attempt to eliminate poverty, delinquency, and unemployment in Italy and to assist the culturally, economically, mentally, and physically handicapped child is not a new activity. What is new is the vigorous national effort to abolish these problems. Increasingly, the major emphasis is being placed on the school system and the efforts of the Ministry of Public Instruction. The activity there to make education reach more, to provide scholarships for needy students, and to obtain funds to assist educational improvement at all levels is impressive.

51

Education and the Poor
in India

Margaret L. Cormack

These mute, depressed and ignorant people
must be endowed with education.
These spent-up, withered and broken-hearted men
must be rejuvenated with hope.

Rabindranath Tagore

What teacher's heart does not resonate to these human sentiments—written by one of the world's greatest masters? But, to be honest, the horrendous truth is baring its teeth—"access" to education and other rejuvenating processes is no automatic utopia. It works for a few, whose success-sagas are reiterated in countless classrooms for decades, but, for most people entrenched in subsocial sludge, mere "access" is an empty pot of rice.

There are more than 500,000,000 Indians today, their numbers multiplying from 12–20,000,000 each year. The annual per capita income is about Rs. 500[1] (about $66) and only a small fraction of the population earn enough to be eligible to pay taxes and, thus, to contribute to their nation's welfare. Perhaps 100,000,000 subsist at submarginal levels, mute victims of monsoons, malnutrition, and a social system in which they have been taken for granted. For those who survive disease and famine, the material and human resources in the rural communities afford some succor. Furthermore, there are some real political, agricultural, and educational changes in village India—and fewer families live through every hot season in semistarvation. Urban India is another matter. The plight of the urban poor is the sole result of reliance on money as medium for all needs; occasional "welfare" is

[1] The Government of India figure for 1965, as published in *India 1966*, is Rs. 421.5. The London *Economist* gives $72 for 1966.

helpful but inadequate. Urban families have become nuclear units, and, thus, do not have the traditional social security. In the cities live not only the established rich and the burgeoning nouveaux riches and middle classes— but also the multiplying poor. Riots in city streets have become more common than festival dancing.

Where is the capital, human and financial, to rejuvenate this massive quantum of inertia? Where is the will—and where is the skill? In India, to be blunt, nothing short of a total political, economic, and social revolution— a total "rebirth," as some Indians put it—would stimulate most of the sub-human poor to the riches and reaches of the mind. Benign gestures of ameli-oration add nothing but the pain of aroused hope when little is hopeful.

Why has Indian "development" not accomplished more—via the Five Year Plans and substantial foreign aid? Perhaps we should add a third slogan to the classic formulas for improvement analyzed years ago by Gunnar Myrdal: "Let's educate them! Get a leader! Give them technical assistance!" It has been easy to commit ourselves to these principles, perhaps especially in our time to help others to help themselves. We believe in it, but do we know under what conditions it works? Men in mass, if sufficiently numerous and sufficiently subjected, respond only sluggishly to any or all of the above stimuli. As a matter of fact, rapid development tends to widen socioeconomic gulfs. Just as the developed nations are largely progressing more rapidly than the developing, due to the larger knowledge-skill base and to progress atti-tudes, within India the ranks of the rich swell—but so do those of the populous poor, many of them at the distant end of a widening spectrum. Progress or poverty are more than matters of mathematical projections, but not more than matters of projected human aspirations and habits. How to energize the enervated? That is the question—of development—and the ra-tional mobilization of resources is but one means to this end. The human element (or what we still call the irrational because we have not defined the variables) has not been considered, scientifically or via common sense.

Indian efforts in the field of education only can be described as massive but not productive. For obvious political and humane reasons, after Inde-pendence, clear priority was given to getting every child in school and reduc-ing illiteracy. This goal has not been achieved, and, certainly, the quality of education has been neglected. Educational planners now concede that selec-tive focus would have been wiser than the comprehensive approach, but political pressures and vested interests have increased in favor of egalitarian patrimony. There is no doubt the nation is trying to do too many things for too many people. Initial emphasis on the stimulation of innovation and leadership probably would have benefited the masses sooner, and, with hindsight, it is clear there should have been planned phases in relation to political autonomy, democracy as a political system based on the adult franchise, democracy in terms of social justice, science and technology in agri-culture and industry, and economic self-sufficiency. On the whole it may be impossible for production and equalization factors to be achieved at the same time, even under conditions of maximum good will and substantial foreign aid.

Unfortunately, the educational base—the potential manpower base—has remained so disfunctional to the innovation and leadership skills and atti-tudes needed that mere expansion of this base has contributed to a vicious circle of descending standards—and to the continuance of disfunctional content. Nehru said in 1948 that "the entire base of education must be revolutionized," but, as late as 1965, J. P. Naik, chief architect of the *Report of the Education Commission, Education and National Development*,[2] re-marked that no inherent change had taken place in the general character of education since 1940.[3] This *Report* is the latest in a continuous series of Government of India efforts to improve, as well as to extend, the national system of education. The Commission was formed "to advise Government on the national pattern of education at all stages and in all aspects."[4] It is the first time Indian education has been analyzed as a whole, and the first time education has been related to development. The recommendations must be passed by the Parliament if they are to be put into effect; political viability and the chances of implementation, therefore, are highly uncertain. The urgency of comprehensive reform, however, is increasingly recognized in India. To quote from the *Report* itself, "The population of India is now about 500 million,[5] and half of it is below the age of 18 years—India today is essentially a land of youth. Over the next 20 years, the population is likely to increase by another 250 million. . . . The total student population which is now about 70 million will be more than doubled in the next 20 years, and by 1985 it will become about 170 million or about equal to the total popula-tion of Europe."[6] The sheer quantitative challenge is so formidable that quality may continue to be sacrificed, but never before has India been so serious about developing a national system of education that is Indian in character and purpose.

The three great streams of educational influence in India, prior to the significant postwar American influence, could be said to be "gurus, Great Britain, and Gandhi." The "Gurukela System," in which boys generally lived

[2] *Report of the Education Commission, Education and National Development* (New Delhi: Government of India, 1966).

[3] J. Paul Leonard, *The Development of the National Institute of Education* (New Delhi: US/AID TCCU Team in India, 1967), p. 17.

[4] *Report of the Education Commission*, op. cit., Foreword, p. i.

[5] Ibid. The 500,000,000 mark was registered in August, 1966.

[6] Loc. cit.

with their gurus and identified with them psychologically and philosophically as they studied the great religious classics, was the Indian form of humanities. It was designed to enlighten and ennoble, not to provide vocational training. The tutelage was relatively inexpensive, thus available to all but the lowest classes, and the humanizing and disciplinary results were culturally pervasive. Indian culture, therefore, was preserved throughout many centuries, but the hierarchical and differentiated character of the culture naturally was not challenged, and there was no place for modern science or new social patterns. The poor continued to accept their lot with patience and resignation.

The British, their early presence in the form of the East India Company, came to need a large corps of clerks and minor bureaucrats competent in the English language. Four patterns were set early: a government educational policy made explicit by Macaulay's famous Minute, which emphasized the need for "a large class of intermediaries between the British rulers and the ignorant masses," this new educated class to influence those below via "downward filtration"; education to be handled largely by private agencies, including foreign missions, and to be the responsibility of the provinces; government administrative and financial assistance toward this end; and Western-style education. The British Raj later developed new social concerns and attitudes, but educational reforms largely were pressed by Indians determined to formulate an Indian system of education that included Western science.

By Independence there already were many institutions in effect, and most schools were conducted in the regional languages, with English in the higher secondary and university sectors. Literacy was estimated to be about 15%, and the educated population at least had tripled since the turn of the century. Education as an intrinsic factor of childhood was yet to be established, however, and the educated Indians' abhorrence for any form of manual labor or technology persisted.

Gandhi, political leader of the Independence Movement and spiritual father to all, including the untouchables and the poor, devoted considerable attention to the formulation of an indigenous system of education available to all children. His Basic Education scheme, in fact, was adopted by the Congress administration after Independence. For the most part, his educational influence was pertinent and persuasive, but, unfortunately, his theories of learning by doing and "doing what makes economic sense in India—via craft education" narrowly were conceived on his part and misunderstood by his followers. With all due respect to this saint, Gandhi romanticized poverty and promoted what might be called a nondevelopment system of education. Hand-ginning, spinning, and rice-husking are poor curricular bases for a society trying to become a modern industrial state (to be sure, Gandhi did not share this dream). They have proved not even to provide individual economic self-sufficiency in the preindustrial stage. Basic Education now generally is conceded to have been a failure, but Gandhi's emphasis on the dignity of labor, on eliminating the gulf between "mind and hand," and on the right of every child to attend school have had an influence. His greatest contribution was the element of caring for all.

The Constitution, adopted in 1949, continued the tradition of education as the responsibility of the (now) states and private agencies, and mandated Central Government assistance. Increasingly, there has been guidance in addition to grant-in-aid assistance, and a growing number of "institutions of national significance" have been handled exclusively by the Ministry of Education. Three Five Year Plans have been completed, with education a factor of secondary importance in them; the Fourth Plan, which began in 1969, has substantial allocations. In general, the planning has shifted from priority on primary schools to the development of secondary and vocational education—and now to advanced training and research. Appropriate administrative structures have been established—such as Advisory Committees, Central Institutes, Regional Colleges of Education, and the highly significant National Council of Educational Research and Training (NCERT) and National Institute of Education (NIE).

Expansion planning and the establishment of administrative organs are one thing, however, and the nature and quality of education is another. The Education Commission, mentioned above, was asked to examine the entire corpus of education and make recommendations for total reform. Even if parliamentary approval is only partial, this exercise has resulted in the organization and publication of sobering statistics, especially in relation to the potential school population and "wastage."[7]

The increase in school enrollment seems impressive; in 1950 the total number of children in classes 1–12 was 18,500,000 and by 1965 was 56,400,-000. However, this gain represents progress toward the goal of universal education only to the point that 40.3% of the children 6–7 years of age entered class 1 in 1965–1966, and, of those who did enter, only 15.4% reached class 8. Similarly, literacy has been raised from about 15% in 1947 to 24% in 1960 (boys 34 and girls 13%). Since 1960 there has been an estimated 2% gain, but the total number of illiterates has grown. Of particular concern are the dropout and failure rates and the inadequate educational expenditures, published on the following page.

The Commission has pointed out that, in 15 years, enrollments have increased 185% but expenditures only by 175%—in a period, moreover, when the rupee seriously declined because of inflation and devaluation (from 4.75 to 7.5 rupees to the dollar in June, 1966). Various figures are cited for the

[7] Ministry of Education figures, used in the *Report*, pp. 147–182.

Table 1

School Enrollment, 1965

Classes	1–4	37,100,000
	5–7	12,500,000
	8–10	6,000,000
	11–12	830,000
Undergraduate		760,000
M.A. level		90,000
Advanced professional		70,000

Dropouts, 1960

Class	1—35%	
	2—56%	
	5—66%	
	5–8—31%	

Secondary Failure Rate, 1960

Class 10—55%
    11—40%
Private tutoring—70%

Teachers Salaries, 1960

Primary	—Rs.	873/year plus allowances
Middle	—	1058/year plus allowances
Secondary	—	1681/year plus allowances

Educational Costs, 1965

Primary	—Rs.	33/pupil/year
Middle	—	50/pupil/year
Secondary	—	101/pupil/year
College	—	301/pupil/year
Teacher training	—	520/pupil/year
Agriculture	—	1521/pupil/year
Commerce	—	227/pupil/year
Engineering	—	984/pupil/year
Professional	—	1008/pupil/year

---

proportion of the national income utilized for education; the 2.6% reported by the Commission is considerably higher than other estimates. This percentage is conceded to be grossly inadequate, but the low priority given to education in the annual budgets and Five Year Plans is not likely to change radically.

Educational reform effort on the part of many educators and planners, thus, is sincere and substantial, but ineffective. Whether the vast poor will find education an accessible and useful vehicle for upward mobility, or even a more decent survival, will depend in large part on the ability of these educators and planners to convince economists, politicians, and legislators of the urgency of reform and the necessity of allocating the required resources. This, indeed, would be a revolution—in any part of the world—but will prove especially difficult in an India currently pressed on every front. There is little professional or public credence given to a long-range educational plan as a solution for border wars, depleted foreign exchange, inadequate exports, the devalued rupee, and riots on campuses and city streets. The weakening government administration, moreover, is not in position or mood to exert educational pressures.

Some of the problems of the poor have a universal psychological twist— with particular Indian relevance. Classically, the social utility of the poor has been greater than their liability. Who else will perform the disagreeable, polluting, and occasional tasks that exist? It is no accident that elites consistently have understood education as both derivative and preservative of power, thus denied or made too difficult for the masses. By now, reluctant ground has been given, and education is becoming the route to wealth and power all over the world. Not all have used it, and not all education has been fit to use, but it is the most revolutionary institution in human society. This is true even when it is largely disfunctional to the needs of the society, as in India's case. Why, then, do so many of the underprivileged fail to take advantage of this way up and out?

It is difficult for Americans to comprehend conditions of poverty in which the price of a postage stamp is the price of a meal. The latest available figures relate to the National Sample Survey of 1959–1960 (the cost-of-living index has risen about 5% a year since then).[8] In rural areas (where the average family size is 5.2) the consumer expenditure is Rs. 20.30 per person per month, 69.2% allocated to food. In urban areas (with average family size of 4.8) the consumer expenditure is Rs. 27.50 (40.4 in the four major cities), with 61.4% utilized for food. The relationship of this expenditure to family incomes can be seen in the Madras distribution tables (rural figures are not given but would be lower). In the defined working class about 9% earn less than Rs. 60 a month; 56% earn Rs. 60–120; and 50%, Rs. 120–210. In the middle class, 12% receive less than Rs. 100 a month; 38%, Rs. 100–200; and 40%, Rs. 200–300. Anything less than Rs. 15 a month ($2.00) per person for food represents starvation. Many families cannot afford education—because of the cost of books, fees, clothing, and transportation, and especially because every able-bodied member of the family must work if there is to be food. Child labor is essential to the domestic economy, and most children are economic assets, not liabilities.

Furthermore, the poor rarely have gone to school willingly or stayed when they got there—let alone stormed the gates of higher academe. They have had a place in their society, miserable though it may be, and in a way could count on protection and family perpetuity. Their very social utility made

[8] *India 1966* (New Delhi: Government of India, 1966), pp. 163–165.

them less vulnerable to elimination or ruination than rajahs and money-lenders. They suffered privation, but supplication is not degrading to those already degraded—and usually works in the appeal to "superiority benevolence." Moreover, many pains are dissolved in the solaces of Saturday night toddy, gyrations or gluttony on festival day, or pious placations to the gods. What changes have seemed possible? Those poor in body and spirit, who lack the physical and psychic energy to revolt or change, find the "dreary desert sand of dead habit" has consolations in the predictability of routine and the possibility of survival. One lives—or dies—according to one's destiny.

Peculiarly, Hindu is the belief, conscious or unconscious, in the personal wheel of life—an infinity concept, to be sure, that now is giving way to the temporal. Any given birth determines the "varna" (caste, kin), which prescribes the "dharma" (duty, role). How one performs this function, thus developing one's "karma" (destiny), is an individual matter. Passive acceptance to the role moves one "up," while active resistance moves one "down." Virtue, perhaps especially when accompanied by suffering, consists of resignation, and detachment makes resignation possible. This is a social philosophy serving physical and psychic survival, but not individual progress or social responsibility. It promotes social separation, not integration. A starving man, therefore, is experiencing his just retribution. Others may see fit to give him alms—more often for credit than in compassion—but starve he will as long as his shriveled tissues are more a private desiccation than a public indecency.

India's non-science has been more than a matter of religious influence. A rational and observant culture in some areas, there has been a curious detachment from most natural phenomena. Indian farmers, for instance, did not develop the sciences of seed selection, soil fertilization, pruning, grafting, and tool improvement. They did learn to irrigate and leave fields fallow, but the vast stretches of leached and mined soil are the results of farming without the understanding of cause-and-effect in nature. Similarly, the Indian diet is nutritionally one of the poorest in the world—not only for the poor. These two unscientifically handled areas particularly affect India's poor—in the products of their labor and in their energic capacity. National programs currently are applying science to agriculture, but only minimally and ineffectually to nutrition, at the very time when human energy should be viewed as the *sine qua non* of progress.

The complex language dilemma cannot be discussed here except in relation to its impact on the lower socioeconomic groups. The need of one or more link languages in a country with hundreds of dialects, 15 major Indian languages, and English as the long-established medium in universities and the government is assumed. The Education Commission, which necessarily considered language in relation to learning as well as national and international communication, has recommended a flexible three-language formula.[9] In essence, it will result in Hindi as the link language for the rural and lower classes and Hindi and English as link languages for the more highly educated. No other compromise seems possible, but the absence of the "higher link" will perpetuate the social and economic distance between the privileged and the less privileged. The advantages of English are widely recognized by the educated, for most of them, including politicians promoting regional languages, send their own children to English-medium schools.

The last universal problem with particular Indian relevance in this discussion—population pressures—is also widely recognized. The rate of growth negates gains, the numbers of unemployed and illiterate grow, and the necessary capital for "take-off" is not accumulated. Ironically, real progress in medicine has reduced so sharply infant and child mortality that the youth sector has mushroomed; it might be called the "educational sector" or the "fertility sector of tomorrow." Propagation, in fact, is defeating the Plans. Few countries are tackling the subject more vigorously or openly, but as in all countries the poor and uneducated are less amenable to control measures than the higher classes; hence, the population balance becomes increasingly skewed. There is no doubt that social coercion will have to be added to persuasion and that even a new philosophy will have to supplant the traditional "children are wealth."

Development analysts know that nothing can succeed in any aspect of development without a "critical mass." Somehow the poor as well as those not so poor must learn to sow the seeds of their own construction. This self-generating condition, however, probably will not pertain without many forms and degrees of social coercion heretofore inimical to free societies. This will require qualities of leadership not yet utilized and communication concepts and systems not yet developed, but nothing less will reach the multitudinous poor.

The injunction of the Bhagavad-Gita, "Let man lift himself, by himself," is futile unless coercion and stimulation are added to access. Nothing, however, will have the self-regenerating effect unless education becomes—and rapidly becomes—both economically rewarding and intellectually creative. Education should be not only the general thing to do, but for each child "my thing." Too utopian? Probably, for most educators in most countries—developed and developing—are as ignorant as Indian farmers about input and output. There still may be time for radical change—in India, in America —but, unless we make it happen, the poor will inherit the earth.

[9] Education Commission, op. cit., p. 192.

Bibliography of
Selected References

The School and the Children of the Poor: A Bibliography of Selected References

Francesco Cordasco and Maurie Hillson

Introduction

Since the enactment of the Economic Opportunity Act in 1964, American society has been preoccupied with poverty, and a good share of this concern has been directed to the urban slum school and the deprived[1] children whom it serves. A vast literature on the children of the poor and their schools has emerged, and, in the main, it has been concerned with the contemporary urban milieu. In a broad sense, an American society which is multiracial, ethnically variegated, and socially heterogeneous in its very origins is a society which has dealt, since its beginnings, with the minority child, whatever the anchorage of his minority status. If the term "minority child" is used, and the social context is one of deprivation (whatever form it takes, viz., ghettoization; segregated schools; cultural assault and enforced change, etc.), the term may be enlarged to comprehend the urban black in-migrant poor; Puerto Rican migrants to mainland cities; the Mexican-American poor of the Southwest; the economically displaced white poor (the euphemism is "Appalachian poor"); reservation Indians and migrant Indians; the ethnic poor who reflect relaxed immigration quotas; the agricultural seasonally-employed poor caught in migrancy and rootlessness; and, in the broad historical sense, the ethnic poor of other eras.[2]

---

[1] Our age has fashioned a constellation of euphemisms to characterize the children of the poor: if "deprived" or "disadvantaged" most often are encountered, they are no less awkward than "culturally deprived," "slow learners," or others which have been in use. See Helen E. Rees, *Deprivation and Compensatory Education* (Boston: Houghton Mifflin, 1968), pp. 8–9.

[2] Generally, the American poor of other eras have not been adequately studied, and the study of the education of the children of the poor has been neglected by American historians, until very recently (cf., in this regard, the English studies of Victorian poverty and 19th-century society, e.g., Charles Booth, *Life and Labour of the People*

This bibliography is a guide to selected references dealing with the education of the children of the poor. Although the entries have been arranged under five main categories (Role of the School; Dropouts and Delinquency; Characteristics of the Disadvantaged Student; Teaching and Teacher Education; Programs and Materials), the categories, themselves, are very flexibly defined and many of the entries could have been placed in more than one category.

Socioeconomic Conditions of the Disadvantaged

In dealing with the education of the poor, inevitable attention must be given to a whole range of problems which are implicit in poverty; to unemployment, housing, and the ghetto; to race and segregation; to life-styles and family patterns; and to the very ethos which is poverty itself. Many of the entries in the bibliography deal with these phenomena, but those materials which deal with them exclusively and do not have the school as their main concern have been excluded. However, some basic references to poverty, and the socioeconomic correlates which are the fabric of deprivation (beyond what is found tangentially in the bibliography's entries), are pulled together here for general reference. One of the best and most incisive commentaries, in a huge literature on poverty, is Thomas Gladwin, *Poverty: U.S.A.* (Boston: Little, Brown, 1967); and further reference can be made to Sidney Lens, *Poverty—America's Enduring Paradox* (New York: Crowell, 1969); to Henry P. Miller, *Poverty American Style* (Belmont, California: Wadsworth, 1966); to Daniel P. Moynihan, ed., *On Understanding Poverty* (New York:

in London, 3rd ed., London: Macmillan, 1902–1903, 17 vols. [Selections from this vast work are in Albert Fried and Richard M. Elman, *Charles Booth's London,* New York: Pantheon, 1968]; and the earlier Henry Mayhew, *London Labour and the London Poor,* London: Griffin, Bohn, 1861–1962. 4 vols.). See Francesco Cordasco, ed., *Jacob Riis Revisited: Poverty and the Slum in Another Era* (New York: Doubleday, 1968); and Robert H. Bremner, *From the Depths: The Discovery of Poverty in the United States* (New York: New York University Press, 1956). Lawrence Cremin's *The Transformation of the School* (New York: Alfred A. Knopf, 1961) is a good introduction to the history of the American school and the poor (*en passant,* in its study of the Progressive Movement); and Sol Cohen's *Progressives and Urban School Reform* (Bureau of Publications, Teachers College, Columbia University, 1964) is an invaluable study of the Public Education Association of New York City, the dynamics of urban poverty, and social reform. See also William W. Brickman, "Notes on the Education of the Poor in Historical and International Perspective," *McGill Journal of Education,* vol. 3 (Fall, 1968), pp. 141–150, which in many ways defines the perimeters of the vast areas of deprivation and the school which await study.

Basic Books, 1969) ; and to James L. Sundquist, ed., *On Fighting Poverty* (New York: Basic Books, 1969). To these should be added, Frank Riessman, *Strategies Against Poverty* (New York: Random House, 1969) ; David N. Alloway and Francesco Cordasco, *The Agony of the Cities: Urban Problems in Contemporary America* (Washington: American Association of State Colleges and Universities, 1969) ; on social class, one of the best references is S. M. Miller and Frank Riessman, *Social Class and Social Policy* (New York: Basic Books, 1968) ; the phenomenon of social welfare is adequately dealt with in Thomas D. Sherrad, *Social Welfare and Urban Problems* (New York: Columbia University Press), and in Richard Titmuss, *Commitment to Welfare* (New York: Pantheon Books, 1968), if in very theoretical terms; the social dynamics of the slum are best studied in Gerald D. Suttles, *The Social Order of the Slum: Ethnicity and Territory in the Inner City* (Chicago: University of Chicago Press, 1968) ; the "culture of poverty" concept is best explored in the studies of Oscar Lewis—*La Vida: A Puerto Rican Family in the Culture of Poverty* (New York: Random House, 1966) and *A Study of Slum Culture: Backgrounds for La Vida* (New York: Random House, 1968) —vast portraits of *Kulturpessimismus* and decadence; but a contrary view should be read in F. Cordasco, "Another Face of Poverty: Oscar Lewis' *La Vida*," *Phylon: The Atlanta University Review of Race & Culture*, **29**: 88–92, Spring 1968. The most comprehensive study of ethnicity, the children of a minority, and the American school in the context of poverty is Leonard Covello, *The Social Background of the Italo-American School Child: A Study of the Southern Italian Mores and their Effect on the School Situation in Italy and America*, edited and with an Introduction by F. Cordasco (Leiden: Brill, 1967) ; the vitality of the *Landsmannschaft* (benevolent societies) and the immigrant social service organizations of the immigrant urban ethnic enclaves (e.g., the Educational Alliance; the Henry Street Settlement; the Baron de Hirsch Fund; the Hebrew Immigrant Aid Society) are graphically recreated in Allan Schoener's *Portal to America: The Lower East Side, 1870–1925* (New York: Holt, Rinehart and Winston, 1967) ; and in Hutchins Hapgood, *The Spirit of the Ghetto*, ed. by Moses Rischin (Cambridge: Harvard University Press, 1967). The mammoth *Equality of Educational Opportunity* [the Coleman report] (Washington: U.S. Office of Education, 1966) is one of the most important social documents of our time and should be consulted along with Daniel P. Moynihan, "Sources of Resistance to the *Coleman Report*," *Harvard Educational Review*, **38**: 23–36, Winter 1968. Lastly, a serviceable general bibliographical guide to poverty is Freda L. Paltiel, *Poverty: An Annotated Bibliography* (Ottawa: Canada Welfare Council, 1966), with continuing reference made to *Poverty and Human Resources Abstracts* (Institute of Labor and Industrial Relations, University of

Michigan), which is issued bimonthly and contains review articles, an annotated bibliography, and recent legislative developments related to all aspects
of poverty and human resources.

Bibliographical Aids

A main source of bibliographical information on the education of the disadvantaged child is the *IRCD* Bulletin (Informational Retrieval Center on
the Disadvantaged [Teachers College, Columbia University]), which is published five times a year by the Center, operated under a contract with U.S.
Office of Education Educational Resources Information Center (*ERIC*); a
vast resource of 1,740 documents (*Selected Documents on the Disadvantaged*)
dealing with the special educational needs of the disadvantaged is available
from the U.S. Office of Education (*Number and Author Index,* OE 37001);
(*Subject Index,* OE 37002). Periodicals which contain bibliographical information include the *Journal of Negro Education; Urban Education;* the
Urban Review; and *Education and Urban Society.* The NDEA National Institute for Advanced Study in Teaching Disadvantaged Youth (initiated June
1966) has completed two years of study, research, field programs, and
dissemination; its *Bulletin/Final Report* (December 1968) should be consulted. A critical review of the literature is available in Bernard Goldstein,
Barbara Steinberg, and Harry C. Bredemeier, *Low Income Youth in Urban
Areas* (New York: Holt, Rinehart and Winston, 1967), which is both a critical
exposition of major concerns and a keyed annotated bibliography; and this
should be supplemented by H. Helen Randolph, *Urban Education Bibliography: An Annotated Listing* (New York: Center For Urban Education,
1968), which derives from Project TRUE (Hunter College). Neglected
sources of great value are *Master Annotated Bibliography of the Papers of
Mobilization For Youth* (New York: Mobilization For Youth, 1965); and
Alfred M. Potts, *Knowing and Educating the Disadvantaged: An Annotated
Bibliography* (Alamosa, Colo.: Adams State College, 1965). Some value lies
in the awkwardly structured Robert E. Booth, et al., *Culturally Disadvantaged*
(Detroit: Wayne State University, 1967), which is a comprehensive classified
bibliography and a key-word-out-of-context index. The education of migrants,
Mexican-Americans, and Indians has as a principal bibliographical resource
the publications of the ERIC Clearinghouse on Rural Education and Small
Schools (New Mexico State University), e.g., *Migrant Education: A Selected
Bibliography* (Las Cruces, New Mexico: New Mexico State University, 1969);
and *Research Abstracts in Rural Education* (Ibid., continuing); and these
should be supplemented by the publications of the Southwest Educational
Development Laboratory (Austin, Tex.) which operates under Title IV of the

Elementary and Secondary Education Act. Bibliography for the Puerto Rican child is found in Gertrude S. Goldberg, "Puerto Rican Migrants on the Mainland of the United States: A Review of the Literature," *IRCD* Bulletin, vol. **IV** (January 1968), pp. 1–12; and in F. Cordasco and Eugene Bucchioni, *Puerto Rican Children in Mainland Schools: A Source Book For Teachers* (New York: Scarecrow Press, 1968), pp. 435–461, a comprehensive listing of over 450 entries. Although essentially a critical exposition, some programmatic bibliographical references are in Richard J. Margolis, *The Losers: A Report on Puerto Ricans and the Public Schools* (New York: Aspira, 1968) which chronicles visits to sixteen schools in seven cities.

Guides to Programs for the Disadvantaged

The most comprehensive guide to programs for the disadvantaged is Edmund W. Gordon and Doxey A. Wilkerson, *Compensatory Education for the Disadvantaged* (New York: College Entrance Examination Board, 1966); with further reference made to *Education: An Answer to Poverty* (Washington: U.S. Office of Education and Office of Economic Opportunity, 1966). Of particular importance are the *Disadvantaged Children Series* published by the U.S. Office of Education: *Educating Disadvantaged Children Under Six* (1965); *Educating Disadvantaged in the Primary Years* (1965); *Educating Disadvantaged Children in the Middle Grades* (1965); *Administration of Elementary School Programs for Disadvantaged Children* (1966); *Educating Disadvantaged Children in the Elementary School: An Annotated Bibliography* (1966). A useful guide to centers of study of deprivation and compensatory education is Helen E. Rees, "Centers of Study and Sources of Information," *Deprivation and Compensatory Education* (New York: Houghton Mifflin, 1968), pp. 237–260.

Role of the School

Bernstein, A. *The Education of Urban Populations* (New York: Random House, 1967).

Berube, M. R., and Gittell, M. *Confrontation at Ocean Hill-Brownsville: The New York School Strikes of 1968* (New York: Frederick A. Praeger, 1969).

Bloom, B. S. *Compensatory Education for Cultural Deprivation* (New York: Holt, Rinehart & Winston, 1965).

Brameld, T. *Cultural Foundations of Education: An Interdisciplinary Exploration* (New York: Harper, 1957).

Brameld, T. *The Use of Explosive Ideas in Education: Culture, Class, and Evolution* (Pittsburgh: University of Pittsburgh Press, 1965).

Brickman, W. W., and Lehrer, S., Eds. *The Countdown on Segregated Education* (New York: Society for the Advancement of Education, 1960).

Burgess, E. *Values in Early Childhood Education.* 2d ed. (Washington: National Education Association, 1965).

Chandler, B. J. *Education in Urban Society* (New York: Dodd, Mead, 1962).

Clark, H. F., and Stone, H. S. *Classrooms on Main Street* (New York: Teachers College Press, 1966).

Clift, V. A., Ed. *Negro Education in America: Its Adequacy, Problems, and Needs* (New York: Harper, 1962).

Clift, V. A. "Factors Relating to the Education of Culturally Deprived Negro Youth," *Educational Theory,* 14: 76–82, April 1964.

Coleman, J. S., et al. *Equality of Educational Opportunity and Supplemental Appendix* . . . (Washington: U.S. Office of Education, 1966). 2 vols.

Commission on School Integration. *Public School Segregation and Integration in the North* (Washington: National Association for Intergroup Relations Officials, 1963).

Conant, J. B. *Slums and Suburbs: A Commentary on Schools in Metropolitan Areas* (New York: McGraw-Hill, 1961).

Conference on Integration in the New York City Public Schools, Columbia University, 1963. *Integrating the Urban School: Proceedings* (New York: Bureau of Publications, Teachers College, Columbia University, 1963).

Cordasco, F. "Educational Pelagianism: The Schools and the Poor," *Teachers College Record,* 69: 705–709, April 1968.

Cordasco, F., Hillson, M., and Bullock, H. A. *The School in the Social Order: A Sociological Introduction to Educational Understanding* (Scranton: International Textbook Co., 1970).

Corwin, R. G. *A Sociology of Education: Emerging Patterns of Class, Status, and Power in the Public Schools* (New York: Appleton-Century-Crofts, 1965).

Cowles, M. *Perspectives in the Education of Disadvantaged Children* (Cleveland: World Publishing Co., 1967).

Crain, R. L. *The Politics of School Desegregation* (Chicago: Aldine Publishing Co., 1968).

Crow, L. D., Murray, W. J., and Smythe, H. *Educating the Culturally Disadvantaged Child: Principles and Programs* (New York: D. McKay Co., 1966).

Decter, M. "The Negro and the New York Schools," *Commentary,* 38: 25–34, September 1964.

Edgar, E. E. *Social Foundations of Education* (New York: Center for Applied Research in Education, 1965).

Educational Policies Commission. *American Education and the Search for Equal Opportunity* (Washington: National Education Association, 1965).

Educational Policies Commission. *Education and the Disadvantaged American* (Washington: National Education Association, 1962).

"Education for Socially Disadvantaged Children," *Review of Educational Research,* **35:** 375–426, December 1965.

Fantini, M., and Weinstein, G. *The Disadvantaged: Challenge To Education* (New York: Harper & Row, 1968).

Ferrer, T. *The Schools and Urban Renewal: A Case Study from New Haven* (New York: Educational Facilities Laboratories, 1964).

Frierson, E. C. "Determining Needs." *Education,* **85:** 461–466, April 1965.

Frost, J. L., and Hawkes, G. R., Eds. *The Disadvantaged Child: Issues and Innovations* (Boston: Houghton Mifflin, 1966). (2nd ed., 1970.)

Fuchs, E. *Pickets at the Gates* (New York: Free Press, 1966).

Giles, H. H. *The Integrated Classroom* (New York: Basic Books, 1959).

Gittell, M. *Participants and Participation: A Study of School Policy in New York City* (New York: Praeger, 1967).

Gittell, M., and Hollander, T. E. *Six Urban School Districts. A Comparative Study of Institutional Response* (New York: Praeger, 1968).

Greene, M. F., and Ryan, O. *The Schoolchildren: Growing Up in The Slums* (New York: Pantheon Books, 1965).

Havighurst, R. J. "The Educationally Difficult Student: What the Schools Can Do," *Bulletin of National Association of Secondary School Principals,* **41:** 110–127, March 1965.

Havighurst, R. J. *Education in Metropolitan Areas* (Boston: Allyn and Bacon, 1966).

Herriott, R. E., and St. John, N. H. *Social Class and the Urban School: The Impact of Pupil Background on Teachers and Principals* (New York: Wiley, 1966).

Hickerson, N. *Education for Alienation* (New York: Prentice-Hall, 1966).

Hillson, M., Cordasco, F., and Purcell, F. P. *Education and the Urban Community: Schools and the Crisis of the Cities* (New York: American Book Co., 1969).

Hunnicutt, C. W. *Urban Education and Cultural Deprivation* (Syracuse: Syracuse University, 1964).

"Indian Education," *Research Abstracts in Rural Education* [New Mexico State University, January 1969], pp. 30–37.

[Indian Education] Wolcott, Harry F. *A Kwakiutl Village and School* (New York: Holt, Rinehart & Winston, 1967).

Jaffe, A. J., Adams, W., and Meyers, S. G. *Negro Higher Education in the 1960's* (New York: Praeger, 1968).

Kaplan, B. A. "Issues in Educating the Culturally Disadvantaged," *Phi Delta Kappan,* **45:** 70–76, November 1963.

Kerber, A., and Smith, W. R., Eds. *Educational Issues in a Changing Society* (Detroit: Wayne State University Press, 1964).

Kerber, A., and Bommarito, B., Eds. *The Schools and the Urban Crisis: A Book of Readings* (New York: Holt, Rinehart and Winston, 1965).

Kerckhoff, R. K. "Problems of the City School," *Journal of Marriage and the Family,* **26:** 435–439, November 1964.

Knapp, R. B. *Social Integration in Urban Communities: A Guide for Educational Planning* (New York: Bureau of Publications, Teachers College, Columbia University, 1960).

Kvaraceus, W. C. "Social Stresses and Strains on Children and Youth: Some Implications for Schools," *High School Journal,* **47:** 140–145, January 1964.

Landes, R. *Culture in American Education: Anthropological Approaches to Minority and Dominant Groups in the Schools* (New York: Wiley, 1965).

Levine, D. U. "Integration: Reconstructing Academic Values of Youths in Deprived Areas," *Clearing House,* **39:** 159–162, November 1964.

Levine, L. S. "Imposed Social Position, Assessment and Curricular Implications," *Bulletin of National Association of Secondary School Principals,* **50:** 44–74, May 1966.

Lewis, G. M., and Murow, E. *Educating Disadvantaged Children in the Elementary School.* (Disadvantaged Children Series, No. 5) (Washington: U.S. Office of Education, 1966).

Loretan, J. O. "Problems in Improving Educational Opportunities for Puerto Ricans in New York. Third Annual Conference for New Yorkers of Puerto Rican Background," *High Points,* **45:** 23–31, May 1963.

MacKintosh, H. K., Gore, L., and Lewis, G. M. *Educating Disadvantaged Children in the Middle Grades.* Disadvantaged Children Series, No. 3. (Washington: U.S. Office of Education, 1965).

MacKintosh, H. K., Gore, L., and Lewis, G. M. *Educating Disadvantaged Children in the Primary Years.* Disadvantaged Children Series, No. 2. (Washington: U.S. Office of Education, 1965).

MacKintosh, H., Gore, L., and Lewis, G. M. *Educating Disadvantaged Children Under Six.* Disadvantaged Children Series, No. 1. (Washington: U.S. Office of Education, 1966).

Marbinger, C. "Educational Problems of Culturally Deprived Children and Youth," in Mahar, Mary H. *School Library Supervision in Large Cities* (Washington: U.S. Office of Education, 1966), pp. 25–35.

McKendall, B. W., Jr. "Breaking the Barriers of Cultural Disadvantage and Curriculum Imbalance," *Phi Delta Kappan,* **46:** 307–311, March 1965.

Miller, H. L., Ed. *Education for the Disadvantaged* (New York: Macmillan—Free Press, 1967).

National Conference on Education of the Disadvantaged. *Report* (Washington: United States Department of Health, Education, and Welfare, 1966).

National Education Association. Department of Elementary, Kindergarten, Nursery Education. *Prevention of Failure* (Washington: National Education Association, 1965).

National Society for the Study of Education. *The Changing American School.* Pt. 2. Yearbook 1965 (Chicago: University of Chicago, 1966).

National Society for the Study of Education. Committee on the Educationally Retarded and Disadvantaged. *The Educationally Retarded and Disadvantaged.* Ed. by Paul A. Witty. Pt. 1, Yearbook 1966 (Chicago: University of Chicago Press, 1967).

O'Hara, M. "We Heighten the Child's Self-Image Through the School: A Selected Bibliography," *High Points,* **48:** 71–79, June 1966.

Ornstein, A. C. "Effective Schools for Disadvantaged Children," *Journal of Secondary Education,* **46:** 105–109, March 1965.

Passow, A. H. *Education in Depressed Areas* (New York: Bureau of Publications, Teachers College, Columbia University, 1965).

Passow, A. H., Comp. *Education of the Disadvantaged: A Book of Readings* (New York: Holt, Rinehart and Winston, 1967).

Passow, A. H. *Toward Creating a Model Urban School System: A Study of the Washington, D.C. Public Schools* (New York: Teachers College, Columbia University, 1967).

Phi Delta Kappa. Commission on the Study of Educational Policies and Programs in Relation to Desegregation. *Action Patterns in School Desegregation: A Guidebook* (Bloomington, Ind.: Phi Delta Kappa, 1959).

Proctor, S. "Reversing the Spiral Toward Futility," in *Eighteenth Yearbook of the American Association of Colleges for Teacher Education* (Washington: AACTE, 1965).

Rees, H. E. *Deprivation and Compensatory Education: A Consideration* (Boston: Houghton Mifflin, 1968).

Reiss, A. J., Ed. *Schools in a Changing Society* (New York: Free Press, 1965).

Riese, H. (P.). *Heal the Hurt Child: An Approach Through Educational Therapy with Special Reference to the Extremely Deprived Negro Child* (Chicago: University of Chicago Press, 1962).

Roberts, J. I. *School Children in the Urban Slum* (New York: Macmillan, 1967).

Rodgers, D. *110 Livingston Street: Politics and Bureaucracy in the New York City School System* (New York: Random House, 1968).

Rosenthal, A., Ed. *Governing Education: A Reader on Politics, Power, and Public School Policy* (New York: Doubleday, 1969).

Sexton, P. C. *Education and Income: Inequalities of Opportunity in Our Public Schools* (New York: Viking Press, 1961).

Smiley, M. B., and Miller, H. L., Eds. *Policy Issues in Urban Education* (New York: Macmillan—Free Press, 1968).

Steinberg, E. R. "Middle-Class Education for Lower-Class Students," *Education*, **86**: 67–74, October 1965.

Swanson, B. E. *The Struggle for Equality: School Integration Controversy in New York City* (New York: Hobbs, Dorman, 1966).

Thomas, R. M. *Social Differences in the Classroom: Social-Class, Ethnic, and Religious Problems* (New York: McKay, 1965).

[Urban Education] "Problems of Urban Education," *Phi Delta Kappan*, **48**: 305–376, March 1967.

U.S. Commission on Civil Rights. *Racial Isolation in the Public Schools* (Washington: U.S. Government Printing Office, 1967). 2 vols.

Vairo, P. D., and Perel, W. M. *Urban Education: Problems and Prospects* (New York: McKay, 1969).

Vontress, C. E. "Our Demoralizing Slum Schools," *Phi Delta Kappan*, **45**: 77–81, November 1963.

Weinberg, M. *Integrated Education: A Reader* (Beverly Hills, Calif.: Glencoe Press, 1968).

Wise, A. E. *Rich Schools, Poor Schools: The Promise of Equal Educational Opportunity* (Chicago: University of Chicago Press, 1968).

Work Conference on Curriculum and Teaching in Depressed Urban Areas, Columbia University, 1962. *Education in Depressed Areas* (New York: Bureau of Publications, Teachers College, Columbia University, 1963).

Dropouts and Delinquency

Cervantes, L. F. *The Dropout: Causes and Cures* (Ann Arbor: University of Michigan Press, 1965).

Dentler, R. A. "Dropouts, Automation and the Cities," *Teachers College Record*, **65**: 475–483, March 1964.

Dentler, R. A., and Warshauer, M. E. *Big City Dropouts and Illiterates* (New York: Praeger, 1968).

Duncan, B. "Dropouts and the Unemployed," *Journal of Political Economy*, **73**: 123–134, April 1965.

Elam, S. L. "Poverty and Acculturation in a Migrant Puerto Rican Family," *Teachers College Record,* **70**: 617–623, April 1969.

Equal Educational Opportunity [Harvard Educational Review] (Cambridge, Mass.: Harvard University Press, 1969).

Farrow, R. B. "Schools and Help for the Offending Child," *Childhood Education,* **41**: 123–134, April 1965.

Fleisher, B. M. "Effect of Income on Delinquency," *American Economic Review,* **56**: 118–137, March 1966.

Glazer, M. Y., and Creedon, C. F., Eds. *Children and Poverty* (Chicago: Rand McNally, 1968).

Gowan, J. C., and Demos, G. D., Eds. *The Disadvantaged and Potential Dropout: Compensatory Education Programs: A Book of Readings* (Springfield, Ill.: C. C Thomas, 1966).

The Juvenile Delinquency Prevention Act of 1967 (Hearings before the General Subcommittee on Education of the Committee on Education and Labor, House of Representatives, 90th Congress, 1st session on H.R. 7642, 1967).

Kelly, F. J., et al. "Multiple Discriminant, Prediction of Delinquency and School Dropouts," *Educational and Psychological Measurement,* **24**: 535–544, Fall 1964.

Liddle, G. P. "Secondary School as an Instrument for Preventing Juvenile Delinquency," *High School Journal,* **47**: 146–152, January 1964.

Purcell, F. P., and Hillson, M. "The Disadvantaged Child: A Product of the Culture of Poverty, His Education, and His Life Chances," *Eugenics Quarterly,* **13**: 179–185, September 1966.

Schreiber, D., Ed. *Guidance and the School Dropout* (Washington: Project: School Dropouts, National Education Association and American Personnel and Guidance Association, 1964).

Schreiber, D., Ed. *The School Dropout* (Washington: Project: School Dropouts, National Education Association, 1964).

Strom, R. D. "A Realistic Curriculum for the Predictive Dropout," *Clearing House,* **39**: 101–106, October 1964.

Willie, C. V., et al. "Race and Delinquency," *Phylon,* **26**: 240–246, Spring 1965.

Zirbes, L. "Dropouts in Long Perspective," *Childhood Education,* **40**: 345–348, March 1964.

Characteristics of the Disadvantaged Student

Beymer, L. "Pros and Cons of the National Assessment Project," *Clearing House,* **40**: 540–543, May 1966.

Black, M. H. "Characteristics of the Culturally Disadvantaged Child," *Reading Teacher*, **18**: 465–470, March 1965.

Brussell, C. B. *Disadvantaged Mexican American Children and Early Educational Experience* (Austin, Texas: Southwest Educational Development Corporation, 1968).

Cordasco, F. "Puerto Rican Pupils and American Education," *School & Society*, **95**: 116–119, Feb. 18, 1967.

Cordasco, F. "The Challenge of the Non-English-Speaking Child in the American School," *School & Society*, **96**: 198–201, March 30, 1968.

Cordasco, F., and Bucchioni, E. *Puerto Rican Children in Mainland Schools: A Sourcebook for Teachers* (New York: Scarecrow Press, 1968).

Cordasco, F., and Redd, J. "Summer Camp Education for Underprivileged Children," *School & Society*, **23**: 299–300, Summer 1965.

Daniels, V. "Concerning the Validity of Standardized Tests," *Clearing House*, **39**: 12–14, September 1964.

Deutsch, M., et al. *The Disadvantaged: Studies of the Social Environment and Learning* (New York: Basic Books, 1967).

Duncan, J. B., and Mindlin, A. "Municipal Fair Housing Legislation: Community Beliefs and Facts," *Phylon*, **25**: 217–237, Fall 1964.

Eells, K. W. *Intelligence and Cultural Differences: A Study of Cultural Learning and Problem-Solving* (Chicago: University of Chicago Press, 1951).

"Evaluation: Case Studies," *Nation's Schools*, **77**: 59–66, May 1966.

Feldmann, S., and Weiner, M. "Use of a Standardized Reading Achievement Test with Two Levels of Socio-Economic Status Pupils," *Journal of Experimental Education* **32**: 269–274, Spring 1964.

Frierson, E. C. "Upper and Lower Status Gifted Children: A Study of Differences," *Exceptional Children*, **32**: 83–90, October 1965.

Grebler, L., Moore, J. W., and Guzman, R. C. *The Mexican American People: The Nation's Second Largest Minority* (New York: Free Press, 1969).

Green, R. L., and Farquhar, W. W. "Negro Academic Motivation and Scholastic Achievement," *Journal of Educational Psychology*, **56**: 241–243, October 1965.

Havighurst, R. J. "Unrealized Potentials of Adolescents," *Bulletin of National Association of Secondary School Principals*, **50**: 75–114, May 1966.

Heller, C. S. *Mexican American Youth: Forgotten Youth at the Crossroad* (New York: Random House, 1966).

Hewer, V. H. "Are Tests Fair to College Students from Homes with Low Socio-Economic Status?," *Personnel and Guidance Journal*, **43**: 764–769, April 1955.

Hunt, J. M. "How Children Develop Intellectually," *Children*, **11**: 83–91, May 1964.

Iscoe, I., and Pierce-Jones, J. "Divergent Thinking, Age and Intelligence in White and Negro Children," *Child Development,* **35**: 785–797, September 1964.

Jones, J. L. "Assessing the Academic Achievement of Negro Students," *Clearing House,* **39**: 12–14, September 1964.

Katz, I. "Review of Evidence Relating to Effects of Desegregation on the Intellectual Performance of Negroes," *American Psychologist,* **19**: 381–399, June 1964.

Loretan, J. O. "Decline and Fall of Group Intelligence Testing," *Teachers College Record,* **67**: 10–17, October 1965.

Loretan, J. O., and Umans, S. *Teaching the Disadvantaged: New Curriculum Approaches* (New York: Teachers College Press, Columbia University, 1966).

Metz, F. E. "Poverty, Early Language Deprivation and Learning Ability," *Elementary English,* **43**: 129–133, February 1966.

[Mexican-Americans] *The Invisible Minority. Report of the N.E.A. Tucson Survey on the Teaching of Spanish to the Spanish-Speaking* (Washington: N.E.A., 1966).

[Mexican-American Education] Manuel, Herschel T. *Spanish Speaking Children of the Southwest* (Austin: University of Texas Press, 1965).

[Mexican-American Education] "Viva La Raza: Mexican-American Education. A Search For Identity," *American Education* (Washington: Government Printing Office, 1968) (OE-38011).

Miller, C. H. "Counselors and the Culturally Different," *Teachers College Journal,* **37**: 212–217, March 1966.

Moore, J. W. *Mexican-Americans: Problems and Prospects* (Madison, Wisconsin: Institute For Research on Poverty, 1968).

Morrill, R. L. "Negro Ghetto: Problems and Alternatives," *Geographical Review,* **55**: 339–361, July 1965.

Ornstein, A. C. "Who are the Disadvantaged?," *Journal of Secondary Education,* **41**: 154–163, April 1966.

Pearl, A. "As a Psychologist Sees Pressures on Disadvantaged Teen-Agers," *NEA Journal,* **54**: 18–19, February 1965.

Richey, E. "Tenant Oppression: Our Smouldering Housing Scandal," *Antioch Review,* **24**: 337–350, Fall 1964.

Riessman, F. *The Culturally Deprived Child* (New York: Harper, 1962).

Rude, H. N., and King, D. C. "Aptitude Levels in a Depressed Area," *Personnel and Guidance Journal,* **43**: 785–789, April 1965.

Savitsky, C. "Social Theory Advances on the Disadvantaged," *High Points,* **43**: 785–789, April 1965.

Scales, E. "Measured: What is the Standard?," *Clearing House,* **39**: 195–202, December 1964.

Schorr, A. L. *Poor Kids: A Report on Children in Poverty* (New York: Basic Books, 1966).

Schwebel, M. "Learning and the Socially Deprived," *Personnel and Guidance Journal*, **43**: 646–653, March 1965.

Stalnaker, J. M. "Scholarship Selection and Cultural Disadvantage," *Bulletin of National Association of Secondary School Principals*, **49**: 142–150, March 1961.

Warden, S. A. *The Leftouts: Disadvantaged Children in Heterogeneous Schools* (New York: Holt, Rinehart & Winston, 1968).

Webster, S. W., Ed. *The Disadvantaged Learner: Knowing, Understanding, Educating* (San Francisco: Chandler, 1966).

Teaching and Teacher Education

Arnez, N. L. "Effect of Teacher Attitudes on the Culturally Different," *School and Society*, **94**: 149–152, March 19, 1966.

Arnez, N. L. "Teacher Education for an Urban Environment," *Improving College and University Teaching*, **14**: 122–123, September 1966.

Bereiter, C., and Engelmann, S. *Teaching Disadvantaged Children in the Pre-School* (New York: Prentice-Hall, 1966).

Bettelheim, B. "Teaching the Disadvantaged," *NEA Journal*, **54**: 8–12, September 1965.

Bilingual Education. Hearings before the Special Subcommittee on Bilingual Education of the Committee on Labor and Public Welfare. (U.S. Senate, 90th Congress, 1st session on S. 428, Pts. 1–2, 1967). 2 vols.

Bilingual Education Programs. Hearings before the General Subcommittee on Education of the Committee on Education and Labor. (House of Representatives, 90th Congress, 1st session on H.R. 9840 and H.R. 10224, 1967).

Blatt, B. "Preparation of Special Education Personnel: Culturally Deprived," *Review of Educational Research*, **36**: 155–156, February 1966.

Brunson, F. W. "Creative Teaching of the Culturally Disadvantaged," *Audio-Visual Instructor*, **10**: 30–32, January 1965.

Chamberlin, L. J. "Teaching in the Large City," *Clearing House*, **39**: 483–486, April 1965.

Cordasco, F. "Teachers for Disadvantaged Youth: The City University of New York Program," *The New Campus*, **22**: 7–10, Spring 1969.

Cordasco, F., and Croman, C. "The English Maiden and the Poverty Dragon: The Social Imperatives of Educational Change," *College English Association Critic*, **29**: 1–6, November 1966.

Cordasco, F., and Romano, L. A. "The Promethean Ethic: Higher Education and Social Imperatives," *Peabody Journal of Education*, **44**: 295–299, March 1967.

Cuban, L. *Teaching in the Inner City* (New York: Macmillan—Free Press, 1969).

Eddy, E. M. *Walk the White Line: A Profile of Urban Education* (New York: Doubleday, 1967).

"Evaluating Educational Programs: A Symposium," *Urban Review* (February 1969) **3**: 4–26 [includes an appended bibliography (pp. 27–31) on evaluating educational programs by Dorothy Christiansen].

Haubrich, V. F. "Culturally Disadvantaged and Teacher Education," *Reading Teacher*, **18**: 499–505, March 1965.

Kauffman, J. F. "Responsibilities of Teacher Education Institutions for Expanding Educational Opportunities," in *Eighteenth Yearbook of American Association of Colleges for Teacher Education* (Washington: AACTE, 1965), pp. 179–184.

Koenigsberg, S. P. "Teaching Disadvantaged Youth in Secondary School," *Journal of Secondary Education*, **41**: 17–24, January 1966.

Kozol, J. *Death at an Early Age: The Destruction of the Hearts and Minds of Negro Children in the Boston Public Schools* (Boston: Houghton Mifflin, 1967).

Levey, S. "Are We Driving Teachers Out of Ghetto Schools?," *American Education*, **3**: 2–4, May 1967.

Lohman, J. D. "Expose Don't Impose: Introducing Middle Class Values to Disadvantaged Children," *NEA Journal*, **55**: 74–76, January 1966.

MacKintosh, H. K., Gore, L., and Lewis, G. M. *Administration of Elementary School Programs for Disadvantaged Children*. Disadvantaged Children Series, No. 4 (Washington: U.S. Office of Education, 1966).

Moore, G. A. *Realities of the Urban Classroom: Observations in Elementary Schools* (Garden City, New York: Anchor Books, 1967).

Noar, G. *Teaching the Disadvantaged* (Washington: National Education Association, Department of Classroom Teachers, 1967).

Ornstein, A. C. "Teacher Training for the Difficult School," *Peabody Journal of Education*, **41**: 235–237, January 1964.

Ornstein, A. C. "Learning to Teach the Disadvantaged," *Journal of Secondary Education*, **41**: 206–213, May 1966.

"Preparation of Teachers for Depressed Urban Areas, Panel Discussion," in *Eighteenth Yearbook of American Association of Colleges for Teacher Education* (Washington: AACTE, 1965), pp. 111–125.

"A Proposal from Metropolitan College for a Summer Institute for Thirty Supervisors and Classroom Teachers of Disadvantaged Children in 1965," in *Eighteenth Yearbook of American Association of Colleges for Teacher Education* (Washington: AACTE, 1965), pp. 100–110.

Rivlin, H. N., Ed. "Teaching & Teacher Education for Urban Disadvantaged Schools," *Journal of Teacher Education,* **16**: 135–186, June 1965.

Rivlin, H. N. "New Pattern for Urban Teacher Education," *Journal of Teacher Education,* **17**: 177–184, Summer 1966.

Simon, S. "Wanted: New Education Professors for the Slums," *Teachers College Record,* **67**: 271–275, January 1966.

Storen, H. F. "Making up the Deficit. Special Problems Facing Those Who Teach in Culturally Deprived Areas," *Clearing House,* **39**: 495–498, April 1965.

Strom, R. D. *Teaching in the Slum School* (Columbus, Ohio: Merrill, 1965).

Strom, R. D. *The Inner-City Classroom: Teacher Behaviors* (Columbus, Ohio: Merrill, 1966).

Taba, H. *Teaching Strategies for the Culturally Disadvantaged* (Chicago: Rand McNally, 1966).

Tiedt, S. W., Ed. *Teaching the Disadvantaged Child* (New York: Oxford University Press, 1968).

Trubowitz, S. *A Handbook for Teaching in the Ghetto School* (Chicago: Quadrangle Book, 1968).

Tuckman, B. W., and O'Brian, J. L., Eds. *Preparing to Teach the Disadvantaged: Approaches to Teacher Education* (New York: Macmillan— Free Press, 1969).

U.S. Office of Education. *Staffing for Better Schools Under Title I, Elementary and Secondary Education Act of 1965* (Washington: U.S. Department of Health, Education, and Welfare, Office of Education, 1967).

Walker, E. V. "In-Service Training of Teachers to Work With the Disadvantaged," *Reading Teacher,* **18**: 493–498, March 1965.

Willie, C. V. "Anti-Social Behavior Among Disadvantaged Youth: Some Observations on Prevention for Teachers," *Journal of Negro Education,* **33**: 176–181, Spring 1964.

Wisniewski, R. *New Teachers in Urban Schools* (Detroit: Wayne State University Press, 1968).

Programs and Materials

Anderson, V. "Teaching English to Puerto Rican Pupils," *High Points,* **46**: 51–54, March 1964.

Andersson, T. "New Focus on the Bilingual Child," *Modern Language Journal,* **49**: 156–160, March 1965.

Antes, J. M. "Implications for the Elementary School of the Oberlin College Special Opportunities Program for Culturally Disadvantaged Children," *Childhood Education,* **43**: 370, February 1967.

Carlton, L., and Moore, R. H. "Culturally Disadvantaged Children Can Be Helped: Self-Direction Dramatization in Reading," *NEA Journal*, **55**: 13–14, September 1966.

Carlton, A. S. "Poverty Programs, Civil Rights, and the American School," *School & Society*, **95**: 108, Feb. 18, 1967.

Coin, H. "English as a Second Language," *High Points*, **48**: 55–58, January 1966.

Conference on Improving English Skills of Culturally Different Youth in Large Cities, Washington, D.C., 1962. *Improving English Skills of Culturally Different Youth in Large Cities.* U.S. Office of Education. Bulletin 1964, No. 5 (Washington: U.S. Government Printing Office, 1964).

Conference on Teaching Children and Youth Who are Educationally Disadvantaged, Washington, D.C., 1962. *Programs for the Educationally Disadvantaged: A Report.* U.S. Office of Education. Bulletin 1963, No. 17 (Washington: U.S. Government Printing Office, 1963).

Dale, E. "Vocabulary Development of the Underprivileged Child," *Elementary English*, **42**: 778–786, November 1965.

Dawson, C. B. "A Cooperative Plan for Helping the Culturally Disadvantaged Reader," in Conference on Reading, University of Chicago, 1965. *Recent Developments in Reading . . .* (Chicago: University of Chicago Press, 1965), pp. 201–205.

Elkin, S. M. "Minorities in Textbooks," *Teachers College Record*, **66**: 502–508, March 1965.

Elkins, D. "Instructional Guidelines for Teachers of the Disadvantaged," *Teachers College Record*, **70**: 593–597, April 1969.

Esser, G. H. "Widening the Horizons of the Culturally Deprived," *ALA Bulletin*, **60**: 175–178, February 1966.

Fagan, E. R., Ed. *English and the Disadvantaged* (Scranton: International Textbook Co., 1967).

Fantini, M. D., and Weinstein, G. *Toward a Contact Curriculum* (New York: Anti-Defamation League of B'nai B'rith, [1966]).

Fantini, M., and Weinstein, G. *Making Urban Schools Work* (New York: Holt, Rinehart & Winston, 1968).

Ferman, L. A., Ed. *Poverty in America: A Book of Readings* (Ann Arbor: University of Michigan Press, 1965).

Fries, C. C. *Teaching and Learning English as a Foreign Language* (Ann Arbor: University of Michigan Press, 1957).

Giddings, M. G. "Science Education and the Disadvantaged," *Science Education*, **50**: 206–212, April 1966.

Gordon, E. W., and Wilkerson, D. A. *Compensatory Education for the Dis-*

advantaged: Programs and Practices—Preschool Through College (Princeton: College Entrance Examination Board, 1966).

Gray, S. W. *Before the First Grade: The Early Training Project for Culturally Disadvantaged Children* (New York: Teachers College Press, 1966).

Harrington, M. *The Other America: Poverty in the United States* (New York: Macmillan, 1962).

Haubrich, V. F. "Teachers and Resources in the Slum Complex," in *Claremont College Reading Conference. Yearbook*. Claremont, Calif., **28**: 40–50, 1964.

Hillson, M. "Sociological, Psychological and Educational Correlates of Gradeless Schools," *Hillson Letter #3: The Nongraded Elementary School* (Chicago: Science Research Associates, 1966).

Hillson, M. "The Nongraded School: An Organization for Meeting the Needs of Disadvantaged and Culturally Different Learners," *Hillson Letter #17: The Nongraded Elementary School* (Chicago: Science Research Associates, 1967).

Hillson, M. "The Reorganization of the Schools: Bringing About a Remission in the Problems Faced by Minority Children," (Phylon: *The Atlanta University Review of Race and Culture*), **28**: 230–245, 1967.

Isenberg, I., Ed. *The Drive Against Illiteracy* (New York: Wilson, 1964).

Klemm, E. "Appropriate School Programs," *Education*, **85**: 486–489, April 1965.

LaBrant, L. "Broadening the Experiences of Deprived Readers," *Education*, **85**: 499–502, April 1965.

Lanning, F. W., Ed. *Basic Education for the Disadvantaged Adult: Theory and Practice* (Boston: Houghton Mifflin, 1966).

Levy, M. "Upward Bound: A Summer Romance?," *Reporter*, **35**: 41–43, Oct. 6, 1966.

Lewis, H. P., and Lewis, E. R. "Written Language Performance of Sixth-Grade Children of Low Socio-Economic Status from Bilingual and from Monolingual Backgrounds," *Journal of Experimental Education*, **33**: 237–242, Spring 1965.

Macauley, R. K. S. "Vocabulary Problems for Spanish Learners," *English Language Teacher*, **20**: 131–136, January 1966.

[Migrant Children] *A Guide for Programs for the Education of Migrant Children* (Austin, Texas: Texas Education Agency, 1968).

[Migrant Children] *Guidelines For the Education of Migrant Children* (Sacramento, California: California State Department of Education, 1965).

Mingoia, E. M. "The Language Arts and Deprived Pupils," *Education*, **85**: 283–287, January 1965.

Mintz, N., and Fremont, H. "Some Practical Ideas for Teaching Mathematics to Disadvantaged Children," *Arithmetic Teacher*, **12:** 258–260, April 1965.

National Council of Teachers of English. Task Force on Teaching English to the Disadvantaged. *Language Programs for the Disadvantaged: The Report of the NCTE Task Force on Teaching English to the Disadvantaged* (Chicago: National Council of Teachers of English, 1965).

New Jersey Education Association. *The Disadvantaged Child: A Program for Action* (Trenton, New Jersey: N.J.E.A.). [1965]

Niemeyer, J. H. "The Bank Street Readers: Support for Movement Toward an Integrated Society," *Reading Teacher*, **18:** 542–551, April 1965.

Olsen, J. "The Verbal Ability of the Culturally Different," *Reading Teacher*, **18:** 552–556, April 1965.

Orem, R. C., Ed. *Montessori for the Disadvantaged: An Application of Montessori Educational Principles to the War on Poverty* (New York: Putnam, 1967).

Ornstein, A. C., and Vairo, P. D. *How to Teach Disadvantaged Youth* (New York: McKay, 1969).

Passow, A. H., Ed. *Developing Programs for the Educationally Disadvantaged* (New York: Teachers College Press, Teachers College, Columbia University, 1968).

Passow, A. H. *Reaching the Disadvantaged Learner* (New York: Teachers College Press, Teachers College, Columbia University, 1969).

Perales, A. M. "Audio-Lingual Approach and the Spanish-Speaking Student," *Hispania*, **48:** 99–102, March 1965.

Phelps, D. W. "Project Headstart: A Professional Challenge," *Adult Leadership*, **15:** 41–42, June 1966.

Ponder, E. G. "Understanding the Language of the Culturally Disadvantaged Child," *Elementary English*, **42:** 769–774, November 1965.

"Poverty and Employment," *IRCD Bulletin*, **5:** 1–12, March 1969. [Strategies for Closing the Poverty Gap"; "Rich Man's Qualifications For Poor Man's Jobs."]

Prator, C. "English as a Second Language," *Bulletin of National Association of Secondary School Principals*, **48:** 113–120, February 1964.

"Project Head Start," *NEA Journal*, **54:** 58–59, October 1965.

Reid, R. D. "Curricular Changes in Colleges and Universities for Negroes," *Journal of Higher Education*, **38:** 153–160, March 1967.

Riessman, F., Cohen, J., and Pearl, A., Eds. *Mental Health of the Poor; New Treatment Approaches for Low Income People* (New York: Free Press, 1964).

Rojas, P. M. "Instructional Materials and Aids to Facilitate Teaching the Bilingual Child," *Modern Language Journal*, **49:** 237–239, April 1965.

Ross, F. E. "For the Disadvantaged Student: A Program that Swings," *English Journal*, **54**: 280–283, April 1965.

Smilansky, S. *The Effects of Sociodramatic Play on Disadvantaged Pre-School Children* (New York: Wiley, 1968).

Smiley, M. B. "Gateway English: Teaching English to Disadvantaged Students," *English Journal*, **54**: 265–274, April 1965.

Smith, L. "Literature for the Negro Student," *High Points*, **47**: 15–26, October 1965.

Stroheker, E. C., Ed. *If They Read: A Report of the Workshop in the Reading Problems of the Culturally Disadvantaged Child, July 12–13, 1965* (Louisville, Ky.: Department of Library Science, Catherine Spalding College, 1966) (Mimeo).

Stull, E. G. "Reading Materials for the Disadvantaged: From Yaki to Tlingit to Kotzebue," *Reading Teacher*, **17**: 522–527, April 1964.

U.S. Office of Economic Opportunity. Project Head Start. *An Invitation to Help Head Start Child Development Programs: A Community Action Program for Young Children* (Washington: Office of Economic Opportunity, 1965).

U.S. Office of Education. *A Chance for a Change: New School Programs for the Disadvantaged* (Washington: U.S. Government Printing Office, 1966).

U.S. Office of Education. *Guidelines: Special Programs for Educationally Deprived Children, Elementary and Secondary Education Act of 1965, Title I* (Washington: U.S. Department of Health, Education, and Welfare, Office of Education, 1965).

U.S. Office of Educational Research Information Center. *Catalog of Selected Documents on the Disadvantaged* (Washington: U.S. Office of Education, 1966).

Ward, B. A. *Literacy and Basic Elementary Education for Adults: A Selected Annotated Bibliography* (Washington: U.S. Department of Health, Education, and Welfare, Office of Education, 1961).

Watt, L. B., et al. *The Education of Disadvantaged Children: A Bibliography.* Education Materials Center (Washington, D.C.: U.S. Office of Education, 1966). [Professional Resources; Elementary and Secondary School Textbooks; Children's Literature.]

Washington, B. B. "Books to Make Them Proud," *NEA Journal*, **55**: 20–22, May 1966.

Wolk, E. "Teaching English as a Second Language in the Elementary Schools of New York City," *Hispania*, **49**: 293–296, May 1966.

Addendum: Additional Selected References

Alloway, David, and Cordasco, Francesco. *Minorities and the American City: A Sociological Primer for Educators* (New York: David McKay, 1970).

Brickman, William W., and Lehrer, Stanley, Eds. *Conflicts and Change on the Campus: The Response to Student Hyperactivism* (New York: School & Society Books, 1970).

Burma, John H. *Mexican-Americans in the United States* (Cambridge, Mass.: Schenkman, 1970).

Cordasco, Francesco. *Italians in the United States: A Bibliography of Reports, Texts, Critical Studies and Related Materials* (New York: Oriole Editions, 1972).

Cordasco, Francesco, Ed. *Poverty: Sources for the Study of Economic Inequality and its Social Consequences* (New York: Augustus M. Kelley, 1971). [A collection of over 100 vols.]

Crossland, Fred E. *Minority Access to College* (New York: Schocken, 1971).

[Education] *Needs of Elementary and Secondary Education for the Seventies: A Compendium of Policy Papers* (Washington: U.S. Government Printing Office, 1970).

Fantini, Mario, Gittell, M., and Magat, R. *Community Control and the Urban School* (New York: Praeger, 1970).

Fitzpatrick, Joseph P. *Puerto Rican Americans* (Englewood Cliffs, N.J.: Prentice-Hall, 1971).

Gordon, Ira J. *Parent Involvement in Compensatory Education* (Urbana, Ill.: University of Illinois Press, 1971).

Havighurst, Robert L., and Levine, Daniel U. *Education in Metropolitan Areas.* 2nd ed. (Boston: Allyn and Bacon, 1971).

Hellmuth, Jerome, Ed. *Disadvantaged Child* (New York: Brunner/Mazel, 1969–1970). 3 vols.

[Immigrant Children] *The Children of Immigrants in Schools. With An Introductory Essay* by Francesco Cordasco. (Metuchen, N.J.: Scarecrow Reprint Corp., 1970; originally, 1911). 5 vols.

Janowitz, Morris. *Institution Building in Urban Education* (New York: Russell Sage Foundation, 1969–1970).

John, Vera P., and Horner, Vivian M. *Early Childhood Bilingual Education* (New York: Modern Language Association, 1971).

Jones, W. Ron. *Finding Community: A Guide to Community Research and Action* (Palo Alto, Calif.: James E. Freel, 1971).

Levin, Henry M., Ed. *Community Control of Schools* (Washington: Brookings Institution, 1970).

Meranto, Philip. *School Politics in the Metropolis* (Columbus, Ohio: Charles E. Merrill Co., 1970).

Miller, Harry L., and Woock, R. R. *Social Foundations of Urban Education* (Hinsdale, Ill.: Dryden Press, 1970).

Mink, Oscar G., and Kaplan, B. A. *America's Problem Youth. Education and Guidance of the Disadvantaged* (Scranton: International Textbook Co., 1970).

Passow, A. Harry, Ed. *Reaching the Disadvantaged Learner* (New York: Teachers College Press, 1970).

Passow, A. Harry, Ed. *Urban Education in the 1970s* (New York: Teachers College Press, 1971).

Piven, Frances F., and Cloward, Richard A. *Regulating the Poor: The Functions of Public Welfare* (New York: Pantheon Books, 1971).

Rever, Philip R., Ed. *Open Admissions and Equal Access* (Iowa City, Iowa: American College Testing Program, 1971).

Riles, Wilson C. [Chairman] *The Urban Education Task Force Report. Final Report of the Task Force on Urban Education to the Department of Health, Education, and Welfare* (New York: Praeger, 1970).

Rubenstein, Annette T., Ed. *Schools Against Children: The Case for Community Control* (New York: Monthly Review Press, 1970).

[Socially Disadvantaged Children] "Education for Socially Disadvantaged Children," *Review of Educational Research*, **40:** 1–179, February 1970.

Stone, James C., and DeNevi, Donald P., Eds. *Teaching Multi-Cultural Populations* (New York: Van Nostrand Reinhold, 1971). [Blacks; Puerto Ricans; Mexicans; Asians; and Indians].

Totten, W. Fred. *The Power of Community Education* (Midland, Mich.: Pendall, 1970).

Weinberg, Meyer, Ed. *The Education of the Minority Child* (Chicago: Integrated Education Associates, 1970). [A bibliography of over 10,000 references]

Willingham, Warren W. *Free-Access Higher Education* (New York: College Entrance Board, 1970).

Index